INSECURITIES OF
EXPULSION

I0099578

Insecurities of Expulsion

Afro-Asian Entanglements in Transcontinental Uganda

ANNEETH KAUR HUNDLE

DUKE UNIVERSITY PRESS
Durham and London
2025

© 2025 DUKE UNIVERSITY PRESS
All rights reserved
Project Editor: Michael Trudeau
Designed by A. Mattson Gallagher
Typeset in Minion Pro and Source Sans 3 by
Westchester Publishing Services

Library of Congress Cataloging-in-Publication Data
Names: Hundle, Anneeth Kaur, [date] author.
Title: Insecurities of expulsion : Afro-Asian entanglements in
transcontinental Uganda / Anneeth Kaur Hundle.
Description: Durham : Duke University Press, 2025. | Includes
bibliographical references and index.
Identifiers: LCCN 2024033412 (print)
LCCN 2024033413 (ebook)
ISBN 9781478031918 (paperback)
ISBN 9781478028680 (hardcover)
ISBN 9781478060895 (ebook)
Subjects: LCSH: South Asians—Uganda—History—20th century. |
Forced migration—Uganda—History—20th century. | Deportation—
Uganda—History—20th century. | Uganda—History—1971–1979.
| Africa—Foreign economic relations—South Asia. | South Asia—
Foreign economic relations—Africa.
Classification: LCC DT433.283 .H86 2025 (print) | LCC DT433.283
(ebook) | DDC 305.89140676109/04—DC23/ENG/20241213
LC record available at https://lccn.loc.gov/2024033412
LC ebook record available at https://lccn.loc.gov/2024033413

Cover art: Ugandan Asians departing Uganda at Entebbe
Airport. Courtesy of the Mohamed Amin Collection, Nairobi.

For my parents

CONTENTS

ABBREVIATIONS

AAA	Asian African Association
ACFODE	Action for Development
BJP	Bharatiya Janata Party
BLM	Black Lives Matter
BPP	British Protected Person
CBR	Centre for Basic Research
CEDOVIP	Center for Domestic Violence Prevention
DAPCB	Departed Asians Property Custodial Board
DRB	Domestic Relations Bill
EAC	East African Community
FDC	Forum for Democratic Change
FIDA	Uganda Association of Women Lawyers
FMF	Fees Must Fall
GMF	Gandhi Must Fall

HAR	Hope After Rape
HSS	Hindu Swayamsevak Sangh
IAU	Indian Association of Uganda
IMF	International Monetary Fund
INC	Indian National Congress
IPA	Investment Promotion Agency
IWA	Indian Women's Association
IWO	International Women's Organization
KIBP	Kampala Industrial Business Park
KY	Kabaka Yekka
MISR	Makerere Institute of Social Research
MoFPED	Ministry of Financial Planning and Economic Development
NAM	Non-Aligned Movement
NRA	National Resistance Army
NRI	Non-Resident Indian
NRM	National Resistance Movement
OAU	Organization of African Unity
OCI	Overseas Citizen of India
PIO	Person of Indian Origin
RMF	Rhodes Must Fall
UCW	Uganda Council of Women
UIA	Uganda Investment Authority
UNCTAD	United Nations Conference on Trade and Development
UNHCR	United Nations High Commission on Refugees
UNLF	Uganda National Liberation Front
UNRCA	Uganda National Records Center and Archive

UPC	Uganda People's Conference
UPDF	Uganda People's Defence Forces
URB	Uganda Resettlement Board
UWONET	Uganda Women's Network
YWCA	Uganda Women Christian Association

From Diasporic to Transcontinental Entanglement

It is perhaps ironic that a book about transcontinental Uganda—one that seeks to de-exceptionalize the critical event of the 1972 Ugandan Asian expulsion from normative South Asian diasporic understandings—is itself rooted in South Asian and Punjabi Sikh diasporic experience in the United States. *Insecurities of Expulsion* is grounded in my life history of growing up in the quintessentially Black American city of Chicago and its sprawling suburbs. Histories of frontier mercantilism and settler colonial expansion across the Great Plains, European settlement, indigenous land dispossession, and the labor of Black fugitive slaves and freedmen were all key to the development of this grand city on the southern shores of Lake Michigan. Black American descendants of slaves from the South settled in the city after the Civil War, during Reconstruction, and during the Great Migration of the twentieth century. My father arrived late on this roiling urban scene, from the rural *doaba* region of the land of five rivers, the Punjab, just as immigration restrictions eased and permitted his entry in the 1960s. Against the turmoil of the civil rights struggle, he made his way to the Windy City, working scrappy jobs until he was hired as an industrial engineer with a major automaker before returning to India to marry my mother through traditionally arranged *zaat-biradari* (caste and kin-based tribe) marriage networks. Chicago remained that symbol of American promise, prosperity, and modernity—economic and social mobility, industrial transformation, a mecca for architecture, art, and education.

Orientalized at times within a Hinduized formation of Indianness and at other times within an Islamicized formation of a South Asian or Arab Muslim—within the Black-white hierarchies of US nationalist racial formation—we participated in a Christian and secular public sphere, even as we practiced Sikhism in our homes and in the *gurudwara*. If public life felt like a series of deracinations from ancestral origin and tradition, of being remade into a singular South Asian American, Indian American, or even *desi* identity, then community and domestic life became sites of reconstructing and asserting tradition, culture, religion, and minority identity. I became adept at moving flexibly across these nested and interlinked identities, public and private domains. Traveling between the United States and the Punjab, I was working out the legacies of colonial and communal violence brought about by the Partition of the Punjab in 1947, followed by the growing oppression and militancy in post-partition Indian Punjab and, finally, by the events of 1984 in India, which culminated in anti-Sikh pogroms and a brutal counter-insurgency in the Punjab throughout the 1990s, the fallout of which continued to reverberate in the global Sikh community. Diasporic Sikh lifeworlds were wrought through racial, religious, and gendered precarities and intergenerational violence, the remembering and narrating of collective and individual histories. Spoken English—and even Punjabi—were limited vehicles for expressing traumas and displacements. Embodied practices—the performance of devotional music (*kirtan-sangeet*) and Punjabi poetry, folk music, and dance—offered paths to sacred heritage and healing. This lived experience of navigating society, similar to what W. E. B. Du Bois described in *The Souls of Black Folk* as "double consciousness,"[1] was the underneath of things, that which belied the secular and multicultural making of "hyphenated" American identities in post–civil rights–era United States.

A corollary diasporic theme was the forging of Black-Punjabi-Sikh (Afro-Asian) identifications and affiliations. The postwar and post-partition migration of Punjabis to the UK had already led to new encounters between British Asian youth and Afro-Caribbean diasporas. For example, the traditional Punjabi rural folk music and dance of *bhangra* and *giddha* had taken on elements of reggae and dancehall and, later, elements of Black American music like house and hip-hop. The new sound was rooted in the plural devotional cultures of the Punjab (Muslim, Sikh, and Hindu identities) and the ways in which Blackness—culturally and politically—had become an idiom of Punjabi working-class marginalization and the racial and religious

Othering that the community, especially visible minorities like Sikhs, experienced.[2] It was a formative moment in creating transracial Black British identities and solidarities as working-class communities confronted the neoliberalism of the New Right, violent policing, and white supremacist groups in the UK in the 1970s and 1980s. Back in Chicago, and working with these inheritances, I was absorbed in the writings of slave abolitionists and Pan-Africanists—who critiqued the denigration of Blackness and who mobilized a unified Black global consciousness to fight for the self-determination of all indigenous people and diasporas of African ancestry—along with Chicago-based novelists, poets, and jazz and blues musicians. The intimacies between Black Atlantic and Indian Oceanic histories (a product of the modern world's capitalist racial system that links Black and brown people together) were becoming more apparent to me as I continued to read Du Bois and Richard Wright and listened to musicians like John and Alice Coltrane and Yusuf Lateef, the latter a prominent figure in the Black American Ahmadiyya Muslim community. I was also studying the pluralistic and liberatory potential of the Sikh scriptural and secular traditions; Guru Nanak's radical rupture from Brahmanism and casteism; from patriarchy and other religious orthodoxies; and the tradition's egalitarian, anti-casteist, antiracist, and feminist possibilities. These literary, musical, and poetic compositions allowed me to integrate the ways that Punjabi performative cultures—Sufi *qawwali*, *gurbani-kirtan*, *bhangra*, and *giddha*—were also braided with Afrodiasporic expressive repertoires, producing a "vernacular modernity"[3] and a unique diaspora aesthetics.

As Sikh youths embodied a more marked and visibly Othered position in post-1984 India and in the post-9/11 United States, both community-based *and* Black-Punjabi-Sikh racial- and class-based solidarities were also becoming more apparent. Black-Punjabi-Sikh transracial identifications and alignments signified the possibilities of an emerging subjectivity and revealed the internal fractures within universalizing group categories of "Indian," "South Asian," and *desi*. Encounters with Blackness were reshaping what *Sikhi* and being Punjabi Sikh American meant, and vice versa. This was the "remix culture" of the diaspora in which one traversed categories of Sikhness and Punjabiness; racialized ethnicity and religion; stigmatized gender, queer-, and caste-based identities; and ideas of brownness and Blackness. These cultural formations challenged the parochial boundaries of communal life, the high commoditization of hip-hop and *bhangra*, and the singular straightjacketing of racial and cultural identities in the United States. It was an embrace of what Vijay Prashad, drawing on Robin Kelley, argues in *Everyone Was Kung-Fu Fighting* is an antiracist "polycultural" sense of being—the idea that "people live coherent lives made up of a host of lineages," a lived practice that relies on "a ferocious engagement with the political world of culture, a painful embrace of the skin and all its contradictions" (xii).[4] At the same time, there were severe limitations to horizontal Afro–South Asian transracial identifications—a sense that "the political" in struggles for Black and brown self-determination and South Asian investments in Pan-Africanism and Black internationalism had been lost—that internal religious and caste-based ideologies and practices, sexism, elitism, and deep-seated anti-Black racisms and racial tensions persisted.

After 1984, my parents' generation grappled with their loss of national belonging and committed to the idea that securing futures in the United States would offer us more safety from the brutal violence unfolding in the Punjab. Benefiting from policies that enabled upward mobility, our family had already moved to the suburbs, which symbolized aspirational whiteness and economic stability. Here, we could better integrate into the mainstays of middle-class life, including the curation of the bourgeois home. This transition maintained an essentializing and ahistorical South Asian American racial script based on an adherence to US nationalist liberal exceptionalism and minority-making tropes: that South Asian Americans were exceptionally hardworking and successful in the diaspora and thus assimilable. Claire Kim in "The Racial Triangulation of Asian Americans" has described this as a national racial discourse that constructs Asian people as "model minorities" positioned vertically between white and Black people, but one that also maintains immigrant Asians as perpetually foreign, alien, and unassimilable to the nation. It requires the maintenance of anti-Black racism and the reproduction of racial ideologies among immigrants and racial minorities that positions Blackness at the lowest rung of humanity and as an undesirable community, despite one's own racial exclusion. In her 1993 essay, "On the Backs of Blacks," novelist Toni Morrison argues that this is "the organizing principle of becoming an American." Among segments of the Sikh community in the United States, race and caste consciousness melded with class status, bourgeois respectability politics, and the production of anti-Black racism. Race has multiple origins and is also entwined with caste identity, beginning with the earliest Punjabi Sikh migration to the Californian American West at the turn of the nineteenth century. In 1923, Bhagat Singh Thind was racialized as "Hindoo" and barred from full citizenship rights in the United States on the basis of his nonwhite racial identity. Although he was Sikh and a revolutionary anticolonial intellectual affiliated with the California-based

Ghadar Party, he also asserted his upper-caste identity and Aryan racial origins, laying claim to a Caucasian racial identity and thus an entitlement to citizenship. Many North Indians and individuals of the larger Punjabi diaspora continue to assert a politics of both assimilation and resistance to white supremacy and social injustices through the lived experiences of class and performances of racialized ethnicity and caste, demonstrating the enduring legacy of histories of citizenship, race, and empire.

Despite my ongoing interests in Black-Punjabi-Sikh political and cultural formations, navigating the US scene meant contending with the profound inaccessibility of entangled imperial, oceanic, and territorial histories—transcontinental entanglements. My embodied diasporic experience—migration, mobilities, and displacements; negotiations of racial, religious, and citizenship entitlements and precarities; overlapping registers of violence; collective memory and trauma; the weightiness of key historical events; aesthetics and poetics; trans-racial alliances and tensions; and the enduring resonances of Black internationalism, Pan-Africanism, and Afro-Asianism—compelled me to pursue fieldwork in East Africa and the Great Lakes Region of Africa in Uganda and to study the 1972 Asian expulsion through the lens of the ethnographic present. This touchstone event felt less personal to me and my own family, yet familiar when viewed through the lens of the Punjabi Sikh diaspora's connections to Black Africa, Africans, and racial Blackness. The ways in which my aunties and uncles from East Africa interspersed Kiswahili into their Punjabi had always left an impression on me; the languages melded into each other and were overheard at the *gurudwara* and at other community functions. The indentured laborers building the Uganda railway from Mombasa on the Swahili Coast to the shores of Lake Victoria in Entebbe; the figure of the Kenyan *kalasingha* (a colloquial term for turbaned Sikhs in Kenya); histories of anticolonial freedom fighters like Kenyan trade unionist Makhan Singh and famed rally car drivers like the "Flying Sikh" Joginder Singh; the importance of the Makindu *gurdwara* (a commemoration site for the Indian labor and lives lost in building the East African railway in Kenya); and the entwined histories of the Indian Punjab with East Africa had all shaped a shared sense of the global Sikh and Punjabi experience.

In addition to racial scripts about Black Americans then, images of Black Africa, Africans, and racial Blackness moved surreptitiously and obliquely into and out of my view in the diaspora community. Here were South Asian community-based origin stories of Uganda, Idi Amin, and the Asian expulsion, imaginaries of Africa that intersected with and departed from Black American imaginaries of the African continent that I had also absorbed. There were the hauntings of Afro–South Asian racial estrangement, resentments, and racial conflict—all these complicated signs, affects, and histories circulating and shared through collective memory and in a *kahani* (story), shared over a cup of tea while eating *besan mittai* (chickpea flour sweet) or a warm bowl of *kheer* (rice pudding). My uncle often recounted the rags-to-riches story of Indar Singh Gill, a prosperous *sardar*, industrialist, and Ugandan settler, who owned a sawmill factory in Jinja. From his living room in the Detroit suburbs, he shared his own version of Idi Amin mythology, the expulsion of Asians, Gill's loss of home and wealth, ending with a spiritual and ethical lesson in material detachment and immigrant resilience, reciting a *pauri*, or poetic verse from the *Adi Granth*. I could easily connect to this experience of forced exile and the negotiation of loss of entitlement and loss of privilege, of sentimental memories for lives once lived in Africa, despite the limits of language itself. In contrast to the larger East African Asian diaspora, the expulsion of the Ugandan Asian diaspora was compelling because theirs was a narrative shaped by sudden and forced exile and estrangement from Black Africans. Their silences were not absences but presences, racial traumas reworked into new nation-based landscapes, becoming louder as I confronted them. These silent presences revealed a strong South Asian (via Africa) racial, caste, and class consciousness; feelings of victimization and resentment; loyalties to imperial citizenship and its racial hierarchies; new deracinations from African-Asian identity; and the making of new South Asian diasporic and liberal nationalist identities and desires for racial proximity to whiteness and the denigration of Blackness. But in other cases, and much to my interest, deep feelings of grief, love, and affection for Black Africans tinged these displaced Afro–South Asian cultural formations. More specifically, East African Asian–Punjabi identities persisted in cultural and performative domains, in the everyday stuff of diasporic aesthetics: in sartorial choices, language, sports, food, and musical cultures.

Yet the legibility of the 1972 Asian expulsion was an epistemic conundrum for me, especially in the US academy. It was clear to me that the itineraries of diasporic youths like me—our identities, subjectivities, orientations—were deeply entwined with internationalist histories of Africa and South Asia. But our recognition was obstructed by US nationalism and liberal multicultural and model-minority identities, the institutional operations of 2000s-era neoliberalism, and postracial colorblindness; it was obstructed even by the territorial limitations of US-based ethnic studies, which reproduced nationalist narratives that erased imperial and other intimacies. All the books I read on Ugandan history were limited to the scholarly field of African studies, tracing Afro–South Asian racial conflict and the expulsion back to world-historical processes of British imperialism, experiments in colonial capitalism, and Anglo-European racial supremacy and usually ending in 1972. But histories of Afro–South Asian racial conflict persisted in lived and embodied ways: a sensation of pressure in my chest, a tension headache, anxiousness in my belly. They became heightened as I negotiated intimacies and estrangements with the Black and African diaspora, working across registers of family, communal, social, and academic life.

In the US university, South Asian studies courses often examined issues of communal violence, caste, gender, and patriarchy—but they excluded an analysis of racial politics and their relationship to caste discrimination, colorism, and communal violence. This was so despite the extensive nature of African-South Asian encounters and the presence of old and new African diaspora communities in South Asia, which I read about separately. The tendency was that these courses had a dominant focus on Indian nationhood and an elite postcolonial politics that contended with anticolonial stuggle, communalism, or the racial discrimination experienced by South Asians in Global North (Western) diasporas; but they could not attend to South Asian sources of anti-Black racist prejudice, casteism, colorism, or the multiple origins of racial consciousness. There were other challenges, too. African studies in the US-based academy often excluded race and the South Asian diaspora from understandings of the African continent and its diasporas, albeit with some limited focus on Eastern Africa and South Africa. There were the many intellectual fractures between African studies and African diaspora studies (or Africana studies), and what eventually became Black studies and African studies departments in the university, making it challenging to access earlier intellectual genealogies of Pan-Africanism and Black internationalism that were inclusive of Afro–South Asian dialogue—especially Afro–Dalit studies and other third world internationalisms that crosscut area studies and disciplinary concerns. And then there was the tricky business of navigating the racial, religious, and caste politics of various disciplines and departments: the "racial flattening" of identifications that displaced Black-Punjabi-Sikh and Afro–South Asian diasporic consciousness. Here, queer Africa-based scholar Keguro Macharia offers a similar critique of navigating the knowledge politics of African studies outside of the African continent.[5] Finally, and more intimate to my own ethno-religious community, working through internal racial, color, caste, and gendered discriminations was challenging, for we were already minoritized, combating layered racial and religious oppressions and discriminations in academia. Engaging the university required from us what Edward Said, in *Culture and Imperialism*, has described as "contrapuntal reading": participating in, but not being completely produced by, dominant knowledge formations, subjectivities, and agendas. Envisioning a university that was more habitable to lived histories and practices was a parallel endeavor to the existential questions I had inherited from the Sikh tradition, namely, how to live in a world shaped by the challenges of everyday life, the self, and ego and yet transcend them via struggles for social justice and the cultivation of an ethical and poetic consciousness oriented toward the Divine, ultimate reality.

In addition to unmaking conventional understandings of the 1972 Asian expulsion then, this book aims to complicate facile or overly determined understandings of Black/Afro–South Asian connections. Racial identities, racial conflict, and racial resentments are usually presented as timeless and primordial rather than historical and contextual phenomena. Postcolonial events like the expulsion often obfuscate the significance of European empire, racial capitalisms, and white supremacy in fomenting race and class tensions between unevenly colonized communities. Racial divisions are often positioned as a by-product of exclusively European encounter. Yet colonial determinisms and single-origin stories about the making of racial hierarchies and supremacies are also problematic. At the same time, progressive scholars usually have investments in emphasizing global interracial solidarities, even romanticizing Afro–South Asian connection with a sole focus on anticolonial and anticapitalist solidarity. They might focus selectively, or in reductive ways, on recuperating the early internationalist solidarities examined in W. E. B. DuBois's Pan-Africanist thought and the nascent connections between enslaved and colonized people; Afro-Black-Dalit solidarities (race and caste analogy); mid-twentieth-century histories of Afro-Asian nonalignment and the 1955 Afro-Asian Conference in Bandung; transnational connections in abolitionist, anti-imperialist, anticolonial, and civil rights organizing; and most recently, optimistic narratives of South-South cooperation between postcolonial elites and policy pundits as they strive to meet development goals; or even the romance of academic collaborations across Global South geographies. In this book, I show that the insecurities of expulsion enable a critical feminist engagement with the multiple (historical and geographic, South Asian) sources of racialism and other inequalities, with the asymmetries, ambivalences, and tensions intrinsic to projects and performances of reconciliation, cooperation, and solidarity, and with unequal domains of knowledge and power. Here, I strive to center the experiences of Black Africans, the caste-oppressed, religious minorities, and others with vulnerable gender and sexual identities.

The 1972 Asian expulsion is significant precisely because it is a difficult and uncomfortable *racial* event; but it is one that has the potential to unfold into a more robust anthropological engagement with transcontinental Afro–South Asian entanglement. Entanglement suggests the complexity that is constitutive of Afro–South Asian encounters: it comprises both intimacies and estrangements. And so while this book speaks more immediately to new scholarly directions in Ugandan studies, African studies, South Asian diasporas, Indian Ocean studies (and connections to what Paul Gilroy has described as a distinctive and modern cultural world of the Black Atlantic[6]), and global Afro–South Asian studies, I am in dialogue with an African continental intellectual tradition of study that must continue to engage with race and racial entanglements. Here, I am committed to an ongoing project of "reinventing the Left" in ways that take seriously critical feminist approaches to race, ethnicity, and class; religion and caste; gender and sexuality.

These scholarly investments are grounded in my location as a feminist anthropologist with experience working in the African university and now based in the US academy. This book was written during a time of great political and social upheaval in the United States, where I confronted the (often frustrating) exclusion of the African continent from US-based South Asian studies and the limitations of transnational feminist, Black internationalist, Pan-Africanist, Afro-Asian, and Global South solidarities. I did this while making sense of US imperialism and the aftermath of 9/11 and the Bush and Obama "global war on terror" both abroad and in the US; Islamoracism and racial and religious minoritization; the ascendancy of Obama-era postracialism and the neoconservative and neoliberal consensus; and finally, the assertion of Trump-era White Christian racial nativism and the Biden-Harris–era normalization of late neoliberalism and identity politics (the latter both strategically necessary but also reductive and limiting in its potential for anticolonialism). I found myself also unexpectedly encountering the currency of racial pessimism in US social movements and the US academy, and I hope that this text reveals the complexities of anti-Black racism and anti-Blackness globally and the shifting logics of race, empire, labor, and capital through the lens of Afro–South Asia specifically.[7]

Transcontinental Uganda is thus a key geographical center from which to study the dynamics of Afro–South Asian racial violence while maintaining possibilities for Afro–South Asian universalisms and futurisms. And since I completed the research, the excesses of US imperialism and shifting global geopolitics (the rise of BRICS, Russia's war on Ukraine, and Israel's offensive war and genocide in Gaza), coupled with the apparent waning of liberal democracy; the rise of late neoliberalism, militarism, and repression; and the resurgence of Black and Palestinian protest movements—both solidarities and tensions—compel me to dwell on Afro–South Asian universalisms in the United States as well. Ultimately, however, I aim to universalize transcontinental Uganda instead, thus enabling multiply conceptualized analysis.

Far from a purely analytical or written exercise that privileges the epistemologies of Western modernity, feminist and anticolonial knowledge production is an embodied, vernacular, and intersubjective experience wrought through intimate and affective encounters. Kinship and relationship-building nurture ethical and spiritual commitments in research partnerships, community collaborations, and higher education. Small ripples of growing political, ethical, and spiritual consciousness gradually build oceanic and cosmic waves of transformation, but always in the messy materiality of living with difference and imagining other universals via particular histories, locations, and experiences. In this way, I write with insistence that this book, via the study of a complicated and enduring history, might trace paths to a present abundant with possibility for becoming and being co-liberated across the many lands and waters—Chicago, Kampala, the Punjab, and California—that I travel.

Unforeseen by me, this project has spanned many years and benefited from the support and critique offered by many individuals and institutions. It would truly be impossible for me to try to thank each person here. The writing of this book coincided with a significant expansion in my research program and several job transitions, so I am especially thankful to those who have understood my multiple intellectual commitments and supported my journey with great sensitivity and encouragement. My work began at Northwestern University in Evanston, Illinois, where this project took root as a senior thesis; and it continued at the University of Michigan, Ann Arbor, where that thesis eventually became a chapter of a much more elaborate dissertation. At Northwestern, I thank Micaela di Leonardo, Kearsley Stewart and Mary Weismantel; and at Michigan, I am indebted to my co-chairs, Kelly Askew and Damani Partridge, without whom succeeding in academia would have been impossible. My committee members Gillian Feeley-Harnik, Mamadou Diouf, Derek Peterson, and Farina Mir also offered

me countless office hours, readings suggestions, and advice on the develop-
ment of my research. I also thank Tom Trautmann, Arvind Mandair, Bruce
Mannheim, Andrew Shryock, David William Cohen, Julie Skurski, Amal
Hassan Fadlalla, Frieda Ekotto, and Miriam Ticktin for their support
and mentorship as I navigated African and South Asian studies, Punjab,
and Sikh studies. I continue to learn from Devon Keen, Rebecca Carter,
Xochitl Ruiz, Purvi Mehta, Haydar Darici, Nishaant Choksi, Nafisa Essop
Sheik, Stephen Sparks, Edgar Taylor, Andy Ivaska, Hafsa Kanjwal, Harjeet
Grewal, Sara Grewal, Sean Singh Chauhan, and many, many others in the
Michigan network. I am indebted to many Uganda studies colleagues and
scholars at Makerere University, but especially Nakanyike and Seggane Musisi,
and to several community members in the Uganda-based and exiled Ugan-
dan Asian communities who made this research possible—especially the late
Vali Jamal, Arafat Jamal, Rajni Tailor, Sarita Alam, Musarait Kashmiri, Mira
Nair, Maggie Kigozi, Humma Ahmad, Deepa Verma, Farah Benis, Doris
Kimuli, and Harriet Namaganda, among others, for their conversations and
insights into the project. I am deeply thankful for knowledge and experience gained while working with Mahmood Mamdani and colleagues at the
Makerere Institute of Social Research (MISR) from 2013 to 2015, including
Okello Ogwang, A. B. K. Kasozi, Adam Branch, Guiliano Martiniello, Pamela
Khanakwa, Manuel Shwab, Stella Nyanzi, Lawyer Kafureeka, Florence Ebila
(and others!), and I am likewise thankful for the support of a wonderful network of African and Uganda studies colleagues and feminist scholars, including Alicia Decker, Corrie Decker, Shobana Shankar, Sarah Ssali, Josephine
Ahikire, Sylvia Tamale, and former students Noosim Naimasiah, Netsanet
Gebremichael, and Jackline Kirungi (and others!). I thank colleagues in the
anthropology program and interdisciplinary humanities program during
my short time at the University of California–Merced, especially Ma Vang,
Kit Myers, Mario Sifuentez, Sean Malloy, Kathleen Hull, and Robin DeLu-
gan. Finally, I thank my colleagues in the Anthropology Department at the
University of California, Irvine (UCI), which has been my intellectual, and
Pacific Coast, home since 2019, with special thanks to Dean of Social Sciences Bill Maurer, Eve Darien-Smith, Kim Fortun, Eleana Kim, and Karen
Leonard for their incredible vision to bring Sikh studies and my research
program to UCI Anthropology. My deepest appreciation to Kris Peterson,
David Goldberg, Samar Al-Bulushi, Victoria Bernal, and Ruchi Chaturvedi
for their wise friendship and careful readings of draft chapters of the book
manuscript; and to Valerie Olson, Tom Boellstorff, Mei Zhan, David Goldberg, Leo Chavez, Justin Richland, and Nina Bandelj for their mentorship

and support for my journey to tenure promotion amid the fallout of the global pandemic emergency. I am thankful for the intellectual community fostered by Gabriele Schwab, Beheroze Shroff, Rajagopalan Radakrishnan, Vinayak Chaturvedi, Mark Levine, Judy Wu, Sohail Daulatzai, Angela Jenks, Sherine Hamdy, George Marcus, Keith Murphy, Lilith Mahmud, Damien Sojoyner, Sal Zárate, António Tomás, Sylvia Croese, Rudo Mudiwa, Cecelia Lynch, Tiffany Willoughby-Herard, and Yousuf Al-Bulushi. Long Bui, Sandra Harvey, and Chelsea Shields deserve special thanks for their friendship, delicious food, humor, and wit. In the UC system, thank you to African studies network colleagues, and especially to Andrew Apter, Bettina N'gweno, Amina Mama, and Rachel Jean-Baptiste for our intellectual community; and thank you to the larger Sikh and Punjab studies network, especially Guriqbal (Bali) Sahota, for his comradeship and support. Thank you also to Gabriel Dattatreyan, Neilesh Bose, Renu Modi, Sunaina Maira, and Neha Vora for being wonderful conversation partners over the years. Finally, I have delighted in nurturing the intellectual and personal growth of a number of graduate students at UC Merced and UCI, including Amrit Deol, Gabrielle Cabrera, Tavleen Kaur, Tawfiq Alhamedi, Nima Yolmo, Misbah Hyder, Muneira Hoballah, Yvette Vasquez, the late Tarek Mohamed, Tenzing Wangdak, Damanjit Gill, Preetika Nanda, Mridula Garg, Rishi Guné, and other colleagues who have been part of the Sikh Feminisms Working Group at UCI—I learn from you as much as you learn from me! Thank you to Melissa Valdez, Monica Briseno, and Aubrey Bayoneta at UCI Anthropology, and to all of the support staff at MISR and Makerere University Library, the Centre for Basic Research (CBR), and the Uganda National Records Center and Archives (UNRCA) and other institutions I have worked at; your camaraderie and goodwill are with me always.

The generous financial and institutional support from the National Science Foundation, the Wenner-Gren Association for Anthropological Research, and the UC President's Faculty Fellowship in the Humanities at UCI in 2019 helped to support the research and writing of this book. Additional institutional support from the Makerere Institute of Social Research (MISR) and the School of Women and Gender Studies at Makerere University, and a visiting professorship at the Center for African Studies at UC Berkeley in 2018, coordinated by Leo Arriola and Martha Saavedra, offered me crucial opportunities to conduct follow-up research and publish articles. Invited talks, workshops, and panels helped me to organize my data and refine chapters and arguments. Many thanks to Renu Modi at the Centre for African Studies at the University of Mumbai; Dilip Menon and Edgar Taylor at the Center for

Indian Studies in Africa at the University of Witwatersrand and the University of Johannesburg; Ruchi Chaturvedi, Victoria Collis-Buthelezi, and Suren Pillay at the University of Cape Town; Inderpal Grewal in Women, Gender, and Sexuality Studies at Yale University; Ashley Rockenbach at the Carter G. Woodson Institute at University of Virginia; Neilesh Bose at the University of Victoria; Gaurav Desai and James Ocita at the African Studies Association; Hannah Appel and Jessica Cattelino at UCLA Anthropology; and Faisal Devji at Oxford University. Earlier versions of some of the material presented here have appeared in two previous publications: parts of chapter 2 draw on "Exceptions to the Expulsion: Violence, Security and Community among Ugandan Asians, 1972–79," published in the *Journal of Eastern African Studies* 7, no. 1 (2013): 164–82; and chapter 6 further develops "Postcolonial Patriarchal Nativism, Domestic Violence and Transnational Feminist Research in Uganda," published in *Feminist Review* 121, no. 1 (2019): 37–52.

At Duke University Press, I possess deep admiration for my editor Elizabeth Ault, who has been passionate about this project since our first conversation about it, and who has nurtured the manuscript and its intellectual commitments at every turn. Many thanks also to Benjamin Kossak, Michael Trudeau, and the entire Duke Press team; to Christine Riggio, for her labor on the visuals in the book; and to Laura Helper and Shazia Iftkar for earlier developmental and copyediting support. Salim Amin at the Mo Amin Foundation offered generous copyright permissions for numerous photographs. More gratitude to the anonymous reviewers of my manuscript; your insightful comments have worked their way into the following pages. The deepest love and respect for my parents and their labor and sacrifices, Shivjit Singh Hundle and Preminder Kaur (Sukerchakia) Hundle, who have trusted and supported me in my life path even as they did not have the opportunities I had; and especially for my mother, my aunt, Sarbinder (Gikki) Gill (Michigan-*walle*), and my late grandmothers, *sardarnis* Mohinder Kaur Sandhu and Harjinder Kaur Gill, who have modeled feminist courage and ethics for me. Thank you to Seerath, Rami, Shaun, Nathek, Sohava, Nanak for all the love, affection, and humor, and to many others in my family and community for the ethos of *chardi kala* (ascending spiritual energy) they have instilled within me, always offering welcome distractions and creating a sense of home for me amid my journeys and many transitions. Along with my parents, this book is dedicated to the diverse communities who trace their heritage to Uganda, and to all those who were part of my research: your generosity and trust in me to convey the insecurities of expulsion remains with me still.

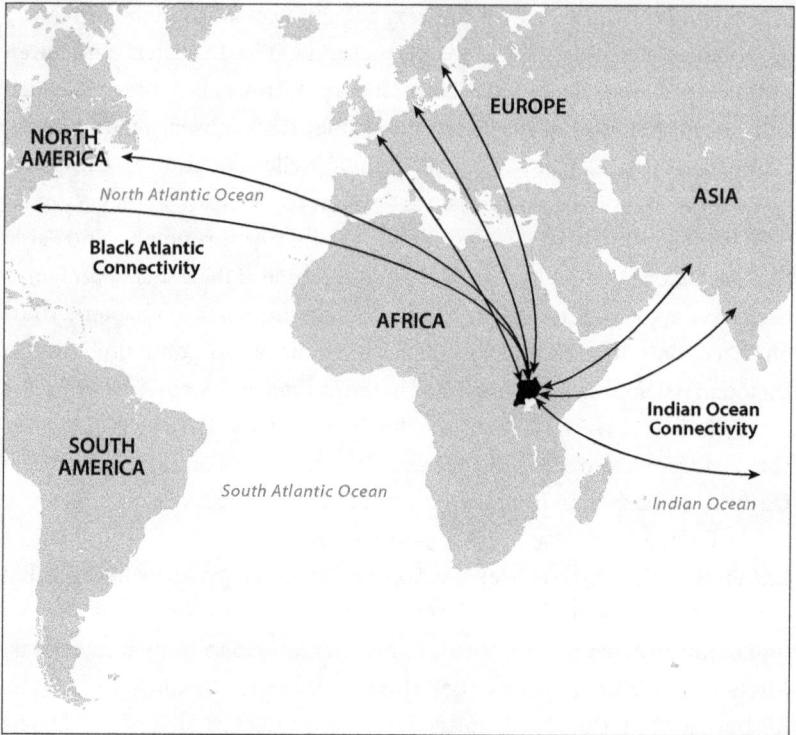

Map 1 Transcontinental Uganda: Differentiated migration and mobilities of Black African, African Asian and South Asian (imperial, post-partition, and postcolonial) diasporic communities.

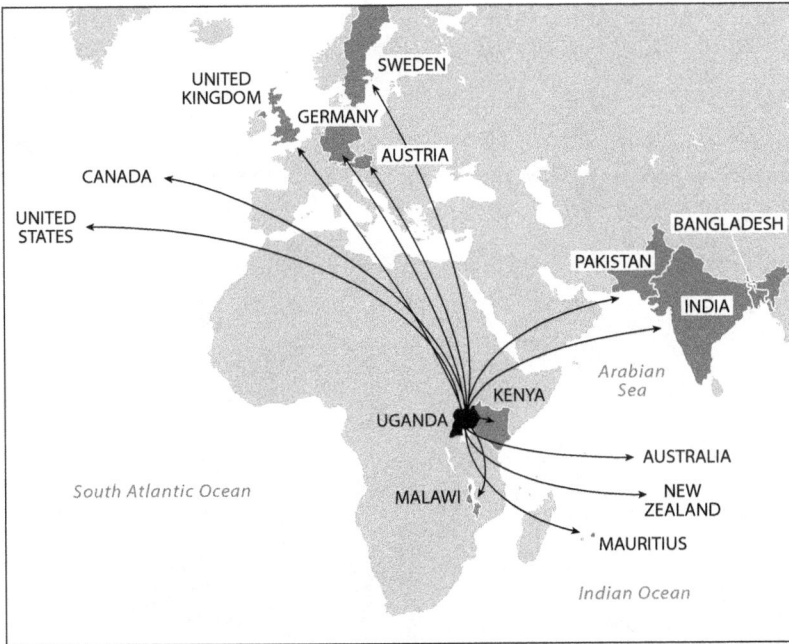

Map 2 Postcolonial Uganda and Ugandan Asian displacement in 1972.

Map 3 Uganda: Selected regions and traditional kingdoms.

Map 4 Uganda: Selected major cities and towns.

PART I

Imperial
Entanglements

Introduction

Expulsion as Closure, Expulsion as Opening

The recent story of Indians in Uganda—the summary expulsions en masse, the harassment from security and bureaucratic personnel, the detentions, "disappearances," and deaths, and the lack of any compensation for any abandoned property and businesses—is tragic indeed. But we must not lose sight of the fact that Uganda as a whole is truly an African tragedy.

Hasu Patel, "General Amin and the Indian Exodus from Uganda," 1972

Fused into the paradox of heroic evil was Idi Amin—at once a hero and a villain, at once a subject of applause and denunciation. As a villain he was a symbol of tyranny. Hundreds of thousands of his fellow compatriots died under his rule. As a hero, Amin had four meanings for Africa and the Third World. Economically he attempted to strike a blow against dependency and foreign control of his country's economy. Culturally, he signified a reaffirmation of cultural authenticity. He helped to foster cultural discovery among Africans. . . . Politically, Amin was often in rebellion against the northern-dominated power structure of the twentieth century. He made fun of the mighty—and sometimes helped to inspire self-confidence in the ranks of the Third World. Morally, Amin signified a basic leverage between the liberal values of the Western world and the nationalistic concerns of much of the Third World.

Ali A. Mazrui, "Between Development and Decay: Anarchy, Tyranny, and Progress under Idi Amin," 1980

In fall 2008, I met again Dr. Vali Jamal, a self-described "returnee" of Ugandan Asian origin and Ismaili Khoja Muslim background. A retired academic and economist, he had returned to Kampala in the early 2000s, and lived there permanently, running a small eatery as a retirement activity. He welcomed me warmly to his café, and we settled at a table across from each other, sharing tea and roasted groundnuts. I mentioned that I had read some of his articles in the local Ugandan dailies and that I appreciated seeing Asian (often used interchangeably with Indian) representation in political affairs as well as in discussions of the infamous 1972 decree by President Idi Amin to expel all Asians from the nation. Upon hearing this, Jamal retrieved a frayed and yellowed copy of a newspaper from his back office. Together we gazed at the large block headline: "ALL ASIANS MUST GO."

I was surprised that for so many years he had kept a copy of the newspaper announcing his expulsion; and he began to share with me his life story and memories of the expulsion event. Jamal explained how, in the early 1960s, Prince Karim Aga Khan had envisioned a multiracial society in East Africa and had advised Ismailis to take on Ugandan citizenship and play an active role in nation-building through their daily lives, grounded in spiritual and ethical principles. As a doctoral student at Stanford, Jamal had been in Kampala in 1972, collecting dissertation research at Makerere University when he was ordered out of the country. Although he was himself a Kenyan citizen at the time, he described how, as mostly stateless refugees, the Ismaili community was especially affected by the expulsion order. Jamal narrated his and his family's eventual resettlement in Vancouver, Canada, followed by his career at the International Labour Organization. The British colonial administration had socially engineered enormous Indian and African racial and class disparity in Ugandan society, he explained, which led to anti-Asian sentiment and his expulsion following Uganda's political independence from Britain. Jamal had researched the political economy of the cotton cash-cropping industry and the role of Indian merchants in the colonial era. Now, inspired by Cynthia Salvadori's *We Came in Dhows*, a collection of oral histories that documents the settlement of the Indian diaspora in East Africa, he was beginning to compile interviews from Ugandan Asian returnees and exiles in the global diaspora.

Just beyond the open café doors and across the busy traffic on Kampala Road, we could make out City Square, a public garden and park in front of the Ugandan courts of justice. It was there, Jamal recounted, that Idi Amin had made an influential anti-Asian speech just prior to announcing the expulsion decree. Wistfully, Jamal recalled when he would picnic in the park

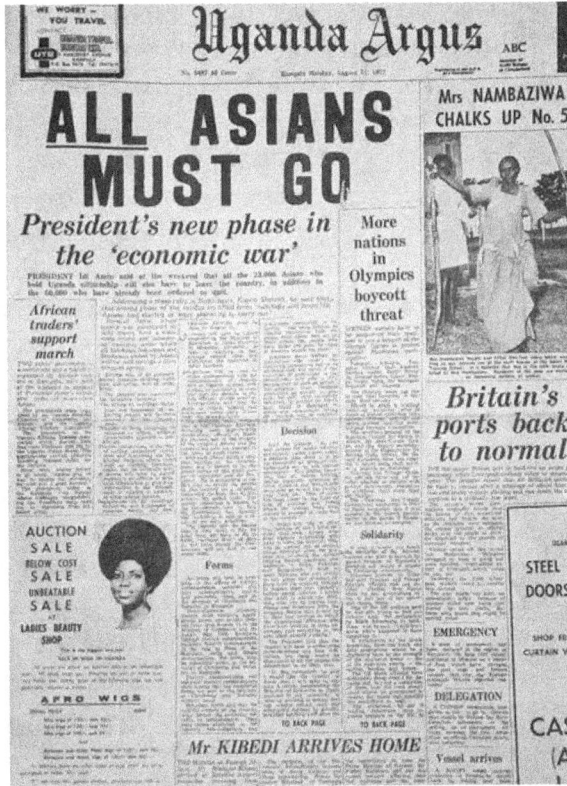

I.1 Newspaper clipping from the *Uganda Argus*, August 21, 1972.

before strolling to an afternoon matinee of a newly released Indian film at one of the theaters in the city. He paused in his recollections, taking a sip of tea, as he peered at me from behind his black-rimmed glasses. Hinting at the racial issues that had made Ugandan Asians so vulnerable to expulsion, he said, "But we were also arrogant. We thought we were superior, and we were a minority." I could sense his unresolved pain and disquiet, his careful unearthing of community complicities. Sitting with me in a sensory and figurative zone of "cultural intimacy,"[1] we became friends and colleagues, sharing observations about our research and writing, discussing global and local political issues when we met and over email communications, and attending community events together.

This book is a study of the persistent afterlives of the 1972 Asian expulsion in contemporary and transcontinental Uganda; it is an anthropology of an expulsion event. Although this particular expulsion—defined here as the process of forcing someone to leave their homeland (not just territory but modern nation)—may be unknown to a general reader, I argue that it is a *global critical event*. This book makes legible the *insecurities of expulsion*, a term that encompasses the interrelation between (1) the consequences and effects of the 1972 Asian expulsion; (2) the circulating global representations, discourses, and imaginaries of the event and the state, individual, and collective memories and narrations of the expulsion and their affective resonances; and (3) the logics, practices, and performances of citizenship that have flourished subsequent to the event. The expulsion is neither a parochial nor an exceptional moment of postcolonial Afro–South Asian racial estrangement and closure. Instead, the event and its aftermaths linger—materially, discursively, ideologically, and affectively—in *transcontinental Uganda*, which I define as the modern, territorial Ugandan nation-state and its intimate connections with trans-Indian Oceanic and Black Atlantic migrations, mobilities, and displacements and territorially based intra-African, South Asian subcontinental, European, and North American geographies inclusive of specific transnational circuits of connection. In fact, the insecurities of expulsion offer us an epistemological opening into a transcontinental study of Afro–South Asian entanglement. This orientation toward theorizing citizenship through racial entanglement is not concerned with an either/or dichotomy of inclusion or exclusion, nor is it concerned with a singular narrative of Ugandan Asian victimhood, Afro–South Asian racial conflict, or a redemptive search for Afro–South Asian racial solidarity. Rather, this book foregrounds the enduring residues of a critical event and the evolving terrains of citizenship practice that are fragile, tense, and ambivalent—even strategic, embodied, subaltern, and performative.

In the pages that follow, I trace old and new assemblages of empire—Indian sub-imperialist ambition and anticolonial solidarities; nationalisms, governance, sovereignty, citizenship; race, labor-capital and class relations, religion, caste, gender, and sexuality—all from the vantage of contemporary urban Uganda that is itself constituted through transcontinental processes. Building on growing scholarly interest in the production of "noncitizens" or "impossible citizens" in both so-called liberal and illiberal contexts,[2] I demonstrate that successive Ugandan authoritarian and militarized state projects have shifted from practices of Asian/Indian racially nativist expulsion to the interlocking logics and practices of racial expulsion, exclusion, and noncitizen incorporation. These new incorporations are constituted by the unresolved legacies of the 1972 Asian expulsion and by a normalized politics of racial nonreconciliation. Through ethnographic analysis, I explore the classed, raced, ethno-religious, caste-based, and gendered hierarchies within racially privileged yet noncitizen Ugandan Asian and other South Asian–descendant communities, laying out gradations and combinations of formal, structural, and substantive inclusions and exclusions and parsing the complexity of citizenship practices in the post-expulsion era with respect to Black African aspirations for self-determination and sovereignty. I show how those individuals, racialized as "Asian"—Ugandan Asians and postcolonial South Asian migrants, and all those who are structurally, substantively, or legally noncitizens and unofficial citizens—continue to negotiate the tensions between formal and substantive citizenship and settler/ citizen, native/immigrant, insider/outsider, and racial Black African/South Asian identities. These practices are never wholly reduced to or defined by a top-down hierarchy; rather, nation-building and state-building are constantly produced and contested by subjects as they negotiate governance, inclusion, and exclusion.

Despite the attempts of Ugandan nationalists and state actors to reshape the nation through population demography and ideas of indigeneity, autochthony, and racial Blackness (defined here via imputed biological and phenotypical notions of Black identity, accompanied by other criteria such as claims to autochthony and indigeneity to African territory or homelands), people of South Asian heritage (both African Asians, or Ugandan Asians, and new post-expulsion South Asian migrants) and racial South Asianness (defined here via imputed biological and phenotypical notions of South Asian identity and ancestral and heritage claims to the South Asian subcontinent) are an entrenched feature of the Ugandan nation. Ugandan Asian and South Asian migration, labor, capital, and community formation are necessary for, or even constitutive of, Ugandan national identity, state formation, citizenship, and belonging, both within and outside of the nation-state. This has been the case from its very inception. Ugandan national identity and normative citizenship are constituted by those who embody its limits: the expelled and exiled; the returned; migrants, dependents, transients, and sojourners; transnationals and expatriates. In other words, Afro–South Asian connections, communities, identities, and subjectivities are at the heart of what we call Africa or the South Asian/Indian diaspora in Africa—they also persist in Uganda's racially diverse global diasporas.

Departing from abstract analysis that examines the limits of settler inclusion in the postcolony or the study of majoritarian-minoritarian relations in the nation, this book demonstrates that there are multiple, transnational scales of governance and sovereignty that produce people of Ugandan Asian and South Asian heritage as simultaneous racial noncitizens and economic citizens. More specifically, I track how imperial citizens and Subject Races–turned–postcolonial–citizens[3] straddle ambivalent positions of global racial privilege and postcolonial racial exclusion vis-à-vis Black African global and national racial exclusion. Working with and past the dominant conceptual apparatus of liberal-nationalist, multiracial, and secular citizenship, contestations between and among Black African and South Asian racialized sovereignties become paramount. Some might argue that the insecurities of expulsion are relevant only to the Ugandan Asians who were directly expelled; but they are also relevant to Ugandan Black African–identifying communities. And they are relevant to theorizing the production of racial difference and racial Blackness and racial South Asianness; to the production of racially nativist nationalism; and to the connections between Black African, African Asian, and South Asian diasporic communities in transcontinental scope.

Studying the insecurities of expulsion and the often-fraught nature of Afro-Asian encounters enables new approaches to studying citizenship in Africa in a shifting geopolitical context. While anthropologists of citizenship in liberal nation-states study the exclusion, deportations, and expulsions of minoritized racial groups with less power than normative citizens in host societies, this book focuses on postcolonial Uganda and the complicated and uneven inheritances of imperial and colonial violence on racialized and colonized communities, the possibilities and limitations of democratization and decolonization, and histories and presents of authoritarianisms, illiberalisms, neoliberalisms. It looks at expulsions, repatriations, and ongoing migrations and mobilities, including new South-South migrations, and builds on existing conversations in political anthropology and debates on citizenship in anthropology in particular. Centering Weberian notions of disenchantment with liberal and legal-juridical citizenship,[4] I write amid the perceived crisis of liberal democracy in Western nation-states and other signal events of geopolitical shift.[5] Anthropologist Deborah Thomas has argued that we are living through and witnessing the death of "the West" (naming our contemporary moment as an "epochal shift" rather than "crisis"); that "we have reached the limits of liberal forms of sovereignty that were themselves rooted in plantation-based slavery and imperialism."[6] She uses the phrase "conceptual disenchantment" to underscore the limitations of the liberal vocabulary that we have inherited and that continue to be universalized to capture complex historical, political, and cultural formations.

Transcontinental Uganda allows us to study existing citizenship practices that may be inflected by the material histories, ideologies, and practices of European imperialism, liberalism, and decolonization; but it showcases other important political practices, too, such as the interactive elements of what I am bracketing as *liberal, illiberal,* and *nonliberal* modes of governance, sovereignty, and citizenship. Most anthropological studies that contend with the limitations of liberal, legal-juridical citizenship and its abstract utility still tend to be centered within the universalized Eurocentrism of Europe and North America (previously referred to by postcolonial scholars as "the West" and by left-identifying scholars as the wealthy, developed nations of "the Global North"),[7] locations where the imputed and assumed civilizational and racial divisions between liberal and illiberal nations are widely accepted and from which the African continent and its complex diasporas continue to be excluded. While this book builds on anthropological studies that have focused on the (formal, legal-juridical) exclusion of minoritized subjects, or on the production of noncitizens through "technologies of exclusionary incorporation" in liberal-democratic nation-states,[8] it centers debates in the anthropology of citizenship in Africa and the postcolonial world, or the Global South, with attention to postcolonial Uganda specifically.

Here, disenchantments with liberal and legal-juridical citizenship have been apparent since at least the 1960s, and they continue to circulate within urban and global geographies, imaginaries, and affective economies. The multiplicity and complexity of postliberal democratic practices and performances of citizenship require new conceptual vocabularies that can speak to a normalized politics of nonreconciliation and the ambivalences that continue to characterize Afro–South Asian encounters as we enter a transformative era of global geopolitics and the escalation of militarism, authoritarianism, rightist populisms, and even neofascist movements globally. In other words, we must study how individuals negotiate citizenship and belonging in what are usually defined through a Eurocentric lens as exceptionalized states and geographies of illiberalism and authoritarianism but that are fast becoming a global condition.[9]

Anthropology, unlike other disciplines, is limited in offering us sufficient ways to think and write relationally across colonized and minoritized groups that have been situated unequally across European imperial and colonial experiments. Nor has it offered deeper contributions to the development of global or transnational Afro–South Asian studies. Beyond its contributions to an anthropology of citizenship then, *Insecurities of Expulsion* introduces a transcontinental anthropology of Afro–South

Asian entanglement. This requires new conceptual and methodological tool kits that center relationalities of *violence, interdependency, intimacies*, and *estrangements*—that which binds racialized Black Africans and South Asians subjects together across shifting projects of empire and sub-imperialist ambition, postcolonial nation-building, geopolitical transformation, solidarity, and cultural connection—with transcontinental Uganda as a critical center of the study.

Encountering the Expulsion in the South Asian American Diaspora

Jamal's narrative of his expulsion, which took place between the months of August and November 1972, was very familiar to me, as I had heard similar versions and recollections of expulsion from fellow community members. The sudden and violent nature of mass expulsion targeting Uganda's entire Asian population required immediate responses by government officials from the United Kingdom, Canada, and India as well as from the United Nations Human Rights Commissioner and influential religious and community leaders. In short, it required the willingness of numerous advocates to convince many nations to absorb large numbers of stateless refugees. To be sure, it was an unparalleled event in postcolonial Africa that rippled across the continent and the world, receiving both media and scholarly attention.[10]

As a displaced population, some Ugandan Asians completely moved on from this difficult chapter in their lives, cutting off their connections to the Ugandan nation and Africa completely. Others attempted to return or revive connections to the nation when later governments introduced property repossession processes as a mode of repatriation. Some never returned, nurturing attachments to their homeland and fellow Ugandans from afar, digitally and virtually via social media or through community gatherings and official commemorations of the expulsion among resettled communities in the UK and Canada. And some became global citizens, engaging in a kind of cosmopolitan lifestyle across multiple states, moving across imperial geographies. (For example, I recall unexpectedly meeting an exile during a family wedding party in Jalandhar, the Indian Punjab, during my research. He had first temporarily resettled in Europe as a refugee, then moved to Malaysia, and finally settled in Vancouver.) The large-scale movement of the majority of Ugandan Asians from East Africa to the UK and Canada meant that these communities were formative to nation-based projects of postimperial multiracialism and liberal multiculturalism as well as to the negotiation of racial and cultural difference in those contexts (see map 2). Many exiled Ugandan Asians embraced new British, Canadian, and other national identities, processing their sudden displacement from what had become an exclusionary and racially nativist African society, focusing instead on integrating into Western societies with white European demographic majorities. Their Ugandan (and African) cultural and political identities were marred by a sense of unwantedness, their unwilling estrangement from Black Ugandans and from African nationhood. In my encounters with exiles from different racialized ethno-religious communities (addressed in more detail in the next chapter) in Canada, the United States, and the UK, many positioned themselves ambivalently as "ex-Ugandan Asians": as if to designate this unwantedness but also to demarcate that they had once been Ugandan Asians (a persistent claiming of African and Ugandan identity, despite its ongoing disavowal).

I was also familiar with expulsion stories through film and literature. I first watched Mira Nair's *Mississippi Masala* in an undergraduate South Asian diaspora studies class in college; and I later screened *The Last King of Scotland* (starring Forest Whitaker as Idi Amin, and based on Giles Foden's novel), which led to my explorations of other, lesser-known films and documentaries about this period of Ugandan history, including representations of Idi Amin.[11] These films helped to solidify the 1972 Asian expulsion in a global, Western imaginary, conveying representations of East Africa, Uganda, Idi Amin, and Ugandan Asians that made the event accessible to many viewers. They have been joined by numerous other narrative accounts by Ugandan Asians, both autobiographical and fictional, about their own expulsion experiences.[12] Taken together, films, novels, memoirs, and other cultural productions constitute a powerful archive of Ugandan Asian identity and the experiences of expulsion, exile, and resettlement. Each contribution is worthy of analysis on its own terms, and each is central to key debates within postcolonial and other dominant intellectual strands in South Asian diaspora studies in Western contexts that explore themes of exile, displacement, trauma, memory, identity, and cultural hybridity. These works present the 1972 Asian expulsion as one of the most important moments of African–South Asian racial estrangement and of the broader East African Asian out-migration from postcolonial Africa; and they continue to offer both conventional and critical analyses of the event, its historical context, and its diasporic aftermaths, discussed further below.[13] Here, expulsion is typically posited as a rupture or crisis that exemplifies South Asian racial victimhood and estrangement from Black Africans, followed by a negotiation

I.2 & I.3   Representations of the 1972 Asian expulsion in Hollywood: Movie posters for Mira Nair's *Mississippi Masala* (1991) and Kevin Macdonald's *The Last King of Scotland* (2006).

of an African Asian identity in exile that is eventually deracinated and absorbed into South Asianness writ large. And often, the very eventfulness of the event, its spectacular nature, and its mass-media representations exceed its context, the "facts" of the event itself.

In more recent years, research on the resettlement of Ugandan Asian refugees and their descendants in the UK, Canada, the United States, and other countries has increased in number; and much of it is being carried out by exiles and their descendants.[14] This research has helped to establish academic and other community archives of Ugandan Asian exile experiences, including oral history and museum projects, a significant feat as members of the expelled generation are now in their retirement years.[15] They reveal that throughout the 1970s and the ensuing decades, Western governments such as those of the UK (the former imperial power) often extolled Ugandan Asian refugees, or the so-called twice migrants,[16] for their entrepreneurial success, constructing them as ideal integrated and successful immigrants by British officials, by Ugandan Asian community elites, and by conservative politicians and ideologues alike.[17] In the UK, the forced expulsion of Ugandan Asians was actually a sedimented migration, building on earlier displacements of other East African Asians to the UK, such as the Africanization-era out-migrations of Kenyan Asians. Ugandan Asian migration complicated earlier migrations of former British Indian subjects to the UK in which new postimperial migrants were experimenting with "Afro–South Asianness" though working-class encounters and identifications with Afro-diasporic identity and eventually with antifascist, working-class, and feminist experiments with Black Britishness, a political expression of Black identity.[18] These alternative configurations of Afro–South Asian identities continue to warrant deeper examination, especially as they developed alongside the arrivals of Ugandan Asian exiles.

Together, the rise and fall of scholarship on expulsion, cultural productions of the event, and the sense that the exiled population is now integrated into liberal nation-state contexts lends an air of finality to, even a sense of closure around, the 1972 Asian expulsion, indicating the total "de-Indianization" of Uganda. It produces a teleological course to the migration of Ugandan Asian exiles from Africa to the dominant geographies of settlement in the Global North. *Insecurities of Expulsion* recenters contemporary urban Uganda in this unidirectional story of Ugandan Asian exiles' minority integration in liberal states of inclusion. The expulsion is far from over; the event remains unresolved, with residual effects and affects that reverberate in transcontinental Uganda. It is a persistent expulsion, an ongoing technology of nativist nationalism and racial exclusion, a source of meaning-making, still central to nation-building and statecraft and even to imperial and sub-imperial formations that encompass the United Kingdom and the Indian nation. The expulsion is also a structural, material, and affective reality that, as we will see, shapes logics of governance and sovereignty and practices of citizenship and belonging; this includes contestations over whether race and nation are mutually exclusive, or if national territories can be plural across Afro–South Asian encounters or across zones of racial and religious encounter, cultural productions, and exchange.

Somewhat surprisingly, and despite the global consequences of the 1972 Ugandan Asian expulsion, few scholars oriented within and across the South Asian and African postcolonial intellectual tradition have seriously reassessed the 1972 Asian expulsion and its aftermaths in the context of contemporary debates. This is true despite the ways in which we might characterize the Asian expulsions and other exoduses of South Asians from decolonizing East Africa as the great "racial partitions" that are at the center of global histories and imaginaries of Afro–South Asian racial conflict and solidarity. Indeed, compared with the decolonization of Kenya and Tanzania and the transition to postapartheid South Africa, Uganda's expulsion of its Asian population was one of the most extreme policies of postcolonial racial exclusion.[19] Yet the event remains relegated as a minor topic within the study of global South Asian diasporas (as was my own experience as a college student) or understood as an exceptional or provincial event in African studies. Ideas and meaning-making about the expulsion and its Ugandan Asian exiles—like ideas of Africa, Uganda, and the notorious dictator Idi Amin—are constructed as exceptional rather than as located in dynamic historical and global processes; they are also not universalized to engender new contemporary arenas of discussion and debate. However, the 1972 Asian expulsion is a landmark event constitutive of epistemological concerns in South Asian and African/diaspora studies, global Afro–South Asian studies, and Indian Ocean and Black Atlantic studies as well as in themes of citizenship, refugee, and migration history in anthropology.

Expulsion Exceptionalism: Identifying Terrains of Exceptionalism

In this book, I use the term *expulsion exceptionalism* to refer to a global assemblage of normative discourses, imaginaries, and representations of the 1972 Asian expulsion. I contend with existing common-sense knowledge that circulates in Ugandan Asian and other South Asian diasporic communities, mass-media representations, cultural productions, and even scholarly assessments of this period. There are many registers of expulsion exceptionalism, beginning with media representations of the three-month period during which the expulsion took place. Here, the event is rendered as a spectacle. In "Race and Nation in Ugandan Public Discourse," Edgar Taylor has observed that this is because of numerous factors, including the relocation of a large population of South Asians into European and North American nations that impacted British and Canadian demographics, the simultaneous shift (at that time) of Ugandan president Idi Amin's government away from Western influence, and the global racist and classist perceptions that the expulsion of fairly prosperous Indians (many of whom were British citizens) was more important than the displacement of and violence against Black Africans.[20] Ian Sanjay Patel has argued further that the British government made the so-called Ugandan Asian crisis and the refugees' British nationality a global responsibility (addressed further in chapter 1).[21] Indeed, the ensuing refugee crisis in the UK and Canada, which received the majority of Uganda's Asians, and the international press's existing preoccupation with Ugandan president Idi Amin shaped the entire episode as a global media event.[22]

One of the consequences of expulsion exceptionalism is that it constructs expulsion in reductive and singular ways, preventing a deeper investigation of the why and how of expulsion, and even contributing to a deep erasure of Black African experience of South Asianness. While some individuals, like Vali Jamal, have understood the expulsion as revealing the violence of colonialism and relationships between the imperial metropole and its postcolonial territories (even after the so-called end of colonialism), others have focused exclusively on the racism and illiberalism of Black Ugandan nationalism and Asians' racial victimization by Idi Amin and fellow Black-identifying Ugandans. Major media representations emphasize the dynamics of postcolonial violence but are limited in their ability to offer us a sense of the historical and structural processes that gave way to the rise of Idi Amin, his military dictatorship, and the racial tensions that led to the mass expulsion of Ugandan Asians. Expulsion exceptionalism can inadvertently legitimize ideas of Black Africa and Africans as inherently nativist and exclusionary, of anti-Asian or racial South Asianness as *equivalent* to immigrant foreignness, and of Asians as essentialized victims of racism and racial estrangement.[23]

Eurocentrism and the ensuing liberal Western (read: global) imaginaries of racial Blackness, Africa, Uganda, and Idi Amin are central to configurations of expulsion exceptionalism. For instance, the Punjabi diaspora community I am part of in the United States typically views Africa through civilizational, settler, or racializing/racist imaginaries of Blackness that are understood through postcolonial crisis, failure, underdevelopment, and "lack." In this framing, Africa is the exceptionally inferior illiberal Other to an exceptionally superior liberal West. Uganda, in particular, occupies a central position within these circulating epistemologies about the African continent. It is viewed as the premier site of political conflict and war, illiberalism, autocracy, and corruption—as represented by the exceptional brutality of military dictator Idi Amin. However, scholars such as Mark Leopold continue to unravel the distinctions between the myth and reality of Idi Amin, documenting the ways in which Western journalists constructed racist images of him as "Africa's icon of evil" through both personal and political notions of evil. Leopold observes that these notions of evil encompassed ideas of Amin's supposed, but unfounded, practices of cannibalism and sadistic pleasure, violent hypermasculinity and heterosexuality, illiteracy and buffoonery, and his excesses, thus constructing meanings about Africa, Africans, and Blackness itself.[24]

Even after the expulsion, some commentators simply assumed that the institutionalization and effective enforcement of liberal citizenship laws in the African postcolony would naturally enshrine substantive and equal rights for new citizen-subjects across racial, class, and other lines of difference. Mobilizing Eurocentric and liberal-democratic paradigms of modernization and development, they argued that individual rights on the basis of citizenship, backed by substantive content, would eventually overtake deeply entrenched racial and tribal (ethnic) conflicts and thus pave the way for norms of individual freedom and liberty and the interpersonal civility and respect common to multicultural and multiracial societies. In their efforts to perpetuate liberal-democratic norms in African contexts, they minimized the effects of empire and colonial violence and the role these played in the making of postcolonial racial, ethnic, and class identities; and they overlooked the agency of African and South Asian subjects in shaping the trajectory of the nation. Instead, their focus was on debating whether President Idi Amin's decree that expelled Asians was a violation of existing international human rights laws and norms, and legal strategies became a central modality of redress for many expelled Ugandan Asians.[25]

In response, Ugandan and East African intellectuals deployed analyses of political economy, dependency theory, and Marxist theory to underscore that European imperialism and colonial capitalism were central to fomenting racial and class tensions between Indian and African communities.[26] Mahmood Mamdani further developed the relationship between imperialist intervention, neocolonialism, and the ensuing emergence of military dictatorship and fascism in postcolonial Uganda, and later, the enduring logics of racialist and native rule in producing antagonistic postcolonial political identities and violence.[27] Others underscored the minoritized position of mercantile communities in new postcolonial nations and developed their analysis of expulsion according to Marx's study of the inequalities embedded in the modern liberal bourgeois capitalist nation as presented in his "On the Jewish Question." Here, they highlighted the circulation of anti-Semitic and other racial tropes that were applied to Indian merchants in Uganda as part of the nationalist bourgeoisie's visions of purifying the nation of minority groups made "alien" and "internal Others."

Decades after these scholarly interventions were introduced, both expulsion exceptionalism and colonial determinism continue to be

I.4   Ugandan Asian refugees deplaning upon arrival at Stansted Airport in the UK, September 18, 1972. This is a dominant visual representation of expulsion that circulates at commemorative functions; it is part of a global visual archive of expulsion exceptionalism. Courtesy of Keystone/Hulton Archive by Getty Images.

the preferred lenses through which to understand this particular historical event: either by rendering opaque imperial and colonial violence, capitalism, and global white supremacy and constructing instead postcolonial Afro–South Asian conflict as primordial and inevitable; or by explaining away Afro–South Asian conflict solely as the byproduct of European colonialism and European racism. And thus, expulsion becomes transformed into a spectacle of illiberalism imbued with reductive racial analysis. Images of racially victimized Asians leaving the nation via the Uganda Railway, and images of more well-to-do Asians boarding international airline carriers at Entebbe International Airport and deplaning as refugees in Stansted Airport in the United Kingdom, accompany references to the expulsion, (re)producing a collective global and diasporic memory of the event. These images are part of a global visual archive that depicts Asian/Indian eviction from an illiberal Africa due to the whims of an African dictator, leading to the incorporation of victimized, stateless refugees into Western liberal multicultural nation-states. Expulsion continues to be associated with powerful

1.5 & 1.6   Ugandan Asians forced to return to India: Uganda Asians arriving by train in Voi; and Asian passengers aboard the vessel SS *Karanja* arriving in Mombasa. Courtesy of the Mohamed Amin Collection, Nairobi.

I.7   Ugandan Asians departing Uganda at Entebbe Airport. Courtesy of the
       Mohamed Amin Collection, Nairobi.

racial imagery of Africa, of Idi Amin as the archetypical African autocrat,
and of Black Africans in general as a racially threatening body politic inca-
pable of liberal governance, civility, or even civilization. These associations
linger, like waves, in our Eurocentric consciousness.

But the illiberal exceptionalism associated with racial Blackness, Africa,
Uganda, Idi Amin, and the expulsion is not only rooted in a Western, white
imaginary. From the vantage of other locations in the Global South such
as South Africa and India—officially designated and self-defined as liberal democracies—Uganda continues to occupy an exceptionally illiberal
position. For the larger global South Asian diaspora and many subcontinental South Asians, Uganda is associated with the exceptional figure of
Idi Amin and his associated imagery, and especially with his sovereign
decree to expel all Asians from the nation. This perpetuates South Asian
racist imaginaries of Blackness and Africanness through South Asian source
idioms and practices, which also indicates that there are multiple origins of
race and civilizational thinking.

Importantly, in pointing out discourses and narratives that mark historical events through racialized binaries of liberalism and illiberalism, I do not
wish to minimize Ugandan Asians' legitimate experiences of racial violence

and trauma during their expulsion; rather, I wish to interrogate their lived historical experiences and their interpretations and representations of the event, which are themselves dependent upon historical location, identity, power, and privilege. Moving away from the idea that expelled Ugandan Asians are either singular or a monolithic community, or exceptional racial victims of Idi Amin, I am interested not only in how they negotiated the violence of their expulsion but also in how they continue to understand and construct ideas about expulsion many years on.

Finally, contemporary British and Canadian nationalist celebrations of Ugandan Asian exiles as exceptionally successful refugees and immigrants are also constitutive of the global landscape of expulsion exceptionalism I am mapping here. Formal and legal-juridical notions of citizenship are connected to normative notions of Western liberal democracy, civilization, the rule of law, and the successful integration of legal-juridical citizenship status with substantive rights and entitlements. This is exemplified by the making of exceptional refugees and immigrants who successfully embody citizenship in liberal nations. Commemorative practices and memorializations of the 1972 Asian expulsion are at the heart of reproducing and challenging aspects of expulsion exceptionalism, as they tend to focus on the time between the issuance of Idi Amin's decree to expel Asians and the ninety days following, during which Ugandan Asians were forced to flee. Indeed, commemorative events are usually racially compartmentalized, reproducing Ugandan Asian–centric understandings of the event.[28] I am interested in the weightiness of the expulsion as a traumatic event, the limitations of language in accessing the past, and the limitations of its more official representation through discourses of expulsion exceptionalism and official state narratives. What might be unearthed if we begin to work through and past these registers, centering the unresolved nature of the event, its tensions, and ambivalences?

This is important because it is not only Ugandan Asian exiles and their descendants who are working through their unresolved experience of expulsion and the enduring politics and practices of race, empire, and citizenship.[29] Ugandans of Black African heritage (also not a singular or monolithic group) continue to debate and discuss South Asian presence in the nation, and their entanglements with racial South Asianness remains persistent and complicated. Many young Black African–identifying Ugandans—both in Uganda and in global African diasporas—are becoming knowledgeable about the expulsion and are thinking through South Asianness. South Asians of Ugandan Asian heritage in the global diaspora are becoming more interested in their African heritage and in Uganda's place in the world. For many, their inheritance of racial exclusion from Africa and their continued racial discrimination in white majoritarian contexts are entwined with other complicated sentiments, such as discomfort and shame at working through elitism, casteism, anti-Black racism, and anti-Blackness within their South Asian communities. And as I will show, African–South Asian encounters are intensifying, not only in the African and South Asian diasporas in Global North contexts but also in the Global South and contemporary Uganda.

From Exceptional to Global Critical Event: Unraveling Expulsion Histories and Afterlives

Expulsion exceptionalism is both pervasive and illuminating. The excessive nature of the expulsion event is productive of its own occlusions. In "Asians and Africans in Ugandan Urban Life," Taylor has argued against a teleological narrative of racialization that posits "Africans" and "Asians" at odds with each other and in which "the 1972 Asian expulsion constitutes a totalizing legacy of Ugandan Asian history."[30] Such an understanding, Taylor maintains, obscures other historical contestations over race, class, identity, and citizenship before 1972. It also conceals other moments of anti-Asian violence that help us better map the run-up to the expulsion event as well as the complementary expulsions of the numerically larger communities of Kenyan Luos and Banyarwanda communities from Uganda by the first Ugandan president, Milton Obote; these communities were also constructed as nonindigenous to the nation.[31] With respect to Obote's civilian government and Amin's military government, the Asian expulsion is actually consistent with long-standing colonial tactics of identifying, persecuting, and eliminating social groups that came to be branded as "foreigners," "enemies," "saboteurs," or "anti-nationals" in the name of creating a new national and moral order. Other scholars have documented a range of "slow" evictions and deportations alongside the more radical expulsions of Black African "ethnic Others" considered nonindigenous during the decolonization eras of numerous African nations.[32] More recently, immigration restrictions, deportations, and expulsions have been more closely associated with a transforming global political economy, late neoliberal capitalism, and intensified migration; and there is specifically a growing literature on intra-African violence and migrant xenophobia in South Africa.[33]

While expulsion exceptionalism has concealed important precursors to Idi Amin's regime and the events of 1972, it leaves us without a sense of the *afterlives of 1972* in the Ugandan nation. I argue that the expulsion is an example of what Veena Das has described—in the context of divided societies created in post-partition South Asia—as a "critical event."[34] Das argues that critical events institute "new modalities of historical action" and that "new modes of action [come] into being which redefine traditional categories such as codes of purity and honour, the meaning of martyrdom, and the construction of the heroic life. . . . New forms were acquired by a variety of political actors, such as caste groups, religious communities, women's groups, and the nation as a whole. . . . They are also located across many terrains and institutions."[35] While Das examines critical events in post-partition and postcolonial India with respect to communal (religious-based) violence and pogroms, her concept is useful for studying the violence constitutive of postcolonial settler–Subject Race–native relationalities in the racially plural societies created by British indirect rule.[36] Elaborating upon Das's theorizations of violence, events, and the everyday allows us to reposition the 1972 Asian expulsion as a *global critical event*.[37] In general, anthropologists have argued that we should approach events "not as aberrations of the normal state of affairs but [as] elements of the everyday," which suggests that "social structure is a dynamic form shaped and remade through events."[38]

In this book, the expulsion is less of an "event as a historical construct that constitutes a rupture," or one that is framed singularly around Ugandan Asian experiences of expulsion and resettlement in the West.[39] The expulsion event is critical in the sense that it cannot "be subsumed within existing repertoires of thought and action" and it is constitutive of what I describe as the insecurities of expulsion.[40] This alternative positioning allows for deeper ethnographic engagement with persistent Afro–South Asian entanglements, including racial intimacies and estrangements. Expulsion as global critical event contends with both the continual reconstitution of racially nativist nationalism via transnational processes—and the colonized native subject's Manichean desire to rid, or "purify," the postcolony or nation of the settler-turned-citizen via expulsion—as well as with ongoing resistance to these same impulses.[41] This is a specific inheritance of the decolonization process that not only persists within Black African Ugandan and Ugandan Asian diasporic imaginaries but, like a haunting, lingers in contemporary urban Uganda.

In this book, I counter those who might exceptionalize a Ugandan postcolonial "culture of violence," including militarism and dictatorship (primarily and incorrectly associated with the Idi Amin regime), ethnic-based politics, and failures to arrive at modern political formations. Instead, I posit postcolonial Uganda's trajectory within interrelated scales of structural and societal-based violence that derive from European imperialism and colonialism, neo-imperialist and sub-imperialist formations of power, nativist nation-building, the excesses of political elites, militarism, and racial and ethnic, communal and gendered violence in everyday urban life. Das's conceptualization of "violence in the weave of life"[42] is useful here in considering the ways in which the familiar rhythms of postcolonial urban life were transformed into new and uneven domains of political and cultural practice and performance in the years that followed the expulsion. She considers the "mutual absorption of the event and the ordinary . . . So I end up thinking of the event as always attached to the ordinary as if there are tentacles that reach out from the everyday and anchor the event to it in some specific ways."[43] I approach the expulsion event in similar ways among Ugandan Asians—as silenced, politically regulated, constituted by the experience of trauma, a psycho-socially repressed domain of discourse that constitutes urban life.

Expulsion exceptionalism has both oversimplified and overdetermined the historical event of expulsion and its aftermaths. It fixes essentialized Black African and South Asian identities in opposition to each other in a binary logic, concealing the complexity of Afro–South Asian identities, subjectivities, and relationalities and concealing other persistent, if fragile, connections in post-expulsion years. When scholars stress either the event of expulsion via sovereign decree by the African autocrat (Idi Amin) or a historical-materialist analysis that resulted in Asian expulsion, they fail to see that both options prevent us from thinking about the everyday, productive tensions between historical process (structure) and the event and its circulations; they fail to consider the ways in which events may or may not illuminate structural processes, and how structural processes accrue and erupt in spectacular violence.

In other words, in this book, I examine how subjects understand and articulate the tensions and ambivalences between the two dominant themes constitutive of the expulsion as each claims, practices, and performs citizenship: first, as the failure of liberal nation-statehood and multiracialism; and second, as the failure of decolonization. While I am suspicious of a Western liberal worldview that posits the expulsion as the epitome of "failed citizenship," I am invested in working out how those I interacted with (across their relative positions of imperial and racial privilege, power, or precarity) navigate the aftermath of violence and continue to construct liberal and illiberal binary imaginaries. How do the subjects draw upon or forget colonial histories to make or disavow claims to citizenship and belonging, and what imaginaries of decolonization continue to persist?

When I began my research, I was struck by the ways in which the exoduses and expulsions of European settler and Subject Race communities of Indians and Arabs who left Africa in the 1960s and 1970s had foreclosed ethnographic research on South Asian presence in contemporary Uganda and on themes of race, citizenship, and belonging in East African nations, despite their neoliberal transformation since at least the 1980s. About 150 or so individuals who came to identify as Ugandan Asians—holding Ugandan, Indian, Pakistani, or other South Asian national citizenship— remained in the nation during the Amin regime; two thousand of the expelled generation and their descendants (usually third-, fourth-, or fifth-generation Ugandan Asians) returned to the nation after two separate state attempts to repatriate Ugandan Asian exiles during President Milton Obote's second government (1980–85) and President Yoweri Museveni's National Resistance Movement (NRM) government (1986–present). In addition, the state was engaged in a project to attract South Asian foreign investors (primarily Indian nationals) to settle in the nation as expatriate-citizens; and a growing population of noncitizen postcolonial migrants (estimated between 25,000 and 30,000) from India, Pakistan, and even Bangladesh and Sri Lanka had settled in the nation. Despite the growing urban presence of South Asians once again, there was a complete absence of an open discussion about the expulsion in national public life (although racial tensions and internal feelings of racial precarity among old and new "Asians" in Uganda were apparent once again). And unlike other (usually European settler) contexts in Africa, Uganda's postcolonial trajectory involved both Asian expulsion and state property expropriation *followed by* repatriation and property repossession for Ugandan Asian exiles—an unparalleled (and understudied) process in Africa.

The normalization of the contradictions between Ugandan Asian racial privilege and racial exclusion in urban Uganda (a vulnerable sense of noncitizenship—structurally, legal-juridically, and for some, substantively) became my entry point for studying what Aihwa Ong, in *Neoliberalism as Exception*, has astutely described as "mutations in citizenship and sovereignty."[44] How was it that despite attempts to de-Indianize the nation via expulsion and rid the new nation of a community with accumulated colonial, racial, and class privilege, numerous South Asian–descendant communities were still residing in the nation? How were their experiences of citizenship, belonging, inclusion, and exclusion shaped by the historical legacy of politics and policies of Africanization and expulsion, including Ugandan debates over Indian assimilation and social integration with Africans in the nation? Or how were their experiences being shaped by novel formations of power, sovereignty, and governance? How were they negotiating both privilege and precarity in the nation?

Open the Field: Remapping Citizenship, Sovereignty, Governance

Exceptionalities accrue. The propensity "to do history by analogy,"[45] alongside standard political commentaries, has produced Uganda as an epistemological foil to teleological Western liberal-capitalist norms of modernity and Eurocentric notions of development. Working from a descriptive and comparative perspective, the effect is that much knowledge production on Uganda buttresses policy frameworks that are used by international or global governance institutions, further normalizing the interventionist roles of such institutions. Knowledge experts position themselves as custodians of modernity, development, progress, and civilization through their discussions of distorted African political formations and their failure to arrive at supposedly universal metrics.[46]

Drawing on the postcolonial intellectual tradition that has underscored the historical and relational development of nationalism, the state, citizenship, and subjectivity within global and structural systems of power and violence, *Insecurities of Expulsion* unsettles the geographic and racialized epistemological distributions of liberalism and illiberalism (and their respective associations with a predominantly white Euro-American Global North and a predominantly Black African Global South) as mediated by South Asian communities and Asian nations in a hierarchy of nation, civilization, and race.[47] It is more fruitful to work from a baseline that acknowledges the entwinement of liberal, illiberal, and "nonliberal" modalities of governance in *both* Africa and the Global North. Ugandan state projects are modern phenomena, with state actors participating in their own nationalist and geopolitical projects, shaping citizenship and racial regimes, and negotiating interactive liberal, illiberal, and "nonliberal" domains of governance and sovereignty. (Here, I place the "nonliberal" in quotes to indicate that the term includes ideas and practices of Pan-Africanism and other practices of Black self-determinism; Afro-Asianism; racialized and patriarchal ethnic, religious, and caste formations; moral economies; and non-Western African political cultures—all deeply historical and social practices—that often become slotted under the signs of illiberalism, culture, tribalism, corruption, neopatrimonialism, clientelism.) Uganda is not exceptionally illiberal, backward, crisis-ridden, or pathological. Contemporary Uganda is a site from which to theorize more universally about what postliberal democratic citizenship formations might look like, even contemplating possible futures of what is understood as the exceptionally civilized West.[48]

By unbundling the category of citizenship from its assumed liberal, legal-juridical, nationalist, European, and heteropatriarchal associations, this book advances anthropological approaches to citizenship and noncitizenship.[49] Citizenship is neither a matter of legal-juridical status, nor is it delimited by an abstract or prescriptive assessment of citizen or subject status in postcolonial society.[50] Mahmood Mamdani's powerful analysis of the bifurcated nature of the colonial state and its construction of a domain of civil citizenship (for nonnative Subject Races), positioned in hierarchical relationship to ethnic citizenship (for native or indigenous Africans), showcases the exclusion of most Black Africans from citizenship. Mamdani analyzes the partial reform of the colonial state ("deracialization without detribalization"), and the resulting nativist construction of national identity and the exclusion of white settler and immigrant Subject Race populations, such as South Asians and Arabs, from the postcolony. Mamdani focuses more intensively on the ethnic domain of citizenship and does not offer us an analysis of the *ongoing incorporation* of nonnative or nonindigenous racialized subjects into the nation in relation to the persistence of citizen and subject hierarchies. I build on Mamdani's insights ethnographically by continuing to focus on the racial (civil) domain of citizenship; and I examine the transnational and multiple logics of governance, sovereignty, citizenship, and subjectivity even after the supposed de-Indianization of the nation. Attention to governmentality, to biopolitical and disciplinary power, and to necropolitics allows for a focus on the production of various racialized Asian subjects as both economic citizens and racial noncitizens who participate in citizenship-like effects with respect to specific gradations of Black African inclusion and exclusion from citizenship.[51] Black African, Ugandan Asian (or African Asian), and South Asian heritage communities are constructing projects of inclusion and exclusion, making claims to or even disavowing legal-juridical (formal) citizenship, and ultimately creating the assumed and naturalized binaries between citizen and noncitizen and state and national identity.

Likewise, by unbundling sovereignty from its associations with an ideal state that maps neatly onto the boundaries of a national territory, I follow those who have argued for the study of the dispersal of power and sovereignty across postcolonial societies and the state through the study of "sovereign bodies."[52] This is especially relevant for African states that continue to be shaped by external forces like donor-aid dependency, humanitarian and military intervention, NGO-ization, and neoliberal market encroachments from both Western and other Global South nations. Sovereign actors and entities like state officials who represent the UK, Canada, and the Indian nation-state, Ugandan Asian firms, self-appointed Ugandan Asian/Indian "big men" and other intermediaries, Indian entrepreneurs, community organizations, gender-based NGOs, and women activists all shape projects of governance, citizenship, the state, and national identity. And in order to avoid the so-called Agamben effect that often pervades the study of citizenship and sovereignty in anthropology, this research foregrounds political economy analysis and Indian Oceanic approaches to racial capitalism in its analysis of the shifting nature of empire, sub-imperialism, race, and capital.[53]

I trace liberal, illiberal, nonliberal, and neoliberal logics of governance, power, sovereignty, and citizenship. Here, different registers of citizenship appear across domains of structural racial exclusion, formal or legal-juridical status, and other substantive dimensions of inclusion and exclusion (or inclusion that according to Neha Vora is "both within and through conditions of legal impossibility").[54] As Damani Partridge observes, "An analytic of noncitizenship opens up a space for thinking about how the foreign subject is incorporated into social and political life without being totally excluded."[55] I examine this noncitizen racial and economic incorporation of "Asian" subjects—Ugandan Asians and other South Asians—as they negotiate gradations of inclusions and exclusions in postcolonial Ugandan society. Ugandan statecraft is characterized by autocratic and illiberal governance, and although political leaders have consistently positioned themselves as anti-Western imperialists, in practice, they have incorporated elements of liberal, nonliberal, and neoliberal governance as they undertake nation-building and citizenship projects. Taken together, I assess postcolonial racially nativist governance, neoliberal governance, and nonliberal forms of governance as assemblages of power central to the dynamics of inclusion and exclusion.

A persistent challenge in Uganda studies is the "methodological nationalism" that obscures Western imperial and Indian sub-imperial formations and that participates in the construction of Uganda through a lens of exceptional illiberalism.[56] This is so, despite the ways that African nations have to be legible in an international system of liberal nation-states, even as their sovereignty is continually undermined by imperialist and neocolonial interventions. This does not mean that nation-based illiberal governance should not be critiqued; it does, however, require transnational and geopolitical analysis. Those who analyze Western imperialism as an ongoing structure of power in contemporary Uganda often utilize reductive frames to understand Uganda's relationship to empire. For instance, with respect to US empire specifically, they assume that the Ugandan state is a client state or puppet regime of the United States, or simply a derivative regional or proxy ally in the United States' more recent Global War on Terror. At worst, they become apologists for the excesses of Ugandan state violence and militarism and romanticize Uganda's new strategic relationships with China and, to a lesser extent, with the Indian nation. Others take the position of critiquing only Ugandan postcolonial state violence, thus invisibilizing or implicitly defending Western influence in Africa and instead adopting simplistic discourses that analyze the influence of BRICS nations like China and India in Uganda through the lens of neocolonialism. They point to the role of new Indian and Chinese elites in helping to consolidate illiberal, authoritarian regimes in Africa under the reductive sign of "corruption," with little historical mapping or complexity that anchor these projects.[57]

Insecurities of Expulsion emphasizes the agency of Ugandan postcolonial elites and state officials alongside the changing nature of Western imperialism and the Global South's geopolitical shifts, including Indian sub-imperialist and nationalist ambitions, Afro-Asianism, and South-South cooperation. An ethnographic approach to governance, sovereignty, and citizenship highlights the agency of postcolonial elites, transnational expatriates and migrants, and other marginalized communities as they both participate in and contest imperialist and settler-colonial projects; the approach specifically highlights how subjects claim, disavow, or remake citizenship, inclusion, and belonging through domains of racial noncitizenship and economic inclusion in urban Uganda. This is especially crucial for studying the state that, vis-à-vis militarization, has long participated in its own interventions, counterinsurgencies, and political repression domestically and in East and Central Africa.[58] And as much as I am attentive to the ways in which Afro–South Asian connections have been mediated by historical processes of Western imperialism, colonialism, capitalism, and white supremacy, I track the contradictions embedded in emergent South-South connections and the resurgence of ideas and practices of Afro–South Asianism as South Asians continue to migrate to East Africa and to Uganda, specifically.

Feminist Anthropological Approaches to Transcontinental and Racial Uganda

This book is grounded in feminist anthropology regarding ethnography, theory, and methodology. Drawing on classical studies of nation, race, and citizenship in postcolonial East Africa and the anthropology of transnationalism and transnational feminist theory, *Insecurities of Expulsion* posits the territorial Ugandan nation as *a transcontinental formation* that is produced and constituted by circuits of Ugandan Asian (or African Asian) and South Asian capital, labor, migration, and mobility. Here, I am working past vague notions of "the global." The transcontinental lens encompasses a methodological parsing of the analytics of diaspora, imperial, national, transnational, and geopolitical scales of analysis while being attentive to the specificity of Uganda's transnational connections to specific nation-states that harness both imperial and sub-imperial ambitions. While the analytic of transnationalism attends to nation-to-nation connections and can at times inadvertently recenter "the West" or even "US empire," the transcontinental emphasizes the Ugandan nation's relationships to Western imperialist geographies and to *both* Indian Oceanic and Black Atlantic territorial geographies and historical processes, showcasing entanglements between empire, sub-empire, postcolony, nation, and diaspora (see map 1).[59] In doing so, I study how territorial-based state formation and citizenship are constructed and contested transcontinentally and both internal and external to the contemporary Ugandan nation.

Feminist anthropology that is informed by intersectional, postcolonial, and transnational feminist theories allows me to visiblize and foreground the experiences of Asian women and their relationalities to Black African men and women, the construction of racialized masculinities and femininities, and the changing structures and practices of heteropatriarchies central to imperial and colonial violence, anticolonialism, decolonization, and postcolonial statecraft and nation-building. Moreover, feminist theory advances new directions in classical studies of nation, race, and class as well as race and racialization in contemporary Uganda.

Race, like citizenship, is entwined with the rise of modernity, secularism, and racialized formations of ethnicity, religion, and caste. Ideas of Africa, India, Blackness, Africanness, Indianness, and South Asianness are contingent across time and space. Uganda and the East African region are shaped by distinctive landscapes of racialism and racialization practices, what we may describe, borrowing from David Goldberg, as a site of "racial regionalization."[60] Africa as an idea and as a continent is also racialized as Other to Western liberal modernity, which itself produces a hierarchy of nation-states, races, cultures, and civilizations.[61] Jemima Pierre's interventions on race, Africa, and the African diaspora parochialize South Africa's exclusive purchase on racial analysis, suggesting that non-European-settler colonized nations like contemporary Ghana and Uganda are also shaped by global white supremacy and global racial hierarchies, thus framing the African continent within discussions of "global Blackness" to include, rather than exclude, global racial regimes and their relationship to the specificity of regional racial formations.[62]

Africanists who deploy liberal "race-avoidant" practices based on the socially constructed nature of race tend to invisibilize the dynamics of whiteness and white supremacy as central to colonial and postcolonial rule, especially in non-European-settler contexts. In Uganda studies, paradigms of African ethnicity and ethnic conflict became dominant in the aftermath of the postindependence out-migrations of the British European administrative class and Ugandan Asians. In chapter 1, I discuss how the production of a (heteropatriarchal and militarized) racially nativist nationalism, the expulsion of Ugandan Asians in 1972, and the dominant ethnicity paradigm in academia, coupled with "race relations" analyses,[63] have marginalized the study of racial formation and racialization with respect to the structuring of African ethnic identity in postcolonial Uganda.

Building on more recent scholarship on East Africa, South Asia, and the Indian Ocean world that examines histories of racial thought and practice, this book is invested in the interactive elements of global and regional racial formations of Blackness and South Asianness. So, in addition to studying the production of anti-Asian sentiment and exclusion through Black African sources of Orientalism and racial nativism, I argue that both Western or Eurocentric and South Asian sources of racialism are implicated in anti-Black racisms and the denigration of African people, particularly through the intimacies of racial and caste consciousness.[64] Here, this research grapples with the ways in which Africa as an idea and as a continent is also rendered Other to ideas of Indian liberal-democratic national and civilizational modernity, which is itself under contestation, given the ascendancy of illiberalism and the Hindu right in contemporary India as well as other supremacist projects elsewhere in South Asia. To be sure, both Black African and South Asian–descendant people are racialized through global white supremacy and imperial or colonial race-making. Yet South Asian sources of civilizational, racial, and caste consciousness are central to understanding "race" in the Indian Ocean world and wherever South Asians migrate. So, while Indians, Arabs, and Africans are all subject to racial regimes that emanate from Western conceptions of race hierarchy and difference, I am working past any theorization of a single origin of race or what has become an either/or formulation of Western-centric racial analysis versus South Asian–centric religious and caste analysis. Racialisms have multiple sources, and the race, religion, and caste nexus, in addition to gender and sexuality and class formation and labor-capital relations, is critical to unpacking these dynamics. Finally, race is relational and mutually constitutive. African identities and ideas of racial Blackness are constituted by and through ideas of racial South Asianness, and vice versa. Both are mediated by ideas of racial whiteness and supremacy. Racial Uganda is produced within a transcontinental system of racial meanings and hierarchies in which Africa itself is racialized as a location of Blackness and continues to be configured as a racialized space by South Asians as they encounter racial Blackness and Africans in Africa.

Feminist analysis reveals that earlier studies of the Indian (or Ugandan Asian) diaspora in Uganda struggled with theorizing *both* class and racial formation; while other recent engagements with race in Uganda or East Africa are typically positioned in a white-Black binary framework, with no attention paid to Asians, Arabs, or other multiracial and religious communities. Historical-materialist histories of Indians in East Africa highlight the "masculinized migrant narratives"[65] of men or "Indians" who are unmarked and gendered male, with little attention to the dynamics of trans–Indian Oceanic patriarchal marriage and kinship; the racialized and gendered production of religious, sectarian, and caste-based communities; or the reproductive and productive labor of Indian and African women. Gendered, communal, sectarian, and caste-based identities are themselves nested within larger racial structures and labor-capital relationships, implicating both Black Africans and South Asians/Indians. Race is gendered and sexualized, and gender and sexuality are fundamentally raced.[66] A feminist undertaking of changing systems of race, capitalism, and patriarchy is foundational to the domains of citizenship and noncitizenship that I study. And while each of these domains is deserving of in-depth treatment, *Insecurities of Expulsion* offers more robust interventions in the discussion, advancing standard race and class analysis in East Africa.

From Diaspora to Theorizing Afro–South Asian Entanglement

This book is in conversation with existing studies of the global South Asian and East African Asian diasporas—works that have largely explored postcolonial themes of nation-based racial and cultural alienation and belonging, identity, migration, displacement, and nostalgia as South Asians migrated to the Global North.[67] It joins scholarly critiques of South Asian diaspora studies that argue that these studies have typically focused on majoritarian communities in Western liberal states, with less attention paid to the ways in which diaspora communities continue to be implicated in the material and discursive construction of the homeland.[68] New studies have expanded focus to the historical and more recent diasporic migrations of South Asians in the Caribbean, Middle East, and Africa, emphasizing themes of Arab-Asian and Afro-Asian connectivity, empire, and trans-Indian Ocean and Black Atlantic mobilities.[69]

The complexity of colonial and postcolonial African Asian and South Asian migrations, settlements, displacements, return migrations, and new migrations requires attending to British imperial diasporas and their descendants (whom I refer to as Ugandan Asian exiles, *stayees*, and returnees; they are also part of a larger "African Asian" global community). The overseas British Indian community (that is, the overseas Indian diaspora) that eventually came to see themselves as Ugandan Asians was deeply affected by the 1947 division of British India and the further division of Punjab into an officially Islamic (majority Muslim) Pakistan and secular (majority Hindu with Sikh, Muslim, Christian, and other minority religions) India; this division included the partition of East Bengal and the creation of Bangladesh in 1971, and the creation of the semi-autonomous, contested, and now Indian-occupied Kashmir. From the vantage of the African continent, the notion of "India" is not static and discursively shades into prepartition and premodern notions of "Hindustan" and "the subcontinent" as well as into contemporary nation-states. This is especially the case as I trace post-1990s South Asian migrations to Uganda (I variously describe these new migrants as investors and entrepreneurs, newcomers, and sojourners) from the postcolonial Indian nation, with scope for more attention to be paid to Pakistan and other South Asian nations. I examine how the Indian nation has come to be increasingly defined by Hindu majoritarian and Hindu nationalist tendencies, exclusionary to the ethno-religious plurality of the earlier East African Asian migrations, and more critical to the construction of the new post-expulsion South Asian communities in East Africa.

The multiple diaspora communities that move into and out of the Ugandan territory are characterized by different political, ethnic, and religious affiliations—with distinctive histories, loyalties, and identifications—all in flux and all of which changed during my fieldwork.

Many East African Asian heritage scholars studying their own displacements from Africa have critiqued any monolithic ideas of a South Asian diaspora, or even the idea that diasporic communities maintain attachments to a singular homeland in South Asia. Parminder Bhachu studies the "twice-migrant" East African Punjabi Sikh settlers in Britain; Avtar Brah, of East African Punjabi heritage, highlights "cartographies of diaspora" and the persistence of a "homing desire"; May Joseph analyzes the "nomadic identities" and the "performance of citizenship" among Tanzanian Asians; and most recently, Maya Parmar writes of "the double diaspora" in her study of the East African–Gujarati community in the UK.[70] This book follows Stuart Hall in his arguments that the location and "emplacement" of diaspora communities matters.[71] Returnee Ugandan Asians and newcomer South Asian migrants are a minority presence and are subject to structural and even interpersonal racial discrimination, or they have experienced racial discrimination in the West. But they also retain racial and (often) class privileges, and they can participate in settler ambitions, strong racial and civilizational consciousness, and racially prejudiced attitudes toward indigenous Black Africans. Interlaced with state and populist anxieties over the past and present of South Asian/Indian and foreigner presence in the nation, their citizenship practices, developed through multiple diasporic mobilities and displacements, inform the insecurities of expulsion I explore in this book. I work past the traditional anthropological study of diaspora communities as monolithic, with singular attachments to homelands and without the possibility of return; rather, I study their reception by their host nation and communities, the possibilities and limits of their repatriation to Uganda, their tensions with new migrants, and the construction of public and private narratives of racial victimization, privilege, belonging, and exclusion.

In this transcontinental analysis, the notion of diaspora is not only a scholarly analytical concept but also increasingly central to Ugandan, Indian, and other state-based ambitions. In a shifting geopolitical and political-economic context in which diaspora, South-South cooperation, and Afro-Asianism are being increasingly mobilized in international diplomacy and neoliberal economic policy, a focus on Afro–South Asian entanglement allows us to attend to wide-ranging configurations of connection: from the remaking of racial capitalisms and resurging racial resentments to notions of hospitality-guest relations, neighborliness, strangerhood, and intimacy to strategic cooperation and diplomacy. In general, Afro-Asianism has become a mode of describing cross-racial, national, and continental connections, including particular historical moments and shared experiences of oppression, politics, and aesthetics. Christopher Lee, in *Making a World after Empire*, concurs that "Afro-Asianism" is "an ill-defined term that has signaled both a cold war ideology of diplomatic solidarity and a more general phenomenon of intercontinental exchange and interracial connection."[72] My book engages with ideas of Afro-Asianism (and Afro–South Asianism more specifically) through ethnographic analysis of the state, citizenship, sovereignty, and governance. The geopolitical and neoliberal capitalist emergence of BRICS nations and South-South cooperation is recasting earlier Afro-Asian histories to new ends. It is not a linear, temporal progression from earlier Afro-Asian visions but a remaking of earlier historical moments and ideas, grafted into new practices. I trace how ideas of Afro-Asianism are becoming both nonliberal and neoliberal resources for practices of sovereignty, governance, and citizenship in the aftermath of the expulsion. As Afro-Asianism is increasingly authorized by state actors, these practices do not necessarily lead to less social distance between Black Africans and South Asians (both Uganda Asians and new South Asian migrants); instead they reveal both racial tensions and internal racial community oppressions—indeed, the unresolved nature of the expulsion event.

Conventional approaches to methodological nationalisms, area studies, and even anthropological research methodologies are limited in their ability to attend fully to entanglement. We cannot think of Africa as compartmentalized from South Asia, nor of South Asia (and its diverse diasporas) as isolated from Africa and its diasporas. Following Pan-Africanist Ugandan scholar Ali Al'amin Mazrui, who describes Africa's "triple heritage," and Paul Zeleza, who argues for "rewriting the African diaspora," this book asserts a notion of Africa that makes space for "Afro–South Asia" as territory, geography, and imaginary.[73] It is in dialogue with research that makes legible the transcontinental intimacies forged by European imperialist endeavors; and it expands upon research on what is being described as "Afro-Asian worlds" and "Afrasian imaginaries" among postcolonial scholars and others engaged with the possibilities of premodern Indian Ocean commercial cosmopolitanisms and pluralistic cross-cultural and religious encounters that were fostered in this region prior to the onset of European imperialism, colonial capitalism, and Western onto-epistemological conceptions of the human (including the ideas and practices of slavery, indenture, race).[74] However, it builds on more recent postcolonial insights on "brown over Black" and the uneasy nature of African-Indian entanglements, raising questions about the possibilities and limitations of the work of the anticolonial, postcolonial, and decolonial in research and scholarship.[75]

Methodological Notes and Plan of the Book

Insecurities of Expulsion is based on two years of ethnographic field research (2008–10), supplemented with follow-up research conducted while working on a national archive project (2011–12), while researching and teaching at Makerere University (2013–15), and during follow-up fieldwork in summer 2017. It includes additional online and virtual research tracking relevant developments up to 2022, focusing on the fifty-year commemoration of the Ugandan Asian expulsion. Most of my ethnographic research was carried out in central Uganda (Kampala and Jinja; Buganda and Busoga regions), with additional trips to small towns in other regions of the country to carry out interviews (see maps 3 and 4). I conducted participation-observation and made use of informal conversations, attended community events, and spent time at government institutions. The last chapter builds on an earlier phase of research carried out in 2003–4. I consulted print media in major national newspapers (since the expulsion) and analyzed archival documents. I also examined Ugandan Asian expulsion survivors' testimonies and cultural productions that circulate in the diaspora; I followed online social media engagement and commemoration events as they were planned by community leaders over email, social media (and after the COVID-19 pandemic, virtually); and I helped to organize community events in Kampala, especially in 2013–15. While this book foregrounds ethnography in contemporary urban Uganda, mapping the transcontinental nature of the insecurities of expulsion required following the partial and situated knowledge productions and practices emerging in the UK, Canada, and India—the contexts most significant to this study.

A significant challenge in my study was the high degree of political violence and political repression encountered in Kampala. The fallout of the Amin and Obote years, Asian expulsion, and civil war has resulted in enduring antagonisms and tensions within communities and in broader society, sensitivities that I, naively, did not always understand. Extended family connections were necessary for introductions and to build long-term relationships with affected families over many years. Given the economies of mistrust and suspicion that circulated in urban Uganda, my positionality and social location mattered a great deal, but often in unexpected ways. Although I was not quite a native anthropologist with Ugandan Asian heritage, my cultural familiarity with the Ugandan Asian community lent itself to varying degrees of insiderness and outsiderness and to accessing certain kinds of information; this varied by context, of course, due to my ethnicity, religion, age, gender. Moreover, among Ugandan Asians who had experienced the expulsion, what people talked about with me in private was different from their more self-conscious positioning in urban life. The management of trauma, of self and community representations, and of racial stereotypes were all micropractices that shaped the social fabric and everyday life. This study is not empirically exhaustive and does not intend to be. Instead, it opens up interpretive and subjective terrains of knowledge–with the realization that the act of writing is constituted by the limits of its ability to render legible violence and trauma or to engage with silences that surround critical events like expulsion and its aftermaths.

In contrast to persistent state discourses and even scholarship on the Asian presence in East Africa, there never was, nor is there now, any essential community to study. Rather, my subject of study is the continually unfolding insecurities of expulsion as viewed through critical themes of interest. Methodologically, I used the unfolding experiences of (racially defined) Ugandan Asian or African Asian and South Asian subjects as starting points from which to theorize entanglement and gain insight into the perspectives and agency of Black-identifying Ugandans, presenting empirical context in each chapter in relation to the discursive and representational constructions of the "Asian" or the "Indian" and the "Black African." Due to the specter of another possible expulsion and feelings of racial precarity among returnees and others, and in light of the fact that community networks are small, I maintain the anonymity, confidentiality, and privacy of those mentioned in this study. In some cases, I have used strategies such as composite figures and vignettes to convey meanings and ideas. In the case of public figures who gave me permission to use their real names, I have used them only after weighing the risks of doing so in an evolving political context.

Despite my efforts to share this research with and integrate perspectives of Ugandan (Black-identifying) intellectuals and researchers, government workers, journalists, artists, writers, and political activists, the very act of doing so raises methodological questions about anthropology and ethnography and how one develops a project that speaks to the relational but that might also peripheralize some voices and center others, and how one might imagine collaborative Black and South Asian ethnographic methodologies in places like urban Uganda and its geographies of connection. If I was worried about internalizing nationalist and nativist norms and anti-Asian sentiments, I was also concerned that my racial and cultural access to Ugandan Asian and other South Asian communities would lead me to reproduce the exceptionalisms I sought to undermine and to inadvertently highlight sympathetic representations of Ugandan Asians as singularly victimized subjects. Through the centering of Black African and other marginalized perspectives and by having others read and discuss my work with me, I hope that threads of scholarly accountability are woven into the text. The denigration of Blackness and African lifeworlds, often framed indirectly through discourses of cultural difference and connected to civilizational and religious ideology, casteism, and colorism, was emotionally difficult to confront. Apprehending and discussing racial practice with sensitivity were persistent ethical quandaries, especially during moments of heightened political violence, such as during elections, when anti-Asian discourses could quickly transform into racial violence. At the same time, I attempted to write without losing sight of racial, nativist, xenophobic, gendered, casteist, and other chauvinisms. Those who shared their lives with me also made strategic choices about what they presented. The ethnographic dynamics of what was "off stage / on display," both deeply intimate and very public, simultaneously secret and overt, was central to the insecurities of expulsion and constitutive of dynamic relationships and conversations unfolding during research.[76]

Asian, Indian, South Asian, Black, and African are discursive categories of colonial racial rule and anthropological knowledge-making that are still in common use in everyday life. But they must be denaturalized—even decolonized—in analytic and scholarly practice. I consider all racial categories to be mobile signifiers, and their meanings are shaped and reshaped dialogically and according to context. *Asian* and *Indian* are often used interchangeably in East African scholarship and in common parlance; but in this book I demarcate shifts in racialization and identification practices, attending to racialized ethnicity and religion. I refer to the older, British imperial diaspora of East African Asians as Ugandan Asians and as African Asians, especially as they distinguish themselves from post-expulsion migrants from South Asia. Newcomers are referred to as postcolonial South Asian migrants or more specifically, as Indian capitalists and entrepreneurs, as sojourners and migrants, or as immigrants and expatriates. Ugandan host communities are referred to as indigenous or

Black-identifying Africans or Ugandans. I use the figure of the "Asian" or the "Indian," the "Asian man/woman," the "African" in quotes to refer to the discursive register of race-making—recall that discursive and legal categories of native and nonnative shape racial distinctions in everyday life. I offer attention to racialized ethnicity and religion and to sect and caste identities as well, since *African* and *Asian* or *Indian* are incomplete in their ability to account for numerous communities that each have their own complex histories, traditions, and vernaculars (as addressed in chapter 1).[77] I am aware of a Gujarati and (Ba)ganda-centrism that might come to inadvertently stand in for "Asian" and "African," respectively, and thus unpack the multiplicities (and majority-minorities) that might be concealed by racial signifiers.

In positing the categories I use, I am aware that they still reassert the fixity of racial, ethnic, and cultural identities. Unlike the presumed essential and biological nature of race or the racial, ethnic, and caste purity of bloodlines, no one lives in isolated silos where cross-cultural borrowing and identity formations are not in flux, or where Afro–South Asian identities, subjectivities, and communities are not emergent, even if and when difference and hierarchy are regulated and reinforced. People with multiracial identities from mixed-racial and ethnic heritage communities also appear in this book. There is a dynamism to identity and subjectivity—the lived substance and fluidity of what becomes fixed racial identity—even as I write about nationalist, state, and community projects of racial, ethnic, communal, caste purity. I trace evolving categories of self-identification and Othering in order to make this complexity tangible, mapping categories of practice in contrast to my own categories of analysis. Finally, I use the category of Afro-Asian (and Afro–South Asian more specifically) because I am interested in how actors mobilize this category for governance (and its capacity to mask cross-racial inequality and internal hierarchies within racial communities) as well as its liberatory power to denaturalize imperial or colonial racial power and Eurocentric epistemologies and to forge solidarities across racialized groups. I attend to the circulation of Afro–South Asianness in grounded contexts and to the contingency of all categories as they emerge, strengthen, fade, and are remade anew.

The arguments evolve over six chapters that unravel the fallout of the expulsion and the continuity of Ugandan Asian and South Asian presence in the nation via a narrative of Ugandan statecraft and nation-building: the Idi Amin military government (roughly 1972–79); Milton Obote's second government (1980–85); and the post-1986 Yoweri Museveni–led NRM government. The exiled global Ugandan Asian diaspora community is not absented here but central to post–Liberation War statecraft and nation-building. Working from the ethnographic present then, part I of the book, "Imperial Entanglements," contends with expulsion as an epistemic and scholarly problem. Extending the discussion from this introduction, chapter 1 offers an analysis of the historical processes that shaped the rise of Idi Amin and the key anti-Asian themes that led to the 1972 Asian expulsion order, my interventions into existing scholarly debates on "Asians" or Indians in Uganda, and the scholarly distortions surrounding 1972 in knowledge production. Part II, "Entanglements of Expulsion," explores the shifting nature of imperialism and neocolonialism and postcolonial nation-building through the political and economic transformations of the post-Amin period. Chapter 2 examines the narratives of those who were "exceptions to the expulsion" and who lived as racial denizens in Amin's Uganda after the displacement of the majority Ugandan Asian population. In chapter 3, I examine the return of Ugandan Asians and (British-origin) Ugandan Asian capital via property repossession, all in the midst of structural adjustment, liberalization, and experiments with "No-Party Democracy," which marked a new era of racial noncitizenship and economic inclusion for those constructed as "Asian" and a normalized politics of racial nonreconciliation.

Part III, "South-South Entanglements," takes on recent geopolitical shifts of empire and sub-imperialism through a retheorization of Indian sub-imperialist and nationalist ambition, South-South cooperation, Afro-Asianism, and related concepts in contemporary Uganda. It also takes on three critical themes and points of racial tension that were central to the events of 1972, namely, economic exploitation, social integration, and interracial intimacies. Chapter 4 examines how Ugandan postcolonial elites at a state agency work to attract foreign direct investment from Indian capitalist entrepreneurs, all while remaking histories of Asian expulsion and facilitating "neoliberal Afro-Asianism" and noncitizen racial incorporation. Chapter 5 explores new South Asian migration and community-building practices and obstacles to social integration, state-community governance and citizenship practices, and community-based tribal citizenship claims by examining contestations between Ugandan Asians and new South Asian residents surrounding the moral and substantive content of citizenship in the aftermath of 1972. Chapter 6 unravels the heteropatriarchal nature of state- and community-building projects as the nationalist discourse surrounding Asian womanhood comes under public scrutiny for the first time since the expulsion, eliciting novel, but also tense and ambivalent, practices of cross-racial feminist organizing between Ugandan (Black

African), Ugandan Asian, and South Asian women. Finally, the concluding chapter and postscript shift back to transcontinental Uganda and its relationships with empire and sub-imperialism, postcolonial nation-building, geopolitics, and diaspora as I deepen my discussion of an *anthropology of transcontinental Afro–South Asian entanglement*. I reflect on the knowledge politics of the 1972 Asian expulsion and the transcontinental nature of contemporary social movements surrounding race and caste liberation and university-based student movements in the midst of intensifying South-South connection, all of which require rethinking empire, nation, race, caste, area, and discipline as separate domains of analysis. More immediately, I assess the possibilities and limitations of post-expulsion racial reconciliation, emphasizing that the conceptual and theoretical tool kit developed in this book is necessary for any substantive project of decolonizing citizenship and the liberation of Black and co-colonized people.

If Ugandan postcolonial experiments with liberal nation-building, interracialism, and social integration have proven fallible, then we might focus on an analytic of "arrested decolonization."[78] In my efforts to de-exceptionalize and deparochialize this difficult history and context, I argue that transcontinental Uganda can tell us much about the problems of democracy and decolonization, of uneasy paths to reconciliation, of interracial pluralisms, and of the need for more robust engagements with Black and Afro–South Asian study. But we must first begin by dwelling in the uncomfortable and unromantic labor of how people tentatively remake encounter in the aftermath of violent events and processes; this is a labor that requires epistemological possibility to flourish.

1

Becoming a Racial Exile, Becoming a Black Nation

Colonial and Postcolonial Orientations

"There's a sense of finality about the expulsion, a lack of desire to visit the past," I wrote in my notes. It appeared that Kampala, the capital city of Uganda, had been successfully refashioned into a racially Black city, consistent with Idi Amin's remaking of the racial demographics of the nation, not least because of the small numbers of South Asians living in Kampala: Ugandan Asian returnees, Indian merchants, newcomer migrants, entrepreneurs, and expatriates like myself. I was working through my embodied sense of racial South Asianness, both familiar and strange to urban Black African Ugandans, both *mzungu* (white or foreign) and *muhindi* (Indian) in Luganda, which is the language of the Baganda, or Ganda, people and other Ugandans of different ethnic affiliations and histories who resided in central Uganda and spoke Luganda. It was unclear to me whether I fell into the category of *muhindiness* that had been applied to the expelled Ugandan Asian community. I knew that among the Baganda, I represented the notion of a racial stranger or foreigner encompassed by the category *bagwira,* an unexpected stranger, one whose origin was unknown.[1]

Parsing out both public and private narratives about the expulsion was proving to be a challenge. Among older generations (of both Black African and South Asian–Ugandan descent), those who had lived through the political terror of the Amin and Obote years and the subsequent governments, there was a morbid fear of talking about the past. Embodying and managing traumas, avoiding overt discussion of the past, and constructing everyday life through silences or through freeze-frame images of the past had become an effective strategy for forging ahead. Some (Black African) Ugandans simply described the 1970s and the military dictatorship as the time when "Asians went away" (*abahindi abagenze*, in Luganda); among those of South Asian descent, the period was described as the time when "Amin chased us away" (*Amin ne humme bhagaya tha*, in Urdu/Hindi). Others recounted the past in perfunctory ways, like reading a textbook of chronological events, reciting political histories routinized through tales of coups and countercoups. As I drank coffee and ate *sukaali ndiizi* (small bananas) in the mornings, I scoured the daily newspapers, coming across occasional ministerial advertisements for the public auction of an "expropriated" or "repossessed" Asian property. I noted that many Kampala-based Ugandans who had prospered under the political stability of the current government, the National Resistance Movement (NRM), juxtaposed the present with the tyranny and violence of the past, acknowledging the historical importance of the Ugandan Asian community and their return, and dismissing anti-Asianism as a phenomenon among "uneducated" and often, rural Ugandans.

While for Black African–identifying and multiethnic Ugandans the expulsion was one of a series of violent events in the nation's uncertain trajectory, for Ugandans of South Asian heritage, the expulsion was *the* defining event of their lives; it destroyed the existing Ugandan Asian community and completely determined their ensuing life trajectories. While many Black African Ugandans had lost their lives or fled into exile during the worst years of political violence, Black African Ugandan youths born post-1972, unlike their parents and grandparents, had not grown up with sizable urban Indian communities in their midst. Here, I am mapping the multiple, "disjunctive temporalities"[2] experienced by differing generations of the racially diverse Ugandan diaspora, Black African and Asian/Indian communities who navigated differing postcolonial trajectories and forms of political violence: those who were killed; those who were expelled; those who fled into exile; those who were displaced and who migrated elsewhere; those who remained or returned; and those who were being birthed into a new national order.

Beyond population demographics, I was becoming attuned to more overt and subtle registers of South Asian/Indian presence in Kampala and other towns and cities in Uganda. Visible on the streets of many of the small, historical, colonial, and frontier towns that dot the countryside are the well-built, often ornate, buildings established by expelled Ugandan Asians. Expropriated by the Amin government in 1973 after the Ugandan Asian population fled the country, some had been repossessed by diasporic exiles or returnees in the mid-1990s, while others had been rented out to new tenants. Some had never been reclaimed and had been under the stewardship of the state since the 1970s. This infrastructural network of shops, homes, temples, and schools was in varying states of ruination and restoration. Religious, sectarian, and caste identifications, including Indic terms for "community" such as *samaj, mandal,* and *sabha,* were evident on these buildings, showcasing the significance of internal divisions within the historical "Asian community." They were a sustained urban record of the past, revealing the colonial racial ordering of urban space and the postcolonial processes of Africanization, expulsion, and neoliberalism, a veritable archive of the multiracial Ugandan city.

There were other visual and sensorial registers of South Asian presence. Street names that celebrated significant Ugandan Asian "settlers" or "pioneers"; Gujarati merchants plying their wares in small commercial shops on Kampala Road; expatriate returnees remaking transnational lives; the Ugandanized versions of Indian dietary staples like *samosas, chapati*, and *chai* consumed by all on a daily basis; and the cosmopolitan mishmash of Luganda, Swahili, Gujarati, Punjabi, and Urdu phrases. All these signs and symbols created ambivalent messaging about South Asian presence. For example, if the degradation of properties was suggestive of racial resentments and disinterest in the past, the memorialization of streets like Allidina Visram Street and the celebration of rags-to-riches Asian "pioneers" (merchants-turned-business tycoons) in Ugandan primary school textbooks seemed to celebrate the nation's South Asian heritage and its connections to the South Asian subcontinent.

Like the properties that cling tenaciously to the urban landscape, in this chapter I argue that the past—the 1972 Asian expulsion as a historical event and the processes that culminated in it—constitutes the present. Discourses and imaginaries of expulsion exceptionalism often construct the figure of Idi Amin, or "Asians" and "Africans," into singular and monolithic entities; and they construct postcolonial Uganda as an exceptional site of illiberalism, racial primordialism, and racial conflict culminating in a totalizing project of de-Indianization. Yet South Asianness, expulsion, and Afro-Asian entanglements persist, albeit precariously. The aim of this chapter is to map the European imperialist processes of colonial capitalism, race, and citizenship-making and unmaking that are otherwise masked

1.1 A reclaimed, freshly painted "Asian" property next to one in decline in Jinja. Photograph by the author.

1.2 A once-striking "Asian" property in ruin in Jinja. Photograph by the author.

by the spectacular nature of the expulsion and its seeming exceptionality. While historical contextualization of the 1972 Asian expulsion is hardly new in Uganda studies, I offer a critical reading of these histories and a scholarly analysis that de-exceptionalizes and deparochializes the event. More pointedly, the post-1972 scholarly focus on Ugandan postcolonial (read: Black African) ethnic conflict has produced epistemological closures surrounding the study of race, citizenship, and Afro-Asian entanglements. I focus on race and related social categories because they have always been insufficiently analyzed by postcolonial scholars and are necessary for contemporary analysis. The dominant scholarly focus on the Ugandan postcolonial structuring of African ethnicity and ethnic conflict must encompass the transcontinentalism that constitutes the nation, which means that African ethnicity should be considered a Black racialized formation in relation to global whiteness and South Asianness.

Ugandan Asians—those who remained in the nation after the expulsion, or those who returned later on—helped me to understand their progressive racial exclusion and alienation from the nation prior to 1972. Their memories were selective and constituted by colonial subjectivation; state, ethnoracial, and gender-based violence; ensuing trauma and silences; remembering and forgetting; fragments of reconstructed memories, or "rememories,"[3] that told me as much about their negotiation of their present conditions as the past. Their accounts departed from the dominant Western Ugandan Asian exile memorializations that tend to focus on Idi Amin as an exceptional figure, the expulsion decree, and the ninety-day expulsion period during which they fled the nation. Rather, they revealed longer temporalities of the expulsion event, including the persistence of claims to racial belonging despite racial alienation, even as they desired to "beat back the past"[4] and make way for potential futures. Memories and narratives further reveal complexity in the singular figure of "the Black African" during a time of heightened Black racial and nationalist consciousness in Uganda, across the African Continent, and globally.

Older Thematics in the Study of Asians in Colonial and Postcolonial Uganda

British imperialism was both a material and ideological project. It was about reshaping indigenous territories (seen as peripheral, uncivilized, and unChristian) into colonies that would become economically profitable. Imperialists used civilizational, developmental, and racist ideologies to foster colonized subjects' participation in the project of colonial conquest through the making of new identities and subjectivities. A key technology of colonization was to create gradations and hierarchies among subjects, both across empire and in specific territories. The imperial conquest of India (1858–1947) and the territory of what would become the Uganda Protectorate (1894–1962)—and the interrelation of the two—is an exemplary case of these processes.

Prior to European conquest, the lands between the Great Lakes heading north along the Nile were integrated into a world economy through indigenous modes of production and regional commercial trade networks developed by Arab traders.[5] Trade gave way to the expansionist and militaristic impulses of the Buganda Kingdom, the influence of Arab traders, followed by the settlement of Christian Protestant and Catholic missions in Buganda, creating pluralistic religious traditions and religious conversions that combined African indigenous spiritualities with Islam and Christianity. Within the Buganda Kingdom, Christian and Islamic rivalries and religious wars would become connected to the politicization of religious identity during the colonial and the postcolonial era.[6]

The early travelogues of European explorers such as John Hanning Speke and Henry Morton Stanley served as the ideological, racial, religious, and secularizing scaffolding of imperial designs. Mobilizing biblical mythologies and Victorian-era racial and civilizational thought, these travelogues argued that the southern kingdoms of the Great Lakes region were centralized and thus more developed than the segmentary societies of the north, ascribing their social organization and development to "Hamitic" or "Nilo-Hamitic" influences and to the civilizational virtues of the "Bantu."[7] In a parallel project, eighteenth-century European Indologists codified language families on the South Asian subcontinent. These language families, Aryan and Dravidian, then corresponded to the construction of indigeneity and migration histories as well as to phenotypical and biological constructions of race.[8] Building on the tactics of indirect rule as developed in the British Raj, which had already "invented" or defined religious and caste communities in relation to linguistic and racial criteria, and coupled with early anthropological research on African "tribes" in the region, the British successfully cultivated the Baganda people of the Buganda Kingdom as a collaborating ruling class.[9]

The 1900 Buganda Agreement consolidated colonial control of indigenous lands that would eventually become the Uganda Protectorate. The land treaty parceled "freehold" (or *mailo* land, in Buganda) from existing land, transforming these parcels into "Crown Land" administered by the Buganda royalty (the *kabaka*, or the king of Buganda, and other landlords and chiefs). This British-Buganda alliance and the creation of a native elite allowed the Buganda Kingdom to expand farther northwest, expropriating lands from other polities and territories, most notably from the Bunyoro Kingdom. By sending Buganda chiefs and later Indian colonial subjects— such as Sikh soldiers who had been defined as a "martial race" and deployed across the empire—to more remote regions, the colonial administration effectively quelled anticolonial insurgencies. Divide and rule tactics and the imposition of a decentralized Buganda authority throughout other native territories consolidated British control.

Although the administration initially wanted to transform the Buganda Protectorate into a European settler- and plantation-based colony like the highlands of Kenya or South Africa, their attempts at such settler schemes and economic productivity failed in the fertile regions. Over time, and in the process of privatizing precapitalist land tenure arrangements into landlord-tenant relations, they established instead a *nonsettler* peasant-based colony that would produce cash crops such as cotton, coffee, tea, and tobacco for the British-based manufacturing economy. This required a small British (European) administrative strata, the pacification and incorporation of native elites, the extraction of more labor, and the development of urban infrastructure.

As a result of the triangular Indian Ocean trade, Indian settlement in Africa had preceded the British in places like Zanzibar and the Swahili Coast. The Omani sultanate's move from Muscat on the Arabian Peninsula to Zanzibar in the late 1840s helped formalize Indian participation in commerce, creating a wealthy mercantile class of Indian and Arab traders and financiers involved in the trans–Indian Oceanic slave trade and the trade in ivory, spice, and gum-copal, thus connecting the East African coast to the Arab Peninsula and to India.[10] In contrast, Indian settlement in the Great Lakes region and what would become modern Uganda was more directly shaped by British colonization of the territory and world events. After the abolition of the transatlantic slave trade in the United States, a global cotton shortage imperiled the textile industry, and the British began to introduce new systems of coercive labor. Hugh Tinker, in *A New System of Slavery*, describes a "second slavery," or the indentured labor system of exporting and contracting Indian labor overseas to colonial territories through exploitative means. Indian indentured labor was necessary for the British-financed construction of the Uganda Railway that ran from Mombasa on the Swahili Coast to the shores of Lake Victoria.[11] By 1902, the British had forced African peasants in Buganda and other regions to grow cotton for export, followed by other lucrative cash crops, such as coffee, tea, tobacco, and sugar. The railway was critical for the transport of these agricultural products to the coast and for the overall transfer of wealth from the Great Lakes region to Europe. As their lands and livelihoods became sources of labor and economic exploitation in a global and colonial economy, colonized Africans—with many different linguistic, ethnic, and spiritual affiliations, the boundaries of which were always in flux and changing—were now loosely identified as "Ugandans" based on a common British colonial experience (rather than being identified traditionally as of the Baganda people and their many clans).

The British referred to indentured Indian railway laborers from Northern India pejoratively as *coolies*. It was primarily Punjabi Hindus, Muslims, and Sikhs and other low-caste Hindus from Kutch and Kathiawar in Gujarat who built or serviced the rails. Railway indenture was rather short-lived in comparison to Indian indenture in South Africa and the Caribbean. Nonetheless, many of the indentured remained in the Uganda Protectorate after their railway labor contracts were completed, seeking wage labor and economic opportunity. Between 1890 and 1920, the migration of "free" or "passenger" migrants grew as "overseas Indians" continued to seek economic opportunities in East Africa to escape exploitation and oppression in the British Raj. In fact, East Africa became such a sought-after migration destination for Indians escaping poverty that the British began to refer to the Ugandan and East African Protectorates as "The America of the Hindu."[12] Thus, unlike the settler plantation colonies of Natal that predominantly exploited indentured labor from the descendants of Southern India, the (mostly) Gujarati and Punjabi Indians who settled in East Africa came from (but not exclusively) dominant caste communities and were understood as " "voluntary" labor migrants and merchants, despite the fact that their mobilities were compelled by oppressive imperial and colonial forces.

Already established Indian merchants and trading firms in Zanzibar and on the Swahili Coast took advantage of the colonial context to expand their entrepreneurship into inner East Africa. Through Indian Ocean–based chain migration and endogamous kinship and caste-based capital and credit borrowing and lending practices, specific dominant caste Hindus and Islamic religious sects, known generally as *banias*, had traditionally dominated mercantile trade in coastal Surat and Gujarat; as a result, Gujarati Hindu Patidars (Patels) and Lohanas, Jains, and the Shia Muslim (Khoja

Ismaili, Istha-sheri, Bohras, and Memons) dominated mercantile trade in the East African interior. Serving as middlemen, they bought cotton and other agricultural products from African peasants and sold them to small-scale ginners or, later, to larger processing firms of both British and Indian origin.[13] In exchange, the so-called *dukanwallas* (shopkeepers) sold small, manufactured commodities and textiles produced in factories in Britain or in the British Raj to Africans in remote areas. Other labor migrants, such as clerks and civil service workers (Goans and Sikhs), soldiers and transporters (Sikhs and Muslims from Punjab), and carpenters and artisans (largely Ramgariah Sikhs from the Punjab) were recruited for administrative purposes, for security, and for building urban infrastructure.[14] Africans had little access to the agro-processing, manufacturing, and commercial aspects of the colonial economy that Indians and Europeans performed, which resulted in racialized class stratifications and urban- and rural-based racial disparities in colonial society.

In his foundational work on Ugandan political economy—*Politics and Class Formation in Uganda*, published after his own expulsion in 1972—Mahmood Mamdani convincingly argues that the integration of the Uganda Protectorate into the European world–capitalist system led to the "underdevelopment" of the region, thus refuting the idea that it was ever *innately* underdeveloped with respect to Western ideologies of development.[15] Colonialism, Mamdani argues, required indirect rule, or the establishment of "a class of collaborators who would receive partial treatment in return for helping to maintain law and order."[16] This class was found among the natives or brought from other dependencies. Structurally, "Asians," defined by the colonial administration through the legal and racial category of "non-native," were an "alien" collaborating class. Mamdani also describes Indians in Uganda as a "comprador class" essential to British metropolitan capitalist accumulation.[17] The scholarly language of "middle figures"[18] became important here as intellectuals positioned Indians in East Africa as both "intermediary colonists" and as "intermediary capitalists" within the territory. Furthermore, and as Indian settlement continued, political economy and class analysis deconstructed images of a monolithic or singular Asian or Indian community by distinguishing traders (the petit bourgeoisie) from capitalists (the commercial bourgeoisie), offering more nuance to representations of "Asians" as *banias*, or Gujarati merchants, even if Indians were still understood rather exclusively as traders and capitalist entrepreneurs.[19] While the class dimensions of the Ugandan-based Indian community were demystified, issues of the different ethnic, religious, sectarian and caste-based dimensions, including the significance of women and gender, were sidelined.

At that time, scholars understood the expulsion and Afro–South Asian racial conflict in postindependence East Africa primarily through the lens of class formation, which took primacy over the study of racial formation. Commentators often described "the deterioration of race relations" or an antagonistic "race consciousness." In a more nuanced formulation, race was conceptualized as a class-based identity, so that class was expressed as race. In a nonsettler colony like Uganda, Indians were "the visible settlers,"[20] and class status had a racial nature. Race, however, was considered epiphenomenal to labor-capital relations and the historical-material process of class formation. Racial categories like "Indian" or "Asian" and "African" tended to have a fixed and timeless nature to them, with little attention to race-making as a process.

In actuality, colonized subjects were made into "Indians" or "Asians" and "Black Africans." "Whiteness," "Asianness," and "Blackness" came into being through mutually reinforcing racializations (and secularizations) in which Christianity and Anglo-white supremacist race-thinking, including Orientalism, constructed race hierarchies, with Europeans at the top; Indians as less civilized but still within the civilizational ambit; and Africans at the bottom with no civilizational contributions.[21] European conquest relied upon the primacy of work-discipline, productivity, and the profitability of capital, rationalized through the civilizational and racial progress of the colonized and the infrastructural and technological development of native territories. Race was made material through experiments in statecraft and governance (the creation of institutionalized "native" and "nonnative" identities, the maintenance of law and order, the making of liberal institutions) and primitive accumulation (taxation and land enclosure). Racial difference was made into fact through labor-capital relations and the legal apparatus of the state, and through knowledge formations about supposed inherent and essential cultural traits, behavioral features, and physical attributes. Colonized subjects themselves internalized this Western racial consciousness and subjectivity, imbibing and reproducing racialisms.

In a shift from the study of political economy to political and legal governance, Mamdani, in his *Citizen and Subject*, returned to the question of race and ethnicity-making. He argued that British indirect rule required the construction of a "bifurcated state"[22]—one that entrenched rights on the basis of racial and native rule among urban-based "citizens" and rural-based "subjects," the latter exclusively defined by ethnicity and governed by customary authority. He identified this mode of governance and power, operating through racial and native rule, as the "decentralized despotism" that was deployed by institutions of native and customary authority.[23] So not only were the British successful in defining and governing different racial and ethnic communities,[24] but the bifurcated state would institutionalize racial and native identities, such that they would continue to shape the contours of political resistance to colonialism and the nature of postcolonial politics. Crucially, the urban-based nonnative or immigrant communities in Africa (Indians, Arabs, Tutsis, Somalis, and others) are understood as Subject Races. The (European-supremacist nature of) the colonial state offered the urban-based nonnatives more citizenship rights and entitlements than the majority African peasants, who were excluded from the domain of citizenship (the former was civil citizenship, as opposed to ethnic citizenship). Racial and native (ethnic) identities are thus not biologically or culturally inherent but become formalized, "political" and "politicized," through the violence of colonialism and its state and legal institutions, creating racial and ethnic antagonisms in the postcolony.[25] This significant intervention into the nature of the colonial state and governance complicated earlier discussions of the tripartite racial hierarchy in which Indians played an intermediary role in colonized East Africa, what J. S. Furnivall has described as the "plural society" created by the British and Dutch empires.[26] Mamdani actually offers an analysis into the differential and relational nature of governance between Indians (nonnatives and Subject Races) and Africans (natives), through his account of the hierarchical position of Subject Races in relation to Black Africans, distributed across urban and rural domains of colonial society.

In addition to the limitations of an exclusively structural and institutional account of race and colonial violence, Jemima Pierre argues for more attention to the global dimensions of race and racial formation. These, she maintains, offer an account of the racialization of native African identities as racially Black in relation to global white supremacy in postcolonial Ghana, whether through case studies of African-Americans' racialized encounters with Ghanaians, or through the popularity of skin-lightening creams and the colorism that continue to afflict beauty standards for Black Ghanaian women.[27]

I also develop Mamdani's discussion of decentralized despotism, which focuses on the ethnic dimension of the bifurcated state. In this book, I attend to the complementary and changing nature of the racial dimensions of the bifurcated state, even after Asian expulsion, assessing customary governance and the practice of decentralized despotism among racial community patriarchs.[28] Postcolonial feminist and gender scholars have argued for more attention to be paid to the heteropatriarchal and gendered nature of the state and to the gendered dimensions of racial and native rule, the constant refashioning of existing indigenous (native) and communal (Indian or Asian) patriarchies.[29] Colonial conquest was as much about defining ideas about gender and sexuality as it was about defining racial and ethnic identities. Decentralized despotism is a heteropatriarchal despotism.[30]

Multiple Sources of Race Consciousness: Racialized Ethnoreligious, Sectarian, and Caste Community; or, The Race, Religion, and Caste Nexus

Colonial racial governance, racial hierarchies, and racial boundaries were made material through the everyday stuff of life: racialized urban infrastructures, anti-miscegenation laws and racial endogamy, and the social experience of work and home life. Racial segregation policies required that Indians live in designated "Indian areas" of small towns, while the majority of Africans lived in more impoverished urban areas or rural villages. On one occasion, Vali Jamal and I drove to Old Kampala, a historic Indian area, to explore middle-class residential areas with conspicuous Indian place-names like "Bombay Gardens" and "Delhi Gardens. After that, we toured Jamal's former racially segregated primary and secondary schools nearby. We then drove to the grounds of the beautiful Ismaili *jamatkhana*, walking past Indian commercial storefronts on our way home. Together, we imagined the liveliness of Old Kampala, prior to the expulsion, and compared our visions with the more limited South Asian presence today and the many other African migrants, including Somalis and Ethiopians, who had moved into the area.

Racial segregation meant that Indian-African encounters were often limited to urban workplace interactions on the merchant's shop floor or in local government offices. Some Indians, depending on their traditional and colonially conceived occupations, labored more closely with Africans who served as apprentices as artisans, carpenters, builders. As Indians became more prosperous, they developed hierarchical and racially paternalistic relationships with Africans, employing them as shop attendants, as domestic servants in their homes, or as drivers and security guards. Racial and civilizational consciousness commingled with class consciousness, such that Indians treated Africans in impersonal and dehumanizing ways. Both colonial racial and native governance and antagonistic labor-capital relations fueled urban racial tensions.

But while Mamdani focuses on the racial and native governance and divisions fostered by the colonial state, and while Pierre examines the significance of global racial regimes of whiteness and Black Atlantic conceptions of racial Blackness to contemporary Ghanaians, I focus here on South Asian subcontinental (Indian diasporic) regimes of race and the development of Asian or Indian racial consciousness.[31] It is also true that South Asian racial consciousness was cemented through patriarchal kinship and religious, sectarian, and caste-based endogamy as well as by the intimacies and intersections of race and caste-based social systems. The caste system, which, according to B. R. Ambedkar, is a graded system of hierarchy,[32] has its origins in early Vedic sources and the spiritual ideals of Brahmanical Hinduism. It encompasses an embodied logic of purity and pollution in which birth status determines occupation, marriage prospects, ritual practice, forms of commensality, access to spiritual liberation and enlightenment, and all other aspects of everyday life. Casteism has complex origins and expressions on the South Asian subcontinent, both within Hindu society and in non-Hindu religious communities. Although the caste system is ancient and predates Western conceptions of race, caste, and religious groups, like ethnicity and ethnic groups in Africa, caste groups and caste-based divisions were politically defined and redefined in relation to the British conquest of the Indian subcontinent.[33]

In fact, the dominant ideology of Hinduism-Brahminism—and its ideals of upper-caste superiority over others within Hindu society—constructs Dalits, indigenous Adivasi communities, and "internal others" such as Muslims as beyond the line of pollution and thus within the realm of untouchability. Increasingly, Brahminism is related to modern projects of Hindu nationalism and Hindu supremacy over minority religious traditions and especially traditions now constructed as nonindigenous to the nation, binding Brahminism and casteism to linguistic and racial theories of Aryan invasion and settlement and the imputed boundaries between the descendants of ancient Aryan and Dravidian groups. This Aryan racial identity thesis instantiates the phenotypical logic of colorism and connections between dominant caste Hindu supremacy and Anglo-European/white racial supremacy (especially in Northern India), such that light skin and other aspects of sacred Brahmanical Hindu life are considered pure and closer to God than the darker-skinned individuals in other parts of the subcontinent, especially those with supposedly Southern or Dravidian origins.[34] In India, *adivasis*, Afro-descendant communities like the *Siddis* of Gujarat, who are descendants of African slaves and soldiers and even more contemporary Black African migrants, are positioned within this racial and caste purity and pollution matrix.[35] This, of course, does not mean that Brahmanical casteism operates exclusively according to colorism, but there is an affiliation between the two.

All South Asian religious traditions continuously underwent processes of change and reform in relation to the Moghul and then the British conquest of the subcontinent, with both older and more recent traditions like Buddhism, Jainism, Christianity, Islam, and Sikhism often serving as resources for religious conversion out of the oppressions of Brahmanism and casteism for discriminated Dalits and other communities. Non-Hindu South Asian traditions also contended with the deeply seated practices of Brahminism, casteism, racism, and colorism. In the nineteenth century, new religious nationalist and religious reform movements—responding to European presence, Christian missionaries, and the desire to especially reform casteism and sexism in Indian society—became central to a growing anticolonial and nationalist consciousness and to the Indian Independence Movement.

As Indians migrated across the *kala pani* (literally "Black water," ocean crossing) and settled in East Africa, they brought their communal and caste-based attachments with them, even as they negotiated Anglo-European racial supremacy and civilizational norms. In his major work, *The Indians in Uganda*, anthropologist H. S. Morris argued that "no representative cross-section of society of any district in India was transplanted to Africa, partly because members of certain sub-castes did not migrate at all . . . there was, therefore, no caste system, in the strict sense of the term, in Africa."[36] Instead, Morris focused on the "caste categories," or *jatis* (defined loosely as sub-castes), that were derived from the traditional Brahmanical four-fold *varnas*, which had previously determined hierarchical labor occupation and prestige according to ranked status in India, noting that primarily (non-Brahmin) dominant mercantile castes—sustained via transoceanic systems of patriarchal kinship and marriage endogamy—settled in East Africa.[37] Morris traced the development of "caste associations" that were used in the formation and organization of "caste communities." He argued that "the caste category gave way to a larger field of recruitment for the emerging 'community' and allowed people to come together who, at home, in the rural districts of India, would probably not have associated with one another."[38] For Morris, who closely studied the Gujarati Hindu

Patidar and Lohana caste communities and the Shia Muslim Khoja Ismaili, Istha-sheri, and Bohra communities in townships in Buganda and Busoga, "the Asian community" was more or less a fictive British administerial political and legal category, while the organizing units of everyday life and the basis of institutionalized community-building were actually religious, sectarian, and caste-based.

Morris emphasized the caste-based nature of trans–Indian Oceanic capital and trade networks and, unlike in India, the importance of merchants' securing of *both* consanguineous and affinal marriage alliances in the development of endogamous caste-based commercial and kinship networks in East Africa.[39] Among the Hindu communities, he explored religious practice and the caste-based nature of ritual purity and pollution—including the phenomenon of what M. N. Srinivas has described as "Sanskritization," or "up-casting," among certain caste-based groups as they gained occupational and economic mobility and prestige in relation to their counterparts back in India (this was especially true for the Lohana caste community but was also the case in other caste communities).[40] Likewise, Morris examined religious practice and sectarian divisions among the Muslim communities in East Africa, arguing that contestations over religious ideology, orthodoxies, and heterodoxies contributed to community elites' political claims upon the colonial state to establish distinctive places of worship, funerary sites, schools, and other communal organizations. Under the leadership of the Aga Khan, the Ismaili Khoja community, for example, emerged as a modernizing, "pace-making group" for other Indian communities, who followed suit in institutionalizing their own organizations in urban areas.[41] The Ramgharia Sikhs, whose traditional *misl* (sovereign state) became landless in the Punjab, flourished in East Africa, establishing a network of separate *gurudwaras* in East Africa.[42] Others have examined the reach of religious reform (especially neo-Hindu) movements in the Punjab and Gujarat, and the institutionalization of the Sanatan Dharm, Swaminarayan, Brahmo Samaj, Arya Samaj, and even the Hindu Swayamsevak Sangh (HSS), affiliated with the Sangh Parivar, or the Hindu right-wing movement, in East Africa and Uganda; others have explored the Punjabi Singh Sabha (Sikh reformist), Shia Muslim (Gujarati and Kutchi-speaking), and Sunni Muslim and Ahmadiyya Muslim Jama'at (Punjabi) movements and related institutions in the region.[43]

Religious community could also foster both affiliations and tensions between Indians and Africans. Richa Nagar has argued:

Shiite Muslim traders from Ismaili, Ithna Asheri, and Bhora sects felt a religious affinity with the Islamic culture of Zanzibar and the Swahili coast . . . the constructions of ritual purity and pollution among Hindu trading castes of Bhatias, Lohanas, and Jains, on the other hand, initially discouraged the permanent settlement of Hindu families in Zanzibar. These Hindu castes were characterized by strict social taboos against Muslim ways, especially their non-vegetarian dietary habits. Hindu-ness and caste purity for upper castes and classes was defined in opposition to Muslim ways and the Islamic environment of Zanzibar and the Swahili coast was thought to threaten and pollute this purity.[44]

Thus, for caste Hindu communities, Africa was symbolically understood as "alien" and "unsafe" for women, and men maintained close ties to their home villages on the Indian subcontinent, maintaining trans–Indian Oceanic marriage alliances. For them, Islam came to be associated with Africa, Blackness, pollution, and the lack of civilization.

The racial construction of Africa and Africans as "alien" and "unsafe" was thus predicated upon Brahmanical Hindu cosmologies (ritual and caste-based notions) of purity and pollution and related institutionalized and ritualized discriminations within South Asian communities. In the upper-caste (class) Hindu imaginary, both Africans and Muslims could be viewed as "polluted" due to food taboos and other seemingly foreign and "primitive" practices. These prohibitions were more flexible among caste-oppressed or low-caste Hindus, and especially among segments of the Punjabi community and others who participated in shared religiosity, were nonvegetarian, drank alcohol, or who worked closely and side-by-side with their African counterparts in working-class occupations.

South Asian religious and caste-based endogamy relies upon patriarchal kinship and marriage endogamy and involves the patriarchal control of women's reproductive labor, sexual desire, and marriage alliances. Dominant-caste and elite Indian women are especially regarded as the custodians of patriarchal family and community honor through the maintenance of individual honor, especially sexual morality and sexual purity, or what I loosely describe through the category of *izzat*.[45] In the aftermath of 1947 and the communal and gendered sexual violence that accompanied the partition of British India into the new nations of India and Pakistan, overseas Indians in East Africa came to be more strongly identified with new postcolonial religious nationalisms that were reconfiguring both internal religious divisions and boundaries in East Africa as well as racialized boundaries between Indians and Africans, especially through the figure of the Indian woman and her honor, a theme I reengage with in chapter 6.

Morris did not address the relationship between race and caste-based systems and social structures in East Africa, or the ways that casteism has its own racial features—both embodied and phenotypical notions of hierarchical difference—which commingled with Western ideas of race and the British system of racial and native governance for Indians and Africans. What I describe as the *race, religion, and caste nexus* reinforced South Asian racial and civilizational consciousness in relation to a caste consciousness connected to religion and spirituality, reinforcing hierarchies and boundaries between Indians and Black Africans. Anthropologist Agenandha Bharati, in *Asians in East Africa*, describes this as Indians' "matrix of spiritual condescension," or ethnocentrism, in East Africa.[46]

Although traditional religious, caste, and sectarian affiliations and related occupations and domestic life guided everyday life for Indians in Uganda, there was always flexibility in these structures. In our interviews, many Ugandan Asians remembered the East African–style South Asian cross-ethnic and religious pluralism they enjoyed, attending each other's social and religious functions and learning each other's languages, even as religious ideology and caste difference shaped communal consciousness and as language shaped ethnic consciousness. Most East African Asians followed rules of ritual ceremony and purity, commensality, and marriage endogamy, even as they changed and adapted to East Africa. The race, religion, and caste nexus did not mean that intercaste, intercommunal, and interracial intimacies did not exist; instead, they often took place when suitable (endogamous) marriage alliances were not available. Moreover, as anthropologists Aidan Southall and Peter Gutkind observed, interracial intimacies were typically between Indian men and African women and were patriarchal and hypogamous in nature, a pattern found in intercommunal and intercaste alliances as well.[47] Interracial intimacies between Indian men and African women were more prominent in the early colonial period, as Indian settlers, laborers, and merchants pursued a range of relationships with Black African women, from concubinage and extramarital affairs to official marriage unions. This was so despite European anti-miscegenation policies that especially restricted these intimacies and African women from settling in urban Uganda.[48] As more Indian men settled permanently in East Africa, more Indian women arrived on the scene, sharpening racial, religious, class, and caste boundaries. Cross-racial intimacies—based on both European and South Asian notions of race—were regarded as improper and taboo. Nonetheless, cross-racial intimacies persisted as Indian men possessed patriarchal racial and sexual access to African women and participated in intimate relationships with African and mixed-racial heritage women.[49]

In a striking parallel to anthropologist Karen Leonard's research on mixed-race Punjabi Mexican marriage alliances in early twentieth-century California,[50] a small minority of East African men from Punjabi communities (primarily Sikh and Muslim) and the more Europeanized Goan community formalized marriage arrangements with African women in frontier regions of Uganda and Kenya despite their restricted and taboo nature. New multiracial Afro-Asian communities emerged, joining and marrying into existing Indian, Arab, Swahili, and Nubi communities and becoming part of existing urban racial and color hierarchies. Shared religiosity—especially via Christian, Sunni Islam, Sikh, and other religious institutions—also created spaces for cross-racial intimacies and for the inclusion of multiracial families within the racial margins of racially endogamous Indian communities.

What we take to be fixed racial identities or naturalized distinctions between Indians and Africans are, in fact, products of complicated processes of race-making, themselves shaped by religious, caste, gender, and sexual dynamics. These dynamics, in turn, became the basis for racialized labor-capital relations and the making of racial and class consciousness. Racial distinctions and boundaries were always in flux, even as they came to be redefined through colonial governance and legal administrative processes and subsequently reworked in the postcolonial era. The race, religion, and caste nexus and associated ideas and practices of patriarchal kinship, marriage endogamy, purity, pollution, and colorism are foundational to community-building, labor-capital relations and class formation. All this belies the framing of a primordial and inevitable postcolonial Afro–South Asian racial conflict and violence, deepening our understandings of the multiple sources of South Asian civilizational and race consciousness and the degradation of Black and African communities in Uganda.

Newer Thematics in the Study of Asians in Colonial and Postcolonial Uganda

Integrating and developing insights from existing studies, we are in a better position now to theorize the imbrication of the material and social relations of production (productive and reproductive labor, labor-capital relations, class formation) with social analysis (the race, religion, and caste nexus; patriarchal kinship, gender, and sexuality). For example, if we take seriously a more internationalist application of the insights of scholars from the Black radical tradition, like Cedric Robinson (*On Racial Capitalism*), who have argued for the racialized nature of systems of imperial and colonial capitalism, slavery, and labor exploitation, contemporary Uganda offers us a distinctly Afro–South Asian reading of colonial racial capitalism and political economy analysis.[51] I deploy the notion of *racial-caste capitalism* to best describe the racialized system of capitalism and the dominant role of traditional merchant communities from coastal Gujarat and Surat that relied upon endogamous kinship-based caste-capital networks shaped by structures of colonial racial governance.[52]

Legally and politically, the colonial administration facilitated "Indian" dominance in trade, commerce, and industry and "African" dominance in agricultural labor through several mechanisms. First, the British created legal and racial discriminations that prevented nonnative Indians from owning (freehold, or *mailo*) land and establishing an "ethnic homeland" in African territories. Additionally, Africans (especially those from the north) were prevented from migrating to urban areas and entering commercial trade. Second, the bifurcated nature of the colonial state created two parallel and hierarchical systems of citizenship: "civic citizenship" for Indians and "ethnic citizenship" for Africans; and both racialized groups experienced a deferral of full citizenship rights in relation to Europeans. This meant that colonial administrators governed an invented "Asian" or "Indian" racial community that lived in urban areas and various African "tribes" that lived in their ethnic homelands. In actuality, very complex religious, sectarian, and caste-based communities became nested identities within this fictive "Asian" racial community;[53] and likewise, complex indigenous collectivities were racialized as "Black" and "African" by the colonial state.

Shifting away from scholarship that has focused exclusively on the spatial dimensions of the colony/nation, I am invested in engaging the history and complexity of the British Empire in the Indian Ocean arena. I build on what Thomas Metcalf, in *Imperial Connections*, has described as the British Raj's and overseas Indians' "sub-imperial role" within the British empire. Sub-imperialism marks the ways in which different colonial territories and their subjects are positioned differentially, and even hierarchically, within the spatial dimensions of empire, thus becoming complicit in imperial designs and the colonial domination of other colonized groups. For instance, we know that the large-scale transplantation of Indian labor and merchants into inner East Africa was entwined with the institutionalization of colonial technologies developed in the British Raj: legal systems, currency, administrative systems, all of which became very profitable not only for the British but also for the British India–based native elite and capitalist class, and eventually, in Uganda, for the entrepreneurial Ugandan Asian capitalist class. Extending Metcalf's analysis to studies of imperial citizenship and its attendant notions of race and civilization, sub-imperialism is useful when thinking about the ways in which British Indian subjects (or legally defined British Protected Persons in the colonial Ugandan Protectorate) had an elevated racial and legal status in relation to Black Africans, a status that afforded them certain political and economic entitlements, including access to mobility, trade, and entrepreneurship opportunities across the British Empire.

Even with these British imperial and British Indian sub-imperial dynamics, the colonial administration in the Uganda Protectorate strongly regulated the labor migration and settlement of less privileged Indians as well as their day-to-day lives. The foreign and colonial office was concerned with the "uncontrollable" and "polluting" Indian presence moving from the coast into the "African interior," and it imposed immigration restrictions and exercised deportations and discriminatory policies that prevented Indians from attaining certain kinds of political and economic entitlements—while they were also exploited for their labor, skills, and expertise. Despite these obstacles, some entrepreneurial Indian merchants gradually built intergenerational wealth, purchasing agricultural land and establishing independent manufacturing firms in competition with British firms and capital interests. Nanji Kalidas Mehta's autobiography *Dream Half-Expressed* and Muljibhai Prabhudas Madhvani's *Tide of Fortune: A Family Tale* illustrate this intergenerational process of pioneering *dukan-wallas* becoming successful family firms, the Mehta and Madhvani Groups.[54] In fact, Indian capital interests and entrepreneurship prevented both Kenya and Uganda from becoming fully fledged European/white settler colonies like Rhodesia and South Africa. British policies continued to establish limits on Indian immigration and business enterprise, rationalizing the restrictions through paternalistic discourses of safeguarding and protecting "African interests," thus preventing Indians from converting their economic power into political power. So, despite the sub-imperialist and even settler-colonial ambitions of a small number of Ugandan Asian entrepreneurs, on the whole, the British were successful in pitting Indians and Africans against each other and fomenting racial and class tensions, all while maintaining political, economic, and social control.

But Indian sub-imperialist and settler-colonial ambition was also challenged by a laboring Indian proletariat that forged horizontal working-
class, cross-racial, and anticolonial solidarities with Africans, especially in
Kenya. East Africa–based Indians were deeply influenced by the Indian freedom struggle, and especially by Mohandas K. Gandhi, among other anticolonial leaders, who advocated for civil disobedience, nonviolent resistance,
and *satyagraha*, or self-rule. In fact, Gandhi's first *satyagraha* campaign
concerned the condition of Indian *coolies* in Natal, South Africa, with the
abolition of Indian indentured labor finally taking place in 1916. Here,
the Indian diaspora in Africa (both South Africa and Eastern Africa) was
central to a more inclusive notion of "Indianness" promulgated by Gandhi
and the transcontinental reach of Gandhianism.[55]

After Indian independence and the partition, Indian prime minister
Jaharwal Nehru and other new nationalist leaders helped to cement a notion of diplomatic Afro-Asian solidarity and South-South cooperation,
exemplified by the proceedings of the 1955 Afro-Asian Conference in
Bandung. The political ideology of nonalignment (the Non-Aligned Movement [NAM], established in 1961) and resistance to imperialism, colonialism, and racism would define diplomatic relationships between postcolonial
India and emerging African nations during the Cold War and prior to the
1972 Asian expulsion, even as the new Indian nation was at geopolitical odds
with China, Pakistan, and its own illiberal political interventions over territorial Kashmir. Significantly, the Nehruvian Indian project shaped a more
exclusive notion of "Indianness" in which "overseas Indians" in Africa were
encouraged to take on the citizenship of their host nations and integrate into
new African nation-states.[56] Nonetheless, third world anticolonial struggle
and the struggle for autonomy from the global powers continued to shape
the discourses and imaginaries of horizontal solidarity between "Indians"
and "Africans."

Much of the debate about overseas Indians' middling status as imperial
citizen-subjects who straddled both freedom and unfreedom—and their access to differential and elevated civilizational rights, benefits, and privileges
denied to Black Africans—has been refracted through a related scholarly
debate on Mohandas K. Gandhi and his life in South Africa, which I do not
take up extensively in this book. In brief, we now know that Gandhi's South
African itinerary reveals an early accommodation to the European imperial
matrix of civilizational and race hierarchies at the expense of Black South
Africans like the Zulu in the Natal, who, for Gandhi, appeared to remain outside of the civilizational ambit. Gandhi's South African itinerary, attention to

his writings on race and caste, and both the secular and nonsecular nature of political and ethical praxis serve as a foil to an exclusive or parochial Indian nationalist historiography of Gandhi as well as to understandings of the Indian diaspora in Africa as exclusively one of colonial collaboration or resistance. Rather, Gandhi's South African trajectory reveals the importance of studying the multiple sources of, and the changing nature of, Indian imperial, race, and civilizational consciousness; the internal differentiation and inequalities within Indian communities; and the continued significance of material histories, symbols, and ideas of Gandhi and Gandhianism on the African continent, which I address further in the conclusion.

Given the dominant and stereotypical representation of the figure of the "Asian" as a Gujarati merchant in postcolonial Uganda, there are a few other ways of reading Asian presence in the scholarship. After 1972, many sociologists posited comparisons between Indians and Jews as similar "alien" and endogamous "internal others" in East Africa. Some have deployed the "Simmelian stranger paradigm"—see, for example Gijsbert Oonk's discussion of "settled strangers" in his analysis of Indian business elites in East Africa[57]—to describe the mix of strangeness and familiarity between immigrant Indian mercantile and African host communities. In South Africa, Thomas Blom Hansen, in *Melancholia for Freedom*, focuses on phenomenological race analysis, describing a "mutual nonrecognition" or sense of incommensurability between Indians and Africans in a township in Durban, South Africa; and Jon Soske deploys the category "other colonized" to refer to South African Indians.[58]

I shift away from all-encompassing theories or representational frames to explain South Asian presence and Black African–South Asian relationalities in postcolonial Uganda, engaging instead with the complexities of racial entanglement after the expulsion. Ugandan postcolonial scholarship leans toward structural analysis, such that there is less attention paid to the contextual and contingent ways in which Ugandan Asians and other South Asians have negotiated their racialized expulsion, exclusion, and incorporation, both privilege and victimization. Siba Grovogui's use of the "quasi-sovereign" in international relations theory is helpful in conceptualizing the ambivalent quasi-subject, quasi-settler postcolonial subjectivities of Ugandan Asians and other racialized subjects, the not quite "beyond settler or native" positionality.[59] The insecurities of expulsion are thus animated by vertical and horizontal dimensions of intimacy and estrangement; of subimperialist, settler colonial, and nationalist ambitions; of the unmaking and remaking of racial and civilizational supremacies; and of the reciprocal and equalizing ideas and practices of Afro-Asian interracialism and connection.

Anticolonial Nationalisms, Racial Nationalism, Black African Racial Consciousness, and Anti-Asian Populism

The sturdy, middle-class Indian homes that Jamal and I visited in Old Kampala were evidence of midcentury Ugandan Asian prosperity, residences that would last for generations. By the end of World War II, the Indian or Asian racial community was settled and multigenerational, identifying as Ugandan Asian, speaking Luganda and other regional African languages in the towns in which they lived, investing their capital and savings in their homes and businesses, creating a secure future. By contrast, Black Africans had less access to political and economic rights and entitlements, and they encountered the wealthier Ugandan Asians in their everyday lives. Black Africans, however, did not passively accept the exploitative racial and economic conditions to which they were subjected. They articulated racialized class grievances against Ugandan Asians through political activism, including economic boycotts and expressions of growing populist anti-Asian sentiments and violence.

If Ugandan Asians possessed a diasporic racial, religious, and caste consciousness, Africans had developed their own ethnic and Black racial consciousness from multiple sources, including colonial racial and native rule. A unifying Black racial consciousness was forged from colonial subjugation and inflamed by local and urban interactions with Ugandan Asians and through a growing African anticolonial nationalist consciousness. This expanding Ugandan Black racial consciousness was in dialogue with internationalist Pan-Africanist, decolonizing Black liberation and Black consciousness movements across the African continent. Here, Pan-Africanism refers to numerous ideologies—articulated by key thinkers dating back to the Atlantic slave trade and late nineteenth- and early twentieth-century intellectuals such as W. E. B. Du Bois and Marcus Garvey—that elevate the connectedness between the African diaspora and indigenous Africans on the continent via a common history and ancestry, and a unified Black racial and cultural consciousness, with ideas to unify and uplift the descendants of slavery and colonization. While Pan-Africanism has also historically been less defined by racial criteria and has been a source of Afro–South Asian dialogue and solidarity "across the color line," and while Uganda would become a key center for Pan-Africanist political action after independence, in the colonial period, the core concern for Ugandans was their oppression via the visible, yet minority, Indian community, especially Indian traders in urban areas. Throughout the 1940s and 1950s, H. S. Morris documents that the numbers of African traders grew and that they were numerically larger than the Indian traders; but the latter handled almost three times as much business, such that both Europeans and Africans felt that Indians had a stranglehold on the economy.[60] The concentration of Indians in urban areas of Buganda and Busoga as well as in other frontier towns in the countryside, in addition to their conspicuous prosperity, provoked the growth of anti-Asian sentiment among urban Africans. Ultimately, the entire Asian racial community was scapegoated for the ills of the colonial system: Asians, it was said, were unfairly dominating the economy and exploiting Africans.

Rajivbhai is a third-generation Ugandan Asian of Gujarati Hindu (Lohana trading caste) heritage who had managed to stay in Uganda even after the expulsion deadline (see chapter 2). He was in his late seventies at the time of our interview, and through his life history narrative, he illustrated the racial privileges and precarities that came with his commercial success in the run-up to Ugandan independence. His experience echoes those of Asian traders in more rural areas who were victimized by anti-Asian violence in earlier decades. Rajivbhai began his story by detailing his memories working as a clerk for the colonial civil service and by describing the racial discrimination he experienced at the hands of the Europeans before he decided to leave Buganda and open his own wholesale shop near Lake Katwe, in the southwest of Uganda. Working on the basis of family loans, borrowed credit, and very small profit margins, at one point he had two shops and a petrol station in Kasese. "I was stable," he described. "I had a good name in the [Indian] business community because I was honest. I may have delayed [creditors'] payments, but I never had the intention of not paying. I had credibility in the market. People were giving me credit and I was giving credit to Ugandans as well . . . there was no problem." Positioning himself as a moral citizen by virtue of his integrity in business transactions and the extension of credit to African peasants and traders, he then described the loss of his businesses due to organized African protests against the British administration, including anti-Indian shop boycotts. Indicating his felt proximity to Europeanness, he eventually moved back to Kampala where there was more racial security for Indians. Although Ugandan Asians like Rajivbhai were aware that Africans were protesting Indians' commercial advantages—

access to credit and their dominance in trade—he also countered (from his vantage of post-expulsion vulnerability and insecurity in Uganda) that the Asian community was important because they had helped to develop the colony's monetary economy and extended opportunities and skills to Africans. At the same time, Black-identifying Ugandans who worked in Indian shops during this era felt that Ugandan Asians posed obstacles to their own advancement, and that Indian-African interactions reinforced hierarchical and exploitative racial and class hierarchies and paternalistic attitudes toward Africans. For example, many of the Ugandan African elders I spoke with (primarily those of Banyankole, Hima ethnic heritage) during several visits to Mbarara, a small frontier town in Ankole, and who had later become beneficiaries of the Asian expulsion and businessmen when they were given Indian shops, remembered that Indian merchants were savvy in business, brought unique and exotic commodities to rural areas, gave African customers items on credit, and even included small gifts in their purchases, like matchbooks and safety pins. Many African elders remembered the humiliation they experienced at the hands of British colonial officers when paying their head and hut taxes, or while performing manual and unskilled labor in Indian shops and being referred to in patronizing and emasculating ways as "boys," even when they were grown men.

Despite their unified and growing anticolonial consciousness, Africans were also internally fragmented and politically divided according to class and colonial privilege, ethnicity (the Baganda native elite and the many other disenfranchised Ugandan ethnic communities), and religious affiliation. An anticolonial Baganda urban elite and the growing African urban working class was organizing anticolonial, antiloyalist Buganda, and anti-Indian political agitations. Buganda peasants and landowners, frustrated by the loyalist leadership of the Buganda *lukiiko* (parliament), had established an alliance with Kabaka Mutesa II, the King of Buganda. Urban-based bureaucrats in the civil service were upset over racial discrimination in pay scales; cash-crop farmers were frustrated with colonial marketing boards that extracted profits from peasants; traders demanded an end to state-protected monopolies that denied them access to wholesale trade; and urban workers (domestics and transport drivers) demanded better wages. Buganda nationalists like Ignatius Musazi focused their political campaigns and grievances against the native elite ruling chiefs and Indian merchants. In 1945 and 1949, there were massive general strikes withholding African labor, boycotts of Indian shops, and uprisings in rural and urban areas. The more violent uprisings targeted vulnerable Indian shopkeepers and traders in the countryside through overt racial anti-Asian sentiment and accusations that Indian traders exploited Africans.

By the early 1950s, the African peasantry and working class had managed to gain considerable concessions from the colonial administration, including more democratic and inclusive membership for Africans within the Buganda Lukiiko, the establishment of cooperative societies that would grant Buganda peasants and landowners access to agro-processing, the establishment of an African Trader Association, and the "Africanization" of personnel in the colonial civil service. Here, *Africanization* refers to the incremental policy reforms brought about by colonial and postcolonial governments that increased African participation within government and the economy. These policies delicately balanced African-Indian employment ratios, slowly replacing the majority Indian employees and traders in government service and commerce with indigenous Africans.

India gained independence in 1947, Ghana became independent in 1957, and the nearby Kenyan freedom struggle was underway. In the wake of these developments, new Ugandan-led political parties put forth their own visions for a free and independent nation. Formed in 1952, the Uganda National Congress (UNC) established coalitions across colonially crafted religious and ethnic divisions between indigenous Africans. A section of the Buganda elite was also fighting for the independence of Buganda from the larger territory of Uganda and seeking recognition by the British Commonwealth. When the colonial administration demanded that the *kabaka* of Buganda, Mutesa II, pledge his allegiance to the British Crown and Her Majesty and he refused, he was exiled. By 1954, the UNC strategized a total country-wide boycott of Indian traders and the commercial sector to pressure the colonial administration to bring back the *kabaka*. Politicized Africans identified Indians as a colonial class of settlers and believed that confronting them was necessary to dismantling colonial power.

Upon the *kabaka*'s return in 1955, the UNC had transformed into the Uganda People's Congress (UPC), and the Buganda ruling elite established the separatist Kabaka Yekka (Kabaka Only [KY]) party. The UPC—mostly Protestant Christians—united Africans from the north and east, and it was successful in forging ethnic alliances among urban traders and Baganda civil service bureaucrats who had their own grievances against the Baganda ruling class. In other regions like Ankole, West Nile, and Kigezi, Catholic-identifying Africans under the leadership of Benedicto Kiwanuka organized the Democratic Party (DP), which was primarily concerned with the Africanization of the civil service. By 1959, the Uganda National Movement

(UNM), an alliance of local trading associations, was led by Baganda nationalists like Augustine Kamya, and it successfully organized another major Indian trade boycott. Once again, anti-Asian populist grievances exploded on the national scene, this time more forcefully coalescing around the idea of Indians' economic exploitation of Africans. Indian shops in townships across the country were burned, and Indian traders fled to Kampala or even left Uganda. Many Ugandan Asians involved in retail and commercial trade, like Rajivbhai, detailed their movements from more isolated regions of the country back to major urban centers throughout the 1960s. In doing so, they narrated internal mobilities and temporalities of anti-Asian violence and exclusion that differed from the dominant and exceptionalized narrative of President Idi Amin's three-month-long expulsion in 1972.

African politicization and the institutionalization of party politics continued to grow in the 1960s. The Buganda Lukiiko passed a resolution declaring Buganda an independent state, although the move was not politically recognized by the British. Although Kiwanuka and the DP won the 1961 national elections, their victory was considered futile because of internal disagreements among the Baganda about political representation, which prompted a strategic political alliance between the UPC and the KY. The British administration organized fresh elections, and Dr. Milton Obote, of Northern Langi ethnic origin, won the election, becoming the first prime minister of Uganda, with the *kabaka* appointed as the president. At this time, it was assumed that the problem of Ugandan Asian economic dominance in trade would be resolved through Africanization policies.

Against the backdrop of Ugandan nationalist politics, an East Africa–based Indian diasporic and anticolonial consciousness connected to the freedom struggle in British India was also growing. The political activity of nearby Kenyan Asians was remarkable—they had established the East African Indian National Congress as an extension of the Indian National Congress (INC). Kenyan Asian political activists like trade unionist Makhan Singh, M. A. Desai, Pio Gama Pinto, and the Punjabi-based Kenyan contingent of the internationalist Ghadar Party nurtured racial and class-based solidarities with Africans in anticolonial struggle against the British. In contrast to their Kenyan Asian counterparts, Ugandan Asians were fewer in number, disproportionately in the commercial sector, and less politically conscious and active. However, the British authorities were also intensively surveilling African and Ugandan Asian political activity at this time; colonial tactics of surveillance and repression would continue in the postindependence period under President Milton Obote, as evidenced by the case of Rajat Neogy, a prominent Ugandan Asian political activist and founder and editor of the progressive and nonracialist magazine *Transition*.[61]

Official Ugandan Asian political participation was circumscribed by the British administration, and to attain political gains, it relied upon appointed Indian community elites forging connections with Europeans in the British Legislative Council. Following the imperial model of civilizational and racial mobility, Ugandan Asians in formal political positions often fought for political representation on key institutional boards, voting franchise, and other concessions that mostly benefited their (minority) capitalist and commercial interests. Other activities for which Ugandan Asians advocated included participation in local administrative affairs or community-based (religious and cultural) institutions, because there were few shared spaces of cross-racial political activity that could foster horizontal relationalities between co-colonized groups. Still, Gardner Thompson has observed that as independence approached, there was a shift, "from communal to national politics, from nomination to direct election, and it implied an end to the conducting of Indian politics at an informal level between representatives of pressure groups and officials in government."[62] Ugandans of both Black African and South Asian descent were beginning to imagine a kind of formal equality across racial and class divides as they were now directly contending with each other in the postcolony/nation. During this high era of nationalism, colonial subjects-turned-citizens were beginning to experiment with ideas of liberal democracy, emerging forms of political consciousness, and performing Ugandan and Ugandan Asian, or African Asian, national and cultural identities.[63]

Predictably, Ugandan Asian politics were both conservative and progressive, ranging from strategic participation in formal party politics to developing liberal and radical-left activist collectives. By the late 1960s, most Ugandan Asians were aligning themselves with either the UPC government (Obote) or the KY (the Buganda Establishment). Business elites were concerned with the self-preservationist defense of privileges in the new nation. Others, like Rajat Neogy of the Uganda Action Group (UAG), pushed Ugandan Asians to identify with African nationalist interests by relinquishing their racial and class privileges. Neogy vilified the existing Ugandan Asian leadership for "exploiting Africans unduly, keeping themselves socially aloof, and hindering rather than advancing the 'African cause.'"[64] Neogy and the UAG were creating novel space for inclusive and plural "African Asian" nationalist identities, even as "African" and "Asian" identities continued to become polarized and defined by strict racial criteria.

1.3   Rajat Neogy, the founder of *Transition* magazine,
       image date unknown.

1.4   Sugra Visram dancing in a traditional Buganda *gomesi*, 1962.

Another example of independence-era activism was the liberal bourgeois participation of Ugandan Asian women in voluntary organizations
and other professional societies. Aili Mari Tripp, in "Women's Mobilization in Uganda," has documented a range of women's groups that brought
middle- and upper-class urban African and Indian women together, fashioning new ideas of respectable womanhood and femininity alongside
nation-building. Sugra Visram, an important independence-era politician,
activist, and businesswoman—and the only Ugandan Asian woman member of the Buganda Lukiiko and MP for the KY party—became a symbol for
this modern and newly visible Ugandan Asian womanhood. Having been
adopted into the Buganda Mamba clan and given a Ugandan name, Namu-
biru, she was successful in staging African, Ugandan Asian, and Afro-Asian
identities, crossing racial, communal, and gendered boundaries, exempli-
fying her investments in the new Ugandan nation and "Asian" racial and
cultural integration.

Decolonization Pains: Defining the "African,"
Excluding the "Asian"

Independence was not so much an exit from empire or colonialism as
an entry into a transforming global order that maintained colonial logics, boundaries, and the political and economic marginalization of Africa
through neo-imperialism and neocolonialism.[65] National identity never
mapped onto cultural, ethnic, or racial homogeneity; and statehood, political
authority, and citizenship were contested. The political and legal structures
of colonial states (the bifurcation between civil and ethnic citizenship)[66]
was retained, even as political leaders mobilized abstract liberal ideas of individual freedom and equal citizenship through the legal-juridical contours
of citizenship that were central to the modular nature and the "imagined
communities"[67] of the new nation. As Bronwen Manby observes, "New citizenship laws were adopted, largely based on models from the [European]
power that had colonized them but using the versions that had applied at
home to their own full citizens, rather than in their colonies."[68] Obote and
the UPC adopted liberal constitutional frameworks that asserted the equality of all citizens, despite the fact of glaring institutionalized racial and class
hierarchies and inequities across Ugandans of indigenous African and South
Asian descent.

The 1962 Constitution of the Republic of Uganda defined citizenship
on the basis of *jus soli* (citizenship by place of birth) and *jus sanguinis*

(citizenship by descent) principles. If a person was born within national territorial boundaries prior to independence, or if the person was a British national or British Protected Person with at least a father or paternal grandfather born in Uganda, they could automatically become a Ugandan citizen (there were additional provisions for citizenship by registration or marriage).[69] Could Ugandan Asians become "natives" in the postcolonial context? That is, could they become fully integrated as equal citizens, despite their "visible settler" status?[70] One response was to deracialize the urban sphere of citizenship by expanding the realm of substantive rights and entitlements for Black Africans, thus forcing Ugandan Asians to relinquish their race and class-based entitlements. Obote established a Minister of State for Africanization who was empowered to Africanize the civil service. Other reforms increased and facilitated the entry of African traders and entrepreneurs into the market. A second response was to reshape the demography of the nation through legal restrictions that controlled the migration of noncitizen Indians and their role in commerce, thus effectively maintaining the minority status of nonindigenous communities. Both Africanization policies and immigration restrictions were central to remaking Ugandan nationality and African identity.

The situation was all the more complicated since those racialized as "Asian" did not have the same formal citizenship status at independence, much less substantive commitments to the nation. While many Ugandan Asians automatically became Ugandan citizens at independence, some British Protected Persons and British Indian subjects did not; they needed to register for citizenship within a designated two-year period. Some identified culturally as African and understood Uganda to be their permanent home, while others were invested in other possible futures and the political security that British nationality could provide. Their status as British Protected Persons, a legacy of their inherited imperial racial and civilizational privileges, allowed them to choose their nationality at independence. Against the unfolding management of imperial citizenship privileges, community leaders, Ugandan officials, Indian nationalist leaders like Jawaharlal Nehru, and British officials in the United Kingdom were all weighing in on the possible futures and divided loyalties of Uganda-based Asians and the overseas East African Indian diaspora in general.[71] From the perspective of Ugandan nationalist leaders, it was important that those who understood themselves to be Ugandan Asians demonstrate their willingness to retract their imperial citizenship *both* through formal legal-juridical means and through demonstrated substantive commitments to the Ugandan nation and to Africans.

Meanwhile, Obote's UPC government was drifting toward illiberal governance, authoritarianism, and a one-party state. Conflicts internal to the ruling party led Obote to undemocratically ban more radical Baganda-led African trade unions. By 1966, Obote contested the *kabaka*'s political authority and the Buganda Kingdom's attempt to lay claim to two disputed counties in Bunyoro; this became the so-called Lost Counties controversy. In the fallout, the UPC-KY alliance was disbanded. Grace Ibiringa, a prominent Buganda politician, led an effort to reintegrate Buganda into the UPC by creating a Buganda branch of the party and holding fresh elections. After Ibiringa and other prominent Baganda leaders attempted a coup against Obote and the UPC, they were arrested. Obote then introduced a unitary constitution that abrogated all the federal powers of the Buganda Kingdom, suspending the *kabaka* from his duties. When both parties refused to sign off on the new constitution, Obote escalated the standoff by ordering armed aggression on Mengo Hill, and General Idi Amin, the commander of the Uganda Army, attacked Lubiri, the *kabaka*'s palace. The *kabaka* escaped and fled to the UK, where he later died in exile. The outcome of the so-called Mengo Crisis was that Obote declared all state institutions supreme, and he outlawed traditional kingdoms in the 1967 Constitution of the Republic of Uganda, establishing political norms of increasing dependency on military power and authoritarianism.

Meanwhile, the Ugandan Asian capitalist class had maintained its alliance with Obote and the UPC by expanding their investments into industry and manufacturing, especially as British capital interests receded.[72] This was strategic for Obote and the UPC, because it compromised the political power of the Baganda elite, and it also maintained political security for Ugandan Asian community elites. Obote continued to consolidate political authority, announcing the "Common Man's Charter" and his "Move to the Left" agenda. Utilizing the discourse of African socialism, Obote inaugurated majority state and government ownership of multinational companies. Mamdani points to the fact that the policies, while ideologically socialist in expression, did little to serve the interests of trade unions or the urban working class; they were instead the "practical instance of nationalization as partnership between multinational capital and the ruling class of political elites."[73] Ugandan government officials often became partners in Ugandan Asian firms, and capital circulated back to African politicians who had formal directorships in these same firms. Simultaneously, however, Obote and the UPC maintained the government rhetoric about Asian dominance and the exploitation of Africans in the economy, appealing to the sentiments of

1.5 The *kabaka* Mutesa II (*left*) and Apollo Milton Obote of the Uganda People's Congress (*right*).

the majority Ugandan population. The UPC targeted vulnerable noncitizen Indian traders by imposing restrictions on their commercial activity and stalling the pending citizenship applications of British Protected Persons and others who wanted to naturalize as Ugandan citizens.[74] It became clear that the prospects for and possibilities of "Ugandanization" (the inclusion of different racial groups into an inclusive Ugandan nation and identity) and "Africanization" (the gradual replacement of Asians in the civil service and economy with Black Africans) would be determined by the political and class interests of a new postcolonial elite and its alliances with Ugandan Asian capitalists.

This complex history demonstrates that the dominant narrative of Asian racial expulsion from Uganda—exceptionalized today—has, in fact, a much longer arc and was shaped by many competing interests. Many Ugandan Asians I spoke with in Kampala—some who stayed on after the expulsion, others who had returned—focused on this longer temporality of Africaniza-tion policies and their gradual racial exclusion, in contrast to the spectacle of Amin's expulsion decree and the three-month displacement window for the remaining Ugandan Asian community. Amrita, a returnee of Ugandan and Punjabi Hindu descent who had left the nation with her family during the expulsion and eventually resettled in Kampala at the end of the civil war in the late 1980s, emphasized this alternative temporality of Asian ra-cial exclusion: "Actually, the real exodus had begun by 1968 or so . . . state policies were making it difficult for Asians to naturalize as citizens, to earn a livelihood, so many made use of their 'exit strategy' through their British passports. The Kenyan Asian exodus was also in full swing at that time, so many people began to leave here as their friends and family in Kenya also migrated out of East Africa." In fact, as early as 1965, Indian embassy offi-cials were complaining about the immigration department's foot-dragging on the pending citizenship applications of Indian nationals.[75] The Trade Licensing Act of 1969 forced all Indian traders to obtain a valid license; suddenly they were under new scrutiny. Likewise, the Immigration Act of 1969 required all Indian foreign nationals working in the country to apply for entry permits during an extremely short window, and those not granted permits were required to leave the country or were subject to deportation.[76] That same year, and despite the fact that many Indian noncitizen traders had already left Uganda, Obote—strategically considering the political threat of a growing Buganda-based trading and commercial class that would replace Indian traders—declared that he would reconsider the rights of citizenship for 30,000 British Protected Persons and nonnationals of Indian descent who had pending Ugandan citizenship applications.[77]

In response to these restrictive and changing policies, many individuals who wanted to naturalize as Ugandan citizens were also compelled to hedge their bets, strategizing how best to enhance their sense of security across mul-tiple homelands, leading to greater African nationalist suspicions about their intentions. Sir Amar Maini, a community leader at the time, commented on the atmosphere of anxiety and confusion. "There were a multitude of responses within the Asian community in Uganda to African independence, most of them designed to keep as many options as possible. These resulted in certain inconsistencies of behavior in Asians, which led in turn to inevitable charges of hypocrisy when private actions did not (and could not) match up to publicly stated actions."[78] The fact that some—albeit a minority—of Ugandan Asians retained their British nationality or British Protected Person status worked to further reinforce Black African perceptions that "Asians" as a racial community were strategic, untrustworthy, and not committed to Africans. For their part, for those who identified as multigenerational Ugandan Asians, it was unclear if the formalization of their legal-juridical status as Ugandan could ever map onto substantive inclusion and belonging, or if economic livelihoods would even be possible in the new nation.

The harried transition to independence; Ugandan Asians' middling position as imperial citizens (for whom an "exit strategy" was possible); their colonial, racial, and economic privileges; their strategic position as a wedge group between ruling elites and other politicized ethnic factions; their lack of political organization; and the lack of cohesion across citizenship, class, and communal divides—all these factors prevented Ugandan Asians from developing more effective political strategies to remain and assert national and cultural belonging in relation to the structural and racial closures of the new nation. Ugandan national citizenship was redefined by racial criteria: "African" was constructed through racial Blackness and native political identity, paralleling the discursive categories of colonial governance; and "African" was associated with indigeneity and even autochthonous claims to the nation.

Continued foreign interventions—donor-aid dependency, military aid, and foreign capital interests—maintained Uganda's marginalization in the shifting imperial and global order. And then there was the continuing colonial legacy of illiberal governance and its racial, ethnic, and religious character. Following an assassination attempt on Obote's life at the 1969 UPC Conference, Obote oversaw draconian policies and state violence in the crackdown on and detentions of Baganda political activists and other civilians; he oversaw the mass deportations of ethnic Others; and he strengthened state military and paramilitary organizations, expanding the power of military officials like General Idi Amin. The UPC government was not able to successfully implement gradual Africanization policies alongside African socialism and democracy in an inclusive and multiracial and multiethnic nation. The stage instead was set for escalation, for the further cooptation of state institutions of violence. Decolonization remained an unfinished project.

From Africanization to Racially Nativist Nationalism: Idi Amin, the Economic War, and Asian Expulsion

Upon creating strategic alliances with the Baganda and other dissenting groups in the army, Idi Amin staged a military coup d'état against the UPC government while President Milton Obote was attending the Commonwealth

Meetings in Singapore in 1971. Although the British had supported the coup due to Obote's alignment with the Rhodesian and South African liberation movements, Amin broke diplomatic ties with Britain and Israel, expelling the Israeli population in 1971 and nurturing instead Pan-African and Pan-Islamic geopolitical ties with the Arab world.[79] Meanwhile, Obote and other political exiles from the UPC took refuge in Tanzania, where they formed an army; they attempted, unsuccessfully, to invade Uganda in 1972.

In their recollections, many Ugandan Asians remembered celebrating Amin's rise to power. Sahib, whose family lived in Mbarara, recalled joining the crowds who gathered in town on High Street to cheer on Idi Amin as he embarked upon a presidential tour of the country. He was especially popular among the Baganda, Muslims, and others who had been victimized by Obote and the UPC. Sahib, of mixed Punjabi and Munyankole Afro-Asian heritage, identified with popular African interests and with the larger Ugandan Asian community, who hoped that Amin would create a welcoming environment for them. Indeed, Amin was perceived as charismatic, fluent in many African languages and less comfortable with English; he was also a practicing Muslim, which appealed to everyday Ugandan peasants in rural areas. Ali Mazrui has argued that Amin—from the West Nile region, the home of the Kakwa, Nubi, and Anyanya ethnic-identifying people, defined as "martial races" by the British and cultivated as imperial counter-insurgency forces—was the embodiment of a return to and celebration of African traditionalism and a "peasant-warrior masculinity."[80] He posed a contrast to Obote, who represented a modern, colonially educated and bourgeois model of African masculinity. Amin's popularity increased as he lifted the state of emergency that had been imposed on Ugandans since the Mengo Crisis, released political prisoners, and even oversaw the return of the exiled *kabaka*'s body for burial, earning the support of the Baganda people.[81]

But Amin never introduced democratic elections and a civilian government. Presidential decrees began to consolidate his political authority, and existing repressive state institutions surveilled, detained, incarcerated, and eliminated loyalists to the UPC and any Ugandan dissidents. Amin's newly appointed military officers oversaw the massacres of Northern ethnic Acholi and Langi army officers, who constituted the ethnic base of the previous government's military. More decrees overturned existing constitutional laws and dismantled political institutions, including the parliament as well as district and even local town councils. Rights to speech and assembly were disregarded as political parties, student organizations, trade unions, and other associations were banned. Legal processes and practices were upended as court verdicts were ignored and lawyers could easily be detained. Freedom of movement into and out of Uganda required permits, even among citizens and passport holders. The rumored and actual detentions, torture, disappearances, and killings of high-profile individuals became common.

Amin "ethnicized" the military government by elevating the status of West Nile–affiliated ethnic Kakwa-Nubi-Anyanya officers in the military. He raised the status of the minority African Muslim population by establishing a Department of Religious Affairs and the Islamic Supreme Council, which developed more uniformity in Islamic belief and banned minor religious sects. The Amin government also expanded existing repressive and violent state institutions, creating the Bureau of State Research, Public Safety, and Anti-Smuggling Unit.[82] Military officials and government agents searched and looted homes, creating an environment of fear, paranoia, and suspicion among civilians. A. B. K. Kasozi argues that state violence and terror took on a more spectacular nature during this era, further embodied by Amin's often erratic and unpredictable behavior and the intrigue surrounding his public and private life.[83] For example, there are accounts of ritualized forms of violence that accompanied the torture and killings of Ugandan civilians, whether in state institutions or in open spaces. Public executions were common. Bodies were often dumped in mass graves or in forests, lakes, and rivers, including in Lake Victoria and the Nile River at Jinja.

If global South Asian diaspora scholarship has exceptionalized both Idi Amin and the ninety-day period of Asian expulsion and paid less attention to Black African Ugandan histories, politics, and experiences, then Uganda studies scholarship has also tended to exceptionalize the violence of Idi Amin's military dictatorship and understudied its structural, historical, and institutional development. And if Idi Amin and his associates were at the helm, reshaping the nation, state, and economy along new demographic ethnic (and religious) lines, then this imperative would soon become a racial one. By 1971, the remaining population of legal Ugandan Asians, British Protected Persons, and nonnational Indians was increasingly defined as "Asians" or as "Indian" and constructed as suspicious foreigners and as noncitizens of the nation. New decrees targeted the "economic crimes" of the Asian commercial sector, and Amin began to assure African traders that his government would do everything in its power to place the economy in their hands.

On October 7, 1971, while many racialized "Asians" continued to apply for papers to verify or naturalize their Ugandan citizenship, Amin ordered a national census of all "Asians," after which "Asians" were required to carry a green card.[84] By December 7 of that year, Amin canceled 12,000 pending citizenship applications by nonnationals, mostly those of Indians or of others of South Asian descent. Fueled by an intensified Black African racial and nationalist consciousness, and Idi Amin's rhetoric, media propaganda, and racial stereotypes, Ugandans were becoming more visibly resentful of the "Asians" in their midst. Soon after, Amin convened a heavily televised "Asian Conference" with Ugandan Asian community leaders, during which he accused all Asians of the economic exploitation of Africans through their sabotage of the national economy and economic malpractices, their lack of social integration with Africans, and Asian men's unwillingness to allow Asian women to marry African men.[85] By mid-1972, Amin resumed his anti-Asian rhetoric, even declaring in a televised speech that Uganda was not an "Indian colony" and that he would like to see Africans owning businesses on Kampala Road.[86] On August 9, 1972, upon declaring an "economic war" on the Asian community, and provoked by ongoing conflicts with the British government, Idi Amin announced on radio and television that all noncitizen Ugandans of Asian origin must leave the nation within three months.

Community leaders defended themselves against Amin's televised accusations at the Asian Conference and in published op-eds in the paper. They presented a unified front in their commitment to Uganda and the Amin government, offering evidence of their contributions to the nation, and even devising strategies for addressing issues such as economic malpractices and social integration that had been raised by Amin.[87] Some pointed out that while many Ugandan Asians dominated wholesale and retail trade, many others were renters and working-class laborers or were in the skilled professions—doctors, lawyers, educators, architects, and engineers—all contributing their skills and expertise to Africans and to the nation. Some pointed out that the scapegoating of the Asian community in Uganda invisibilized the role of overseas British and Kenyan multinational firms in exploiting Africans.[88] On the issue of national and social integration, community leaders argued that the problem of citizenship naturalizations needed to be resolved, and they pointed to the role that different communities had played in fostering harmonious race relations, including the Ismaili Khoja community, which at the behest of Prince Karim Aga Khan and an ethics of community service, had established multiracial educational institutions and hospitals in East Africa (and, as Taushif Kara has argued about Ismaili Khoja multiculturalism, even adopted many orphaned African children as their own kin).[89]

In our discussions of this period, Rajivbhai described attending the 1971 Asian Conference, noting the gaps between the perceptions of "the

Asian community" as rich and economically exploitative of Africans and their actual internal class stratifications: "At that time, because of the feelings of political insecurity, those that could move finances were sending the money to UK, India, wherever they want, and they wanted to keep less here because of the risk at that time. Those who could afford to send money sent it out. But I tell you, there were many people who were hand to mouth. I would say those who were in the rural areas were not prospering . . . they didn't have much, they were even poor." He also focused on Amin's preoccupation with the lack of interracial marriages between African men and Indian women. "There was a lot of haranguing. A lot of rubbish talks by Amin. Then people got scared, at that time. They started sending their daughters away to UK, India, wherever. He was saying he would force them to marry Africans. Which was not, I mean, no Indian could even think of it at that time. Now everything is happening in America, the UK, the distance [between races] is getting narrow, people intermarry. But in those times, it was not . . . it was a big fear . . . so many people sent away their young daughters to India, to study, or to stay with other relations. I didn't have any daughters, I had only four boys at that time. I didn't have that problem because I didn't have a girl, but many people started fearing. People got scared that Amin is unpredictable, so people started making their arrangements."

The racialized fear surrounding Indian womanhood and the prospect of interracial sexual intimacies between Indian women and African men was especially salient, given the communal and caste-based gendered purities discussed above, as well as community knowledge of the Zanzibar Revolution of 1964 and the destruction of the Zanzibari Asian community—specifically Abeid Karume's policies of legally enforced marriages between African men in the Revolutionary Council and Asian and Arab women who remained in Zanzibar—as a means of promoting racial harmony and eradicating tribalism.[90] Patriarchal kinship arrangements and marriage endogamy preserved female, and therefore family and patriarchal, honor; they thus preserved communal boundaries as well as racial boundaries and separateness, maintaining both community honor and racial honor. In fact, many Ugandan Asians I spoke with articulated distinctive communal-, class-, and gender-based understandings of their expulsion from the nation, outlining the ways in which elites could leave with their relative privilege and honor intact; how some community leaders assisted poor or vulnerable community members; and the ways in which men ensured that Indian women and children left the nation first.

The expulsion decree canceled "every entry permit and certificate of residency who is of Asian origin, extraction, or descent."[91] In the weeks that followed, Amin vacillated between expelling *all* people of Asian origin and expelling only noncitizen British and Indian nationals. Eventually, many Ugandan Asian national citizens were having their passports and certificates torn up by bureaucrats who had been appointed to "citizenship verification committees," resulting in only small numbers of Asians who were "officially" verified as Ugandan citizens. Most Ugandan Asians initially believed that the decree was a scare tactic or an empty threat; they hung on and waited for it to be reversed. Or, they reasoned, if they had to leave for their safety, it would be only temporary, and they would soon be able to return.

The confusion and turmoil of the moment was enhanced by the discriminatory policies of the British government, which had installed harsh immigration quota systems designed to curb the migration to and settlement in Britain of British passport holders in overseas British territories. The government generally failed to take responsibility for the Ugandan Asian crisis, and especially for Ugandan nationals.[92] The 1967 Commonwealth Immigrant Act had already limited the numbers of immigration vouchers allocated to Kenyan and Ugandan British visa and passport holders, British Protected Persons, and citizens of independent Uganda and Kenya.[93] In Kampala, the British High Commission was extremely discriminatory in processing Ugandan Asians and providing entry permits to the UK. The Indian and Pakistani governments also closed their doors to British passport holders, shifting the responsibility back to the British government and arguing that overseas Indians had failed to fully identify with African national interests when, in fact, their citizenship naturalizations and verifications had been prevented by both the Obote and Amin governments.[94] The Prime Minister of India, Indira Gandhi, in the midst of her own domestic campaigns for demographic control of the population in India, had refused to take responsibility for British passport holders, placing the responsibility back on the British government.[95] In the midst of the expulsion crisis, the Indian government cut diplomatic ties with Uganda.

Eventually, and especially after Amin announced a November 9, 1972, deadline for all Asians to leave the nation, the British government, via the bureaucratic work of the newly formed Uganda Resettlement Board (URB) and the volunteer efforts of Ugandan Asian community leaders who themselves were displaced, admitted close to 29,000 British passport holders in the midst of racist anti-immigrant protests. The exiles eventually settled in small cities in the Midlands region of Britain and elsewhere in the UK, with the majority settling in Leicester. As the British government continued to resist its political, moral, and financial obligations in resettling Ugandan Asians in the UK, Prince Karim Aga Khan and Prince Sadruddin of the United Nations Human Rights Commission (UNHCR) worked with Prime Minister Pierre Trudeau of the Canadian government and other European countries to agree to take on the now majority Ismaili Khoja stateless Ugandan Asians. A UNHCR rescue operation began in Kampala as religious community centers were transformed into refugee processing centers, and most Ugandan Asians left their homeland on evacuation flights. Various European nations offered temporary transit centers to refugees, with the majority (about 6,500) displaced Ismaili Khoja community members settling in Canadian cities like Ottawa, Toronto, Montreal, and Vancouver.[96]

Neighboring East and Central African countries had also closed their doors to the Ugandan Asians. Ironically, large numbers of Indian nationals, the descendants of indentured laborers who had once built the famous Uganda Railway several generations before, now traveled back to India on the same railway. They were repatriated back to India via a railway trip to Mombasa port, followed by steamship to coastal India, dealing with much harassment along the way.[97] Here, elite community members assisted with the resettling of Ugandan Asians in Ahmedabad, Gujarat, securing funds for a state housing project for the expelled.

Almost the entire Ugandan Asian population of Uganda left the nation within three months. Their domestic bank accounts were frozen, and they left behind their property and assets, often turning them over to Ugandan work and domestic associates, bringing only 20 kg of luggage and the equivalent of 55 British pounds with them to their new destinations. Spending time in refugee transit centers, resettlement housing, and the homes of extended family and kin, they eventually rebuilt their lives entirely, estranged from both Uganda and Africa.[98] The expulsion crisis was further complicated by the fact that Ugandan Asian families usually possessed different legal-juridical statuses within each household and across extended families, which meant that families became separated without plans in place for the reunification of kin. In fact, the British government refused to issue British passports to many Indian nationals who had become separated from their (legally) British family members.

We can surmise that expulsion helped to circumvent the loss of life among Ugandan Asians—that their accumulated racial and (for many) class privileges protected them before the political situation worsened. Many Ugandan Asians, both in Uganda and in the UK and Canada, mentioned this to me. Some explained to me that they had the "luck" and "fortune" to have been expelled by Amin and to access opportunities abroad, while some more consciously emphasized that it was their British passports and class privileges that had allowed them to leave Uganda voluntarily and without being harmed during the ninety-day expulsion period. But there are unanswered questions about this period that are lost in the existing narratives and memorializations of the event, including the various classed, religious, ethnic, caste, and gendered experiences of expulsion. For example, while some Ugandan Asians were able to leave in relative privilege without experiencing violence, others experienced brutal military harassment, extortion, and criminal acts, including incidents of physical and sexual assault that were traumatizing and humiliating. We now have some accounts of the Amin military government's disappearance, torture, and detention of key Ugandan Asian political figures associated with Obote and the UPC.[99] We do not fully understand the extent to which various groups of Ugandan Asians of different backgrounds experienced different acts of violence, nor do we know the ways in which rumors of gendered and sexual violence were bound up in actual incidents of violence, given the emphasis on gendered, family, and community *izzat* in the South Asian context.[100] Beyond the actions of Idi Amin, we have little research on the everyday complicity and views of Ugandan state actors and others (and according to their different ethnic, religious, and class groups) who made expulsion possible, including those who may have not necessarily agreed with or welcomed it, but who were bystanders and witnesses as the expulsion unfolded.[101] These unresolved issues, and the trauma and varying physical, emotional, and psychological wounds of sudden mass displacement and expulsion, remain.

Although the Ugandan Asian expulsion was condemned by Western governments and by global South Asian communities as an exceptional act of Black nationalist and racial discrimination against South Asians, we know that it was a popular move among most Black-identifying Ugandans and among many Africans in general during the independence era. East African presidents Jomo Kenyatta of Kenya, Julius Nyerere of Tanzania, and Kenneth Kaunda of Zambia condemned the expulsion of the Ugandan Asian community, they preferred the method of the gradual Africanization of the nation and economy through legal restrictions on Indian entrepreneurship and placing pressure on the British government to increase its quotas for especially British passport holders. The expulsion was nonetheless considered to be a decisive blow to the British and to Western hegemony by proxy, exercised upon the South Asian heritage collaborating class it had culti-

1.6   General Idi Amin speaks to Asians in Uganda. Kampala, 1972. Courtesy of the Mohamed Amin Collection, Nairobi.

vated. In fact, despite political tensions between East African leaders at the time and the violence unfolding against his fellow Black Ugandan citizens, Amin's popularity increased as a Pan-African figure who represented the interests of Black African sovereignty, as observed when he presided over the Organization of African Unity (OAU) meetings in Kampala in 1975. Commenting on the Black American response to Idi Amin and the expulsion, Ali A. Mazrui wrote of the expulsion, "[It] was to many Black Americans a stroke of nationalistic genius. Amin seemed determined to put Uganda's destiny back into Black hands. His dedication was not necessarily to the creation of a kinder or more humane Ugandan society, but simply the creation of a situation where Black people of Uganda wrenched their economic destiny from the hands of non-Black people. Amin's economic war against foreign control of the Ugandan economy aroused memories of Black leaders . . . like

1.7 President Idi Amin clarifies the expulsion announcement, seated with the British High Commissioner, the Indian High Commissioner, Pakistan's Ambassador, and leaders of the Asian community at Amin's command post in Kololo, August 1972. Courtesy of Rolls Press / Popperfoto by Getty Images.

1.8 Asians queue up at the Immigration Office, Kampala, 1972. Courtesy of the Mohamed Amin Collection, Nairobi.

THE WORLD OF KEITH WAITE

DEPARTHEID

1.9   "Departheid," 1972. The World of Keith Waite, Scrapbook 5. Cartoon depiction of Amin gleefully "booting out" bare-footed British Ambassador Richard Slater and a turbaned Indian figure representing "Asians," while keeping jewelry, cash, and property deeds. Courtesy of Mirrorpix by Getty Images.

Marcus Garvey, who had similarly been dedicated to Black self-reliance."[102] Finally, the 1972 Asian expulsion was, of course, a major setback for the decolonizing aspirations articulated during the Bandung Conference and for ideas of Afro-Asian solidarity and interracialism, especially between the Uganda and the Indian nation.

By 1972, Uganda was still far from the aims of liberal democracy and decolonization, or the undoing of the colonial project, that is, the deracialization and denativization of society and increasing economic and social development. The racialized and ethnicized character of colonial society was supposed to have been resolved through the decentralization of political authority and Africanization policies; or the gradual replacement of Europeans and Asians in the civil service and market with Black Africans of different ethnic backgrounds; or via the replacement of an Asian quasi-settler, quasi-colonial subject consciousness with an African Asian nationalist consciousness, animated by the practice of African socialism and Pan-Africanist visions of Black liberation and empowerment, as enshrined in liberal and legal constitutionalism. Instead, the advent of the Amin military government revealed the entrenched racialized and ethnic logics of the colonial state in the practice of postcolonial political authority and governance as well as in the maintenance of the capitalist economy. Racially nativist nation-building via Asian racial expulsion was a violent response to violent colonial processes—it was both a destructive and a creative violence.

For many Black-identifying Ugandans, expulsion was not only a material process but also a psychologically cathartic one, allowing them to reclaim a sense of racial and political empowerment; this was in contrast to the racial and civilizational indignities and humiliations they had experienced under Europeans and by Ugandan Asians, who were structurally and often interpersonally complicit in Black African oppression and discrimination. For his part, Idi Amin was successful in mobilizing and articulating grievances, affects, and racial stereotypes to create a singular figure of the exploitative "Asian," also known as the *muhindi*, and a singular "Asian community" in relation to the victimized figure of the Black African. The Amin military government would further normalize the illiberal state technology of mass expulsion via legal decree, defining the figure of the Asian as non-African, Other, and foreign: as external to the nation. And if Ugandan Asians suffered trauma and violence during their sudden displacement, all Black-identifying Ugandans would soon be permanently marked by the violence and terror of the military dictatorship in the 1970s.

The 1972 Ugandan Asian Expulsion, Expulsion Exceptionalism, and Postcolonial Closure

In his edited volume, *Expulsion of a Minority*, published in the aftermath of the 1972 Asian expulsion, Michael Twaddle observes the surprise that many Ugandan scholars felt about the advent of the expulsion and the degree of hostility that was directed against the Uganda-based South Asian population, arguing that expulsion was not necessarily an "inevitability."[103]

More recently, Edgar Taylor, in "Race and Nation in Ugandan Public Discourse," argues that discussions of the 1972 Asian expulsion assume a sense of inevitability.[104] Historians continue to study intensively the decades between independence and expulsion, excavating alternative paths to multiracial or nonracial citizenship that might also have been possible in postcolonial Uganda. Animated by an ethical sensibility of recuperation—possibly even liberal redemption—they are concerned with how the past and other marginalized histories might be mobilized to make multiracial national futures possible.

I take these critiques about the apparent totalizing and inevitable nature of expulsion a step further. The event, as it was both exceptionalized and parochialized across domains of collective and social memory and scholarship, has introduced other epistemological problems in Uganda studies and in global South Asian diaspora studies. While the latter focuses solely on the expulsion and the migration trajectories of the large Ugandan Asian diaspora that was resettled in Western liberal nation-states, the former tends to reproduce in scholarship the racially nativist and nationalist biases of post-1972 Uganda. Uganda studies scholars now focus on the postcolonial politics of ethnic identity and ethnic violence, and the study of race and racialization has receded, encapsulated by 1972 and the sense of postcolonial closure that surrounds it. Further, as scholars have grappled with the legacies of or have revisited the Idi Amin era, its militarism, and the turbulent years of political violence that followed, often exceptionalizing this historical era, the anthropology of race and citizenship in postcolonial Uganda is sidelined.

Expulsion exceptionalism—the spectacle of the African dictator par excellence, President Idi Amin; Asian expulsion; and Afro–South Asian racial conflict—was followed by the flourishing and then the end of scholarly analysis of the expulsion in the mid- to late 1970s, with historiographical interventions also ending in 1972. A palpable sense of crisis surrounds Uganda's turbulent postcolonial years, both in the nation and in its global diasporas. But expulsion and its aftermaths persist, haunt, live. I push up and against these silences—epistemological and affective closures, and especially racial resentments and insecurities—that surround Ugandan nation-building and its expulsion of South Asians. Beyond postcolonial silence and closure is the nation's disavowal of its relationship to South Asians and South Asianness, and the global African Asian and South Asian diaspora's disavowals of its relationships to Africa, Uganda, Africans, and Blackness.

PART II

Entanglements
of Expulsion

Exceptions to the Expulsion

Racial Denizenship in Amin's Uganda

"I am a Ugandan—why would I have left? My mother was African," Rani explained. She adjusted the shawl around her shoulders and her loose cotton *kanga*. We were watching the evening news after dinner at their family home in the small frontier town of Mbarara in Ankole, in Southwest Uganda, the land of the cattle-keeping Nkore or Banyankore (Hima and Iru people), who were generally referred to as Banyankole among the Ganda. Chatting during commercial breaks, her brother, Sahib, reinforced the social distance they had from the majority of the expelled. "Indians ran off because they were afraid! But we stayed." As we spent time together over the course of many visits, I began to better understand the ways that Sahib understood the category of "Indian" in a pejorative sense, not unlike the ways that *muhindi* or *bahindi* had become associated with negative meanings since the expulsion.

A longtime friend and research contact in Kampala had suggested I spend some time with their family to learn how some communities that had remained behind during the Amin regime had weathered the expulsion. I had arrived the day before, after a four-hour-long bus ride from Kampala, dirt and dust in my hair, despite my attempts to tuck it under a scarf. I learned that although Rani and Sahib were of mixed racial (Afro–South Asian) heritage, they had been officially categorized as "Asian" (nonnative) according to state-based and institutionalized patrilineal kinship rules of citizenship.

They were not only multigenerational residents of the town with deep roots in the region but, due to the expulsion and the displacement of other extended family members, now also had transnational kinship ties to the UK and to Canada. Theirs was an established family that ran a local boarding school and other small business ventures in town; a steady stream of African and Indian guests and patrons regularly visited their home, including many from communities who continue to be considered as outsiders to mainstream Baganda society, including the Banyaruanda or Ruandese (Banywarwanda or Rwandese), Nubians, Swahili, and many new Indian migrants. Amid the liveliness, my visits were welcomed, and I came to enjoy these short stays in their traditional Swahili Coast–style *baraza* home, with all the bedrooms facing an open courtyard and living space. Sahib and Rani's thick connections with townspeople, their ethnic identification with the people of Ankole and their Ruandese heritage (the Banyankore and Banyaruanda), their ability to traverse many communities and adapt to the decline in status of Asians and increasing prestige of Black African communities, their proximity to state actors, and their adaptation to rapid political and economic transformations had all served them well during the expulsion and its aftermath.

Rani and Sahib's father was a Sikh from the Punjab who had migrated to East Africa during the early colonial period; he worked in the British civil service. Like other early settlers who had arrived as bachelors (and who married African women considered to have complementary racial features and attributes, like the Watutsi and the Masai), he married an indigenous African (Munyaruanda) woman—herself a migrant to Uganda—and settled in Mbarara permanently in the 1930s. Over time, I discovered that those with biracial and multiracial descent often eschewed racial self-identifications, although they were described by others as *nusu-nusu* ("halfie," or mixed, in Swahili), or even more pejoratively, through the British racial terminology, as "half-castes."[1] I deeply appreciated the ways that members of mixed heritage communities had dislodged my own conceptions of fixed racial African and South Asian binary identities—in East African Punjabi and Sikh communities specifically. Although they primarily spoke Swahili and English, their words were peppered with Punjabi, Urdu, Runyankole, and Luganda phrases, roiling together into a delightful linguistic soundscape. I saw that the family home was a meeting point of many racial, ethnic, religious communities—Christian and Muslim, Banyankole and Banyaruanda communities; Nubi and Swahili communities who practiced African Islam; and South Asian (Sikh, Hindu, Sunni and Shia Islam, especially Ismaili) communities. Yet I was cautious of romanticizing multiracial communities as a symbol of racial integration or reconciliation after the expulsion. Despite the fact that their indigenous African ethnic heritage had allowed them to stay on, Sahib and Rani experienced exclusion and anti-Black racism and colorism from other South Asian communities (some newly arrived) who considered themselves to be racial or caste pure "Indians." Indeed, biracial racial identities fortified existing racial and caste typologies, hierarchies, and community boundaries, all according to changing transnational logics of racism, religion, casteism, and colorism in East Africa.[2] Moreover, even Amin had "mounted a campaign against those born of inter-racial marriages. . . . He castigated 'half-castes' for creating 'class distinctions,' and warned them not to think that 'they are of higher status than the indigenous Ugandans,'" demonstrating the ways in which Amin's anti-imperialism maintained Black African racial nativism and made communities of mixed heritage racial targets as well.[3]

Still, Rani emphasized her African Rwandese ethnic and Ankole regional identity rather than her South Asian heritage. For his part, Sahib, who seemed to practice both masculinist African and Sikh identities, disassociated himself from the figure of the *muhindi*—not out of communal prejudices but due to the lingering insecurities of expulsion. Equipped with the Black African racial consciousness introduced by Idi Amin, he viewed Indianness through the eyes of many Black-identifying Africans, through their humiliating encounters with merchants or with other urban and elite Ugandan Asians. In emphasizing their Ruandese heritage and their linguistic and regional ethnic affiliations with the people of Ankole, Rani and Sahib together leveraged claims of African indigeneity and mobilized histories of the Banyaruanda in Uganda to define their Ugandanness. Moreover, Sahib's assertion that they "refused to leave Uganda" allowed them to maintain a sense of *izzat*, of personal and moral autonomy, performing and embodying an African political and cultural citizenship, one that had been honed carefully in relation to the political precarity of South Asianness after the expulsion.

Many months later and on a subsequent trip to visit the family, while driving back from a visit to Queen Elizabeth Park, Sahib, aware of my research interests, more directly discussed the expulsion in ways that he had not before. As the patriarch of the family, he was grand in stature and was involved in energetic exchanges with everyone around him. Driving his jeep, navigating dirt roads and swirling clouds of red dust, he turned to me: "Okay, so the expulsion . . . yes, it shouldn't have happened the way that it did. But something also had to happen, you know, to balance things out between Africans and Asians." Slowly yet surely, Sahib was revealing his more complicated readings of postcolonial events, processing the hardships that Ugandan Asians had endured during their expulsion while also arguing that the racial and economic entitlements that most Asians had enjoyed with respect to their Black African counterparts was no longer feasible.

In this chapter, I write against dominant epistemologies of expulsion exceptionalism and postcolonial closure surrounding Afro–South Asian entanglement in the immediate aftermath of the 1972 Asian expulsion. I argue that the expulsion was not a totalizing episode of "de-Indianization" of the nation and displacement but a persistent opening into the sustained presence of South Asianness (in the sense of racialized religious tradition, cultural worlds, history and heritage, and the performance of identities) in Idi Amin's Uganda (1971–79). I focus on the experiences of Ugandan Asians, mixed-racial heritage Afro-Asians, and other newcomer South Asians who managed to remain in, return to, or migrate to and settle in Uganda in the aftermath of the expulsion. While the majority of the displaced and exiled Ugandan Asian community were remaking homes abroad as refugees and as new immigrants in Western liberal nations, transnational financial and kinship networks and strategies between those who remained and those who were displaced abroad remained critical to the maintenance of South Asianness, even during the Amin regime.

More specifically, Idi Amin's Uganda exemplifies an in-between period of racial denizenship for those who could remain or for those who arrived after the expulsion, prior to the more formalized mode of racial noncitizen incorporation in the 1990s. Those who remained and those who arrived after 1972 negotiated new forms of governance, sovereignty, and inclusion and exclusion in a transformed political, economic, and social order with rapidly changing racial, religious, and gendered norms and sensibilities. This new order asserted the sovereignty of African political authority, defined by an assertive and empowered Black racial consciousness, alongside the dominant African masculinities and gender norms of the era—whether material, discursive, or symbolic. Those Ugandan Asians who remained became racial denizens, internalizing and reproducing the dominant order, negotiating state and racialized violence, practicing and performing new ways of relating to this empowered practice of Black African identity and to being "Ugandan Asian" or "African Asian" post-1972. Those who stayed on would become foundational to the small Ugandan Asian community that continues to reside in Kampala and other urban localities of Uganda today.

But before turning to Amin's Uganda, I draw out more of the complicated terrains of expulsion afterlives, racial estrangements, and racial resentments in contemporary urban life.

Fragmented Afterlives, Fragmented Communities

I knew fieldwork would be difficult, but if anything, I underestimated the emotional distress that I experienced. I was negotiating state repression and community silences surrounding the past, even as they were slowly giving way to glimpses of emotion, to the need to process a beleaguered past of painful and persistent racial estrangements and intimacies. Research was not just an intellectual exercise; my body was constantly absorbing the social tensions I was sensing around me. As I developed relationships with those around me, my movements felt heightened and intensely visible, especially since I was willing to engage with people across unspoken racial and other (class, ethnic, religious, and gendered) boundaries.

There were other challenges, too. If Ugandan Asians—often defined as a singular racial community by the state and the majority Black Ugandan population—were already heterogeneous and fragmented at the time of their expulsion in 1972, those who were now in Kampala were also deeply alienated in the aftermaths of the destruction of their ethnoreligious communities; they had formed new relationships and ethnoreligious and racial communities in Uganda while maintaining transnational lives and connections with the majority exiled Ugandan Asian community that had resettled abroad in places like Leicester, Montreal, Vancouver, and California. The Ugandan Asians who remained or returned used terms like *stayees*, *returnees*, and *newcomers* to map differing out-migrations and in-migrations, to draw lines of distinction between old and new communities. And even as a new post-expulsion racialized "Asian" community was beginning to emerge in Kampala—comprising individuals with diverse paths to Uganda—there was still no real state or public narrative about the expulsion, as if it had never happened, or that it had happened, but the event was as ordinary or mundane as any other event. Expulsion was relegated to private conversations at home, to one-on-one exchanges, to my impressions in my notes.

I developed a method to avoid asking anyone directly about their experience of expulsion, not wanting to subject anyone to painful memories of the past, especially in a racially precarious present. Nor did I ever ask anyone directly about their legal-juridical citizenship status(es), because

I was cautious about appearing as though I were questioning their status or right to belong. Many Ugandan Asians who had remained or returned preferred to live quiet and private lives. It was as if talking about expulsion or enunciating an overt claim to African or Ugandan identity, citizenship, cultural belonging, or even a particular entitlement (to property or anything else)—being too visible on the urban scene—might render them vulnerable, exposed, even expellable. My arrival and my research, I sensed, were met with anxiety or uncertainty that I might create more exposure surrounding the past. An unspoken fear was the idea that in talking about the past one might once again seed the idea of expulsion in the hearts and minds of Ugandans. I was as sensitive as possible about these issues, understanding that for many, the past and its presence were too painful a topic, that not creating more vulnerabilities, but being empathetic to them as they unfolded through relationship-building, was the labor of anthropology.

Importantly, political and state repression surrounding the past is not singular to the 1972 Asian expulsion but characteristic of many moments in postcolonial Ugandan history marked by state violence, the terrorizing of civilians, and civil war. Many urban Ugandans, regardless of their racial or ethnic background, and because of the long history and continuity of state practices of repression, surveillance, criminalization, civilian detention, torture, and disappearances, live with a sense that their conversations are being watched and monitored.[4] Research required a level of sensitivity and intuition, an understanding of an urban political culture in which interpersonal and cross-community dialogue is stylized and often strategic, posited euphemistically with respect to the imputed gaze of the state or ruling party or other urban constituents in public life.[5] It was normal practice to regulate conversations according to the perceived or actual gaze of the state and others, and these shifting negotiations of intracommunity, familial, and individual exchanges of knowledge were and remain part of social reproduction, the rhythms of everyday life.

Over time, though, I was able to access more impressions of the past from those who had remained or returned. Here, present circumstances were always alive in narratives of the past, and vice versa, an entwinement of the past and present as a lived social experience. Most individuals were still making sense of their expulsion; of their own and others' perceived racial, ethnic, and cultural differences; of their conflicting experiences of racial or class privilege; and of their racial victimization. They negotiated a persistent sense of anti-Asian sentiment and the racial stereotypes that constructed the figure of the Asian/Indian (*muhindi*) and racial South

Asianness (*muhindi-ness*) as merchants motivated by avarice and greed, exploiting and demeaning Africans.[6] They managed their re-racialized bodies and selves and the imputed gaze of the state, ruling party, and African host communities as they remade relationships with Black-identifying Africans. They were deeply unsettled as they were resettling themselves. And while it seemed that many had moved on from expulsion, those who were victimized during the episode could not simply forget.

Although many mentioned how they avoided "politics," the realm of "the political" included other domains in which they processed the past: spiritual or faith-based practices; the intense following of political news; participation in urban gossip, rumor, and conspiracy theory; and expressive and embodied genres of wry humor, wit, sarcasm.[7] I observed and collected these sentiments across individuals, families, and community networks, bits and pieces of evidence that departed from the more impersonal scholarly works I had combed through. The insecurities of expulsion unfolded gradually, in fragmented and circuitous ways, surreptitiously, unraveling slowly. There were residues of memories, rife with remembering and forgetting, personal and family anecdotes that were difficult to make sense of. As I became more sensitive to the post-expulsion environment, I experienced ethnographic refusals and abrupt, emotional intensities—flashes of anger and cynicism, emotional pain hardened into bitterness, even troubling racist rants. Given this complex and uneven terrain of racial estrangement and resentment, unresolved trauma, and both privileges and victimizations—unfolding in relation to old and new urban infrastructures of state violence, repression, and militarization—I was interested, too, in the affective and embodied terrains of the insecurities of expulsion. The multiple registers and constitutive mutuality of political and racial securities and insecurities can best be understood as Raymond William's notion of a "structure of feeling" in urban Uganda.[8]

Idi Amin occupied a constant, if spectral, presence during my fieldwork. Rumor and myth swelled around the many urban narrations and memorializations of him. He appeared, fantastical and ghostly, in my field notes or in my occasional night terrors on humid, sleepless nights. These dreams were usually accompanied by the visuals and sounds of the swelling waters of the Nile, teeming with feeding crocodiles—an image that stayed with me as many Ugandans recalled those decades of civilian mass terror—and ending by startling awake to the calling of bullfrogs after a heavy downpour. So, in addition to the narratives of expulsion that focused on Idi Amin's expulsion announcement and the ninety days of Ugandan Asians' mass displacement, or even the scholarly interventions of Ugandan intellectuals, in Kampala I found that many individuals continued to focus more on Idi Amin's personal agency and decision to expel Asians than on anything else. Some Ugandan Asians discussed his deep observance of Islam and belief in prophetic dreamworlds, including his dream of "making Uganda a Black country." Some men, with bravado and gusto, possibly wanting to provoke a reaction out of me, talked about his insistence on interracial marriages between African men and Asian women. They described his wishes to marry the widow of the industrialist Jayant Madhvani, Meena Madhvani, symbolically integrating "the Indian community" into the nation through a high-profile marriage alliance; they noted Amin's several public and turbulent marriages to African women of different ethnic communities, and especially his turbulent marriage to Kay Adroa, who had died under mysterious circumstances.[9] The rejection of this marriage proposal by the Madhvani family, they argued, led him to castigate all Indians and expel them.

Then there were the continued Ugandan African conspiratorial readings of racial "Asian" presence in the city. There were continuities with the older racial stereotypes, but some were newly reconfigured, post-expulsion. Pastoral and even anti-Semitic metaphors surrounding an untrustworthy and exploitative Asian urban presence were enduring. Idi Amin had argued that Asians were sabotaging the economy and did not have the welfare of Uganda in their hearts, that "they only milked the cow, but did not feed it to yield more milk."[10] Some Ugandans still argued that "Asians" continued to "milk the economy," that they were "blood-sucking parasites" of African (Black) wealth. Ugandan Africans' encounters with South Asian religiosity, especially the ritual ceremonies and obligations associated with practices of the Hindu faith, led some to believe that wealthy business tycoons and merchants participated in occult practices that cursed Africans, and that Indian wealth would keep Africans intergenerationally poor. Others speculated about the proximity of "Asians" to the government, interested in the possible mutual benefits the president and the ruling party might be securing from "the Asian community," and wondering whether it was "Asians who were milking the economy, or the President who was milking them." Still others argued vehemently against this kind of "Asian" scapegoating and stereotyping. As I listened in, they corrected their friends over beer and roasted *mogo* (cassava) and argued that "the real parasites are our own, and they are in the government."

Another genre of urban discourse surrounding the expulsion concerns Ugandan Asian sources of domestic wealth in the nation: property assets and capital. There were hushed, private conversations about the loss of and repossession of Asian assets, and who now owned, "came into," rented, or inhabited such-and-such property on such-and-such street, in such-and-such city, why and how. If there were resentments and conspiracy theories about the property repossession process among Black African Ugandans and within Ugandan Asian networks (see chapter 3), there were also other readings of Asian property and assets. Some Ugandans (primarily Baganda interlocutors) suggested that the property of Ugandan Asians had been wrongfully taken because it had not been earned; and thus these buildings, critical to city infrastructure, as well as the African beneficiaries (primarily Baganda Muslims and other military and ethnic associates of Amin) of the property appropriation and allocation process after the expulsion, were "cursed." Influenced by the now dominant neoliberal meritocratic ideologies that emphasize individual merit, hard work, and entrepreneurship rather than by ideas of African socialism and the nationalization of private business and assets, many Ugandans, both the Baganda and other ethnic communities in Kampala, explained to me that if things had not been worked for or built on one's own, they could, or would, eventually be "lost" and taken again. Some Ugandan Asians who remained or returned reflected similar discourses, but they also contrasted ideas of exceptional cultural "Asian values" and Asian "business success" with liberal meritocratic and racist notions of Black racial and African cultural expectations of patronage rather than the willingness to work, of criminality and corruption (see more in chapter 3).

There were other post-expulsion urban legends, tales of returnees who arrived decades after the expulsion to locate hidden property deeds in the cracks and foundation stones of crumbling homes, or fantastical stories of Indian women's dowries of gold jewelry and silverware being buried on the grounds of properties, only to be recovered decades later. Women talked nostalgically of sentimental pieces of furniture they had left behind—a prized multigenerational heirloom, an *almirah* (wardrobe) or *sandhook* (dowry chest) that had traveled across the Indian Ocean, arriving from the Swahili Coast through intergenerational kinship and marriage networks. Others spoke of their love for and sense of sorrow over the loss of their beloved Ugandan colleagues, friends, assistants, servants, and workers; of the lives lost during the years of political strife. They shared stories of expelled Ugandan Asians leaving the *chabiyaan* (keys) of their homes, cars, and bundles of cash to their trusted workers, managers, and servants at a time when Amin had forbidden the private sale of Asian/Indian assets. Some even asserted their own moral citizenship by distancing themselves from others whom they felt were more opportunistic or self-serving at the time of expulsion, declaring that they had never tried to move their life savings or capital out of the nation prior to their expulsion—that everything they had worked for and earned in the nation had remained in the nation, eventually contributing to the wealth of Africans. Within Ugandan Asian networks, discussions about those who had achieved ill-gotten wealth in the aftermath of the expulsion and/or the liberalization of the economy—as opposed to those who had lost their wealth and then earned or worked their way back up honestly—were circulating apace with Black Ugandan apprehensions of Asian wealth.

Others recounted stories of broken friendships and betrayals, or of friendships and family relations that had managed to survive the political turmoil—unexpected reunions and reconciliations years after expulsion. One of my research contacts suggested that after the expulsion, the mixed-racial heritage children of Indian men in the Old Kampala area—children who had once been financially supported by their fathers who likely had relationships of concubinage with African women—had roamed town carrying photos of their fathers, asking where they had gone. My contact was hinting salaciously at socially proscribed and taboo cross-racial intimacies, usually secreted away, emerging visibly only at expulsion. Other returnees repeated this tale to me several times: that unlike Indian traders, the African traders who took over the expelled Asians' shops had no business management skills—that they assigned prices to shirts on the basis of the sizes of the shirts. Here, some Ugandan Asians asserted their importance to the economy and the nation, even as their cultural and political belonging as racially defined Asians continued to be questioned in the majoritarian Black African nation.

These circulating urban knowledges about the expulsion—mythologies of Idi Amin, the why and how of expulsion, the circulation and transfer of Asian/Indian wealth (capital, property, assets) into African hands, unanswered obligations of debt and reciprocity, the unresolved landscape of racial estrangements and intimacies—and their empirical elusiveness are examples of what Kristin Peterson has described as "phantom epistemologies."[11] They constitute the insecurities of expulsion, and they circulate across transcontinental Uganda, intersecting with, and at times upending, global discourses and imaginaries of expulsion exceptionalism. They are intimate and communal, shared while eating slow-cooked Ugandan Asian curries that make use of Ugandan food staples, like *matooke* (plantain banana) and *ebijanjala* (beans), and sipping tea made with *tangawizi* (ginger), food I often shared with Mr. Rajni Tailor in his office and workplace on Bombo

Road, a long-standing Buganda Parliament member, business entrepreneur, community leader, and member of the Indian Association of Uganda who had remained after expulsion. These circulating knowledges traveled across East Africa and the global East African Asian/Ugandan Asian networks and reappeared in other locations, like in my Punjabi diasporic community networks in the United States. This global archive of knowledge and meaning-making continues to flourish despite political repression and despite the silence surrounding expulsion from Uganda. The fallout of expulsion continues to be enunciated through Ugandan Asians' heightened racial consciousness and racial and political insecurities; there exists the constant specter of another expulsion. The contradictions between the weightiness of the expulsion and the multiple private, raced, classed, and even communal narrations of expulsion in Kampala revealed heightening urban tensions and an unsteady present and future.

"In the Vacuum": Gendered, Racial, and Religious Denizenship in Amin's Uganda

Although I had the impression that the entire Ugandan Asian population had fled the nation between August and November 1972 (see map 2), I was learning about those who had remained after the November 9 departure deadline. Most Ugandan Asian exiles and refugees had resettled in the UK. As displaced refugees, they would make use of immediate government relief for refugees but also build upon their own ethnic and kinship networks, including their entrepreneurial and labor expertise, to rebuild their lives abroad. However, some Ugandan Asians maintained their residences in Kampala even after 1972 by obtaining official documentation that verified their citizenship and identified them as "exceptions" from the expulsion because they were deemed professionals and laborers necessary to the regime. Others hung on, hoping to retain their businesses, life savings, promised pension funds, or other monies held in bank accounts. Some waited for news while living in temporary homes in exile with families and friends; some attempted to return immediately, others returned only for brief durations during the Amin regime.

Initially, about six thousand officially verified (legal-juridical) Ugandan Asian nationals stayed on past the official November 9 deadline for Asians to leave Uganda, withstanding the racially hostile climate. That number drastically dropped to eight hundred; then dwindled down to 150 or so who stayed on fairly consistently.[12] These Ugandan Asians not only related their memories of their expulsion experience to me but offered me a sense of the aftermaths and their lives during the Amin military dictatorship. Many referred to themselves as *rehen walley* (in Urdu or Punjabi), or as *stayees*, to differentiate themselves from the *returnees*, who would arrive later on. They connected me with others: self-described "old-timers" and "die-hards," those who had experienced anti-Asian harassment but were determined to stay on. Some *stayees* were officially categorized as "Asian" on legal documentation but were of mixed racial heritage, like Sahib and Rani, who continued to reside in small towns away from Kampala. On one trip to Nairobi, I unexpectedly unearthed my own family history, learning that during a visit to Uganda after 1972, a Kenyan Asian uncle had been detained by Amin's men in prison, but was later released—a time in his life I had not known about.

Paradoxically then, although Amin's Uganda is associated with the expulsion and de-Indianization of the nation, it can be reframed to study the continuity of South Asian labor, capital, and presence in the nation. I frame it as an era of South Asian *racialized denizenship* in which formations of sovereignty and practices of governance were rapidly evolving and in which a substantive (both political and racial) noncitizenship was being normalized for raced South Asian subjects and bodies. Despite their substantive exclusion, they maintained their attachments to the nation and to urban Uganda, invested their energies and resources into relationships with different African actors, and continued to rehearse and practice African identities, subjectivities, masculinities, and the nonliberal terrains of substantive citizenship and belonging. The Amin era must be studied closely *precisely* because it begins to illuminate the transition from Asian expulsion to Asian racial denizenship and the nonliberal terrains of Asian inclusion, incorporation, and even assimilation.

I use the term *denizenship* to characterize the in-between state of remaining behind, even with legal-juridical recognition, but in the aftermath of mass expulsion. I am concerned with the substantive experience of precarious inclusion and racial exclusion that denizenship best captures. Eventually, my interviews revealed that the Amin government began to introduce new legal-juridical technologies to formalize this in-between state of being both "exceptionally included" while being racially excluded. My use of racial denizenship moves past the notion of official status or a state of being. It speaks to the agency of those both exceptionally included and racially excluded, of urban dwelling and place-making, of relationalities with urban Africans, and the ways in which those raced as Asian—Ugandan Asians, African Asians, and others from South Asia—created protected enclaves of belonging for themselves, despite their precarious racial status and the military government's state expropriation of their assets, homes, businesses, and communal spaces.

Lal Singh, a third-generation Ugandan Asian of Sikh and Punjabi heritage, was a child when he was expelled with his family as stateless refugees; they were evacuated from Entebbe to Stansted Airport in Britain and were eventually resettled in Birmingham. I met him one afternoon in his office in the industrial area of Kampala, where he recounted to me his father's attempts to stay on after the expulsion deadline. We were interrupted by many phone calls during our first meeting, since Lal was in the middle of overseeing a job site for his construction business, and I was still adapting to the rhythm of setting up meetings at workplaces and during business hours. Lal's father eventually left for the UK in early 1973 due to intensifying physical harassment and a near-death scare. "He was 'frog-marched' and harassed by Amin's soldiers," Lal explained in between phone calls. Later on, Lal would return to Uganda in place of his father, becoming a silent, "behind-the-scenes" business partner with African colleagues and those who had become beneficiaries of the family's lost assets, maintaining a foothold in the sawmill workshop that his father once ran. After Amin fled and Obote and the Tanzanian forces invaded and took power in 1979, Lal would continue to take advantage of other entrepreneurial opportunities and his connections with business associates in Uganda.

I scribbled down notes quickly as Lal shifted from memory to memory. "Don't forget to write about Gurdev. My father told me this. Gurdev refused to go because he had done some work in Masaka. I think he had built a town hall. And the government owed him about half a million shillings. So he said no, you pay me my money, and I'll go. You don't pay me my money, I won't go. And this is actually what happened. He said you pay me my money and I'll go. You don't pay me my money, I'm going to sit here. And he sat." I was fascinated by Lal's own father and the tales of some of these daring men—their assertion of a particular entitlement and dignity, and their embodiment of both African and Punjabi masculinities, despite the threat of violence from Amin and his men, despite their imperiled racial status.

The Amin government initiated a massive transfer of Asian domestic wealth (properties, assets, cash, capital, commodity stocks, and jewelry) both during the expulsion and after, especially as properties were expropriated by the state and transferred to Black African ownership with the help of bureaucrats appointed to a newly created state parastatal called the Departed Asians Property Custodial Board (DAPCB) in 1973.[13] Although there was a short period of looting during the expulsion and its immediate aftermath, the DAPCB officials' allocation of expropriated properties was a rather organized, bureaucratic affair. Ultimately, properties and assets were redistributed selectively to Amin's inner clique of government and military officials composed largely of Baganda Muslims, Sudanese, and West Nile (Nubi) army recruits and other African townspeople. In Kampala today, this beneficiary class continues to be referred to as the *mafuta mingi* (Kiswahili for "dripping in oil or fat"), those who suddenly became very wealthy. Harriet Namaganda, who assisted me in my research, explained to me that the beneficiaries of expulsion and property expropriation are usually described as *aggude mu bintu* in Luganda, or those "who have fallen into things." As the DAPCB-led property reallocation exercise commenced, the remaining Ugandan Asians lost their properties and assets to state officials and army men, or they faced continued harassment and eventually fled Uganda.

The expulsion of the Ugandan Asian business and commercial class meant that the government's urban taxation base was virtually destroyed, creating an immediate commercial vacuum, destroying existing trade networks, and depleting the volume and number of commodities for sale. Agricultural production, retail trade, and foreign exchange all decreased. The government also seized British capital interests. Coffee, one of the primary commodities sold on the international market that created foreign exchange, began to be smuggled into neighboring countries, generating revenue for the ruling elite of government officials, military men, and entrepreneurs. Prices for primary goods skyrocketed as inflation increased, and illicit economies, referred to as *magendo*, flourished.[14] So, although expulsion and property repossession was an economic shock that destabilized existing commercial structures, created a new urban capitalist class of ethnic-based beneficiaries, and ultimately did not engender a model of socialist redistribution, one of its important consequences was that it did, in fact, lead to new entrepreneurship opportunities for urban Africans, including women. Suddenly, Africans who previously had no access to trade in urban areas were empowered; they exercised new skills and participated in commerce and entrepreneurship activities under the new constraints of military dictatorship and terror.[15]

Some Ugandan Asians who managed to stay on or who were mobile across borders during this era were businessmen or civil servants of strategic importance to Amin's government. They had personal connections with powerful men in Amin's inner circle and were plugged into networks of mutual obligation with government and army officials based on patronage, debt, skills, and expertise; essentially, they were able to negotiate their stay after the expulsion deadline. They had enough political and cultural capital that they received protection from officials and were thus incorporated into the polity. Others who stayed on were newly hired civil servants, primarily Indian Punjabi and Sikh nationals, who had been working as labor contractors for government ministries just prior to the decree. They were long-term residents and occupied professional niches necessary to the new regime and were thus entitled to stay on. Well-connected men could provide pathways for the chain migration of other intra-ethnic, religious, and caste-based laborers from India by serving as their patrons.[16] They forged spaces of racial protection for new arrivals through their own relationships with Africans and despite the rapid loss of Asian-owned and -inhabited urban space.

One of the (often overlooked) contradictions of this era is that Amin's government began to allow for the immigration of South Asians as early as 1974, and more vigorously after 1976. In line with elevating the position of Islam nationally and forging new Pan-Islamic geopolitical connections, Amin's government hired Muslim South Asian professionals from Pakistan and (post-1971) from Bangladesh to fulfill certain roles that Ugandan Asians had performed prior to their expulsion.[17] Indian state officials had also made some attempts to maintain relations with the Amin government.[18] Thus, in addition to the civil servants, labor contractors, and traders who remained, a few doctors, engineers, technicians, managers, and other professionals would maintain residence in the nation. The immediate need for South Asian labor, professional expertise, and even merchants who could bring in desired goods reveals the extent to which cross-racial interdependence persisted between Africans and multiple communities of South Asian heritage.

Those who remained could even successfully negotiate for their families' return; and many whom I interviewed spoke of individuals who were able to retain South Asian communal and religious temples under their protection and care, especially Sikh and Hindu *gurudwaras* and *mandhirs*, which unlike the Islamic *masjids* had not already been expropriated by the DAPCB. Many who stayed on or who arrived later resided in these temples, temples that had already been used as refugee-processing centers during the expulsion itself. In addition to the Ugandan Asian and new South Asian arrivals, mixed-race Afro-Asian families and a few Indian women (wives and daughters) stayed on or returned, even in the midst of the excessive state violence.

For some who lost their businesses, livelihoods, and homes, staying behind offered surprising new economic opportunities. This was a distinctive entrepreneurial culture, unique to Amin's Uganda. Some described to me savvy "whiskey runners" or "drivers" who traveled across borders, linking regional and international trade, importing scarce and valuable commodities like alcohol, cigarettes, and other luxury goods; others became sole importers of sundries like sugar and salt as the regime progressed. Still others were smuggling coffee or valuable minerals out of Uganda, activities that were common during this era. Fortune-seekers, profiteers, and opportunists were the focal point of moral discourses surrounding the creation of wealth among a cohort of businessmen. Both Black-identifying Africans and Ugandan Asians who stayed on took advantage of the de-Indianized economy. Ironically then, while Amin castigated Ugandan Asians for economically exploitative practices prior to their expulsion, some profited from community expulsion and displacement, rebuilding wealth domestically and supporting families transnationally (resettled abroad). South Asian labor, skills, capital, and entrepreneurship continued to link communities, nations, and continents.

The colonial "order of things" was decisively overturned and reversed in 1972.[19] For Idi Amin, decolonization was primarily a project of territorial and urban deracialization, an expunging of Asianness from the nation. Notably, the construction of national identity and citizenship in line with racial Blackness was intimately connected to the remaking of urban space, which was "deracialized" or "de-Indianized" in accordance with the material process of expulsion and property expropriation. Here, I am complicating our understanding of deracialization: in the sense of the deracialization or de-Indianization of civil society and economy or "the partial reform of the state,"[20] but also with respect to more material urban geographies (transforming formerly Indian spaces into Black African ones through state expropriation), and the more symbolic, embodied, and psychic-affective domains of deracialization. I investigate the cultural—including racialized and gendered—experience of the new national order in which African identity becomes defined through racial Blackness, in which Black racial and political sovereignty is expressed through a newly empowered and hierarchical relationship in relation to the declining racial and social status of "Asianness" or "Indianness."

The inversion of colonial racial hierarchies was not only racial but also expressed through gendered and sexual domains. Idi Amin and the so-called "lumpen militariat"[21] embodied the dominant militarized masculinities of the era, which elaborated upon existing colonial-era martial masculinities then applied to Amin's ethnic group, the Kakwa, and his homeland in West Nile. Militarized masculinities glorified "war and [celebrated] so-called

2.1 Although this photo most likely was taken at the Asian Conference at Amin's command post in Kololo, Kampala in 1972, some believe it reflects those who stayed on after expulsion. Courtesy of the Gheewala family, 2011.

military values—hierarchy, discipline, obedience, and the centralization of authority" and placed emphasis on "physical strength, courage, endurance, discipline, and heterosexual competency."[22] Amin naturalized a patriarchal and nativist nationalist militarized masculinity through performances of gender and sexuality, especially athleticism, heterosexuality, hypermasculinity, and sexual virility.[23] Gender, sexuality, and masculinity were central to Idi Amin's exercise of sovereign power, especially through the Asian expulsion decree, but also through the military government's material "de-Indianization" of the nation through the three-month spectacle of the Ugandan Asian exodus and through the expropriation and redistribution of Ugandan Asian properties and assets. Black African political sovereignty and authority was expressed symbolically, affectively, and psychically via the emasculation of the figure of the Asian qua merchant-trader. Building on anti-Semitic tropes, the figure of the Asian was constructed as a saboteur of the economy/nation. But the figure of the Asian was also rendered effeminate, weak-bodied, and lacking in character—stingy, greedy, duplicitous, communal-minded, and so forth—in contrast to the empowered and morally superior Black African Ugandan citizenry and their masculinities. The Asian symbolically lost his honor, or *izzat,* and his masculinity during the expulsion; those who remained sought to recuperate their honor, moral autonomy, and manliness.

2.2 Decolonization as a racial, ethno-religious, and gendered project. Amin forces British officials to carry him on a palanquin adorned with the Ugandan national flag, asserting Black African Ugandan political and racial sovereignty, militarized masculinities, and the emasculation of European and, later, Asian racialized political sovereignties. Courtesy of Getty Images.

The dissolution of the pre-expulsion Ugandan Asian community—including communal and religious life and the daily rhythms of work, family, and social life—left those who remained after the expulsion in an environment rife with complex moral and psychic dimensions as they negotiated ongoing state violence against the Black civilian population, anti-Asian violence, their vulnerable racial status, and their proximities to the government and complicities with the regime. In one conversation, a small, tightly knit group of multigenerational Ugandan Asian denizens of the era (and some recent arrivals from India) described Kampala to me as a "vacuum." The vacuum symbolized the end of Asian social life, business enterprise, and commerce—the spectral, ghost town quality of a "de-Indianized" urban world in the 1970s. Formerly Indian urban spaces and properties, especially wholesale and retail shops and other places of business, were transformed into African spaces that asserted Black racial and economic sovereignty. South Asian presence was imperiled. Outright hostility, arbitrary and capricious violence, was a constant possibility for anyone who dared to remain. Those who did embedded themselves in an array of intimate relationships with their Black African counterparts in order to survive in this social context of pervasive and unpredictable violence. Building on long-standing African indigenous traditions that incorporated and assimilated ethnic outsiders, they cultivated relations of protection and patronage with military men, bureaucrats, neighbors, and townspeople in order to attain security and the capacity to remain. Confraternity and conviviality between African men and Ugandan Asians and others were commonplace. Yet the inverse was also true: sodality might unexpectedly be retracted or broken, and thus Ugandan Asian and others expended their energies on shoring up their cultural and social capital, among other "tactics of practice,"[24] to attain political protection and maintain urban denizenship. Visible yet vulnerable, they could even become sovereign "big men" within specialized economic niches or occupational professions; or conversely, they could become fairly powerless and dependent. They were visible in times of relative security, and at other times in hiding, confinement, or retreating into exile across national borders or abroad.

Mainstream discourses of expulsion exceptionalism posit the 1972 Asian expulsion and Idi Amin's Uganda as a rupture emblematic of a crisis of liberalism and democracy, of a civilizational retreat into a Rousseauian State of Nature, a Conradian Heart of Darkness. Even mainstream scholars would agree that Amin's ascent to power and the expulsion led to economic collapse, developmental decline, and the normalization of tyranny and political terror. In addition to the ways in which these lenses on this era displace more critical engagements with the interactive elements of liberal, illiberal, and nonliberal practices—or the relationships between imperialisms, neocolonialism, and postcolonial or Global South dictatorships and fascisms—they also displace the study of actually existing and transforming formations of governance, sovereignty, and citizenship and of changing relationships of race, class, ethnicity, religion, caste, gender, and sexuality during the Amin regime. Here, I am following a trajectory of scholarship that complicates the ways in which Idi Amin usually personifies the state itself, showcasing that "the regime" is more than just the dictator or the personality but "a field of social action."[25] It is replete with an array of government bureaucracies and military and policing institutions, political and social actors, and civilian life—in short, full of complicated practices of governance, subjectification, and agency, all of which need to be understood on their own terms. If the 1972 Asian expulsion was both a violent dictatorial and bureaucratic affair, so too was the practice of South Asian racial denizenship during Amin's Uganda.

I did not anticipate writing about the Amin regime, and perhaps I was avoiding it all along. In writing about Ugandan Asian and other South Asians who stayed on, I do not wish to minimize the immense forms of violence that Black Africans experienced at the hands of Amin and, later, Obote during his second era in power. I also fear that I may risk reproducing aspects of expulsion exceptionalism that I have been problematizing in this book. As a corrective, my approach is to work through the voices of the communities I was able to access—what they offer and what they may occlude in terms of Black African experience—to normalize writing about South Asian presence in Uganda *past* expulsion. Amin and the military dictatorship emerged historically, building upon existing modalities of state violence and governmentality introduced by colonialism and the first postindependence Obote government. These modalities involved experiments in despotic and illiberal forms of authority; the use of law and order and criminalization to target specific communities; increasing militarization, repression, and surveillance; and other biopolitical and necropolitical interventions upon the Ugandan body politic.[26]

Thus, postcolonial statecraft, governance, and sovereignty innovate upon imperial and colonial inheritances. Thomas Blom Hansen and Finn Stepputat have argued that colonial state sovereignties were "the naked version of modern sovereign power"[27]—not necessarily totalizing, but always spectacular, partial, and provisional, often making use of excessive and random violence. So, in addition to European sovereign power and military authority asserted over the indigenous Black African and South Asian social body, African sovereignty itself was also dispersed and fragmented across many different actors and institutions. Following Achille Mbembe then, postcolonial states simultaneously deploy disciplinary, biopolitical, and necropolitical modalities of power.[28] Racialized and heteropatriarchal male entitlements are essential features of the many interdigitating modalities of governmentality and registers of violence during this period, and they circulate among the varied sovereign actors proximate to the state: government ministers and state bureaucrats, army officers, soldiers and mercenaries, security agents and operatives, big men, businessmen, and risk-taking entrepreneurs. Indeed, the men I spoke with possessed a heightened sense of themselves as racialized selves, developed in tandem with the racializing gaze of the state.

The men I encountered also relied upon a liberal ethos of legal-juridical documents and related claims to maintain their racialized denizenship or claims to particular entitlements. These included the official verification of their Ugandan citizenship and other documentation prior to the expulsion decree, including their existing property titles, their trade licenses and work permits, and other liberal contract-style agreements. Even if they were now considered to be substantive (racial and cultural) noncitizens—their communities and kin dismantled and displaced and their businesses and homes expropriated—they continued to make claims for their compensation for labor, for unfulfilled contracts and other unfinished business. Yet their ability to hang on was also dependent upon the capricious sovereignty of government officials and bureaucrats and their intimate relationships with African communities. Staying on required new ways of being "Asian" and integrating into a new Black Ugandan national identity—it required adopting a Black African subjectivity and consciousness, speaking African languages, being "Afro-Asian" and participating in shared masculinities. Practicing racial and cultural humility and treating Black Africans with honor, respect, and dignity was an instrument of survival.

Citizenship Verification: Performative Rituals of Liberal/Legal-Juridical Citizenship and Exceptional Noncitizen Incorporation

I arrived, sweaty and disheveled, at the dimly lit foreign-exchange bureau on Kampala Road for my first meeting with Rajivbhai (see also chapter 1). Slight and frail-looking in his elder years, he sat behind a desk as an old computer hummed loudly; the daily newspapers were spread out before him. Colorful artistic depictions of Krishna, Ganesha, and other Hindu religious deities as well as black-and-white photos of family members adorned the office. Incense burned from careful placements in clutter-filled corners. He explained that although he was retired and his sons now oversaw the family business, he still came to the office every day and was passionate about charitable activities, including overseeing the work at a free homeopathic clinic a few streets away. In a mix of both Hindi and English, the languages we shared, we discussed his memories of expulsion, focusing on his determination to stay on after the deadline and his recollections of life during the military dictatorship. I was struck by how he focused less on Amin's expulsion decree and the ninety-day period of expulsion. He offered instead a detailed recounting of the state-based bureaucratic process by which he was verified as a legal-juridical Ugandan citizen and, later, exceptionally included after the expulsion. He stayed on and adapted to the anti-Asian environment.

After the announcement of the expulsion decree, he arranged for his wife and children's travel abroad. A naturalized Ugandan citizen, he traveled from Kasese to Kampala to have his documents (birth certificate, passport, property titles, and business licenses and permits) examined by an appointed "verification committee" at the Ministry of Internal Affairs' Immigration Department. Unlike the nullified passports and documents of other Ugandan Asian citizens, his documents were "verified," and he was issued a red-colored identity card (figure 2.3). He then began to help other stateless Ugandan Asians and Indians citizens who were leaving the county. Although others like him with verified citizenship documents were leaving due to the anti-Asian harassment they were experiencing, he made the decision to return to Kasese to oversee his shop. He lived with another Ugandan Asian colleague for extra safety. As government officials began the property expropriation exercise in towns and districts outside of Buganda, Rajivbhai returned to Kampala once again.

> I sold my shop to a Ugandan in Kasese before I came back to Kampala in January '73. Almost all Ugandan Asians were gone by then, but I was a Uganda citizen. I had a [identity] card. But I didn't really need a card. You see, they had to prove that you are a Ugandan, then they give you a card. First Amin said people holding Indian or British passports should go, then after that he said that even [Ugandan Asian national] citizens who remain behind will have to go to Karamoja.[29] They must have a second home. If you are in Kampala, you must prove you are a Ugandan, and you must have a second home, like an ethnic homeland. This was his tactic. He was trying to scare away those who remained behind. He never enforced it, but still, many Asians left because of that fear. We didn't leave. We remained behind, we said no, we'll stay behind. They gave us a red card, and I also had a Ugandan passport. A red card was like an exemption. It means your file in immigration is verified, because some people may have gotten hold of Ugandan passports, but their records may not be proper in the files. You see, they put people to verify your record in Immigration, they put laymen from Makerere University who did not know the law, who didn't know . . . so they disqualified many people who were real Ugandans saying that you are not Ugandans. Your records are this and that. So they left. Many cases, they happened like that.

Like Rajivbhai, many *rehen walley* described themselves as "exempt" from the expulsion, referring to their verified citizenship status, red identity

2.3 Ugandan Asian passports and a Ugandan identity card. Courtesy of the Uganda Collection, Carleton University Library.

cards, and other documents—passports, birth certificates, business and trading licenses, property titles—that helped identify and distinguish them as legitimate and authentic, or "real," Ugandans who could remain despite their loss of (substantive) racial and cultural citizenship. Red identity cards made manifest the sovereignty of legal recognition, and they were critical to Asian racial denizenship: protecting *stayees* from anti-Asian violence and harassment; shaping them as legitimate residents, workers, and entrepreneurs; and rendering them legible to military and other state officials who continued to police the boundaries of racial inclusion and exclusion. Others of South Asian descent who arrived after the expulsion also had identity cards or some kind of documentation that established their status as "exceptions to the expulsion."

Legal documentation and other material culture such as uniforms, border posts, and official buildings are central to the (re)production of the sovereignty of the state and its legal technologies; these trappings signify the nation and its territorial boundaries, give context to the work of state officials and bureaucrats, and facilitate the production of citizens, noncitizens, and exceptionally included denizens.[30] Bureaucratic practices and performances of formal proceduralism such as censuses, "citizenship verification" exercises, and the creation and allocation of identity cards were dominant in the memories of those who managed to hang on after the expulsion and central to how they imagined and understood the power of individual state officials in the Amin regime—and crucially, not necessarily Amin himself—to include or exclude them. For Ugandan Asians and others who would arrive after the expulsion, state power was reproduced and asserted through the routine encounters of state bureaucrats, including constant documentation checks and verifications of identity cards. State power was clearly not only about the African autocrat's sovereign power to expel racial and ethnic Others; it was exercised through the mobilization of very modern state and legal-juridical technologies that authorized the precarious racial denizenship of those raced as "Asian," repeatedly defining new racial distinctions and reversals in race hierarchy. It maintained and asserted Black African racial and political sovereignty, a racially nativist Ugandan national identity.

In our conversations, I came to realize that Rajivbhai was still grappling with the formal and substantive unbundling of his citizenship status during the expulsion period and its aftermath: the unmaking and remaking of legal-juridical, national, racial and cultural terrains of belonging and exclusion, and perhaps also the impacts of the traumas he had experienced. At times he discounted official state proceduralism like the citizenship verification committee, which legally authorized him as a formal citizen while still subjecting him to racial and cultural humiliation and indignities. Instead, he took pains to stress to me both his legal-juridical Ugandanness (national identity) and his investments in the universal claims of liberal citizenship and the supposedly universal political belonging across Black and South Asian racial status. At other times, he acknowledged the capricious violence of the Amin government and the expulsion decree, including the arbitrary nature of the law and the mobilization of legal documents. He emphasized that they were ineffective in recognizing him as a "real Ugandan." He rationalized this through noting that many Ugandans were "uneducated" and "did not understand the laws"; at other moments he seemed to understand that his substantive inclusion was no longer possible on the basis of his racial and cultural identity: that as long as he was raced as "Asian," he could not ever be considered Ugandan or African. To be Ugandan or African would be possible only if he were phenotypically racially Black and indigenous to an ethnic homeland in the national territory.

Back in Mbarara, I learned that Sahib's friend Jali had also stayed on, residing in town, separated and later estranged from his wife in exile. Jali was adamant that his Ugandan and African identity came before his "Asianness" or even his Ismaili Muslim identity. When we first met, he talked at great length about the present-day agrarian struggles of small-scale farmers in Ankole, including their lack of access to credit and experiences with exploitative corporate lenders. Sitting together in Sahib and Rani's courtyard, we drifted backward in time, tentatively approaching the past, negotiating feelings of suspicion, connection, and trust, and the constant and heavy presence of expulsion. "I never left. We stayed because during the exodus . . . we were citizens. We were working here. At that time we were doing mining business and farming. We verified that our citizenship was proper and then we stayed, and they [referring to military officers and other Africans in town] never harmed us or anything. But very few people stayed here, about ten families only." Jali paused.

> After '73, after six months, they [soldiers] had taken their [Asian] businesses. For us, they never harassed us in the mining business. At that time, they used to make verifications. There was a deadline, it was 9 November I think, so we went to the RDC office, that time it was the DC office, for verification. Ok, so how many Asians are mining here? We were about . . . twenty. Then for the others, their businesses were slowly taken, and they left. For us, they never took our mine. If it was taken, then we also would have gone, see? We stayed and we lived in our home, right there on High Street. They never harmed me. We are born here and lived here for three generations, and everyone knows us. But once you are not in politics, nobody will harass you. And when you are staying with the people [Nkore, or Banyankore townspeople], *like our own people* . . . once you stay with people nicely, nobody will harass you, for what?

Jali remained due to his specialized expertise in the mining industry and the fact that the mine likely remained under some kind of government control, with capital and patronage circulated back to local state officials. Unlike Rajivbhai, who was forced to move back to Kampala, Jali's deep intergenerational ties to Mbarara and his neighborly relationships with townspeople and local state officials were integral to his ability to remain in or prevent his eviction from his home by local DAPCB officials. His narrative, amid his embodied practices and everyday commitments, offered me a glimpse into the new moral order that those who remained continued to cultivate after the expulsion decree: that if Asians treat Ugandans (Africans) like their own people, or "once you stay with people nicely," it is possible to be treated like and to become Ugandan, to stay, to belong.

In her work, Christine Obbo analyzes the integration and assimilation of "village strangers" in Buganda society, arguing that the Baganda had always encountered numerous kinds of strangers, most notoriously the Ruandese and Lugbara from the north, who worked for or served as tenants on Ganda land. Until 1966, when traditional kingdoms were abolished, "everyone who settled in Buganda was, at the village level, a 'chief's man' (*musajja wa mwami*) and at a societal level a 'king's man' (*musajja wa kabaka*). The visitor might be a guest (*mugenyi*), a traveler (*mutambuze*), a blood brother (*munywanyi*), a kinsman (*waluganda*), or a client (*musajja wange*). Should the visitors decide to stay in the village and acquire some land, they became settlers (*mutuze*) . . . they ceased to be strangers; they became fellow villagers (*munyankalo*), neighbors (*muliranwa*), and new tenant-subjects (*musenze mugya*)."[31] The protection of strangers always relied upon local chiefs, with the relationships between people on a given territory or land taking primacy.[32]

The Ganda, like other traditional kingdoms, have always incorporated new members, usually through sacred blood pacts and related mutual obligations (including the observance of similar clan-based totems and taboos); through forms of assimilation (language and dress); and through marriage alliances. Some communities, like the Nkore and Ruandese, continued to maintain a sense of distinction and ethnic consciousness despite their integration.[33] Obbo's research confirms my own data about the incorporation of a final category of strangers, *bagwira* (foreigners), including *bayindi* (Asians), even after the expulsion. "At Kyetume, there were two Asian families who owned small shops. Each family employed a Ruandese as a laundryman. The villagers felt that these Asian families were not as arrogant as those in Mukono. In fact, one Hindu was married to a Ganda woman . . . in 1972 when the Asians were expelled from Uganda, while the other family returned to India, the Hindu refused to go to Britain or India or any other country. He claimed that his roots were in Uganda. In fact, some of his relatives who resided at Mbale did not leave either. In 1974, he had abandoned shopkeeping and concentrated on running his lumber mill."[34]

While some Ugandan Asians left small towns in regions far from Buganda due to a perceived sense of insecurity, for others, like Jali in Mbarara town, thick connections in small towns based on "fictive kinship" relationships, mutual obligations, and a horizontal relational ethics that shaped the practice of neighborliness combined with a cultural politics of racial humility, were central to cultivating safety. Acclimating to the changing racial order, assimilating into indigenous African Banyankore cultural identities through language and investments in reciprocal relationships with local townspeople, even adapting to the militarized political cultures and new economies of the era, were all central to survival in Amin's Uganda.

Both Rajivbhai and Jali took pains to stress that their citizenship status had been verified, revealing the importance of the aesthetic form, procedure, and performance of legal-juridical citizenship by Ugandan bureaucrats and state officials. Rajivbhai observed that "[they] didn't need identity cards . . . they just had to check." They were both processing the unbundling of legal-juridical citizenship from territorial birthright, naturalization, and substantive citizenship. My presence also offered the men a means of processing the mass expulsion of the larger Ugandan Asian community and their own negotiations of the aftermath, creating new narratives of the expulsion that reframed dominant global narratives. Retelling their stories offered them a means of accessing and reconstructing memories, of sorting out their ongoing embodied experiences of racial precarity and racial privilege, constructing their own ideas of what African Asian cultural identities were. Highlighting one's citizenship status and its verification, presenting a red identity card, and forging new relational ethics with Black Africans served as practical and performative responses to anyone who might question their presence in the absence of the Ugandan Asian population writ large—in the past and even in the present.

The formal terrains of legal-juridical citizenship and ideals of liberal governance as espoused by Western liberal-secular governments continued to be powerful models for those I spoke with, especially as they moved transnationally. Yet legal-juridical and material technologies of inclusion and exclusion, such as legal documents and decrees, are contradictory forms. They perform particular functions in their ability to produce and construct binaries between citizens and noncitizens, but they are also arbitrary signifiers that everyday subjects deploy on their own terms. Legal documentation has no valid discriminating power in itself, especially with regard to enshrining substantive social and political protections or individual rights for racial and ethnic subjects contending with political violence across different state projects. Although the men I spoke with located themselves outside of "the political," they discussed their deep relationships with local townspeople who extended protection and care to them and who helped shield them from many forms of violence. These men were deeply embedded within political and cultural networks of intimacy, including neighborliness, friendship, fictive kinship, sexual intimacies, even marriage alliances—all shaped by relations of reciprocity and obligation and the practice of racial and cultural humility, whether in Katwe, Kampala, or Mbarara. Thus, even if men were discursively invested in the durability of liberal and formal (legal-juridical) terrains of citizenship and belonging, their lived experiences of nonliberal domains of political and ethical practice, substantive citizenship, and popular politics were infinitely more important.[35]

Racialized Political Cultures of Protection and Securitization

Back in Kampala, some Ugandan Asian men narrated their experiences of the expulsion and of racial denizenship in Amin's Uganda through a lexicon of risk, protection, security, and insecurity. This calculus emanated from many sources: dominant colonial and liberal political epistemologies; South Asian civilizational and racial thought; and the nonliberal practices outlined above. Some men mobilized ideas of illiberal exceptionalism and discourses of lack: the absence of abstract Lockean liberal notions of democracy, individual property rights, and contractual notions of citizenship rights made material by state institutions and its legal apparatus. South Asian racial discourse could also equate racial Blackness or Africanness with illiberalism, incivility, and the imputed proclivity for violence, criminality, and corruption. Security referred to the absence of the threat of physical violence and the ability to procure an economic livelihood; insecurity referred to the breakdown of law and order and violent acts of looting, muggings, or physical attacks by soldiers, military men, and state agents considered to be undisciplined. The violence of the regime was racialized, represented through essentialized discourses of an uncivilized Black African nature or personality; the threatening, unknowable, and undeveloped African frontier or bush; and African primitive predispositions to sudden and unpredictable violence and criminality.

At other times, however, the men shifted from these tropes to more intimate registers where they humanized urban Ugandans and discussed their friendships with their associates and coconspirators, identifying with Ugandan and Black African perspectives, even revering the charisma and masculine political authority of Idi Amin and his men. This revealed their persistent race consciousness despite their feelings of racial precarity; lapses of anti-Black African racism alongside expressions of love for and intimacies with Blackness; and their contradictory investments in both racialized geographies of liberalism and illiberalism. Here they participated in the legal-juridical terrains of citizenship and pursued nonliberal practices of security-seeking, emphasizing the racial protection that had been conferred upon them by Amin and his inner circle. In doing so, the Ugandan Asian men were complicit in normalizing the violence of the militarized urban world that they were part of and reproduced.

Some Ugandan Asian men retained their residences and livelihoods in the smaller villages and urban centers of Buganda and Busoga. "Big men" who had access to wealth and expertise and social and cultural capital "couldn't be touched," showcasing the contested nature of racial sovereignties during this era. Rajivbhai's Ugandan–Gujarati Ismaili friend owned two petrol stations that required specialized expertise and large amounts of "cash money" to run. Another influential Sikh industrialist had an "entire platoon" guarding his sawmill and workshops throughout the 1970s and 1980s. These men had successfully built protected enclaves for themselves while forging alliances with local military and government officials, exchanging patronage and other favors for economic entitlements and denizenship. Mutually beneficial arrangements could be initiated by a range of actors, but they did require men to speak African languages, rehearse dominant African masculinities, and accommodate to the new political culture and racial order. Racial protection and other favors could also be retracted, and thus the constant threat of detention, torture, death, or the fear of needing to flee into exile influenced the ways in which these systems and strategies worked.

Rajivbhai describes his experience:

> Initially for two, three years we were doing foreign-exchange business. At least it kept us going. Then in '76, the Minister of Information in Amin's government wanted somebody to look after his business here, to run it. He had also grabbed a business. He had a plastic, polythene bag factory and a sock factory. So he asked one of my friends whether "you got somebody who can manage my business." So my friend told me that the minister wants someone to take over as the manager. I said, I don't mind. My condition is that I must get my wife's permit by the immigration department. And my children. If they give me the permit then I will work for you, otherwise I can't work. The minister talked to the Minister of Internal Affairs. . . . He says, okay we will give permit to his wife. They give me the permit, and I called my wife, while Amin was here, in '78 January. So two of my sons came with my wife. I was living at that time in the *gurudwara*. There were no Sikhs living there, only the priest. I rented four rooms from him. So my wife came with my children. We lived there, about one and a half years, two years in *gurudwara*. Then we rented a house in Kanjokya Street. Then I started working with an Indian in Amin's time. He was also lucky to get a business run by a Ugandan. . . . He knew me, so I joined him, and I worked with him for ten months . . .

because by '79 April, Amin left. So April to December '79 I didn't have any fixed job, but still, I was doing some work here and there. I was getting money. I was sustaining myself. No problem.

Rajivbhai's entrepreneurial activities ranged from handling fees through floating foreign exchange to managing expropriated businesses now in the possession of Amin's ministers. Others described how they became economic middlemen in the foreign-exchange business after 1972; still others worked as accountants and managers, running businesses behind-the-scenes with Black African Ugandans as the front, "in name" owners, a mutually beneficial relationship, and in accordance with the transformed racial sovereign order of Amin's Uganda.[36] Ugandan Asian business knowledge, skills, and transnational access to commodity, capital, and credit chains meant that some Ugandan Asians and others were still significant business intermediaries and managerial experts essential to the regime itself.

While immigration officials were not happy to endorse the return of exiled Ugandan Asians, high-ranking ministers, undertaking their own strategic arrangements, authorized the return of some. Rajivbhai's story illuminates how some Ugandan Asians and their families resettled merely six years after their expulsion, taking advantage of economic opportunities in "the vacuum." Others were not so fortunate. Jali described how he had "lost ten years of marriage" to his first wife in the years after the exodus, eventually divorcing and then marrying his current partner years later. Others maintained and financially supported families who lived abroad; they were mobile and transnational urban denizens, setting themselves up for prosperity in the decades that would follow after the fall of Amin. Remaining behind required careful and intricate exchanges of capital, labor, skills, expertise, and favors. These negotiations were fragile, requiring information, relationship-building, and patronage in a racially hostile climate. Denizens successfully created racialized enclaves of security and protection for themselves, even as they engaged in high-risk entrepreneurialism and flirted with possibilities of violence.

Racialized Enclaves and Networks of Social and Communal Reproduction

Racialized denizenship during Amin's Uganda also relied upon a tentative sustaining and remaking of "Asian" racialized religious community, establishing networks of protection for new arrivals from India. Virdee described to me how the Chief Engineer for the Ministry of Defense, who happened to be of Ugandan Punjabi Sikh heritage, was able to retain stewardship of most Sikh *gurudwaras* and even some Hindu *mandhirs* in Buganda and Busoga. While I was talking and drinking tea with him in his sitting room in his home near Mengo, the location of the Kabaka's palace and the Lukiko, other family members drifted in and out of the room, listening in and adding observations and bits of information to our exchange. Virdee said:

> Four or five families of Singhs came together and lived in the *gurdwara*. We looked after them, and every Sunday we had a program. We kept a schedule that one Sunday we would be at the Sikh Ramgarhia *gurudwara*, one Sunday at the Singh Sabha *gurudwara*, one Sunday in the *mandhir*, one Sunday at Jinja *gurudwara*, one Sunday at the Entebbe *gurudwara* or *mandhir*. Like this, we kept going . . . then in '76, the government began to fight with Obote. After work, in the evening, we would make sure that all our people were together. At this time, no one was saying this is a Muslim, or this is a Pakistani. At that time, there was none of this. Everyone was in complete unity. If anyone was missing, for two days, for four days, after a day we would go looking for him.

Virdee discussed the necessity of inviting army officials and government ministers to weekend religious programs as well as the significance of spirituality to all those who remained behind.

Some Ugandan Asians discussed the importance of cultivating relationships with army and government contacts. One-on-one socializing and public gatherings between Ugandan Asian and African men usually involved cooking meat, sharing food, and drinking whiskey together. Some men had access to bars, clubs, and discos that were frequented by military officers. Others avoided these places and entertained ministers and army men in their homes. Mini, the biracial daughter of a Punjabi Sikh construction worker and his Ugandan (Mutoro) wife, described her memories of the military dictatorship one afternoon with me when I visited her at her home near Makerere:

> I was a child then. I remember, it was a scary time. We were not walking outside. We were indoors. And even food was a problem because we couldn't get everything. We would use what was there. Dad would continue with his work, going, coming. He was given

everything he needed, like cement he would get in loads, building materials in loads, because he was doing government work. The Minister of Information would come to our home. Dad would prepare a meal for them. Slaughter a goat for them. And we would enjoy the feast with my Dad at home. And others would come, other ministers, the colonels, the military. Sometimes Dad had us stay in the other rooms of the house to keep us safe, so we kept the doors closed and locked. Life was not easy for him, but he made it. To survive . . . if you have contacts in the government, you have a little bit of safety.

Lal Singh related several stories about the urban social worlds of *stayees*, spinning his tales, as usual, with a touch of bombast, sharing more information about the big men of Asian descent during the regime.

Okay, then you had this guy, he was the kingpin during the '70s. He was the sole importer of sugar, salt, and cooking oil. You couldn't touch this guy. Yeah, Patel. But he was a very nice man, a gentleman. But in those days, there were such few people. In the evening, you would go to his house, and he would be in his *lungi* [sarong] cooking. And he would love doing it. You know, a bottle of whiskey and he would start cooking his chicken curry. It was so simple, so delicious, done so beautifully. That was the only social structure we had. Just sitting with somebody . . . that was the score. He had a lot of influence. But then they were all corrupt. They were all corrupt. Basically, it was crazy.

Lal paused, thinking back on the past. "It was crazy. I mean, this man [Museveni] has done a lot of good for us. At least, this guy has given you the freedom to talk. In those days, you talked politics, you were dead. And somehow, we made a life around this."

Lal's recollections of Amin's Uganda and of the 1980s, during the Obote II regime, were nostalgic, even romantic, despite the intensity of state violence and political repression that shaped his life after the 1972 Asian expulsion. There was a sense of allure and fascination with the strongman figure and Amin's displays of masculine power and entitlement, of living in the militarized and (later on) war zone in Kampala, the urban style of excess and conspicuous consumption, of high-risk entrepreneurialism, and the ordinariness of the black market, of traditionally taboo cross-racial intimacies. Lal often mentioned the importance of gifting bottles of Johnny Walker whiskey, wine, and other luxury items to army men and state officials—

symbolically and materially, these gifts cemented political and patronage relationships, and they created social connections and mutually beneficial friendships and entrepreneurial and other labor opportunities for those who remained. And although stayees were small in number, some became economically powerful and necessary to the regime, thus showcasing that sovereignty was always contested.

While those who remained could be nostalgic about their dangerous adventures and risk-taking despite state violence, at other times they shared their moral anxieties about the dominant practices of profiteering and the looting of valuable resources, both state and nonstate (put plainly, the "corruption"), showcasing ambivalence about participating in wealth accumulation at the expense of the mass displacement of Ugandan Asians in 1972. If some described the racial and political security that they enjoyed due to their proximity to state actors, others shared more pointed commentary about the excessive violence that surrounded them, such as the public executions, detentions, and torture, or the secrecy surrounding the many disappearances of Ugandan civilians as state violence intensified. While they were themselves subject to the vagaries of arbitrary racial violence, they also embodied racial privilege in their ability to compartmentalize and normalize the degree of violence inflicted upon Black African bodies, or Black-on-Black violence, normalizing the massacres of ethnic Others and state enemies that were occurring around them. It was also true that they were not completely untouched by the violence of the regime, for some shared anecdotes of some Ugandan Asians who were also physically assaulted and harassed, detained and imprisoned, or even disappeared; they also shed tears when recounting the loss of their beloved Ugandan (Black African) friends and coconspirators.

Women's voices and experiences were less accessible to me. Racial denizenship was rerouted through the masculinist and patriarchal social norms of the era. African women's lives were difficult and challenging, as they were the prime targets and victims of Amin's anti-imperialist cultural crusades and made to embody Ugandan political and cultural nationalism and African male honor and prestige. Amin practiced this through the legal and moral regulation of African women's dress, comportment, and reproductive rights—the banning of miniskirts, "hot pants," trousers, wigs, skin-lightening creams, and even abortion.[37] On very rare occasions, the Ugandan Asian and other South Asian men I spoke with discussed their intimate relations with Black African women during the Amin regime. The dominant heteropatriarchal and misogynist racial, gendered, and sexual scripts about Indian, mixed-racial heritage, and African women—in which the imputed moral purity, honor, and respect afforded to South Asian women was elevated with respect to mixed racial heritage and Black African women, who were understood as more impure, immoral, and sexually available—were transforming at this time. Men who remained had a range of relationships with African women—loving and caring partnerships (such as the marriage between Mini's father and mother), long-term intimate companion arrangements, and other intimate encounters. In one telling narrative, Virdee described how after the invasion of Tanzanian troops in 1979, and as Amin fled Uganda, it was Ugandan (African, Ganda) women that harbored and took care of him and his Indian colleagues, assisting them with crossing the border to Kenya as Kampala fell to Obote once again. The more constricted and taboo racial boundaries, always informed by religion and caste, that typically proscribed gendered and sexual intimacies between Indian men and African women were loosened during Amin's regime as the status of racial Blackness increased and those who remained integrated in order to stay on. Cross-racial intimacies proliferated in multiple directions as racial hierarchies were reversed and the majority Ugandan Asian community, including Asian women, was exiled.

Racial Denizenship, Noncitizen Incorporations, Insecurities of Expulsion

There were Ugandan Asians, mixed racial heritage African-Asians, and other immigrant South Asians who never left and who stayed on in Amin's Uganda after the mass expulsion. These racial denizens tethered themselves, in precarious ways, to a national and state project that disavowed its relationship to its "Asians" and to racial South Asianness, despite its continued enmeshment with people of South Asian heritage, capital, labor, and expertise. While it might have been easy to dismiss those who remained behind as collaborators or opportunists of the regime, or even as the archetypical "repugnant subjects" of anthropological fieldwork,[38] their expressions of moral agency and claims to being and belonging in the nation, alongside the militarized and other political cultures that were refashioned during this era, were fascinating to me. Amin's Uganda was not only a prime example of the expression of the development of imperialism and third world (African) fascism, or of an exceptionally illiberal military dictatorship; it was also an era of complicated and overlapping sovereignties and forms of governance—an in-between era of Asian racial denizenship, an experi-

2.4 Singh Sabha Sikh Gurudwara in Kampala, which, like the Ramgariah Sikh Gurudwara, was a site of racial and ethno-religious denizenship during the Amin regime. Photograph by the author.

ment in Asian exceptional noncitizen incorporation, in the integration and assimilation of those who could acclimate to the new racial order and the making of African Asian identities.

The men I spoke with rationalized their complicities with, proximities to, and even affinities with the Amin government in relation to their desires to stay on in Uganda and despite their traumatic experience of expulsion and anti-Asian violence in 1972—situated within their particular life stories, locations, contexts. Their narratives were limited in their ability to express violence and loss, and they were composed of silences, no doubt related to the political repression and censorship normalized during the regime, including any political criticisms of Idi Amin. But their performative and embodied expressions revealed the men's contradictory experiences of racial privilege and racial victimization, which offered them possibilities to retreat—socially, psychologically, and emotionally—from the state and societal violence that many of their nonprivileged Black African urban counterparts were experiencing. Still, I was struck by many fleeting moments of vulnerability, when some of the most hardened and gruff "manly" men I spoke with would suddenly revert to deep grief at the numerous losses from this era. Some wept, not only for their own personal losses, including the loss of community and kin, or due to the violence and harassment they experienced, but also from the sorrow they felt for the loss of a beloved African friend and brother, killed by the Amin regime or, later, by the Obote government.

Although deeper complexities of Ugandan identity, subjectivity, and citizenship in the aftermath of 1972 were being revealed to me, racial identities of "African" and "Asian" continued to appear fixed, heightened, and oppositional; and there is still much sensitivity surrounding who, in fact, represents an authentic "Ugandan" or what attributes represent "Asianness" or "Indianness" in the nation. Some Ugandan Asian returnees cautioned me to pay careful attention to who was an "original" Ugandan Asian—they warned me that many people had arrived just prior to the expulsion or were solicited to work for the government just after the expulsion, self-styling themselves as "Ugandan Asians"—the majority of whom were expelled. By contrast, those who remained after the expulsion and who adapted to the regime considered themselves to be well-integrated Ugandans and Africans; they were concerned about the exiles and returnees who might continue to behave in arrogant and racially superior ways in relation to their Black African counterparts, living among them but maintaining their racial consciousness and their stranger status, socially apart from Ugandans. And both groups were very anxious about the more recent arrival of new postcolonial migrants from India, Pakistan, and other South Asian nations and their seeming "lack of respect" (a euphemism for South Asian racial prejudice against Black Africans), and thus their imputed inability to integrate with Africans. Those who remained embodied and performed gendered practices of respect for the new political order that Amin had created that had empowered Black Africans, a horizontal relational ethics that was based on mutual respect, reciprocal obligations, and humility, all indispensable to maintaining racial denizenship in Amin's Uganda. The fear of—and the specter of—continued racial tensions and another Asian expulsion remained a constant, if unspoken, possibility.

The small numbers of Ugandan Asians and noncitizen South Asian (Indian and Pakistani) nationals who resided in Uganda during the Amin regime left temporarily in 1979 and the early 1980s, after the Uganda National Liberation Forces (UNLF) forces ousted Amin from Kampala (Amin then fled to Libya and subsequently went into permanent exile in Saudi Arabia).[39] Some ventured back during Obote's second government in the early 1980s, settling more aggressively in Uganda after the NRA's Liberation War and takeover of Kampala. The liberalization and structural adjustment period ushered in during the 1980s and 1990s led to new dispensations of Ugandan Asian and South Asian immigration and settlement and new Ugandan state logics of "Asian" racial incorporation. Even as more liberal forms of government came to replace the so-called terror regimes of the high nationalist period in postcolonial Africa, the complex dynamics and tenacious nature of South Asian communal and urban life; nonliberal political and cultural practices of racial security-seeking; and the changing racial and cultural "Asian," "Ugandan Asian," and "Asian African" identities that emerged across the colonial and postcolonial Obote and Amin governments would undergird the next new political and moral order. Meanwhile, unaddressed feelings of racial estrangement, the repressed experience of expulsion, and imperial, racial, and class complicities with anti-Black racism and anti-Blackness would continue to haunt Ugandan Asians and other communities, those both in the nation and in exile in the global diaspora. The insecurities of expulsion linger, like a slowly drifting fog.

Insecurities of Repatriation

From Refugee to Returnee

In 2011, I returned to Kampala for follow-up research. It was a trip that happened to coincide with the February national elections, in which tensions between the ruling party and government, the National Resistance Movement (NRM), and a coalition of political opposition groups that challenged the electoral process and results led to several days of repressive state violence and ethnic-based violence across the city. Traveling from Entebbe to my lodging in Kampala, the roadways and roundabouts were festooned with bright yellow banners, images of Museveni and the campaign slogan *Pakalast* (until the end), revealing the huge sums of money the NRM government had spent on advertising, music, and entertainment. The patriotic celebrations and clever campaign productions posed a jarring contrast to the armored vehicles, military tanks, and riot police that had descended upon the city. Many of my research contacts of Ugandan Asian heritage encouraged me to shelter indoors until the immediate postelection violence subsided due to the possibility of anti-Asian attacks. However, I felt that my expatriate American citizenship status and the ways that I was also often constructed as a Westerner, or *mzungu*, would keep me safe.

Once the hum of normal life returned, I visited Mini in her home near Makerere, where we had planned to discuss her experiences living through the civil war and the unsteady political transitions leading up to NRM governance. As we settled in her sitting room for our chat, her phones—a smart phone and a sturdy Nokia phone—interrupted us, beeping loudly. She glanced at the Nokia, laughing loudly, handing it to me. A message from a phone number composed of all number sevens read, "The Man in the Hat Thanks You." Yoweri Museveni was referred to colloquially as "M-7" and celebrated for his trademark large khaki rancher hat that symbolized his Hima identity from the cattle-keeping region of Ankole. Mini explained that his campaign team was texting the public to thank them for their votes. Like Amin, the figure of the president was a continual urban presence, inserting itself even into my research meetings. For Mini and most Ugandans, the NRM implied the fusion of political authority across party, government, and state; but it was always embodied by the presidential sovereignty and the distinctive militarized and pastoral masculinity of Museveni.

In the first phase of my research, I had discovered that Ugandans of diverse class and ethnic backgrounds and returnee Ugandan Asians in Buganda—those who had experienced some of the worst violence in the previous decades—understood Museveni and the NRM as a stabilizing political force that brought development, peace, and security to the nation: a counterpoint to the tyranny of Idi Amin and Milton Obote, a powerful contrast and knowledge claim that Museveni had himself adopted to shore up political authority and remain in power. Some Ugandan Asians rehearsed NRM narratives that constructed "Asians" as a successful business community, explaining that Ugandan Asians had been invited to return as "partners in development" or "investors" in the nation.[1] Many Ugandan Asians constructed the president as a benevolent father figure, even referring to him as *Mzee*, as someone who oversaw their return, a guarantor of racial and political security and an architect of national development and prosperity. "Postliberal" and nonliberal practices of sovereign recognition and inclusion were deeply significant to Ugandan Asians' immediate lives and were a crucial aspect of postcolonial governance.

But many urban Ugandans were simultaneously negotiating the politics and practice of authoritarianism, militarism, repression, and illiberalism. In fact, many others warned me that "the 1970s are back," or "the days of Idi Amin are back in Kampala." In private discussions, many Ugandan Asian *stayees* and returnees were also ambivalent about the vulnerabilities that their de facto proximity to the NRM and state power had created. If they had been unsettled by their expulsion, they were likewise unsettled by their process of return, an ongoing lack of resolution or sense of peace and closure. Nusrat, a Ugandan Asian returnee from the Ismaili community, was one such example. She had come back in 1997 for the first time since her expulsion in 1972. In her retirement years, she kept busy running a small business marketing organic farm products and was involved in the Ismaili community and in volunteer services. I initially met her at a women's group volunteer meeting, where she described her family's experience of fleeing Uganda during the expulsion. She explained that she had been a bright student and active in politics at Makerere University in the late 1960s, and deeply engaged in debates about Africanization policies in Uganda and East Africa before her life plans were disrupted by her expulsion. At the time, she and her husband temporarily relocated to Nairobi, where they waited to find out if they would be able to return to Kampala. Eventually, they were forced to migrate to Richmond, in British Columbia, Canada, where many Ugandan Ismaili Khoja refugees had been resettled during the crisis. They raised two daughters together in exile, both of whom adopted Canadian–South Asian–Muslim identities in the diaspora.

I met Nusrat at a small canteen across from Tuskers, a relatively new and popular Kenyan grocery chain, in Ntinda, a bustling residential area of Kampala for the growing middle classes, including foreign expatriates. "You know, we resettled in Richmond, and we sort of completely blanked ourselves out from what was happening here [Uganda]. It was too painful to think about what had happened, to keep following what was happening here. We completely checked out, just starting over again," she relayed, as we shared a cold bottle of water. "Then in 1992, my brother contacted my husband. And he said, I have been there [Uganda], there are lots of opportunities. My husband went. Everyone had gathered at the Fairway [hotel]. He visited the farm that we used to have and saw that it was totally down. When he came back home, he told me there is a way to repossess the farm." Nusrat took a deep breath. "I, for one, was so broken, because I felt the Ugandans whom I had been so close to, Ugandans I had been so close to . . . at the end of the day who stood by us? Nobody. At the end of the day, no one said . . . in the heart of their hearts, as today I still think, that on the surface 'investors' and all that, but . . ." She dissolved into tears and was no longer able to speak. I was caught off-guard by her emotions and unsure how to comfort her. Nusrat's silences and suppressed pain offered me a glimpse of her lingering experience of displacement and sense of estrangement from Ugandans, even as she had resumed an unsteady life in Kampala. We sat together in silence, contemplating the unaddressed racial tensions that belied the current government's neoliberal agenda of economic development and market activity. Nusrat's return to Kampala, and even our conversation in the shopping plaza, a public setting, felt too vulnerable; it was a risky exposure of the underside of things, of a neoliberal temporality of repression.

Nusrat then shared her qualms about Ugandan Asian return, which she described as "simply about handing back property and creating investors." Significantly, she was most concerned about the possibility of what some called an inevitable future "regime change": in 2011, Kizza Besigye, once part of the NRM and Museveni's former doctor, was the leader of the main opposition group, the Forum for Democratic Change (FDC), which had formed a coalition with other political parties.[2] Responding to my inquiry about whether she would remain in Kampala for the foreseeable future, she said that she would assess the results of the elections. If the NRM continued to govern, she would stay with her husband—she felt that the president had offered them nominal political and racial security. As Ugandan Asian exiles who were both privileged transnationals and expatriates with entitlements to property and business (yet also subject to racial disenfranchisement), they could leave as Canadian citizens if anti-Asian violence made life in Uganda impossible once again. There were other, practical reasons for her and her husband to stay as long as they could, including the fact that their physical health had improved from eating better food and being more physically active in Uganda in their senior years. I came away from our meeting with a deep sense of Nusrat's own Ugandanness despite her integration into the Canadian nation, her estranged and fragile attachment to urban Uganda and lack of awareness of many Ugandans' deep frustrations with the antidemocratic nature of the ruling party, all of which exceeded the NRM's seemingly progressive project of Ugandan Asian repatriation, national development, peace, and security.

In this chapter, I continue to unravel the insecurities of expulsion, examining expulsion as a continuous, unfolding global critical event. The fallout of expulsion and the racialized denizenship of some Ugandan Asians and South Asians during the Amin military dictatorship normalized practices of integration and assimilation into African communities and nonliberal political cultures of proximity between state actors (especially state officials and military men) and Ugandan Asians and others who could negotiate for the security and protection of themselves, members of their family, others racialized as Asian, and even new laborers and professionals who arrived during the Amin regime. Museveni and the NRM elaborated upon these nonliberal practices of inclusion through the sovereign authorization and recognition of Ugandan Asian returnees, in addition to a formal, state-led process of

Ugandan Asian repatriation through property repossession and the ability to reclaim (liberal) legal-juridical Ugandan citizenship. Nonetheless, I show that the NRM has maintained racially nativist notions of national identity, defining Ugandan and African identities through ideas of racial Blackness, indigeneity, and autochthony while reproducing a racialized binary distinction between "African" and "Asian." The NRM does not exemplify an exclusively authoritarian or illiberal mode of governance; it represents a shift to interactive modes of liberal, illiberal, and nonliberal forms of governance that construct Ugandan Asians and other South Asians as racial noncitizens yet valuable economic citizens. Below, I detail the why and how of these processes alongside the restructuring of racial, ethnic, religious, and gendered national identities in what many scholars describe as "Museveni's Uganda."

Obote II to the Movement: Forging New National Futures

The interregnum between Amin's Uganda and the NRM included two short-lived governments. The first was headed by Yusuf Lule and Godfrey Binaisia; it was followed by the installation of Milton Obote's Uganda National Liberation Front (UNLF) government. From 1981 to 1985, violence against civilians and civil war continued as rebel groups struggled to oust Obote's government, known as "Obote II." His return to power is important because his government passed the Expropriated Asian Properties Act in 1983, which empowered the Amin-created DAPCB (Departed Asians Property Custodial Board) to begin a process of property repossession for exiled Ugandan Asians who were now dispersed globally. In the intervening years since 1972, many displaced Ugandan Asians had deployed legal strategies to file grievances against the Ugandan government (often with the assistance of Uganda-based lawyers), seeking redress and compensation for their expulsion and loss of assets. But the first actual returnees who were able to make use of government and state support for their return were the Ugandan Asian Madhvani and Mehta families, the owners of the two largest sugar plantations and agro-industry magnates, the Madhvani and the Mehta Group, prior to their expulsion. Although Obote and the Uganda People's Congress (UPC) had always had a political alliance with the Ugandan Asian capitalist class, Obote's ministers demonstrated their ambivalence about Ugandan Asian return by accompanying "their invitations to expelled Asians with warnings reminiscent of those from the Africanization campaigns in the 1960s."[3] These family firms were now subsidiaries of multinational companies, which had expanded abroad in the years since the expulsion.[4] Others associated with family firms and industry during these years were able to reclaim national citizenship on the basis of the jus soli and jus sanguinis definitions of citizenship as framed in the 1968 Constitution.[5]

The protracted guerrilla struggle led by Museveni and the National Resistance Army (NRA) during the Bush War, or Liberation War, resulted in the NRM's takeover of Kampala in 1986. Known simply as the Movement, the initial successes of the NRM were its popular support base and the democratization of political power in rural areas through the creation of local resistance councils that engaged all ethnic groups and women. The NRM proclaimed an era of "fundamental change" based on the postapartheid South African ANC-inspired "Ten-Point Programme," which boasted liberal-style political innovations during the African continent's "democratic wave" of the 1990s. It also had international legitimacy, since Museveni was able to control and discipline the military that he had educated and trained with in exile.[6] This undercut cyclical patterns of state violence in which political leaders and their militaries sought revenge on previous ethnic enemies and terrorized civilians. By remaking aspects of the state and the military, Museveni—through political reforms, his personal leadership style, and the movement's ideology—seemed to usher in a new era of peace and ethnic unity, melding strongman leadership and military training, revolutionary aspirations and liberal democratic innovations. Scholars have observed that Museveni was invested in a rational, scientific, and methodical approach to nation-building, one that required from the citizenry a renewed commitment to morality, pragmatism, and discipline.[7] Others have observed the NRM's Evangelical Christian and millenarian religious undertones, as Museveni himself embodied both Christian and secular values.[8]

Representing the NRM as a distinctive rupture from the past, and mobilizing more intensive pastoral, paternalistic, and disciplinary modes of government, the NRM was concerned with transforming the citizenry into morally rehabilitated citizens with a united political consciousness based on ideas of peace, prosperity, and national development. Most recently, as of the early 2020s, and as Museveni and the NRM have maintained power in Uganda, the president refers to the now majority youth population of the nation as his *bazzukulu* (grandchildren), with himself as their *jajja* (grandfather), underlining paternalistic and kinship-oriented forms of governance.[9]

Museveni was actually trained as a Pan-Africanist and a Marxist, and the NRM initially attempted a barter economy and a socialist-dirigiste vision of the economy, developing a modernizing critique of Julius Nyerere's socialist principle of *ujaama* (cooperative economies) in postcolonial Tanzania for its romanticism of peasant traditionalism.[10] This initial left-progressive experimentation sought to protect the autonomy and interests of Ugandans rather than resorting to dependency on the liberal capitalist norms of Western nations and institutions and their neocolonial arrangements with former colonies. However, the combined effects of the 1970s international debt crisis, the long-term consequences of civil war and violence, and pressure from Western finance institutions challenged Museveni and the NRM's autonomous visions of nation-state and economic sovereignty. Like other postcolonial nations of the Global South contending with the violent repression of anti-imperialist and socialist aspirations in the 1960s and 1970s,[11] Museveni and the NRM ultimately secured Western donor aid to fund immediate postwar infrastructural reconstruction. Donor aid was conditioned upon mandated structural adjustment programs (SAPs) that, starting in the 1980s, liberalized markets and deregulated capital and, by the 1990s, privatized many government functions.[12]

Political liberalizations followed economic ones. At the outset, Museveni's "No-Party Democracy" system was a sardonic response to Western liberal democratic mandates to immediately move to a multiparty system.[13] Here, Museveni was astute in appropriating the political language of liberal democracy and using it against Western imperial states, mobilizing anti-imperialist rhetoric to establish what the NRM deemed to be an autonomous and necessary alternative to competitive party politics in the context of colonial racial and native rule and ensuing postcolonial racial and ethnic violence.[14] No-Party Democracy was applied to the economic realm, as Museveni argued that without a stable government, a modern industrial sector, and a diversity of social and economic classes from which to organize, Ugandans would continue to identify with colonially crafted ethnic identities, leading to further ethnic-based violence, referred to as tribalism.[15] Urban youths, women, the military, and a diversifying urban political class of government and business elites became the most important political constituencies of the NRM as Museveni inaugurated a rightward shift via (neo)liberal capitalist logics, even while embracing the language of anti-Western imperialism and Pan-Africanism. Although multipartyism was formally restored—and even traditional political kingdoms, renamed "cultural leaders," were officially reintroduced in 1993—the NRM maintained political authority and ownership of "the political" through its monopoly on violence and its political ideologies and discourses of maintaining peace and security. Militarism and political repression became normalized as it was feared that discussing the past—including ethnic violence—might potentially stoke political grievances and normalize political insecurity.[16] In fact, although the NRM had established a Commission of Inquiry into violations of human rights committed between Ugandan national independence in 1962 and the fall of the previous regime, the Commission did not receive much political support or even publicity; nor did it initiate a public conversation about the past or offer any political or material redress for past injustices that could support a substantive project of democracy and ethnic and racial reconciliations.[17]

Although the NRM was successful in propagating a global image of peace and stability internationally and thus became the recipient of large sums of Western military and donor aid—all while strategically maintaining an image of Western anti-imperialism, Pan-Africanism, and African liberation domestically—and although the NRM had incorporated liberal innovations such that it became described as a "hybrid regime"—the NRM was also implicated in committing acts of state violence against its own citizens and those in neighboring nations. Most notable is Museveni's support of his former top military adviser and president (since 2000) of Rwanda Paul Kagame, who led the Rwandan Patriotic Front (RPF) invasion of Rwanda in 1996; the NRM's counterinsurgency operations in Northern Uganda and subsequent civil war in the early 2000s; and the Ugandan military counterinsurgency and counterterrorism interventions in the Democratic Republic of the Congo (DRC) and Somalia. A consequence of the regional military might of Uganda is that it is now also one of the largest recipients of intra-African refugee migration and settlement. Meanwhile, Museveni and his inner circle in the NRM have repeatedly shunned their constitutional obligations, remaining in power since 1986, sidelining transparent electoral processes, and suppressing opposition political parties and other practices of urban dissent (even other assertions of traditional political authority, especially from the Buganda Kingdom). The NRM's left-revolutionary-turned-authoritarian and illiberal drift, then, is a product of both Western imperialist and neocolonial interventions: donor aid and militarization, neoliberal capitalist transformation, and the illiberal authoritarian and repressive excesses of Museveni and the NRM, its associated political class, and the military.

While much scholarly attention has focused on ethnic politics and the drift to authoritarianism in post-1986 Uganda, I argue that the NRM's government and state-based project of "ethnic unity" is also a racial project and that even indigenous African ethnic groups are subject to state-based racial formations, as is apparent in the new racial logics of inclusion and exclusion that have been applied to new migrant and refugee populations in Uganda in the post-1986 era. The NRM has elaborated upon the racial project of Idi Amin's military government such that Ugandan national identity continues to be constructed according to ideas of racial Blackness, or via an elevation of the racial sovereignty of Black African subjects on the basis of claims to biological and phenotypical notions of race, ethnic identity, indigeneity, and autochthony to territory or land. Racial and cultural Others—the Subject Races of the colonial era (Asians, Somalis, Banyaruanda, Arabs, and others of mixed-race descent)[18]—are constructed as default immigrant aliens or permanent foreigners in the nation. At the same time, the post-1986 emergence of the developmental-aid state and the flow of foreign capital into Uganda—including the settlement of Ugandan Asian returnees and Western (white) expatriates and the reintroduction of especially British (Ugandan Asian) capital and Ugandan Asian–owned capital in the nation—are also remapping logics and practices of race, racialization, and citizenship according to global criteria. Kampala is an important site for the remaking of global (racial) white supremacy, whiteness (*mzungu*-ness), South Asianness (*muhindi*-ness), and Blackness; the relationships between race and class; and the redistribution of formal and substantive citizenship rights and entitlements. Specifically, the reintroduction of Western expatriates and Western and Ugandan Asian–owned capital challenges the elevated prestige and status that was afforded to Black Africans during their period of (militarized, masculine, right-wing, nativist) empowerment during the Amin regime.

Museveni and the NRM have institutionalized a shift from Asian racial expulsion to the maintenance of Asian racial exclusion and economic inclusion via "noncitizen incorporation." Two processes have facilitated this state logic and governance of citizenship: (1) the repatriation of Ugandan Asian exiles through state-based property repossession and (2) the remaking of legal-juridical citizenship criteria in the 1995 *Constitution of the Republic of Uganda*. In both cases, the past—including the 1972 Asian expulsion and its aftermaths—remains unresolved. There has been no state-led political process that has prioritized an inquiry or commission into the expulsion and racial reconciliation, nor has there been a process to define its terms. For Museveni and the NRM, Ugandan Asian return is laced with both strategy and ambivalence while also being crucial to the maintenance of governance and the liberalization of the economy—indeed, it is the first phase in a tightening alliance between politics, business, and security and the normalization of a politics of racial nonreconciliation.

"Property Repossession without Racial Reconciliation,"
"Citizenship via Invitation," and "Sovereign Authorization":
Ugandan Asian Repatriation, Again

In 1992 and in response to pressure from international finance institutions (IFIs), Museveni and the NRM reintroduced the Expropriated Properties Act. This time, the NRM was more successful in harnessing state resources to process paperwork and return property and assets back to their original Ugandan Asian owners. This return or "repossession" of expropriated properties is an unparalleled process in postcolonial Africa. Expropriated properties and assets have not usually been returned to white settlers or to other Subject Race populations like Asians or Arabs in postcolonial Zimbabwe or Zanzibar, other nations with histories of Africanization and property redistribution and land reform. While some commentators, including exiled Ugandan Asians, have assumed that property repossession and compensation served as a material form of redress for the expulsion, even symbolizing post-expulsion racial reconciliation, I argue that property repossession was an economic process rather than a political one because it did not reckon with the causes and consequences of the expulsion, the possible futures of Ugandan Asians and other South Asians in the nation, or majority-minority and race relations in Uganda. Rather, it was an IMF- and World Bank–mandated reform connected to donor-aid conditionality. Thus, property repossession aligned with the NRM's national developmental goals, such that state discourses began to construct Ugandan Asian returnees as primarily business-oriented, entrepreneurial citizen-subjects necessary to promote economic growth and attract other economic investment. Moreover, if property repossession was central to the reconstruction of the economy and a shift toward a liberalized market economy, it also buttressed global racial ideas of capitalist modernity, Western liberal exceptionalism, and African illiberal exceptionalism. IFI experts argued that repossession would eradicate corruption and graft within the state and among parastatals, like the DAPCB, associated with the Amin era. Property repossession would allow Uganda to be part of a global and moral community of modern liberal capitalist nations, reversing historical wrongs of the postcolonial era and especially of the Amin regime.

I use the descriptor *property repossession without racial reconciliation* to refer to these processes, highlighting that the political and cultural deracination of Ugandan Asians as African that occurred during their expulsion was maintained and perpetuated during the property repossession process.

If Ugandan Asians were returnees, they were now also Western expatriates, property owners, businesspeople, and economic investors. State discourses maintained racial divisions: the "African" as racially Black and Ugandan, and the "Asian" or "Indian" as foreign and racially and culturally South Asian or of South Asian heritage. In addition to pressure from Western governments and IFIs, the property repossession process contained nonliberal elements, especially the political authority and sovereignty embodied by Museveni through his leadership, political acumen, and charisma. To regain the trust of exiles and to ensure the success of property repossession, Museveni traveled to the Ugandan embassies of the adopted countries of expelled Ugandan Asians, especially those of the UK and Canada. He offered assurances of political and racial protection for the returnees, their property, and their investments while also identifying areas of national investment, constructing a nonliberal logic of noncitizen racial incorporation for Ugandan Asians, what I call *citizenship by invitation* and *sovereign authorization*.

His visits were often coordinated alongside the first state- and community-based (twenty-fifth) anniversary commemorations of the Ugandan Asian expulsion in the UK and Canada. In contrast to some wealthy Ugandan Asians who had been able to transfer wealth abroad prior to their expulsion, most Ugandan Asian refugees—who had been class-diverse at the time of expulsion—experienced the loss of their property, wealth, and assets once the expulsion commenced in late 1972 and had started over economically in the UK. As the decades passed, they negotiated living in liberal, multiracial societies in which racial and cultural difference was respected abstractly; but in practice, they were the subjects of Anglo-British majoritarian racial discrimination, even as they still benefited from racial privileges vis-à-vis the Black British diaspora within the UK.[19] The first commemoration or "reunion" events surrounding the expulsion of 1972 were extremely meaningful for Ugandan Asians: they were a way to officially and collectively narrate and process the violence and trauma of their sudden expulsion—a history that might otherwise have been forgotten in state and bureaucratic archives or privatized to the domain of family and community memory. Commemoration events also challenged exiles' African political and cultural deracination through recalling and connecting to an estranged Ugandan identity and heritage and by forging links to other displaced Ugandan Asians, even while embracing the multiracial and multicultural ethos of British and Canadian society. These events were usually sponsored by state officials who commemorated the events of 1972, celebrating the contributions of the Ugandan Asian community, especially in the UK and Canada, and establishing official narratives of the expulsion event, or the discourses and ideologies of expulsion exceptionalism. For example, official state discourses often mobilized essentialist ideas of Asian values and Asian cultural exceptionalism to describe the economic successes of the exiled Ugandan Asian community. Official and elite Ugandan Asian narratives narrated the discourses and ideologies of expulsion exceptionalism and extolled the integration of Ugandan Asian exiles into British society. They focus especially on the exceptional economic and professional successes of exiles, which come to define the totality of Ugandan Asian experience in the exiled diaspora. These claims often marginalized or invisibilized the not-so-successful stories of Ugandan Asian displacement and resettlement that were detailed in less official accounts of expulsion, or the pain and hardships that less resilient or less integrated Ugandan Asians in British or Canadian society may have endured.[20] (Similarly, Gisjbert Oonk has observed that Asian entrepreneurial success stories, especially among the *baniya* merchants, tend to be overemphasized by Africanist historians, sociologists, and anthropologists, while downplaying the merchants' failures and precarities in business ventures and aspirations that often led them to leave Africa and return to India to pursue business ventures.)[21]

By the mid-1990s, Museveni and the NRM were also beginning to mobilize transcontinental discourses of Ugandan Asian economic and cultural exceptionalism. At a meeting with exiles in a Hindu temple in Neasden, England, in 1997, Museveni had assured Ugandan Asians that the new (1995) *Constitution of the Republic of Uganda* would provide legal backing for property repossession, that rights to and the security of private property ownership would be respected and protected, that foreign exchange would be accepted, and that the return on any capital investments could be sent out of Uganda. He argued that Ugandan Asians should "forget about what happened with Amin, for Africans had also suffered under his rule." Using the example of the expanding clans of the Baganda people, who had always integrated outsiders into their kingdom, he remarked, "As long as people came to a king and pledged allegiance to a king, these people then became his people. There was no reason to send them away." He congratulated the Hindu delegation on their "strong culture" and participated in a ritual blessing offered by the priest, a symbolic performance of racial reconciliation, citizenship by invitation, and sovereign authorization that made (Black African) Ugandan racial sovereignty and traditional nonliberal notions of integration (including political authority based on the practice of protection, obligation, and loyalty) paramount.[22] The "strong culture" that Idi Amin associated with communal tendencies and the lack of national and social integration was being reshaped by Museveni and the NRM through neoliberal logics that extolled and essentialized "Asians" for their business and entrepreneurial success ("Asian" primarily defined through "Hindu-ness"). Asianness was now critical to Ugandan nation-building.

Here, once again, the state use of "Asian" as a monolithic category must be parsed to attend to the race, religion, and caste nexus. The exiled Ugandan Asian Ismaili Muslim community had settled in Canada, and it was Prince Karim Aga Khan and his efforts to develop the global Aga Khan Development Network (AKDN) that encouraged the Ugandan Ismaili community, including individuals like Nusrat and her family, to return to Uganda, re-possess their property, and reinvest their capital in community institutions such as schools, hospitals, and mosques. Other political leaders based in South Asia also participated in these appeals for Ugandan Asian return. Crucially, while Ugandan state officials continued to construct the Ugandan Asian diaspora through racial categories of "Asian" or "Indian" and tended not to differentiate between their multireligious character (inclusive of Hindus, Muslims, Sikhs, Christians, and others), postcolonial India, Pakistan, and other South Asian nations were now negotiating changing relationships to their own overseas diasporas, including to globally displaced Ugandan Asians.

In the aftermath of 1972, geopolitical tensions between Pakistan and India, neoliberalism, postcolonial India–based communal violence, and especially anti–religious minority and anticaste violence, were exposing both the violence of Hindu majoritarianism and the strength of the domestic and global diasporic Hindu nationalist (Hindutva) movement that was remaking postcolonial Indian national and diasporic identity through a majoritarian Hindu religious identity and the reinvention of "Indian" history ("India" and "Indian" being historical and social constructs).[23] In the 1990s, the Indian economy liberalized and transitioned to an official "market democracy," at which point the Indian government began giving primary importance to its diaspora—especially those individuals who had settled in wealthy Western nations—such that the new "global Indian" was defined as a "tech-savvy entrepreneurial and managerial Hindu-identified expert, one who takes pride in Indian and Hindu culture, civilization and religion."[24] Indians abroad were made into new legal subjects: PIOs, or Persons of Indian Origin, and NRIs, or Non-Resident Indians, such that NRIs were being courted for capital investment in the Indian nation in exchange for diasporic citizenship and other entitlements like Overseas Indian Citizenship (OIC-status) in the Indian nation.[25] The Indian state thus constructed its diaspora through its relationship with India as a civilizational, religious (Hindu), and cultural home, and vice versa; Indian diasporic citizenship was constructed on the basis of ideas of indigenous and even autochthonous heritage, ancestry, and pride in Hindu civilization, affiliation, and nation.[26]

But there was less attention paid to the post-1990s Indian nation's relationship to historically marginalized "overseas Indian" diasporas—especially the ancestors of indentured laborers—in Africa, the Caribbean, and the Middle East. Slowly but surely, the liberalized Indian nation started cultivating strategic diplomatic relationships with African nations and the Indian diaspora in Africa, including the displaced Ugandan Asian community that was repossessing property and that, at this point, aside from major industrialists, had few recent kinship ties (via descent or even marriage) to contemporary South Asia. Building on earlier histories of anticolonial Gandhianism, Nonalignment, and Afro-Asian solidarity between India and Uganda, nation-building projects were converging across transnational and transcontinental geographies. Indian political leaders in Uganda began to construct the Indian nation as the civilizational, racial, religious, and cultural homeland of Ugandan Asians (recall, however, that in 1972, Jawaharlal Nehru and others had shifted the responsibility of the expulsion onto Ugandan Asians themselves and back onto the British government). The NRM also defined Ugandan Asian returnees' ancestral homeland and origins as the South Asian subcontinent and what was now post-partition India and Pakistan rather than Africa. In 1997, the Indian premier Atal Bihari Vajpayee visited Uganda and thanked the head of state for the return of properties to Ugandan Asian exiles, which he hailed as a "show of reconciliation."[27] In response, Museveni strategically remarked that the handover of properties to Ugandan Asian exiles was not only about the "righting of historical wrongs" but also about the "self-interest" of the nation.[28] Here, Museveni focused on a more neoliberal and global notion of Indian diasporic identity for returnees—deracinated from African political and cultural heritage. Reflecting Nehruvian discourse, Vajpayee also repeated expulsion-era discourses, admonishing "the Indian community" (Ugandan Asian returnees) to be loyal to Ugandans (Black Africans). In addition to a "memorandum of understanding," a monument of the bust of Mohandas K. Gandhi was unveiled at the Source of the Nile in Jinja, symbolizing racial reconciliation and ushering in a new era of Uganda-India diplomatic and trade relations.[29] Despite the monumentalization of Gandhi and the remaking of Uganda-India diplomatic relationships, actual Ugandan Asian return itself was a challenging and precarious process.

Between 1992 and 1995, Ugandan Asians in exile began en masse to repossess expropriated properties administered by the (then still extant) DAPCB. Nusrat was part of this first wave of returnees who participated in the property repossession process, deciding to return to Uganda on a temporary basis for the first time since her expulsion. Property owners like Nusrat's husband and brother applied for repossession of their properties and assets from the DAPCB and returned to Uganda to oversee the bureaucratic and material transfer of ownership and the rehabilitation of properties. While some reoccupied their homes, others rented their properties to existing or new (Black African) tenants. Overall, the NRM was not successful in enticing the majority of the expelled diaspora Ugandan Asians (who remained in Britain, Canada, or other nations) to resettle and reinvest in the economy. Many Ugandan Asians who were expelled had been renters themselves and owned no fixed property, and those who did own assets were often small proprietors, who typically sought financial compensation from the government.[30] Others gave power of attorney to a small group of Ugandan Asians in Kampala who served as property agents and who handled the repossession and compensation claims for those who lived abroad.

Just like the process of expulsion, repatriation and repossession were classed, racialized, and gendered. Property titles were in the legal name of male-identified owners, and it was men who took on the labor of repossession, traveling to Kampala, meeting with government officials and lawyers, and negotiating property transfers. In addition to family firms, I was surprised that some of the small-scale proprietors and returnees I spoke with who had decided to return on a more-or-less permanent basis were divorced men whose marriages had not survived 1972 and its aftermath (a few of them remarried and, in a few cases, married African women). For their part, Ugandan Asian women returnees talked about how they were initially very reluctant to come back. Here, they contrasted the social conservatism of East African Asian communities (vis-à-vis opportunities for Asian women) with the liberal freedoms they enjoyed in the UK and Canada, where they could participate in the labor force, pursue higher education, and have more choices in planning their lives, including a greater choice in marriage partners.

Some talked about how the repossession process was smooth because of the NRM and military support for the process; but for many it was a fraught process, both for the claimants and for the existing (Black African) owners or renters of the Asian properties.[31] It was frustrating for returnees who contended with confusing, lengthy, and even fraudulent DAPCB processes or intra-familial property disputes; and it was frustrating for the existing occupants of DAPCB properties, many of whom were suddenly or eventually evicted from reclaimed properties as rents on these properties increased.[32] In my reading of print material from this period, African trade associations and other Ugandans who were evicted from repossessed properties dealt with increased rents or Indian trade competition, and they challenged the Ugandan Asians' return.[33] Recall that in the aftermath of 1972, many more Black-identifying Africans had moved to urban areas, were allocated Asian properties, and entered commerce. In the intervening years, the beneficiaries of expulsion and the Amin regime had become successful entrepreneurs; they bought properties and entered the real estate market. As properties shifted from the state or from Black African ownership back to Ugandan Asians, some Africans described their experience as urban eviction. In these commentaries, racializing and xenophobic language continued to reify discursive racial categories of Ugandans as "nationals" or "Africans" and "Asians" as "foreigners" and "so-called investors."

There were also tensions within the Uganda-based Ugandan Asian community and problems of corruption and graft within the DAPCB. A few entrepreneurial Ugandan Asians who had remained or returned took advantage of those in exile who were fearful of returning, becoming legal stewards of their properties and eventually profiting from the government compensation they received for the properties or from the resale of properties. Profitable real estate businesses emerged, creating concentrations of wealth among a small group of propertied "tycoons," their African business partners, and state officials in the DAPCB. As a result of property repossession, a new urban racial economy of landlord-rentier and creditor-debtor relations (in both real estate and finance) developed. In fact, the legal status of many expropriated properties continues to be disputed, and many unclaimed properties are still in the legal possession of the DAPCB, while some Ugandan Asians in the diaspora continue to fight for the return of their properties.[34] Faiza, a third-generation Ugandan Asian of Kashmiri Muslim descent whose family had stayed on due to her father's profession as a respected medical doctor, detailed the many tensions involved in the property repossession process: those of government corruption and the self-interests of beneficiaries of the process, which, she argued, had undermined a more transparent and democratic process of Ugandan Asian repatriation and a sense of political, rather than economic, inclusion for Ugandan Asians. Unlike others who expressed confidence in the current government and the property repossession process, she had many misgivings about Ugandan

Asian repatriation, arguing that although returnees had been encouraged to repossess properties and could technically reapply for Ugandan citizenship with adequate documentation, "the NRM had never actively encouraged returnees to become legal citizens." Their inclusion, Faiza mused, seemed strategically to benefit the NRM politically and economically and contributed to government corruption.

Property repossession introduced a process of re-racializing (the "re-Indianizing") of urban space—especially in Kampala—where properties and assets were cycling back from the state and de facto military possession to private Ugandan Asian ownership, both those living in territorial Uganda and those among the Ugandan Asian diaspora community abroad. In addition to the properties and assets that were reclaimed in former Indian areas like Old Kampala, returnees were also moving into wealthier areas of the city, which were fast becoming white expatriate–friendly areas. Significantly, property repossession (connected to Lockean notions of liberal citizenship and entitlement to private property) was essential for many Ugandan Asians' own individual sense of healing from their expulsion, and for claims to national and urban belonging and citizenship. I was often invited to visit with returnees in their repossessed homes. Amrita, who lived in her repossessed home in Mbuya in Kampala, described the relationships with government officials required to remove military men from her home. Then she often detailed the amount of labor she had put into rehabilitating, decorating, and making her home a safe and secure dwelling. Her discussions offered a way for her to access some of her more traumatic memories of packing up and being evicted and expelled in 1972. In the absence of public discussion or even official commemoration of the past, and in the face of an ongoing sense of racial precarity, the home was a "haven in a heartless world," even as the securing of properties and the refashioning of them into dwellings were also remaking new race and class boundaries in the city.

As a transcontinental process, Ugandan Asian repatriation and property repossession were essential to the NRM's project of nation-state building—racial South Asianness, once again, became constitutive to the insides and outsides of the nation. Racial South Asianness was being reconstituted through the realm of economics: capital and private property. The figure of the "Asian" (as expelled returnee, businessman, expatriate) came to personify and embody foreign capital and investment. Still, Ugandan Asians continued to levy claims to a substantive belonging as Ugandans and as Africans via their history and heritage, their experience of expulsion, their business success, and now their property repossession and compensation. And while it seemed that the past and its racial tensions had been resolved through property repossession and compensation, this was hardly the case.

Other State Citizenship Projects: Maintaining Racial Exclusion through the 1995 Constitution and Schedule Three

The noncitizen racial incorporation of Ugandan Asians relied upon other legal-juridical transformations in the *Constitution of the Republic of Uganda*. The postwar 1995 constitution continued a precedent of allowing expelled Ugandan Asians to reclaim formal citizenship based on both jus soli (birth in the territory) and jus sanguinis (birth by descent), which had been principles since independence[35] (assuming proper documentation could be produced). In the liberalization period, however, neoliberalism served to disassemble the core elements of national citizenship, such that legal-juridical citizenship status is no longer bound to rights and entitlements, state and legal sovereignty, and national territory.[36] Ugandan Asians could reclaim property and assets as transnational expatriates without needing to reclaim formal citizenship or renounce their citizenship from Western nation-states. In order to attract Ugandan Asian return and investment capital, the NRM followed other nations in facilitating the production of mobile and expatriate global citizens who have access to entitlements within the territorial nation as noncitizen actors. Aihwa Ong has referred to this nexus of globalization, neoliberalism, and citizenship as "flexible citizenship," and to mobile, capital-bearing subjects as "flexible citizens."[37] While Ong focuses on the capitalist classes of emerging economies in Asia and their movement to liberal Western states, the Uganda case reveals the need to study the neoliberal transformation of citizenship in relation to complex histories of race and empire, followed by decolonization, Africanization, and Asian expulsion.

Despite the neoliberalization of citizenship, racial Asian access to rights and entitlements was regulated in other ways. Just as the property repossession process was underway between 1992 and 1997, the 1995 Ugandan constitution was also finalized. The constitution introduced the category of "indigeneity" into its conception of Ugandan citizenship, defining national identity through racial criteria. Schedule Three of the Constitution enumerates fifty-six ethnic, or indigenous, communities whose members are officially recognized by the state as (legal-juridical) citizens. These communities are said to have existed and resided in the Ugandan territory as of February 1,

1926—the date on which the formal territorial boundaries of the Ugandan Protectorate were established by the British colonial administration. "Asians" are not listed in Schedule Three because they were technically nonnative communities at this time. In this way, Ugandan Asian returnees and other South Asians are excluded from full national membership on a racial (and therefore substantive) basis.

The emphasis on indigenous identity is connected to the in-migrations of other ethnic and racial Others, and not just to the return of Ugandan Asians in the 1990s. Joseph Oloka-Onyango traces the shift in notions of citizenship based on jus solis and jus sangunis precedents to a growing politics of autochthony in contemporary Uganda.[38] The NRM's early experiments with democratizing local governance involved the establishment of resistance councils during the 1980s, which led to a shift in the rights of democratic participation and national identity from criteria that were based on descent to criteria based on residence. This expansion of political rights based on long-term residence gave way to political backlash, particularly against Banyaruanda migrants and others who were allies during the NRA/NRM Liberation War and who had gained more political entitlements vis-à-vis others. Despite their long-term residence in Uganda then, the Banyaruanda and others continued to be racialized as "African" but also as migrant outsiders and as nonindigenous to the nation, which was now reflected in the constitutional reforms. Thus, despite the NRM's early attempt to "denativize" the colonial construction of ethnic-based identities by emphasizing cultural assimilation, integration, and residence, exclusion-based ideas of race, autochthony, and African indigeneity constricted national membership and its entitlements for many different communities. In a surprising twist, and an appropriation of the popular politics of autochthony, even the president himself was often subject to claims of being an outsider to the nation. Many urban Ugandans from the Ganda community who were critical of the NRM claimed that Museveni was actually born in Rwanda and not Uganda, and thus framed him and his co-ethnics as political interlopers and illegitimate rulers of the nation.

Schedule Three was expanded in 2003 and again in 2005–6 to include sixty-five indigenous groups (versus the 1995 Constitution's original fifty-six groups).[39] Excluded ethnic groups claim the rights and entitlements associated with indigenous status. Like race, indigeneity and ethnicity are contingent categories, changing over time and place and according to the construction of territorial boundaries. Some Othered communities that are considered nonindigenous immigrant groups to the nation, like the Banyaruanda and

Nubi communities, are included in Schedule Three but continue to suffer discrimination in practice as they are denied passports and entitlements due to their phenotypical appearance or other markers of difference. Groups considered to be racially foreign, such as Asians or Indians (*bayindi* or *bahindi*) and people of mixed-racial heritage (*bachotara*)—of Black and Asian/Indian (Afro-Asians) or Black and European descent (Afro-Europeans)—are all officially excluded from Schedule Three. Likewise, Somalis, those who identify as Swahili, and people of Arab descent, including Omanis and Yemenis, are excluded from Schedule Three.

So, despite Uganda's incredible racial and ethnic diversity, the liberalizing economy, and massive refugee and migratory movements across its national borders, the NRM government is extraordinarily restrictive in its definitions of national identity and membership. For example, Indian foreign nationals (NRIs) who want to become Ugandan citizens can do so via registration or naturalization, but with many contingencies. The state maintains its right to exclude Asians—deemed foreign and nonindigenous—through the retraction of citizenship status; and the deportation of foreign nationals is a constant possibility. In addition to the conventional ways that Indian commercial presence is regulated through trade licensing restrictions, permit fees and visa fees, and other requirements, the government has introduced a Certificate of Residence for long-term residents and permanent residents who are foreign nationals, alongside a complex system of work permits and visas required for expatriate foreign workers and businessmen.[40] The process of registering or naturalizing as a citizen is challenging, and many Ugandan Asians, Indian nationals, and others from South Asia have complained that due to their racial appearance, they pay exorbitant fees, both official and unofficial payments (patronage to state officials and police), and often contend with lengthy bureaucratic processes to obtain paperwork. Finally, and in response to both 1990s-era neoliberal mandates, the 9/11 World Trade Center attacks, and the United States' and other imperial powers' Global War on Terror as well as Uganda's own involvement in the East Africa-based war on terror, the government has introduced "e-governance" processes that use biometric technologies for the identification and surveillance of the population, further entrenching racial and ethnic distinctions between those included and excluded. This has created new pressures on foreign nationals who reside and work in Uganda to naturalize as citizens, despite the difficulties of doing so.[41]

Oloka-Onyango has suggested that "Asians" and other racial and ethnic minorities continue to be discriminated against as the state has shifted from overt policies of expulsion to legalized racial exclusion.[42] Building on Oloka-Onyango and Ong's ideas of flexible citizenship, however, I argue that this exclusion is also accompanied by *incorporation*, particularly for returnees entitled to repossess property—sovereign Ugandan Asian–owned entities (like corporations and firms), and other elites (businessmen and entrepreneurs) who have access to privileges, rights, and entitlements in everyday practice—and as the government has created new citizenship categories that facilitate the business and commercial activities of those constructed as racially foreign. Following global neoliberal norms, for example, the Ugandan government introduced dual citizenship in 2005, further enabling the return migration, permanent settlement, and capital investment of returnees and other foreign nationals who are also able to access the substantive entitlements of citizenship (access to property, land, and the market) while maintaining their non-Ugandan (legal) citizenship status and remaining racial noncitizens.

The simultaneous expansion and restriction of both the formal and substantive elements of citizenship have led to an array of citizenship practices and residential arrangements on the ground. If Mamdani makes too much of a totalizing state structure of postcolonial ethnic citizenship and deracialization that normalizes Ugandan Asian racial expulsion and exclusion (in both a formal and substantive sense),[43] then Oloka-Onyango makes too much of the (formal) citizen/noncitizen binary and Asian legal exclusion after the expulsion. He does not attend to the compromised sovereignty of the Ugandan nation-state with respect to Western imperialism and Indian sub-imperialist ambitions (neoliberal globalization), the sovereignty of capital-bearing subjects and firms, an assertive Indian diasporic capitalist class with backing from the Indian government, and the agency of everyday subjects to negotiate the formalistic terrains of citizenship, especially through illicit and informal economies of patronage and protection. Rights and entitlements traditionally bound to legal-juridical status are giving way to geopolitical and neoliberal processes that make the nation accessible for Ugandan Asian and Indian capital investment. In the aftermath of expulsion, Ugandan Asians and other South Asian–descendant communities are adopting strategies to maneuver around their legal-juridical exclusions from full political, racial, and cultural belonging. What is significant is that the government has also maintained its own racially nativist logics of nation-building, based on the primacy and sovereignty of racial Blackness as the primary association with African identity. The 1995 constitution contains provisions that allow for the possibility of retracting the citizenship of nonindigenous (Black African) citizens, and/or deporting, alienating, and expelling people of South Asian heritage from the nation through legal-juridical criteria.[44]

Liberalization Effects: A (Small) Afro-Asian Capitalist Class, Neoliberal Racial Meritocracy, and Citizenship Practices

Returnees are few in number compared with the original Ugandan Asian community displaced at expulsion. Both returnees and the *stayees* and others who arrived after the expulsion (described in the previous chapter) are also now a comparatively prosperous group of businesspeople, many of whom run family firms, most of whom experienced the expulsion and reflect the demographics of the Ugandan Asian community at that time (dominated by *baniya* Hindu and Gujarati merchant groups and the Ismaili Khoja community, along with Punjabis who worked in other sectors, especially construction and transport).[45] While some returnees are more proximate to the state than others, I conceptualize them and their firms as important quasi-sovereign actors, the fragmented sovereignties that also constitute the African state.[46] I use "family firm" to refer to the traditional model of East African Asian business enterprise in which ethnoreligious, caste, and sect-based mercantile trading networks, rooted in kinship networks and chain migration, gradually developed into corporate firms, usually through patriarchal and patrilineal models in which brothers become partners and majority shareholders. The Madhvani and Mehta Groups have expanded for four to five generations in such a manner, with the Mehta family maintaining ties to Porbandar, Gujarat.[47] Another important nonstate quasi-sovereign corporate entity that maintains a presence and investments in Uganda is the Aga Khan Development Network (AKDN), which connects a globally dispersed post-expulsion Ismaili diaspora in the West and Ismailis in East Africa with other communities, especially in the Middle East and India. The AKDN is based on a religious ethics of service and welfare for all, as well as on a more secular, modernized model of social integration and investments, especially in health care and educational institutions that straddle the for-profit and philanthropic/developmental realms.[48]

Other less wealthy, middle-income returnees and their children, born in the intervening years since the expulsion, were also residing in Kampala semipermanently. In the aftermath of the global financial crisis of 2008 and as postgraduate job prospects declined in the UK and elsewhere, many British and Canadian youths of Ugandan Asian heritage joined an earlier wave of returnee families, assisting their families in reclaiming and rehabilitating homes and businesses that would eventually serve the growing urban middle class and foreign expatriate population of Kampala. Having experienced a generational estrangement and deracination from their African heritage, these youths identified more strongly with British, Canadian, and other South Asian diasporic identities. Unlike their parents, many could not speak regional African languages and were learning about Uganda and Ugandans through a foreign expatriate sensibility. Finally, a number of Kenyan Asian entrepreneurs who identified culturally and politically as African Asian took advantage of the liberalization of policies to establish business ventures and settle in Kampala.

Some Ugandan Asians who remained or returned in the 1970s and 1980s and who had maintained exclusive trading monopolies, sources of unofficial wealth, and close connections to successive governments had become city "tycoons." Sudhir Ruparelia, a Ugandan Asian who returned in 1986, built a business empire in commercial real estate, banking, tourism, hospitality, and even education. He is now the wealthiest Ugandan citizen with close ties to the NRM.[49] In addition to the creation of a small African and Asian capitalist class in post-expulsion Uganda,[50] it is now a small African and Asian political class—tycoons and other family firms that are proximate to the NRM—that is subject to political critique by many Ugandans in general, and even by those internal to the Ugandan Asian community that continues to be viewed as monolithic.[51] Faiza explained that while some continue to trace the source of racial tensions to essentialized cultural differences between "Asians" and "Africans," and while others point to the legacy of European colonialism and the creation of racial and class divides and the anti-Asian actions of Idi Amin, the source of these lingering racial tensions now is economic liberalization, the opportunism of individual capitalists, patronage between state officials and businessmen, and the normalization of nepotism and crony capitalism. In exchange for lucrative government contracts, Ruparelia and others are widely rumored to be bankrolling the NRM, especially during elections, thus normalizing a nonliberal political culture of patronage that is widely understood as securing political and racial protection for all "Asians" in the nation, a gendered and patriarchal "citizenship via patronage."

Museveni and the NRM regularly take up the discourses and ideologies of a universalized neoliberal culture in their governance agendas of peace, development, and prosperity, positioning returnee family firms and tycoons as morally redeemed citizens working in partnership with the NRM, thus tightening the alliance between politics, business, and security. Increasingly, the president has acknowledged that returnees are not only "Asian" but also of Ugandan and African heritage, while also mobilizing discourses of expulsion exceptionalism and the exceptional "Asian cultural values" that Black Ugandans should learn from: a work ethic, an emphasis on savings culture, resourcefulness, a strong culture, and focus on the family. The spokesmen for Ugandan Asian family firms and businesses reproduce and reinforce these ideas, as much as they also make claims to national and cultural belonging, asserting Ugandan national patriotism and support for Museveni and the NRM. They make claims about contributing to the nation and the development process through large tax contributions, the creation of employment opportunities for Ugandans, and the practice of philanthropy, whether motivated by traditional religious-based ethics of social welfare or by more modern notions of corporate social responsibility, all of which are becoming central to the construction of self, identity, and Ugandan Asian community after the expulsion.

The circulation of capital in many different directions and domains of everyday life, indeed, the shifting moral economies of urban life—direct state taxation, petty police and immigration-related patronage, high-level state-based patronage, corporate- and religious-based philanthropy, investments in communal and religious missions, the financial support of many Ugandan patrons and their kin in Asian employ (from workplace employees to domestics to drivers and security guards)—all help secure Ugandan Asian return. As they construct themselves as valuable economic citizens to the nation, Ugandan Asians manage lingering public perceptions about, and populist narratives of, their racial South Asianness as inherently racially and economically exploitative of Black Africans. It is a constant labor of managing representations of the self, one's business or enterprise, and community to an imputed (Black) African majoritarian gaze. After the expulsion, some Ugandan Asian–owned businesses even took on African names to assert their Ugandanness. The Mukwano Group and Rafiki Group of companies (meaning "friend" or "friendship" in Luganda and Swahili, respectively) were developed by Ugandan men of Asian heritage who worked exclusively with African businessmen in the 1970s and 1980s. They mobilized ideas of patriarchal fraternity and friendship between Africans and Asians to signify their social commitments to the nation and their social integration with Africans. Many Ugandans spoke highly of these firms, as they did of the Madhvani and Mehta Groups, arguing that they manufactured essential commodities for the citizenry and had created reliable jobs and livelihoods for Ugandans, in contrast to other business undertakings.

The fact that Ugandan Asian repatriation and return was dominated by and skewed toward those involved in business enterprise, and not toward other skilled and educated professionals, was reflected in how returnees referred to each other by the names of their businesses: the individual embodied capital, commerce, industry, firm, corporation. Family firms retained patriarchal norms in which fathers and first-born sons typically ran businesses together (although many returnee Ugandan Asian women were also taking on important leadership roles in the management of family businesses). The gendered patriarchal and militarized African political culture often melded with Indian business and commercial life, shaping social interactions and everyday life. Ugandan Asian men often referred to their African business associates, employees, and even service workers as "boss," "chief," and "*afande*" (high-ranking soldier), cementing a sense of respect for Ugandans and Black African sovereignty, easing the reinscribing of hierarchical racial and class-based urban relationships and the humiliations and indignities, or loss of social status, that many Ugandans have felt since the return of Ugandan Asians. However paternalistic, these masculine (militarized and commercial) forms of address and social exchange are about the careful management of racial and class tensions, the fearful negotiation of the imputed Black African gaze, and the affective economies of the insecurities of expulsion.

Indeed, liberalization reversed President Idi Amin's vision of a closed, nativist Black African nation and economy. The trading sector diversified immediately, and East Africa–based Indian merchants moved into Uganda starting in the 1980s and more extensively from the mid-1990s onward.[52] Richa Nagar has written about the so-called container economy and "container bourgeoisie" in postliberalization Tanzania, suggesting that merchants were able to use their access to caste-based kin networks, knowledge and skills, credit and capital to dominate the import of new commodities for consumption by East Africans.[53] Similar processes took place in Uganda as existing East Africa–based merchant communities took advantage of the unregulated economy, with government officials earning patronage from untaxed cartons and capital. Some returnees discussed how this wealth was reinvested time and again, and how they eventually shifted from commerce to manufacturing and industry. These revived, post-expulsion merchant networks are organized on the basis of caste (and ethnic and religious)

mukwano

FRIENDSHIP

The Natural Choice

3.1   The branding of post-expulsion Uganda through the promotion of Afro–South Asian friendship.

endogamy, reproducing racialized aspects of the commercial economy and even material infrastructural urban life.[54] Another effect is the increased racialized trade competition with politically organized African traders, who themselves gained knowledge, skills, and networks of capital and credit, and who are also traversing global markets as traders or are laboring in Arab states, India, and China, even as they navigate the racial regimes of these varied nation-state contexts.[55]

While state-based policies and African trade union organizing sustain a norm of Africanizing the trading sector despite the challenges of liberalization, there is little government control of the practices of (Asian-owned capital, racially sovereign) Ugandan Asian family firms, where these practices are carried out at the discretion of business owners. Although business owners were quite guarded about their business practices (as they were also about their experiences of expulsion), I learned that most Ugandan Asians who had stayed behind during the Amin years—and especially those without any multigenerational kinship connections to India—worked (in partnership) with African entrepreneurs or hired only Africans. They explained that they did this even if finding reliable, "trustworthy," and skilled labor, especially after the years of war and violence in Uganda, was difficult. By contrast, a few individuals from my fieldwork (a high-profile returnee business tycoon and a middle-class returnee from Canada running a small restaurant) and new Indian entrepreneurs (see chapter 4) were employing South Asians from their own caste-based kin networks (Gujarati Hindu *baniya* communities, specifically) in managerial positions, while hiring Africans for less prestigious, low-wage work.[56] One of my research contacts emphasized the challenges of finding both reliable and skilled labor but also discussed "security" concerns and described the need for "trustworthy" employees—these euphemisms often served both to shore up racial (and caste-based) endogamy within businesses and to perpetuate racist stereotypes of Africans as inherently lazy, deceitful, criminal. But it also articulated returnees' racial precarities and lack of trust in Ugandans after the expulsion. Some interviewees argued that some Ugandan Asian hired co-ethnics (and even caste-kin) in managerial positions in order to better hold their labor accountable and to cut costs. But other, more integrated Ugandan Asians refuted such racialist ideas that Indians were more trustworthy than Africans, arguing that Indians stole more cash and assets from established businesses, especially since they were sojourners and temporary migrants. Many urban Ugandans discussed their own perceptions and understandings of individual firms with me (old money versus new money, big-time industrialists and tycoons versus small-business entrepreneurs and merchants), noting which ones seemed more ethical and committed to Ugandans than others, revealing the low-level but ever-present scrutiny that returnee Ugandan Asians and other South Asian businessmen are under in post-expulsion Uganda.

Urban neoliberal transformation and the associated free market and economy are legitimized on the basis of existing neocolonial arrangements and universalizing Western and specifically US liberal multicultural experiments with postracialism and notions of meritocracy, individual freedom, and choice. In sub-Saharan Africa, and in Uganda specifically, ideologies of the supposedly universal access of differently racialized subjects to capitalist accumulation within an unfettered market is occurring in the context of "racial neoliberalism," which takes on different forms in different nation-state contexts.[57] In urban Uganda, racial neoliberalisms normalize the idea that both (Black-identifying) Africans and Asians can participate in the business of wealth-creation in a free market where everyone, regardless of racial identity, can prosper. This ideology is reflected in the celebratory neoliberal scripts and rags-to-riches stories that surround prominent Africans and Ugandan Asians; it is discussed in newspaper articles, reflected in commercial billboards and advertisements, and divorced from the history and context of colonial racial capitalism and postcolonial attempts at its reform.

While neoliberal orthodoxy conceals material histories of colonial racial capitalism, postcolonial violence, and differential racial community access to capital and credit, knowledge, expertise and networks, it is also central to remaking a new Black African and South Asian political class of urban elites *and* hierarchical, racialized labor-capital relationships between Ugandan Asian–owned businesses and Black African–identifying Ugandans (usually laborers, with some in the skilled managerial class). Postcolonial and, crucially, post-expulsion urban Uganda is a rich site at which to examine reconfigurations of both racial (and racial-caste) capitalism, albeit on a smaller scale. Racial and class tensions, and the unresolved nature of the expulsion, persist.

Between Expatriate and Returnee: Novel Racializations, Investing, and Divesting in Transnational Lives

As laid out, the unbundling and recombination of the formal and substantive elements of citizenship has impacted Ugandan Asian return and its associated entitlements. Rights and entitlements are not necessarily buttressed by a normative terrain of nation- and state-based legal-juridical citizenship, which remains racially exclusive. Instead, global expatriate citizenship privileges, sovereign authorization, and citizenship by invitation; racial protection, patronage, and philanthropy; and symbolic and performative domains of citizenship have become more significant to the logics and practice of Ugandan Asian and racialized South Asian citizenship after the expulsion. Citizenship practices are imbricated with the entrenchment of global racial hierarchies and multiple sources of racial consciousness and practice. Michelle Christian and Assumpta Namaganda have argued that post-1990s urban Uganda is a site of the production of whiteness and white supremacy in structural and institutional ways through the emergence of the developmental-aid state, and not necessarily through the actual presence of white expatriates (although Western white expatriates working and living in Kampala now actually far outnumber the administrative and missionary class who lived in colonial Uganda).[58] Yet Christian and Namaganda miss the ways in which the production of global whiteness (*mzungu*-ness) is entangled not only with ideas of racial Blackness but also with racial South Asianness (*muhindi*-ness) and the return of Ugandan Asians and Ugandan Asian capital in the liberalization period. Ugandan Asians, with imperial and Western citizenship privileges, embody racial capital, and their association with *muhindi*-ness is also proximate to the *mzungu*-ness of expatriate and Asian commercial and entrepreneurial success. In turn, the NRM constructs and maintains the notion of a modern Ugandan body politic as defined through racial Blackness and Black African political and racial sovereignty while embracing global neoliberal and postracial ideas of universal merito-cratic access to the free market, capital, and wealth and, while also incorpo-rating *muhindi*-ness and its embodied association with capital on the basis of neoliberalized ideas of Afro-Asian partnership in national development.

Ugandan Asian citizenship practices continue to be influenced by a racial consciousness from many sources: inherited imperial civilizational, colonial, and citizenship privileges and proximities to whiteness; experi-ences of Black African racial hostility and racial victimization during the expulsion; exposure to racial scripts in the UK that constructed them as exceptional refugees, entrepreneurs, and integrated British Asians (or suc-cessfully integrated refugees in Canada); and experiences of racial discrimi-nation in White majoritarian liberal Western states and their re-racialization as "Asian" or *muhindi* upon their return. Ugandan Asians straddled their racial and citizenship privileges (with respect to non-elite Black Africans), their deracination and de-Ugandanization via their expulsion, and their privileged status as expatriates and the racialized precarity of embodying *muhindi*-ness in post-expulsion Uganda. Remaking a Ugandan Asian ex-patriate community in Kampala, many returnees in business, commerce, manufacturing, and industry socialized together but were not by any means cohesive as a community. Some participated in the ethnoracial stereotyping of themselves and others, even in anti-Black and anti-African racist discourse, reproducing ideas about "unknowable" African Others they had heard in more parochial racially endogamous community contexts. Some questioned received racial knowledge and the supposedly inherent and essentialist meanings, a mode of working through their unresolved experience of ex-pulsion and repatriation. At times they mobilized expatriate terms or the more dehumanizing and off-putting South Asian terminology to refer to Blackness and Africans: "locals," *kala/kaley* (black); *jadoo/a* (someone who performs witchcraft, occult practices); "half-caste," and so on; in more ma-chismo circles these also overlapped with misogynist gendered and sexual discourses about Blackness that revealed a dehumanizing lens applied to Africans and Black bodies of women in particular. Others contested these practices and showcased their cultural Africanness through their deep knowledge of Ugandan history and politics, their understanding of the complicated histories of and differences between different ethnic commu-nities, and their knowledge of and fluency in Ugandan music, visual art, and languages. Some rejected exclusive intra-racial and communal social-izing, spending time with African colleagues, neighbors, and friends with shared middle-class status and educational pedigrees. I noticed that some youths (descendants of the expelled) had appropriated the term *muhindi* and referred to each other jokingly as *muhindi*, a mode of diffusing the racist, shameful, and embarrassing connotations attached to the term when Black Ugandans referred to them as *muhindi* in hostile and discriminatory ways in day-to-day urban life. They referred to me as *mzungu-muhindi* (a deracinated diasporan, neither African or Indian, nor appropriately Punjabi, born and brought up in the United States), while they described more recent arrivals from South Asia as *muhindi-muhindi*, mapping internal distinctions within an imputed state-constructed monolithic racial community, distinguishing between authentic cultural "Indianness" and varying degrees of intimacy with and estrangement from racial whiteness and racial Blackness and Africanness. Navigating the new landscape of race-making and Afro–South Asian encounters in Kampala, some even created new identifications for themselves to establish their Africanness and their social and political integration in Uganda, as opposed to the "newcomer" South Asians: they were "Ug-Indians" living in "Ug-India."

For many urban Africans, Ugandan Asian returnees were seen as *mzungu*, or Western foreign expatriates (a category usually reserved for whites/Europeans), and they occupied a foreign "stranger status" on par with other expatriates involved in NGO work or in the donor-aid and humanitarian work world. But here the expatriate category was also conditioned by the Ugandan Asian expulsion and the variegated citizenship statuses and privileges of Asians expelled in 1972. Most returnees possessed British, Canadian, American, or other citizenship and passports, and many had also reclaimed their Ugandan citizenship and had Ugandan passports, a process that became easier after the passage of the dual citizenship law in 2005. Dual citizenship had become newly possible with the neoliberal restructuring of the East African Community (EAC) to promote foreign investment capital from diaspora communities and business activities, and on a case-by-case basis for those exiled Ugandan Asians who could prove that they had at one time been citizens of Uganda or who were born in the country.[59] Dual citizenship was also available for individuals of different nationalities who possessed a Certificate of Residency and who wished to eventually naturalize as citizens; but this tended to exclude more recent Indian nationals (entrepreneurs, traders, and migrants).[60] Some returnee Ugandan Asians claimed dual citizenship; others converted their Certificates of Residence to Ugandan citizenship, or vice versa, while maintaining their status as British, Canadian, or American citizens. They spoke of the practical and economic advantages of possessing formal Ugandan citizenship and a passport, given its facilitation of business-related travel and investment across East African member states. The policy changes were reshaping the allocation of benefits and entitlements afforded to different communities with racial and class privileges. In addition to easing property and asset repossession and travel, returnees would not be required to pay visa fees or (ostensibly) other patronage required to open businesses; it was also easier to acquire property or land. Yet for others, reclaiming Ugandan citizenship was more of a sentimental and symbolic action, a way of fortifying their Ugandan national identity and African heritage as adjudicated by the state and reinforced by their substantive commitments.

While some returnees felt that it was important to reclaim their Ugandan formal citizenship and did so immediately, others disavowed Ugandan citizenship and declined their newly granted ability to access it. They were more invested in their expatriate and noncitizen permanent resident status, an arrangement that was strategic and low-investment (materially, psychologically, emotionally) for themselves, mirroring the ambivalent strategies of the NRM to include them. More immediate here was the constant focus on an elusive sense of "security" and potential "insecurity"—a Western expatriate and an embodied expelled Ugandan Asian discourse that reinforced racial associations between Blackness and Africanness and an inherent unpredictability in governance and political instability. Transnational strategies of mobility, semipermanent residence, and organizing kinship networks, livelihoods, and financial investments—arrangements of adapting to national exclusions—had all been normalized since expulsion and continued to be practiced. For some returnees and their families, their strategies were also their primary means of managing the economic risks of the neoliberal economy in liberal states—Uganda was a second home, a backup plan in relation to the growing crises in Western liberal states, and vice versa; their homes abroad could offer stability and security in the event they had to leave Uganda once again, revealing the interconnected transcontinental geographies of empire and nation still critical to African Asian diasporas.

The transnational expatriate reorganization of Ugandan Asian families who returned continues to be a morally and politically sensitive terrain of citizenship practice, as they are also read, through nationalist discourse, as a mode of keeping one's options open, rather than adapting to nationalist exclusion. Their practices feel heightened, given the public scrutiny of Ugandan Asian returnees as well as Ugandan Asians' own practices of managing perceptions of the "Asian" community in relation to the imputed gaze of a Black African majoritarian nation. Birender, a community leader of the

Singh Sabha *gurudwara* in Kampala, is not Ugandan Asian but Kenyan Asian of Punjabi Sikh heritage, with multigenerational roots in Nakuru, Kenya. He moved to Kampala in the early 1990s to take advantage of new opportunities in the construction sector. Although he did not experience the expulsion, he had family members who did, and he recalled his memories of an earlier era of Africanization and Asian racial exclusion that culminated in the Kenyan Asian exodus in the late 1960s, which resulted in the resettlement of British Kenyan Asian families in the UK. Meeting him after the *langar* meal at the Nakasero *gurudwara* one Sunday, we discussed some of the dynamics of Ugandan Asian return and African perceptions of Ugandan Asian presence. "It's similar to Kenya, although we have a different history of political activity there. They [Ugandans] see us as not totally committed, not loyal. You see, most [Ugandan Asians] will want to keep their UK or other passports, even as they keep investing their money in their businesses and in their lives here." Birender implied that despite the neoliberalization of citizenship, the Africanization-era trope of "Asians" as "opportunistic fence-sitters" continued to endure, and that taking on Ugandan citizenship without having another backup plan in place was the litmus test for political belonging and commitment to the nation and to Africans. "Asians" who were truly "African" in their hearts, despite their racial vulnerabilities, would cast their lots, including their businesses and livelihoods, with their Black African Ugandan counterparts.

Birender continued to discuss his efforts at political and social integration in Kampala, explaining how turbaned Sikh men like himself were well-established and integrated African Asians, known among Kenyans as *kala singhas*, unlike in Uganda. Here, he was learning more Luganda and using less Swahili. Reproducing a common ethnoracial managerial discourse about African labor I heard among Asian entrepreneurs, he explained that it was important to him that his firm prioritized employing and training Ugandans, rather than taking the potentially cost-saving route of hiring better skilled and more industrious Kenyans. Visiting him at his office in the industrial area at a later date, my attention turned to how he had posted on the wall behind his office desk official documentation that displayed his legal status as a permanent resident in possession of an official Certificate of Residence. Returnees and other Kenyan Asians and South Asians (including Indian entrepreneurs) who had arrived after the NRM came into power often performed their rights to residence and claims to conducting commercial and business activity by showing me their residence certificates or copies of their pending applications for dual citizenship. Most business owners had mounted framed photos of the president next to portraits of important spiritual leaders, marking the significance of both African political and spiritual sovereigns in their lives. These pictures were carefully positioned next to trading permits and licenses, and building and business operation permits. They were integral to both the material and performative domains of citizenship claim-making, even as many depended upon their expatriate citizenship privileges and relations of protection and patronage to maintain an embodied sense of racial security.

For example, on a weekend drive from Entebbe to Kampala, Gurdeep, whose father had remained behind during the Amin regime and who self-identified as a Ugandan of Indian and Punjabi Sikh origin, excitedly took out his Certificate of Residence from his wallet and presented it to me. Gurdeep was born in India but grew up as a child in Kampala, attending a majority Black Ugandan school near his home in Bakuli. Completely fluent in Luganda, Punjabi, and English, he had recently applied for his residence certificate and was overjoyed when it was approved. "I don't really need it," he admitted, "but it's always a good idea to have it." If local police or military officials stopped his vehicle, he would prefer to have this document in addition to a copy of his passport. In some cases, those who identified as Ugandans of Asian descent, even those who held Certificates of Residence or Ugandan passports, had been detained by immigration police if they did not have their documents with them. He described the necessity of small bribes to handle these situations, or even narrowly escaping these situations through light exchanges of humor and flattery with authority figures, always speaking in Luganda or Lugandanized English slang to perform and demonstrate one's Ugandanness and even Ganda-ness—to differentiate oneself as "a Ugandan of Asian origin," and not just "some Indian from India," as he put it. Gurdeep stressed to me that these situations were rare, that his Ugandan neighbors were familiar with him in the locality where he and his family lived. Gurdeep's more modest class status, relations of neighborliness, and integrated African-Asian identity—even as he maintained affiliations with Punjabi, Sikh, and Indian identities—offered him a sense of racial security and belonging.

Lal Singh, who had been expelled as a child, scowled when I asked him if he would be interested in taking up dual citizenship and officially becoming Ugandan, whether for practical or symbolic purposes. I was surprised by his cynicism when he described how his trust in African governance was completely broken, that he wanted to keep his UK passport and citizenship in order to "travel, do business, and move on." He recounted his experiences of anti-Asian discrimination in both East Africa and the UK, contemplating that perhaps his true "racial" home was in India (despite his never having visited or lived there). I was surprised since Lal was completely African in every way, living more or less permanently in Kampala; he interacted and worked with Ugandans on a constant basis, had primarily Black African friends and associates, ran fairly successful businesses, and supported whole Ugandan families financially. Yet he still positioned himself as a sojourner with little commitment to or investment in the nation or its governance. Lal was deeply broken by his expulsion and ongoing feelings of racialized estrangement. When I approached him about participating in the activities of the Asian African Association (see chapter 5), he expressed disinterest in political and community-based work that might lead to expanded possibilities of inclusion for people of South Asian descent in the nation. In this way, Lal had accommodated and reproduced the ruling party and state's construction of him as a racial noncitizen and economic citizen, including the supposed racial dichotomy between "African" political and "Asian" economic entrepreneurial identities.

Returnees' ambivalence about their return and their race and class consciousness manifested in their practices of constructing and performing African Asian identities, their orientations toward racialized security-seeking, and even their investments in militarized and securitized state governance in the aftermath of expulsion. There was a continual undercurrent of the potential for anti-Asian violence lurking in the present, of the need for hypervigilance, and of mistrust. Many returnees moved in carefully orchestrated ways about the city, cultivated small networks of association, or alternately (like the Ugandan Asian men who married Ugandan women) socialized with Africans only or resided and spent time in areas that were raced and classed as white or South Asian and thus considered expatriate-friendly and safe. The persistent NRM discourses of perceived security threats (combined with its own monopoly on military and state violence) led to an obsessive focus on the security and political situation and a constant preoccupation with potential crime or violence. Since community members knew that I resided alone, I was warned by many returnees to stay away from Black-majority areas—which were constructed as unsafe and dangerous and often rendered as immoral (in conjunction with South Asian gendered ideas of women's respectability and purity). I was warned not to ride public transportation like *matatus* and to avoid certain parts of the city during particular times of the day and night. As the expatriate community in Kampala grew, so did the private security industry. Returnees often employed African guards from reputable firms to protect their homes and businesses; like European and American expatriates, they also shared information about proficient and trustworthy domestics, drivers, and guards one could potentially employ. Others developed and maintained relationships with Africans, especially with African women, by taking care of the medical and school fees of their employees and their dependents. The existing colonial, privatized, and militarized infrastructures of the city facilitated the refashioning of race and class boundaries in Kampala, reproducing the racial tensions of hierarchical (Brown-over-Black) paternalism and elitism.

The heightened sense of a racial consciousness (again, always informed by class status, religious and ethnic differences, caste consciousness, and scripts about gender and sexuality) and investments in racialized security reinforced the significance of domesticity and the home as a site of safety, privatizing an elusive reckoning with the past, of expulsion, of its cause and its consequences. In these private spaces, transnational discourses of expulsion exceptionalism (see the introduction) were produced within parochial and racially endogamous family and community settings. For example, it was common to hear expressions of "colonial nostalgia"—a wistful reimagination of the past that romanticized and celebrated an imagined time of law and order, of development and prosperity for colonial subjects during British rule. William Bissell, for example, examines colonial nostalgia among Zanzibaris born well after the colonial period as providing a means of expressing critique and discontent for current policies of neoliberalism and political violence.[61] In her analysis of autobiographical memoirs among settler communities like white Zimbabweans, however, Astrid Rasch distinguishes "colonial nostalgia" from "postcolonial nostalgia." She describes postcolonial nostalgia as a "Western memory practice" in which "condemnations of racism and colonial inequality" coexist with stories of a prosperous past that have been supplanted by a poorer, more dangerous, and more primitive present, all to the detriment of former settlers-turned-citizens who have lost their sense of status, prestige, and racial entitlement in the postcolony.[62]

I turn to Rasch's framing of "postcolonial nostalgia" to understand some Ugandan Asian returnees' understandings of their expulsion and ambivalent return. In the absence of a public discussion of the expulsion and of repatriation and repossession without racial reconciliation, returnees do not publicly express forms of nostalgia for their lives prior to the expulsion. Their status as singularly racial victims of Idi Amin and Black-identifying Ugandans would be challenged by Black African Ugandans, who themselves feel victimized by Ugandan Asians, either through their own memories of Asian urban presence or through the younger (born-into-the-NRM) generation's "post-memory" understandings of the past.[63] Within the private domain of domesticity, with myself as a racialized South Asian woman, or among parochial community networks, however, it was acceptable to be sentimental about the lives that Ugandan Asians led prior to their expulsion. Building on Rasch's and Janet McIntosh's study of "structural occlusion" among white Kenyans,[64] I encountered four genres of postcolonial (or post-expulsion) nostalgia and uninterrogated racial and class privilege among (some, not all) returnee, middle-class, and elite Ugandan Asians (primarily of Gujarati and Punjabi ethnic heritage) that dovetailed with an uninterrogated settler consciousness in East Africa: (1) nostalgic memories of an easy life and a good standard of living prior to the expulsion, the beautiful tropical climate of Uganda, aspirations for wealth and prosperity; (2) nostalgia for the past and (implicitly) racially compartmentalized nature of urban life, coupled with the paternalistic love and care for African workers and domestics (when in actuality, these relationships were often hierarchical and characterized by a one-way, exploitative dynamic); (3) narratives of unpredictable and decontextualized Black African sources of anti-Asian violence, resulting in the loss of the bourgeois home, other property, and assets and sources of wealth (a singular racial Asian victimhood); and (4) ideas that the 1972 Asian expulsion precipitated the downfall of the Ugandan nation and especially the economy. These narratives—repeated in Kampala by returnees— focused on the ninety-day period of expulsion and constructed the Asian home as a site of racialized morality and respectability, violated by Black African (racial) immorality, criminality, excess, and violence. Merging with the neoliberal conditions of their return and racial and class entitlements to property repossession, a singular narrative of Asian racial victimization concealed the possibility of Black African victimhood and suffering in the colonial and postcolonial order, and it erased Ugandan Asian structural and interpersonal complicities in forces of imperialism, colonial (racial-caste) capitalism, and racial exploitation and oppression.

Many, however, updated discourses of postcolonial nostalgia with a genre of discourse I bracket as "colonial determinism"—meaning they also critiqued colonial-era racial and class inequalities and the divisions that had pitted Asians and Africans against each other, describing how Asians were also treated as "beneath" Europeans and were encouraged to think of themselves as superior to Black Africans (with less reflection on the multiple sources of race consciousness among South Asians in general). They discussed the importance of "Asian contribution" to Ugandan society and the nation—what Aihwa Ong has described as claims for "ethnic succession," or the notion that "having made important contributions across generations, and thus being owed a moral debt by society . . . minorities and ethnic immigrants believe they have a right to become full citizens."[65] And they described the economic decline and crisis after their expulsion and offered narratives of ensuing Black/African (read: racial) political violence, bureaucratic mismanagement, and corruption. Redeemed and more confident about their historical and developmental significance to Uganda, and by their invitation to return and contribute economically to the nation, returnees talked about how they had "worked hard to help explore, open up, develop, and build the infrastructure of the nation"—the visible signs of liberal capitalist modernity, development, and progress. One returnee remarked that "although Asians have built the country, they are not recognized today for their important role in developing the nation; instead, they are constantly scapegoated." Another was very sentimental about the cosmopolitan life he led in Uganda in the 1960s and 1970s prior to his expulsion. Narrating his eventual return in the early 1990s to me, he argued that if Ugandans (meaning Black Africans) had wanted Asians to leave, and if they had wanted to take control of the economy, he could not understand why "no development" had taken place in the meantime. The economic success of Ugandan Asians was usually contrasted with the poorer performance of Africans and used to justify racial and cultural distinctions and inherent and essentialist attributes and traits associated with race, a remaking of racial boundaries and hierarchy.

Ideas that the absence or racial exclusion of settler and quasi-settler or Subject Race communities results in the underdevelopment of African postcolonial nations are quite commonplace. Such ideas equate European, Arab, South Asian, or other "civilizational" outside presences with a sense of progress and development defined through a lens of liberal capitalist modernity, without an accompanying analysis of imperialism, neocolonialism, and the development of authoritarianism and political violence, such that indigenous Black African progress and prosperity can happen only through external influence or intervention. While these ideas are certainly not new, what was significant was that they were fusing with existing transcontinental (transnational, transoceanic, nation-based) circulations of expulsion exceptionalist discourse that had been consolidating since 1972, including ideas of Ugandan Asian refugee and immigrant exceptionalism, inherent

"Asian values," and other racial and cultural scripts that have perpetuated anti-Black racism and anti-Blackness in the UK and Canada.

But then there were those who assertively challenged the consolidation of these scripts and narratives, who rejected essentializing and dehumanizing racial ideologies about Blackness and Africanness, and who more confidently claimed their Ugandan and African identity and belonging by disidentifying with the race and class consciousness of other returnees, even if they maintained or rehearsed allegiances to the NRM. Some returnees argued that despite the prejudices internal to the Ugandan Asian community and the hostilities they still faced from Black Africans on an everyday basis, they were "die-hard Ugandans, no matter what"; that they had returned at the first opportunity. They disavowed their transnational expatriate privileges, arguing that although they had family who lived abroad, none of their own capital or life savings was there—it was completely invested in the "local" (read: Black African, Ugandan economy). If an expulsion were to happen again, they would just have to start over again, and they would still come back to Uganda, even if Ugandans wanted them to leave "once things stabilized." In rehearsing divestments from South Asianness, and investments in Ugandans and Africans, they argued that they were already safe and secure.

Some long-term resident Ugandan Asians, including those who stayed on after 1972, raised their children in Kampala, even if they spent some time receiving education abroad. Mohamed, the Ismaili (Khoja) Muslim son of a *stayee* who came from a modest class background and grew up near Mengo, and who attended racially integrated schools in the 1990s, explained to me his newfound sense of racial visibility since the South Asian presence in the city had grown. "I may look like an 'Asian' on the outside based on my skin color, but I feel I am Black on the inside. I speak Luganda, and I spend all my time with African friends, even when other Asians give me a hard time for it. I see, feel, and think about my life here as a Black person would. I understand their perspectives, why they have problems with how some Asians carry themselves." Even after pursuing higher education as an international student in the United States, Mohamed was keen to settle in Kampala. He eventually married a Ugandan (Ganda) Muslim and Black-identifying woman, despite the pressures he faced within his family to marry endogamously within his own ethnic and religious community. Ultimately, it was through an interracial marriage union that Mohamed has sorted out a way to create a sense of political,

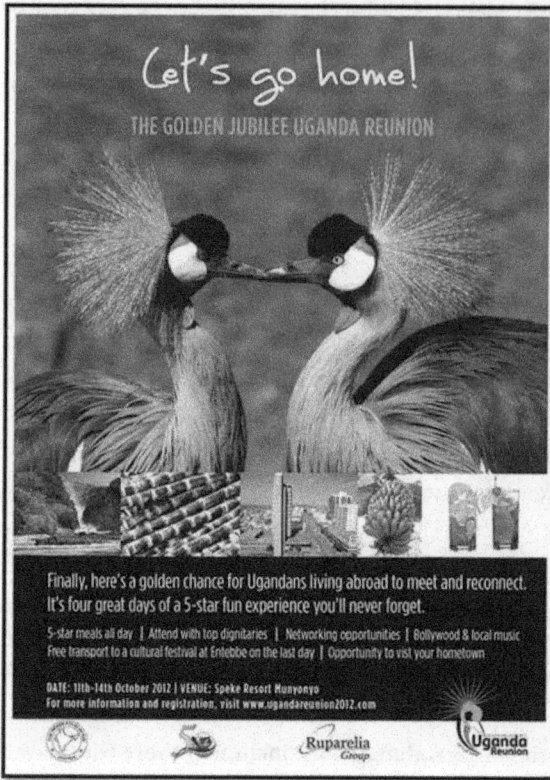

3.2   "Let's Go Home! The Golden Jubilee Uganda Reunion." Poster for the Ugandan reunion event held in Kampala in 2012. Image courtesy of Hon. Rajni Tailor, September 2011.

racial, and cultural inclusion for himself—to be Ugandan, African, South Asian, and Afro–South Asian all at the same time.

On the Possibilities and Limitations of Transcontinental Commemoration

Returnee citizenship practices are continually informed by the diasporic practices of Ugandan Asians who remained in exile and who may have participated in the property repossession and compensation process but who never returned to settle in Uganda. In 2012, Ugandan Asian leaders in the global diaspora in both the UK and Canada planned commemoration events for the fortieth anniversary of the expulsion. The late Praful Patel, chair of the Indian Overseas Trust and the only expelled Ugandan Asian to serve on the Uganda Resettlement Board in the UK in 1972, was busy working on commemorative events with colleagues based in Dubai and London when I met him in 2010 in his home and office in exile at the Taj Mahal Hotel in Mumbai. Back in the United States, I assisted him in developing language for the commemoration website.[66] Although I was not able to attend the event itself, Patel sent me the program, which focused exclusively on the events of 1972 and their aftermath for the displaced in the global Ugandan Asian community: detailing the factors that led up to the expulsion decree; offering thanks to host nations that took in Ugandan Asian refugees; celebrating the achievements of Ugandan Asians who resettled abroad; and giving younger generations an opportunity to learn about their history and heritage. Lord Dolar Popat, a conservative British Parliamentarian, also oversaw a historic debate on Ugandan Asian commemoration in the UK Parliament.[67] Official commemoration events align with Western liberal state discourses and serve as a public mode of contemplating a past that risks being forgotten. Such events exceed the territoriality of the Ugandan nation-state. They place displaced Ugandan Asians within the racial designs of "postimperial" liberal multiracial Britain or the UK and liberal multicultural Canada; they reclaim and reconnect Ugandan Asians to an estranged Ugandan and African identity; and they bridge the gap between the present and past, both reproducing and potentially challenging discourses of expulsion exceptionalism.

There is also what Maya Parmar calls "the virtual memorial."[68] Over the course of my research, social media technologies became increasingly important for connecting diasporic Ugandan Asian exiles, scattered across different countries, with those moving into and out of Uganda. This was especially the case for Facebook groups, transnational digital platforms where members could reunite and connect, share photos and memories of the past, process their expulsion, even share information and photos of their return visits to Uganda.[69] As entrepreneurship in the tourism sector in Uganda has grown, Ugandan Asian–led heritage tours for diasporic exiles are becoming more popular, and exiled Ugandan Asians are virtually documenting their return visits to the small towns of their birthplace and residence while also visiting safari parks and other more touristy, expatriate fare. Internet forums offer another medium for accessing a politically silenced past, for building a collective Ugandan Asian diasporic community and identity online, wrought through emotional and sentimental attachments to Ugandan and African heritage—a virtual platform for forging diasporic citizenship claims to the Ugandan nation despite a lasting and ambivalent sense of racial estrangement. But there are limitations to the dominant politics of nostalgia in these virtual platforms—their racially compartmentalized nature means that there is often an inability to grapple with the exiled community's structural and interpersonal complicities in imperialism, capitalism, and racism and the experiences and apprehensions of Black-identifying Ugandans, an inability to access the multiple meanings and knowledge claims surrounding the expulsion for all, racially diverse Ugandans.

Back in Uganda, there have been (as of this book's publication) no official government or state-led commemoration events surrounding 1972. There are no permanent monuments that might offer a mode of accessing and complicating the past (aside from the aforementioned Mohandas K. Gandhi bust that signified positive diplomatic relations between Uganda and India and—in my own reading—the ambivalent politics of Ugandan Asian repatriation without substantive racial reconciliation). In late summer 2007, I attended the Golden Jubilee celebration of the Aga Khan's accession with Vali Jamal at the Aga Khan Schools in Old Kampala. The Kampala-based Ismaili Khoja community celebrated the Aga Khan's visit and fifty years of his spiritual leadership, commemorating his role in the resettlement of refugees in Canada, and the financing of new projects by the AKDN in education and health care that assert multiracial and integrated African and Asian identities and social commitments to Uganda and East Africans.[70] Later on, in 2012, Sudhir Ruparelia of the Ruparelia Group planned an expulsion commemoration event for the Golden Jubilee celebration of Ugandan independence and the forty-year anniversary of the expulsion, with the president slated to attend; but Ruparelia's controversial connections to the ruling party, coupled with the event's more strategic focus on attracting investment capital from the Ugandan Asians' diaspora, led many to decline attendance, and it was eventually canceled due to a public health emergency.[71]

The privatization of Ugandan Asian expulsion commemoration to exiled communities abroad or hosted among specific ethno-religious communities or community-based elites, the ambivalent and strategic nature of Ugandan Asian return, property repossession without racial reconciliation, the circulation of transcontinental expulsion exceptionalist discourses, the construction of returnees as economic citizens, and returnees' real and perceived proximities and loyalties to the NRM—all these factors have circumscribed a more independent and critical inquiry into 1972 and its aftermaths, of understanding that there are no easy victims or perpetrators when unpacking Afro–South Asian racial conflict and violence, of imagining and practicing horizontal relationalities of political and cultural integration and reconciliation and repair, of accessing other histories and imaginaries of Afro–South Asian interracialisms and universalisms. I predicted that if (and when) the NRM (ruling party) would begin to address the expulsion and Asian presence more officially, it would be to strengthen diplomatic and economic alliances with the Indian nation and to strengthen militarized and securitized neoliberal governance in Uganda.

PART III

South-South
Entanglements

4

Insecurities of Foreign Direct Investment

From Returnee to Investor-Citizen

In 2008, twenty-five Gujarati Indian national industrialists and business-men accompanied Narendra Modi, then chief minister of Gujarat, on a visit to Kampala to meet Ugandan state officials and the Uganda-based Gujarati diaspora. Using the language of South-South cooperation, Modi advertised Vibrant Gujarat, an annual global summit and trade conference held in Ahmedabad, India, to local businessmen. Community leaders—both Ugandan Asian returnees and new entrepreneurs from India—welcomed Modi with an official reception at the Indian Association Uganda headquarters, located on a small plot of land in Nakasero in Kampala that had been repossessed by community leaders in the early 1990s. The visit culminated with a grand investment conference and networking dinner at the Munyonyo Commonwealth Resort, a hotel and convention center built by the Ruparelia Group in Munyonyo, on the northern shores of Lake Victoria. Attending the event with Vali Jamal, I was surprised to see hundreds of "newcomer" South Asian migrants and entrepreneurs making their way to the event as well, suddenly visible and all in one meeting place.

Upon our arrival, we were welcomed at the grand entrance of the hotel by a Ganda artist troupe in traditional dress performing dances and drumming. Guests were dressed in black tie and exquisite saris, *salwar-kameez*, caftans, and *gomesis*. As the late afternoon sun quickly gave way to dusk and a cool breeze wafted into the banquet hall, I observed the Afro-Asian (fashion, music, and food) style on display, recalling the black-and-white photos I had seen of the 1955 Afro-Asian Conference in Bandung, Indonesia. Interspersed with the raucous calls of the Egyptian *hadada ibis*, Indian diplomats spoke of Gujarati business achievements in India and East Africa and the history and prospects of African-Indian relations. Others extolled President Museveni and the National Resistance Movement (NRM) for his visit to the 2008 India-Africa forum summit in New Delhi, India. One Uganda-based Indian business and community leader announced, "Today is a great day! We are bringing Indians and Africans together again in Uganda, and we are representing Gujarat in Uganda. But the history of Indians in this country goes back to the building of the railway." Later, he revised his narration of continuous Gujarati presence in Uganda, noting the "negative episode in Ugandan history," referring to the days of Idi Amin and the 1972 Asian expulsion.

Investment conferences, bilateral diplomatic visits, and networking dinners like this were fast becoming important sites for me to examine the new cultural productions of Ugandan and Indian diasporic nationalism as well as the rescripting of histories and memories of the 1972 Asian expulsion, race relations between Africans and South Asians, and the changing meanings of "Asian" or "Indian" in postcolonial Uganda. Both Ugandan and Indian state officials reimagined the expulsion as an aberration within a longer historical arc of positive collaborations between Africans and Indians through ideas and discourses of Afro-Asianism and South-South cooperation that were being recalibrated according to neoliberal policies in the Global South. Ugandan (Black African) state officials also de-emphasized the expulsion and its aftermaths, welcoming Modi and the Gujarati Indian delegation and describing the Ugandan nation as a "secure investment destination" for Indian businessmen, entrepreneurs, and foreign investors, thus shoring up their political and racial security in the nation.

The Indian and Indian diasporic nationalism on display here was a changing Gujarati ethnic nationalism, built upon Gandhian histories of anticolonialism and the mercantile diaspora's historical connections to East Africa as well as on ideas of spiritual piety, industriousness, and philanthropy. I was also aware of Modi's growing popularity and ascent within the Hindu right-wing Bharatiya Janata Party (BJP) in Gujarat on the basis of his ideas of spiritual *bhakti* (devotion), a hypernationalist strongman masculinity, and neoliberal capitalist development[1]—this, despite the anti-Muslim pogroms in Gujarat in 2002 and despite the growing social and economic disparities in India. The "Gujarat model" was fast becoming the format for an exclusionary Indian and Hindu nationalism and was appealing to some East African and Ugandan Asians of Gujarati and Hindu heritage, especially given their feelings of racial precarity in post-expulsion Uganda. Despite the postcolonial closures to an inclusive ethnic and religious Indian national identity, and despite the historical complexity in Ugandan Asian ethnic, religious (sectarian), and caste identities, the Indian (diasporic) nationalism on display in the events I attended in Kampala were often constructed through a primarily Gujarati ethnic and Hindu religious identity, even as they celebrated an abstract and transhistorical "Indian" or "Asian" community in Uganda. Even more worrisome, Ugandan (Black African) state officials now welcomed the production of a universalized Indian exceptionalism—national, racial, religious, cultural, and civilizational.

Uganda was now a key Africa-based center of South-South connectivities with respect to the formation of BRICS (a geopolitical bloc comprising Brazil, Russia, India, China, and South Africa) and the fiftieth anniversary of the 1955 Afro-Asian Conference in Bandung, Indonesia, which reestablished the principles of its final communiqué, as stated in the *Declaration on the New Asian-African Strategic Partnership*.[2] East African heads of state also reestablished the East African Community (EAC) in 2000—a Pan-Africanist organization originally created in 1967 and disbanded in 1977—in line with new neoliberal principles of advancing trade and business among East African nations.[3] Among development policy pundits, there was renewed hope for relief from the stranglehold of structural adjustment policies and donor-dependency via new alliances with Global South nations and their economies, including the strategic use of Chinese and Indian capital investment and credit lines with little to no interest.[4] By the early 2000s, state visits and bilateral agreements had cemented a new era of Ugandan and Indian diplomacy, including the promotion of trade, education, medical tourism, African-Indian historical connections, and cultural exchange.[5] Now, development experts celebrated "the multi-polar world" and Africa's engagement with "the Asian century."[6] Unlike ideas of "Afro-pessimism," a term first used to describe a sense of fatalism in response to postindependence political violence and economic crisis across the continent, Africa was "rising."[7]

In this chapter, I continue to draw out the insecurities of expulsion, focusing specifically on the noncitizen racial incorporation of the postcolonial Indian diaspora (businessmen, entrepreneurs, and investors) and the incorporation of Indian migrant labor and capital into the nation since the early 2000s. This process has been facilitated by the existing histories of Afro–South Asian connection established during the British empire and subsequent anticolonial movements, Afro-Asianism, and South-South cooperation. It is also related to the neoliberal turn in the postcolonial Global South and the resulting assemblages of governance, sovereignty, and citizenship. These new incorporations rely upon performative assertions of Ugandan and Indian nationalism and gender, state power and performances, practices of security and militarism, and re-narrations of the 1972 Asian expulsion. Racial difference, boundaries, and hierarchies have been made and remade through labor-capital relations; racialized ethnic, religious, and caste distinctions; and gender and sexuality formations. Race, citizenship, and neoliberalism have been articulated in novel ways to facilitate Indian capital and a racialized "Asian" presence in urban Uganda Ultimately, I show that Idi Amin's racially nativist Black African economic nationalism and Asian expulsion have given way to the current government and state-led efforts to attract Indian-owned capital in the service of national development aspirations. While expelled Ugandan Asians remain unsettled by unresolved pasts, the NRM has successfully constructed all South Asian subjects—those racialized as "Asian" or "Indian," both Ugandan Asian returnees and the new Indian diaspora—as "investor-citizens," intensifying urban registers of the insecurities of expulsion.

In addition to the many sites in Kampala where I could study these new performances and celebrations of Ugandan and Indian diplomacy and bilateralism, nationalism, South-South cooperation, and Afro-Asianism, I conducted ethnographic research between 2009 and 2010 at the Uganda Investment Authority, the state-based institution engaged in attracting foreign investment to Uganda.

Negotiating Empire and Global Governance: Global South Neoliberalisms, Race, Citizenship, and Afro-Asianism

The Uganda Investment Authority (UIA) exemplified a reversal of independence-era politics and Africanization and de-Indianization of the nation and economy, showcasing instead the neoliberal state in Uganda (or, rather, the fragmented sovereignties that constitute the African state).[8] Although controversial among Ugandan parliamentarians, the Uganda Investment Code Act was introduced in 1991. It denationalized parastatals, founded a Ministry of Investment and the UIA, and created policies to attract foreign investors and foreign direct investment (FDI) to facilitate economic growth in the nation.[9] First emerging in the "Asian Tiger" contexts of Hong Kong, Singapore, South Korea, and Taiwan in the 1990s, investment promotion agencies (IPAs) were established across all African nations.[10] The

Ugandan version is more or less a modular copy of a Western imperial and global governance template; IPAs facilitate market fundamentalism in post-colonial and Global South nations. The UIA's priorities are "policy advocacy, project facilitation, image building, and investment promotion."[11] State officials engage in these activities to attract global (nonnational) entrepreneurs and their investment capital. They also make decisions surrounding land allocations, tax incentives, and immigration policy for foreign businessmen, managerial expatriates, and other laborers in foreign-run firms. In 1995, the United Nations rated the UIA as "one of the best investment promotion agencies in Africa"; and as a result of Uganda's high economic growth rates, it was named "the best agency in Africa and the Middle East" in 2000.[12]

According to the investment code, a "foreign investor" is "an individual who is not a citizen of Uganda, a company in which more than 50 percent of the shares are not held by a citizen of Uganda, a partnership in which the majority of partnerships are not citizens of Uganda, or a joint-partnership in which the majority of partners are not citizens of Uganda."[13] According to the Uganda National Vision put forth by the NRM, licensed foreign investors should contribute to the development of the nation by investing in targeted sectors of agro-industry, forestry, mineral resources, and tourism.[14] In doing so, state officials expect that private-sector-led (capitalist) development will bring about economic growth—the generation of manufacturing and industry, infrastructural development, a growing tax base, domestic revenue streams for state operations, and jobs-training and skills-transfer for Ugandans—thus increasing wealth and prosperity for all. The intensification of this more aggressive neoliberal capitalism that depends upon foreign investors builds on earlier colonial paradigms of liberal capitalist modernity, progress, and development. Development discourses propose that "national planning" based on a private-sector-led economy that prioritizes foreign investment is beneficial for the nation, its citizens, and entrepreneurs.[15]

While Ugandan scholarship emphasizes the endurance of colonial state institutions and the postcolonial legacies of unequal racial and native governance across African society,[16] there has been less examination of the changing nature of the postcolonial state in Africa and its imbrication with global, or imperialist, and neoliberal governance. While historian Fred Cooper has emphasized the continuities between the African colonial and postcolonial "gate-keeper state"[17] in its facilitation of international (or foreign investment) capital, I argue that some institutions of the African state are actually "global," or Western, in their form and content, reflecting the need to study neoliberal imperialism as a constitutive aspect of the state rather than the state as transformed by neoliberal processes. At the same time, state agencies like the UIA were not only instantiations of neoliberal empire; they also facilitated and were shaped by varied transnational geographies of neoliberal capitalism. In the context of shifting geopolitics, the UIA facilitated these processes within and across postcolonial Global South nations. The Ugandan state and state power, thus, were not derivative of colonial state institutional legacies; nor were they derivative of neocolonial intervention through Western foreign capital interests, military and donor aid, or a singular expression of the sovereign authority of the president and ruling party. Rather, state officials at the UIA had the autonomy to forge new geopolitical alliances and connections as they negotiated Western imperialist and neocolonial processes and the neoliberal transformation of the nation.[18] In fact, the UIA was becoming *more* autonomous from its contractual obligations with the World Bank, such that funding for its activities was routed directly through the government and national budget. State officials had quite a bit of agency to determine the scope of their missions as they worked to attract foreign investment to the nation. They were traveling to regional and international investment conferences; forging new diplomatic relationships with Indian and Chinese diplomats, heads of state, state corporations, and private-sector businessmen; and pursuing different investment strategies with different nations.

I offer two interventions within the scholarly literature on the anthropology of Africa and neoliberal globalization.[19] First, globalization—often equated with a universalizing American-style neoliberalism rooted in the Washington consensus—is abstracted from specific understandings and contexts of Western imperialism and sub-imperial practices of capitalist accumulation, especially as postcolonial nations like Uganda and India enter into intensifying South-South diplomatic and trade relationships. (The Indian nation has also developed assertive diasporic capitalist classes that are active in sub-Saharan African nations like Uganda.) Second, anthropologists of race and the African diaspora argue that neoliberal globalization leaves issues of race and racial formation unaddressed.[20] Contextualized attention to neoliberal transformation and neoliberal authoritarian and militarized governance in postcolonial Uganda requires engagement with not only the white Anglo-European–Black African racial binary but also African–South Asian racial entanglements.

The idea of South-South cooperation in the development world originates in histories of anticolonial solidarity, nonalignment and Third Worldist solidarity, and Afro-Asianism. These cross-continental, national, and racial or cultural historical entanglements between colonies and independent nations of the Global South coalesced materially and symbolically during the 1955 Afro-Asian Conference held in Bandung, Indonesia. The meeting set the stage for the charismatic postcolonial male leadership of the third world, the participation of African and Asian countries in the Non-Aligned Movement (NAM) during the Cold War, the emergence of the G-77 in the United Nations, and the push for the New Economic International Order (NEIO)—which would have given Global South nations more autonomy in the planning of their economies and political alliances. This backdrop of internationalist and tricontinental collaborations—rooted in solidarity claims of imperialist nonalignment, anticolonialism and antiracism, and symbols and discourses of fraternity, diplomacy, partnership, and cooperation—are central to the new economic and trading blocs like BRICS that operate within a twenty-first-century neoliberal framework of South-South cooperation.

In the wake of the 2007–8 global financial crisis, the contraction of labor markets, and casualization of labor in Western liberal capitalist societies, African countries experienced some economic growth based on official development indicators such as gross domestic product (GDP). Development economists who normalized market fundamentalism constructed Africans, and especially the growing youth population, into an overlooked global market of consumers.[21] International donor agency officials had already branded Uganda as a development success story in the 1980s and 1990s. By the mid-2000s, Uganda had become exemplary of the idea of "Africa Rising," itself entwined with continental and Pan-Africanist notions of the "African Renaissance," that was promulgated by former South African president Thabo Mbeki during South Africa's own neoliberal transition in the postapartheid era.[22] Some commentators have suggested that establishing an "alternative global regime of development" will stem the impacts of neoliberal policies initiated by Western imperialist states and international finance institutions.[23] The emergence of continental-based sovereign entities such as the African Union, the New Partnership of Africa's Development, the Economic Community of West African States, and the EAC—including their willingness to forge "lateral" alliances with Global South nations—has provided the grounds for some optimism that African nations will subvert Western imperialist capitalist accumulation and that Global South capital investment will contribute to the developmental needs of Africans on the continent. Yet others have argued compellingly that the BRICS model of South-South cooperation simply reasserts Western imperial and neoliberal capitalist exploitation, establishing BRICS countries as sites of "sub-imperialist power," and enabling predatory capitalism in African hinterlands, capital accumulation and crony capitalism among postcolonial elites, and the support of authoritarian, militarized, and repressive governments.[24]

Examining these processes ethnographically, I refer to the neoliberal capitalist processes that make use of the histories and rhetorics of South-South cooperation and Afro-Asianism as *neoliberal Afro-Asianism*. State officials and elites facilitate neoliberal Afro-Asianism via *(neo)liberal and nonliberal logics and practices*—universalizing logics of (neo)liberal meritocracy and access to capitalist prosperity despite racial identity but also nonliberal discourses and ideologies of South-South cooperation and Afro-Asianism; fraternal kinship, intimacies, and partnerships across business and politics; and patronage and philanthropy. Neoliberal Afro-Asianism and the noncitizen racial incorporation of the Indian diaspora and Indian foreign investment capital are thus facilitated by what I am calling transcontinental (transnational and transoceanic) *Afro-Asian governance*. While the tendency of neoliberal Afro-Asianism is to conceal, or mask, the exploitative racial and economic inequalities involved in Indian diasporic-owned capital (and even the sub-imperialist and settler ambitions of some Indian industrialists and entrepreneurs) through universalizing and equalizing logics, its consequences are often the opposite. And thus, these processes can contain their own undoing. Moreover, neoliberal Afro-Asianism and transcontinental Afro-Asian governance fortify the urban Ugandan political class and Museveni and the NRM's political authority, which also defines and delimits Asian racial inclusion and exclusion.

Visiting the UIA: Facilitating Global South Investment Capital

I was flipping through the UIA's brochures in a conference room when a young female intern from Makerere University interrupted me and announced that Dr. Margaret Kigozi had arrived and that I could meet with her. Affectionately dubbed the "NRM lady" in the early years of the Movement, Kigozi came of age after the Ugandan independence era, imbued with deep love for and patriotic commitment to the young nation. Of both Ganda and colonial British (European/white) ethnicity and ancestry, and from prominent families on both sides, she had studied at the prestigious Gayaza School for Girls in Buganda. She then trained as a medical doctor and worked in the private-sector industry with her late husband before fleeing Uganda during the Amin years. In exile in Kenya, she had supported the youthful, revolutionary Yoweri Museveni in his campaign to take Kampala during the Liberation War. Kigozi then returned and established herself within the National Resistance Movement by organizing national development and gender-related workshops that taught women how to become financially independent and sustain themselves though small-scale entrepreneurship and trade. Her work promoted the presence of Ugandan women in the labor force and in the public sphere, laying the foundations for African women's participation in local and national politics and a national women's movement that fought for powerful constitutional legal reforms and women's rights throughout the 1980s and 1990s.[25]

Given Kigozi's business acumen, leadership skills, and role in women's empowerment, President Museveni appointed Kigozi to the position of Executive Director of the Uganda Investment Authority in 1991.[26] Her fluency in Luganda and loyalty to the ruling party and the Buganda kingdom made her a popular figure of ethnic unity. Unlike urban Ugandan women's more dissident expressions of feminist and queer protest that were confronting state militarism, violence, and repression during the later stages of my fieldwork, Kigozi exemplified the independence-era norms of modern and educated Ugandan womanhood and native elite respectability—gendered ideals of African womanhood and femininity that were required for women to assume political legitimacy within the patriarchal constraints of state institutions and government.[27] I was eager to experience what a woman-led and state-affiliated agency might feel like, and to understand her transformation from a revolutionary "NRM lady" to a figurehead of the UIA. This was especially the case as ostensibly feminist projects of "gender mainstreaming" and "women's empowerment" had also become incorporated into, and even co-opted by, global neoliberal, human rights, gender rights, and humanitarian governance, and, more locally, NRM governance.

At our first meeting, Kigozi explained, "Uganda Asians who stayed on after the expulsion were able to capitalize on the environment at the time, their political connections, and take advantage of the *magendo* economy. Now, the stakes are much higher. The economic landscape of India has entirely changed. Investors who showed up here with only ten thousand dollars in the early 1990s can now invest four million dollars." She encouraged me to pay attention to the areas of investment promoted by the government, what she framed as "the success stories" that had been launched in recent years; many of these were British Asian investors of Ugandan heritage or Indian-owned manufacturing firms and factories. Kigozi framed her comments in relation to recent media attention that had been paid to high-profile foreign investors who had pulled out of major investment projects.[28] Many Ugandans complained to me about empty lots in prime city locations that were now surrounded by corrugated metal fences—projects that had demolished existing buildings and displaced residents in the name of investment but that had failed to materialize. This, in addition to the persistent criticism from opposition politicians that foreign investment was not adequately addressing infrastructural development, unemployment, health, and education— and criticism of corruption scandals, including embezzlement schemes that came to light during the 2007 Commonwealth Heads of Government Meetings (CHOGM)—was an additional motivation for Kigozi and her colleagues to improve the performance and image of the UIA.[29] She described their interest in attracting "committed investors" and "development-friendly projects," describing the successes of recent Chinese infrastructural projects and the construction of major roadways in anticipation of future oil reserve exploitation in the Lake Albert region of Uganda.[30] She also explained her commitment to the education and empowerment of the African women who worked in her office and her loyalty to the Ugandan Asian and Indian business community, noting the importance of Indian entrepreneurship historically. Here, I noticed that while Kigozi discussed Idi Amin and the 1972 Asian expulsion, it was in the context of setting the nation and economy "backward" in its economic development trajectory. Kigozi emphasized that Asian traders and businessmen were critical for bringing Ugandans into commerce and business enterprise, de-emphasizing the structural and interpersonal oppressions that Africans had experienced under the system of colonial and postcolonial racial-caste capitalism.

Once Kigozi had permitted me to conduct research at the agency, I visited the office regularly, finding that it was an example of the NRM's official policies of ethnic unity, gender inclusion, and antitribalism, even as its officials made binary distinctions between a Black (African) and Ugandan citizenry and Asian foreign investors, constructing national identity on the basis of racial Blackness, indigeneity, autochthony. I observed the activities of the Investment Promotion Division (IPD). Three investment officers with different ethnic backgrounds (Bachiga, Basoga, and Baganda) handled Indian, Pakistani, and other foreign investors, and all three officers had long-term relationships with Ugandan Asian returnees and Indian diasporic nationals who owned and ran businesses in Kampala. Another prominent Ganda woman was in charge of the East Asian (largely Chinese, Japanese, and Korean) portfolio of investments and their visiting international investment delegations; she helped me understand the broader dynamics of

Uganda-Chinese and other East Asian trade, investment, and diplomatic partnerships.

Finally, I spent time with a group of women who handled communications, media, research, and event-planning at the agency. They worked with advertising and design consultants to create attractive promotional brochures and websites and organized all major international and regional trade and investment conferences in Kampala. Senior investment officers had especially fascinating personal, political, and professional biographies. Some had even fought in the Liberation War and participated in party politics during the early years of the NRM. Kigozi and many other Ugandan women were public figures and the diplomatic face of the UIA, hosting visiting delegations and promoting the nation for FDI. Senior men usually worked in the more pragmatic logistic departments called Investment Facilitation, Aftercare, and Lands. I had little access to these key gatekeepers who made politically sensitive decisions around the licensing of foreign investors and the allocations of tax incentives, immigration visas, and land and property distribution, although I had informal conversations with all of them. These officials were highly educated professionals with long-term government or private-sector business careers in Uganda and abroad, and they were in close contact with Kigozi and other state officials at various Ugandan ministries of government.

UIA offices are located on the second floor of a recently constructed building called Twed Plaza in Nakasero, near the Ugandan Parliament. Nakasero now has restaurants, hotels, NGOs, and office parks that are frequented by expatriates. During the Amin and Obote II governments, however, this area was notoriously the location of important security, military, and policing institutions, including sites of civilian detention, torture, and killings. Twed Plaza is a new building with a highly modern aesthetic, symbolizing a post-Amin and post–civil war Uganda: cosmopolitan and white, foreign, or expatriate-friendly. The first-floor houses UMEME, the now semi-privatized national electricity company, while the third floor is rented by Hua-Wei, a multinational Chinese telecom company. Private security guards are armed and stationed outside of the building and at every level. On the ground level, a parking lot houses several gleaming white Land Rovers owned by the UIA and used to transport foreign investors and visiting delegations from Entebbe airport and around the city. I often noticed how private vans escorted Chinese expatriates who worked in the building to lunch at a nearby Chinese restaurant. These same vans transport them from their residences to the office every morning and drop them off again at night.

UIA staff presented their offices as modern, global, and secure spaces for non–Black African or local Ugandan visitors like me. The combined modern technologies of an elevator, security devices such as key cards for opening doors, televisions with cable news, air conditioning, a formal receptionist, and investment officers who formally receive guests in the waiting room establish an environment that is familiar to foreigners with little to no knowledge of Uganda or even of Africa, establishing a sense of safety and security. Despite its emphasis on foreign investors, the agency is open to all visitors. At times there are walk-in visits by "locals" as the Ugandan staff themselves referred to visitors, those who have heard about the agency in advertisements and who are interested in "doing business" (*okukola business*) or finding people with whom to do business (*abantu bakola business*).

Visitors are asked to fill out an information form with a section that explains the reason for their visit. After an initial meeting, the officer fills out the rest of the form and enters it into a database accessed via a personal computer in their office.[31] During the meeting, an investor may ask detailed questions about investment policies, specifics on a particular sector of interest for investment, or how to obtain and apply for an investment license. An officer may also bring a representative from the Uganda Revenue Authority or the Ministry of Internal Affairs to the meeting. In turn, these officials handle more specific questions about taxes or visas for expatriate staff. Finally, agents offer visitors glossy brochures, produced by international agencies, that provide a country profile, information on Uganda's "pro-business" political leadership, and details of the advantages of investing in Uganda as compared with other nations. For the most part, UIA officers do not deviate from this official script. Meetings typically end with an exchange of business cards or with the visitor's request to fill out an investment license form.

The UIA and other agencies like it are what Aihwa Ong has described as exceptional sites of sovereignty, where neoliberal governmentality is operating and technocratic norms have come to replace the domain of the political.[32] It is also an example of what James Ferguson has described, in relation to NGOs, as the "anti-politics machine."[33] The norms and mandates of IPAs are continuous with earlier structural adjustment policies that are meant to formalize so-called informal economies and stem government and state-based patronage that is associated with parastatals and earlier postcolonial experiments with socialist transformation. They are also meant to instill Eurocentric/white and liberal capitalist cultures of professionalism, proficiency, productivity, accountability, and transparency among postcolonial elites and state officials. The state officials I spoke with had internalized these institutionalized norms of technocratic and neoliberal professionalism and political repression. They explained to me that although the ruling party's intensive focus on foreign investment and economic growth was politically controversial, unlike other state ministries, the UIA was a place where "business and politics did not meet." A blanket negative category, "politics" was understood as corruption and patronage between and within the business community, the ruling party and its leadership, and government and state officials; it was associated with tensions between the NRM and political opposition groups; or it symbolized ethnic-based political unrest in the city. State agents transformed the UIA into a neutral space in which the transparent processes of market fundamentalism and associated market-based individual freedoms to conduct business were unencumbered by Uganda's complicated historical, political, and social contexts.

Technically a state agency, the UIA actually had the feel of a corporate firm, with office cubicles and boardrooms. Kigozi herself managed the UIA like a business, emulating consumer-oriented practices of customer/client satisfaction and efficient service. The agency's motto, "Your Investment Is Our Business," could be found everywhere. Kigozi continually reminded the staff of their purpose: "Remember, make our investors happy!" All guests and visitors, and all their inquiries—were to be treated with enthusiasm, professionalism, and efficiency, and no visitor should ever be kept waiting. Agents emphasized to potential investors that they should make use of the UIA's services to set up a business rather than relying on their own personal and business networks to navigate Kampala's state ministries and bureaucracies. They warned potential investors that they might encounter "unprofessional behavior," a euphemism for the patronage-client based relationships usually required for nonnational foreigners to reside and settle in the city, obtain official documents, or run a business. UIA staff also often complained to me about the lack of professionalism, corruption, and insufficient "customer care" among Ugandan employees in private business and the government, thus casting the UIA as uniquely transparent, professional, and free of these challenges.

UIA agents assist foreign investors with registering for an investment license or with registering their company by obtaining the required permits, access to land, and property titles. These functions are known as "investment facilitation." The agency is a "one-stop shop" for investment facilitation, which is common to the global template of other IPAs. The government adopted a technocratic "Team Uganda" approach, whereby all public institutions cooperate with each other to attract foreign investors and their business ventures.[34] A "client charter" between government institutions helps streamline the number of steps that expatriates usually contend with when setting up a business, a process that varies according to the type of planned investment in question.[35] By reducing bureaucratic delays, the government has developed a foreigner- and consumer-friendly approach, whereby foreign investors come to enjoy a "privileged pathway" to setting up firms and businesses—and accessing land and property—that ordinary Ugandan citizens do not have access to.

I noted above that government representatives from the Uganda Revenue Authority (customs and tax), Ministry of Internal Affairs (immigration), and Ministry of Lands (property and land titles) all had their own desks at the agency itself. Representatives of these offices were immediately available for foreign investors who wished to license their businesses during their visit to the UIA. In theory, this helps to streamline bureaucratic processes and prevent investors from having to visit numerous brick-and-mortar government offices in the city. The foreign investor does not need to go to various government offices; instead, *the state comes to the foreign investor/client/consumer*, thus containing the mobility of the foreign investor. The "one-stop" shop thus supports the overarching goal of global governance institutions and IFIs to stem government corruption and patronage practices, formalize businesses, and reduce tax evasion and other economic malpractices, legitimizing a Western liberal capitalist (and even racial) worldview that exceptionalizes "corruption" as uniquely African and inherent to African governance—in contrast to the normalized and formalized corruption of Western liberal states and governments.

On a follow-up visit to Kampala in 2017, I was surprised to find that the "one-stop shop" had been repackaged and modified—it was now set up as a booth with multiple compartments in the actual waiting room of the agency, making it even more visible, convenient, and accessible to foreign businessmen. The booth offered services such as investment licensing, personal consultations with investment officers, business networking in an investor's sector of interest, and access to practical immigration and taxation consultations and land and business title services, all in the hope of attracting and retaining foreign investment capital. Not legally mandatory, but recommended, investment licenses, if approved, are processed within a target time frame of one to five days.[36]

Kigozi clarified for me that the "investment pipeline" refers to the large number of individuals who inquire about business opportunities and who set up meetings with agents, regardless of whether they actually start a business. Thus, visits to the agency do not necessarily translate into planned, or substantive, investment. I was surprised when one official, tasked with managing Indian foreign investment and countless meetings with Indian businessmen, estimated that, "for every one thousand investor inquiries, one planned investment actually materializes in Uganda." The sheer number of meetings (in addition to the record-keeping and data entry that accompanies each meeting); follow-up visits and assessments of approved investors and their proposed business, manufacturing, and industrial ventures; and the numerous walk-in inquiries all demand an extraordinary amount of labor from staff, who are already over-extended with many other responsibilities, namely, investment promotion. I would soon discover that both the opaque figure of "the investor" and the actual substantive content of the investment (capital, knowledge, expertise, skills transfer) was difficult to pin down and monitor. What seemed to be more important was the agency's ability to cultivate the *possibility* of attracting foreign investors for an aspirational project of national development and economic growth. UIA agents were acting upon nationalist desires and aspirations to join other developed economies of the Global South like South Africa and India: to enter the abstract world of global capitalist modernity and partake of the peace, development, and prosperity promised to all Ugandans.[37] In the meantime, and more pertinent to my study, the real and imagined figure of the foreign investor, or "investor-citizen," was becoming a technology of governance itself, remaking notions of "Asianness" or "Indianess" and facilitating Ugandan Asian and Indian diasporic capital, labor, and migration into the post-expulsion Ugandan nation once again.

Coproducing Neoliberal Afro-Asianism, Transcontinental Afro-Asian Governance, and Investor-Citizenship

UIA agents preferred to call the long-term benefits of foreign investment a "national development strategy," deploying the rhetoric of South-South cooperation to combat the challenges of Western imperialist neocolonialism and the challenges of the evolving developmental-aid state since independence and, especially, the 1980s. Occasionally, UIA officials encountered representatives of NGOs at the agency, adamantly stating that the UIA served private-sector business and industry only. One official explained to me that NGOs were not "serious business" since they were dependent upon external sources of funding and funding cycles, resulting in failed development initiatives; the official maintained that some were even "briefcase NGOs." Yet agents still deployed the language of *the project* (the term used in the development world) to describe a business venture to me, as in, "We are interested in investment projects that are going to make an impact, that are going to stay here, that are going to create jobs for people . . . projects that are going to contribute to the development process." Here, agents rehearsed the imagined binary between neutral "business" and "politics," marking distinctions between the transparency of one-to-one business transactions within the private sector and the more circuitous routes of capital in the development-aid/NGO sector, invisibilizing the extant circuits of patronage that flowed across private business, state institutions, government officials, even the ruling party. Although British foreign investment capital was central to neocolonial relations between the UK and Uganda at independence, here, sourcing foreign investment from Asian nations especially was posited as a novel and cutting-edge development strategy.

In general, agents wanted to attract investment regardless of the national origin, race, or ethnicity of the investor (businessman or entrepreneur). One official explained, "A good investment is a good project that has good follow-up." However, many officials discussed their preferences for "Asian"— usually meaning Indian and Chinese—foreign investors or state corporations, emphasizing the importance of reputable and established private firms and corporations or the low-interest and nonconditional developmental aid from the Chinese government and the Export-Import (EXIM) Bank of India as a strategy of long-term, sustainable investment and commitment to job creation and skills transfer to Ugandans and Africans. The meaning of "Asian" was changing to describe the wealthy capitalist Indian diaspora, and it was also becoming inclusive of East Asians and the Chinese specifically. The incorporation of Asian capital, capitalists, labor, and migrants in the nation hinged on two state-based neoliberal developmentalist imaginaries of the past: first, a romanticization of Uganda's colonial and postcolonial history of Asian and Indian commerce and business, followed by narratives of Idi Amin's racial victimization of Ugandan Asians, their expulsion, and the economic and developmental decline of the nation; and second, anti-Western imperialist and neocolonialist rhetoric surrounding the limitations of international donor-aid relationships and indebtedness to IFIs (even as neo-imperialist and neocolonial military assistance was accepted by the current government, although not discussed). While the foreign investor could be of any national, racial, or ethnic origin, in practice the figure of the foreign investor was increasingly racialized as "Asian" (Chinese or Indian), gendered male, and more highly valued as compared with other foreign investors. In postcolonial Uganda, the figure of the "Asian" or *muhindi* was being transformed through processes of transcontinental Afro-Asian governance and neoliberal Afro-Asianism, and through specific national, ethnoracial, and gendered configurations. State officials' imaginaries of the category of Asianness were now associated with a more deracinated pan-Asian figure from Asia without prior connections to Uganda or Africa.

In fact, by the early 2000s Indian national investors had become one of the top sources of foreign direct investment in Uganda, outranked by traditional capital investments from the UK, the United States, and other European nations, and joined by Kenya, China, and South Africa. In 2010, India was the top source of FDI to Uganda, usually ranked among China, Kenya, and the UK as well as among other smaller European nations, and it continued to maintain a strong position, especially in 2013–15.[38] In the case of British and Canadian FDI, however, this portfolio also included business investments by expelled Ugandan Asians with UK and Canadian citizenship who had returned during the property repossession process, while Kenyan investments included many Kenyan Asian entrepreneurs who were taking advantage of the incentives of the liberalizing Ugandan economy. While state officials made distinctions between Ugandan Asian origin and Indian national investors generally, both were welcomed to invest in the nation using rhetoric that invoked shared (horizontal) experiences of British imperialism and colonialism, anticolonial struggles for independence, and postcolonial histories of nonalignment and South-South cooperation in the national development process. One official even explained that he preferred working with Ugandan Asian investors and those of Indian national origin and had been doing so since the late 1990s and the establishment of the UIA. He explained that because of Ugandan Asians' experience of expulsion, or due to their knowledge about it (in the case of investors of Indian origin), they usually had more sensitive political and racial concerns about the security of their physical safety, capital investments, property, and other assets. "I understand how they work and how they feel," he explained. "We spent so much time together working on their investment projects I feel that I am now part of their families." Even through the UIA is based on World Bank–related and Western/white norms of corporate professionalism, agents noted the importance of relationship-building with Ugandan Asian and Indian national investors. They observed that these interactions required additional attention in guiding and managing potential investors' fears about the security of their investments and even another possible expulsion.

UIA agents, other Ugandan government officials—including the president, representatives of high-profile Ugandan Asian family firms, and representatives from other established Indian firms and businesses—were all working together to fashion the nation into an "attractive investment destination." Postcolonial elites—straddling worlds of business and politics—worked across transcontinental geographies connected by historical African-Indian entanglements. For instance, Nimisha Madhvani of the Madhvani Group has served as the Ugandan High Commissioner to India, advancing South-South cooperation and connections between returnee Uganda-based Ugandan Asians and their ancestral homeland in Gujarat, India, and simultaneously encouraging Gujarat-based businessmen to bring their investments to Uganda. Madhvani regularly speaks at trade and investment shows and conferences in East Africa and India, merging private business and diplomatic interests as she shares the Madhvani Group's experiences of cross-generational growth from merchants to industrialists, followed by their resilience and tenacity in the face of postcolonial adversity, especially Manubhai Madhvani's expulsion from Uganda. Likewise, Sudhir Ruparelia has participated in trade and investment conferences in Gujarat and New Delhi, but he has also traveled to Ugandan Asian reunion events in places like Vancouver, Canada, to win back the political trust, goodwill, and business investments of Ugandan Asian exiles-turned-investor-citizens. While many of the new investors are therefore from co-ethnic (upper-caste merchant, or *baniya*) communities in East Africa, other Indian nationals of different ethnic and caste backgrounds are also invited to invest in the nation. Nonetheless the category of "Indian investor" in Uganda is increasingly associated with the Gujarati business and political class in contemporary India (largely upper-caste, Hindu, and supportive of the Hindu right wing).

Trade and investment conferences—even Ugandan Asian reunion events—are becoming important sites at which to examine "transnational Afro-Asian governance": an assemblage of global governance and state institutions, state actors, business elites, and community leaders mobilizing shared colonial histories to remake postcolonial ones; participating in diplomatic performances and moral injunctions about national developmental goals; mobilizing affects and performances of racial, gendered, and class-based embodiment; making ethical incitements that are central to the facilitation and success of neoliberal Afro-Asianism. My point here is that the category, discourse, and practices of "Afro-Asianism" constitute a technology of governance, sovereignty, and citizenship. With its origins in nonliberal histories of anti-imperialist solidarity, partnership in national development, and interracial solidarity, Afro-Asianism is fast becoming a new component of Global South–based state governance that relies upon the merging of political and business interests, militarism, and securitization in postcolonial nations like Uganda and India. In Uganda specifically, neoliberal Afro-Asianism is a technology of governance, sovereignty, and citizenship critical for the noncitizen racial incorporation of "Asian" or "Indian" capital and capitalists, migrant labor, and the making of new Indian diasporic communities after the 1972 expulsion.

I continued to observe these processes take shape at events in urban Uganda and in virtual/online venues as Uganda-India ties intensified in the years after my formal field research was completed. Against the backdrop of liberalization in the 1990s, diplomatic and trade relations and the bilateral ties between the Indian nation and African nations increased. By the mid- to late 2000s, the East African community and heads of state in East African nations hosted numerous "India-Africa summits," inviting both state-funded corporations and private firms to learn about trade and business opportunities. While the Indian Association Uganda (IAU) helped support Narendra Modi's visit to Kampala in 2008 to celebrate the revival of Ugandan-Gujarati connections, the (current) prime minister of India, Modi, visited Uganda again in 2017 and 2018, the latter visit ending with Modi addressing the Ugandan Parliament and president, cabinet, and ministers in an hour-long speech on India-Uganda relations more generally.[39] In return, Museveni and high-ranking ministers have regularly attended a number of new forums and conferences in India in order to strengthen the relationship between the two nations.[40]

In Kampala, Indian businessmen participated not only in UIA-sponsored investment conferences and trade shows but also in the annual Presidential Investors' Roundtable (PIRT), a meeting that brings together the president, high-level ministers, and captains of industry and manufacturing in a forum to discuss national development priorities and investment policies.[41] Completely technocratic in its form and organization—and thus, once again, shaped by global governance and developmentalist agendas—the PIRT allowed foreign businessmen and expatriates to advocate for policies that privilege both (1) market fundamentalism at the behest of the state and (2) the political authority of the government. I observed this event in 2010, noting how it legitimized the neoliberal transformation of Ugandan society and Afro-Asian neoliberalism more specifically. PIRT also reproduced the racially nativist logics of citizenship and the noncitizen racial incorporation of Ugandan Asian and Indian businessmen—underscoring that they were primarily "investor-citizens" and guests of a host (Black African) Ugandan nation, embodied by the political authority and sovereignty of the president and the ruling party. This was the case even though the intimacies between state and Asian sources of foreign investment capital also meant that "investor-citizens" were more politically important than they might otherwise appear. Here, industry and businessmen's deference to the political and racial sovereignty of the president—indeed, the president's sovereign authorization of "Asian" presence and capitalist enterprise—was on display.

Some prominent businessmen I spoke with were very excited that they had been invited by the UIA and the president to participate in the PIRT. It was a highly prestigious and much-anticipated event for them. During follow-up visits at their offices, they eagerly presented me with conference programs and framed photos of their participation. Others were recipients of the UIA's "Investor of the Year" award—an event that publicly celebrated the contributions of the Ugandan Asian and Indian business community to the nation. Taken together, these events helped construct people of South Asian heritage as "investor-citizens" and as a business community integral to the prosperity of the nation and Ugandans in general. They also helped to legitimize the presence of racialized South Asian bodies and capitalist enterprise (Asian-owned capital) in the aftermath of the 1972 Asian expulsion, even after the Ugandan Asian repatriation and repossession process, and despite the persistence of anti-Asian populist sentiments (discussed further below).

"Branding Uganda": Recasting Uganda, Idi Amin, the 1972 Asian Expulsion, and Racial South Asianness

Back at the UIA, a major activity of state agents is to organize and host "investment delegations": diplomatic state visits, visits with representatives of Indian and Chinese state corporations, visits with members of trade and industry organizations, and visits with venture capitalists, industry men, and other high-profile entrepreneurs. Planned in advance, the visits are a carefully choreographed process in which foreign visitors are treated exceedingly well from the moment they arrive at Entebbe Airport and are escorted in luxury vehicles along the Entebbe-Kampala expressway to UIA offices and five-star hotel accommodations.

After an initial meeting at the UIA, where delegations are received with tea and refreshments, Kigozi delivers a PowerPoint presentation that promotes the Ugandan nation as an "attractive investment destination" and

answers queries from visitors. There are ceremonial rituals of cooperation and partnership, shaking hands for photo opportunities, and the
exchange of cultural gifts. An appointed agent takes the visitors on a city
tour to visit successful foreign-owned enterprises. An evening dinner at an
upscale restaurant offers a breathtaking view of the sunset and glimmer-
ing lights across Kampala's many hills. Agents continue to accompany the
potential investors to meetings with government officials and industry mo-
guls. In all respects, foreign investors' experience of Kampala is carefully
curated, stressing a sense of political and racial security of personhood,
property, and capital investments; bountiful opportunities; and a life of expatriate privilege. Here, UIA officials have constructed an idea of a developing, prosperous, and modernizing Uganda that is secure and hospitable
to racial and cultural Others and foreign capital, in contrast to Western
and South Asian global imaginaries of an illiberal and racially insecure
Uganda and its historical associations with the Amin regime and the 1972
Asian expulsion. Uganda as a welcoming and hospitable nation for racial
Others is further cemented through Kigozi's warmth and charisma in her
gendered performance of Ugandan and (by proxy) national femininity. The
investment tour exemplifies the new rationalities of transcontinental Afro-
Asian governance and neoliberal Afro-Asianism, consolidating new global
and elite imaginaries of the Ugandan nation.

The UIA, then, has its own historical logic that reinvents the past, framing the rise of Idi Amin and the expulsion of Asians as antimodernist and
antidevelopmental projects. It is not that state agents completely refute colonial and postcolonial racial and class inequality between Africans and Indians. Rather, UIA agents are invested in state projects that construct diaspora
and returnee Ugandan Asians and Indian foreign investors as "modern" and
even rehabilitated, with exposure to Western liberal professional business
practices, including ideas of corporate social responsibility and the importance of contributing to Ugandan society. For example, one state agent explained to me that Ugandan Asian family firms like the Madhvani and Mehta
Groups are "modern Indians"; specifically, although these firms represented
Asian-owned capital in Uganda, they also hired Africans in skilled labor
and management positions, and had helped bring many Ugandans into the
middle class through small tenant farming, showcasing a commitment to
Ugandans. State agents were thus political and cultural workers, transforming the figure of the *muhindi* into a *munaife* (colleague) or a *mwesimbu* (a
trustworthy and genuine person in Luganda). State agents were also invested
in the moral transformation of urban Ugandans, who, they described, now

understood the importance of Asian business, entrepreneurship, and the value of foreign investors.

Beyond the ways in which theorist Michel Foucault has helped us to understand security as a mode of governmentality that is constitutive of the logic of the liberal nation-state and its relationship to territory and population,[42] securitization and militarization in Uganda continue to be central to the alliance between state and capital and for capitalist accumulation by dispossession,[43] including land enclosures and primitive accumulation, the privatization and securitization of property and assets, and the securitized protection of foreign expatriates and businessmen. State agents assured foreign investors that the current government was "pro-business," "friendly to foreign investment," and welcoming to foreigners.[44] They often assured potential investors that Uganda was safe for them and their businesses and that they would not have problems with hiring their own (skilled or specialized) expatriate staff and repatriating capital to their home nations, thus promising bodily and racial security.[45] They insisted, repeatedly, that Amin's actions had not benefited anyone: neither "Asians" nor "Ugandans" (racialized as Black Africans). I was taken aback, when, on a few occasions, state agents went so far as to mention that the military was quick to respond to any "security issues," normalizing the ruling party's authoritarian and militarized neoliberal repression. Indeed, this assemblage of late neoliberal capitalism, authoritarianism, militarism, repression, and securitization is not unique to Uganda and increasingly characteristic of both postcolonial Global South nations and so-called liberal states in the Global North. Yet the particular Afro-Asian dynamic central to racial capitalism—processes of neoliberal Afro-Asianism—juxtaposed with Uganda's postcolonial experiments with decolonization, anti-imperialism, military dictatorship, racially nativist nationalism, and Asian expulsion, meant that the constant focus on the security of personhood, capital, property, and assets of foreign investors was quite remarkable.

There were other state-based cultural productions, too, what Samar Al-Bulushi has described as "nation-branding" in contemporary Kenya.[46] EAC nations are often slotted against each other on international economic indicators and in business rankings such as the World Bank's "Doing Better Business Index." Many state officials believed that Uganda had fallen behind other East African nations—particularly Rwanda—in attracting foreign capital; and thus, UIA agents were working even harder to promote or "brand," the nation through late neoliberal capitalist logics to potential investors. This is significant because foreign investors are very fickle as they

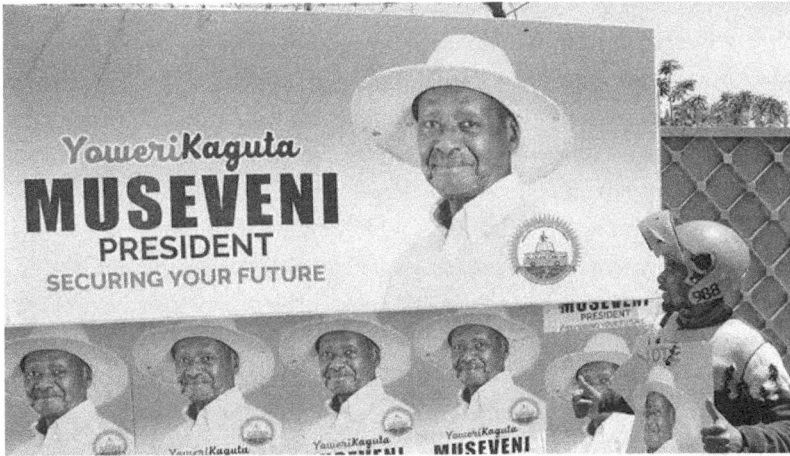

4.1 One of Yoweri Kaguta Museveni's 2021 presidential campaign billboards displaying his campaign slogan, "Securing Your Future."

move and strategize across different nations on the African continent. As James Ferguson has observed, the "foreign investor view" of Africa is one in which the investor does not distinguish among the historical, cultural, and political-economic contexts of different countries. Rather, the category of "Africa" itself, constructed through Western civilizational and colonial ideas of the continent as a frontier region that is undeveloped and antimodern, is more salient, and these ideas are constructed through Asian world-views of Africa as well.[47] The "foreign investor view" of Africa is also produced through racial logics: racialized as Black, coded with civilizational and developmental meanings, and marginalized as a geography with more uncivilized and degraded forms of humanity. Uganda is associated with an exceptionally "illiberal brand": Idi Amin, military dictatorship, and political terror; postcolonial racial and ethnic violence; civil war, and so on.

It is not only foreign investors but also postcolonial elites, including Ugandans themselves, who produce civilizational and colonial frames of Africa's underdevelopment. At the UIA, for example, agents were branding Uganda as a "hub country" that would be attractive to global foreign investors. Some used large regional maps to explain that Uganda was a "gateway nation," nestled between coastal nations and more inaccessible locations in the interior, and that as part of the Great Lakes region it shared five international boundaries. They argued that investors (in this case manufacturers and industrialists) would have the potential to sell their products not only to Uganda's growing population but also to other consumers in South Sudan. By transforming rural African communities into potential markets of consumers with purchasing power, UIA agents argued that Uganda was a "renaissance nation" poised to launch into a future industrial era with infinite capacities for market and economic growth. These discourses, including the visuals and affective incitements that accompanied them, were powerful and impactful at meetings with foreign investors.

In actuality, state agents were increasingly tasked with branding the nation and promoting it for investment, rather than with overseeing the implementation of investment projects once they had been licensed and were operating. More funding was allocated toward activities related to investment promotion and "image building," language taken from the corporate marketing world and applied to the nation itself. For example, UIA's public relations officers created attractive brochures, advertisements, and social media content to promote the nation's ecological diversity, natural resources, and tourism; its labor force (as inexpensive and English literate); its manufacturing and agro-processing potential; its emerging extractive industries such as oil and biofuels; and, most recently, its cultural heritage and tourism, including its traditional kingdoms. Local celebrities, socialites, and popular musicians performed at investment conferences, branding Uganda as open for business. While much of this was intended to attract foreign investors, UIA officials were also at the helm of defining neoliberal and state-based notions of the Ugandan diaspora, here defined as the large global Ugandan or Black African community in the UK, Canada, and even the US, encouraging them to invest in Uganda through "Home Is Best" campaigns, pride in cultural heritage, and patriotic sentiments.[48] It was around this time that many Ugandans working to promote foreign investment were outraged by the US-based "Kony 2012" international humanitarian and social media campaign that they felt perpetuated damaging and racist global representations of Uganda and Ugandans, on par with existing global imaginaries of exceptional illiberalism of Idi Amin. Despite the reality of the victims of the violence and conflict in Northern Uganda, in Kampala, participating in discourses of anti–US imperialism and anti-white saviorism, repairing Uganda's international image, and getting back to the important business of development priorities and attracting committed foreign capital seemed to be on everyone's mind.

Branding Uganda is also a material and infrastructural project. In what Aihwa Ong has described as "graduated sovereignty," a key aspect of neoliberal transformation and neoliberal exceptionality in the Global South in the early 2000s, the Ugandan government began to establish industrial parks that were export processing zones (called EPZs) with tax incentives and privileges for foreign expatriate manufacturers and industrialists.[49] EPZs are standard business parks that follow a global template and contain office parks, residences, and shopping centers for resident expatriates. Ong uses graduated sovereignty and "graduated citizenship" to explain the effects of states "moving from being watertight administrators of a national entity to regulators of diverse spaces and populations that link with global markets."[50] Following this line of thinking, industrial parks have high-quality infrastructure and amenities for foreign workers as well as other regulatory perks to attract foreign investors and assist them with setting up their enterprises and factories in the nation.[51] They are reserved for expatriates who set up factories while enjoying deterritorialized and racialized rights and privileges within spatialities that keep them connected to "the global" and their home nations. I was astounded to learn that as of 2021, the Ugandan government has, using eminent domain clauses, reserved land for *twenty-two* of these industrial parks in all major districts across the nation.[52]

Although the NRM claims to have compensated and resettled existing communities that it displaced in order to secure land and establish these parks, it is unsurprising that their implementation has been extremely controversial. The 1995 Constitution liberalized the land policy such that any (legal-juridical) Ugandan citizen could purchase and own land anywhere; and subsequently, many displaced and disenfranchised Ugandans, especially in northern Uganda, have suffered due to an institutionalized project of military, political, and alleged "foreign" land grabs for commercial agriculture, unrelated to the above-mentioned state-owned industrial parks that are facilitated by the UIA.[53] NRM and UIA officials strategically maintained the rhetoric that all freehold land is owned by (indigenous, Black-identifying) Ugandans, even if, in practice, land can be made available to foreign investors via ninety-nine-year leases and eminent domain policy. The largest industrial park, Kampala Industrial Business Park, is located in Namanve, eighteen miles outside of Kampala, just off the Jinja-Kampala highway. Formerly part of Namanve Forest, it was an infamous dumping-ground for the bodies of tortured and killed civilians during the Amin regime. I often drove on the highway through the forest on my way to Jinja and back to Kampala, shuddering, imagining the mundane and capricious nature of terror and violence in the past. Nowadays, all one sees is advertised park signage and a vast stretch of fenced-off, ocher-colored dirt—all existing trees, scrub, and vegetation have been razed. In 2010, two factories (a Ugandan Asian Khoja

Ismaili–owned steel manufacturing outfit, and an Indian Punjabi–owned construction company) sat on the mostly empty expanse. Although the park was still at an early stage of its development, one of the overseers of the project explained that the World Bank donors who had funded it and who were in charge of its oversight had created massive delays. In the meantime, the industrial park was being managed by the UIA, which provisionally granted land leases to foreign investors for factories and enterprises. In 2010, several returnee Ugandan Asian business families had applied for land in the park. Most, however, expressed doubts about whether its infrastructure would materialize or be completed; they also voiced their concerns about Ugandan perceptions that land was being given to them by the government. In 2020, the UIA finally began infrastructural development of the park through a new public-private partnership, but it remains to be seen if all the lots will be filled, especially by foreign investors without existing connections to Uganda.[54]

Taken together, the logics of governance, sovereignty, race, and citizenship in Kampala and urban Uganda are transforming. It is clear that the 1995 Constitution of the Republic of Uganda, as a legal-juridical document, retains racially nativist notions of national membership by defining normative Ugandan citizenship on the basis of Black African racial identity and sovereignty as well as on ideas of indigeneity and even autochthony within the territorial boundaries of the nation. However, it is now noncitizen racial foreigners and expatriates (many of whom are of Asian or Indian heritage) who have substantive economic entitlements—a privileged pathway to conducting business, access to leases to government-owned freehold land in industrial parks, and even state-based militarized and securitized protection—on the basis of their entrepreneurial identities as foreign investors. The figure of the "investor-citizen" is increasingly racially and politically sovereign in contemporary Uganda, challenging the legacies of Africanization, expulsion, and Black African racially nativist nationalism.

Kiwaani: Real versus Fake Investors

As much as rights and entitlements have been redistributed to the foreign investor, the "investor" and "investment" remained imprecise categories. According to regulatory frameworks, UIA agents were to assess foreign investors on the basis of "the generation of new earnings or savings of foreign exchange through exports, resource-based import substitution, or service sector activities; the utilization of local materials, supplies, and services;

the creation of employment opportunities in Uganda, the introduction of advanced technology or the upgrading of indigenous technology . . . the general contribution to locally or regionally balanced socio-economic development."[55] Agents were to appraise investment license applications by examining whether investors will "employ and train citizens with a view to 'Africanization,'"[56] with explanations for skilled expatriate staff, if any. Finally, investors were to demonstrate that they had at least US$100,000 of planned capital investment (this includes the importation or buying of machinery and the development of contracts to build infrastructure such as offices and manufacturing plants).[57] This capital threshold was intended to minimize "the investment pipeline" and capture committed investment that supports the industrialization and development of the nation.[58] Despite these regulations, global governance mandates to attract foreign investment were often at odds with the labor demands placed upon the state agents. They were also tasked with discerning substantive and committed investment from inauthentic, or "uncommitted," investment in the context of rapid liberalization and the increased transnational mobility of Indian and Chinese entrepreneurs, migrants, and traders.

Although national regulatory frameworks required foreign investors to obtain an investment license, international organizations like the United Nations Conference on Trade and Development (UNCTAD), in the name of advancing neoliberal policies and cutting bureaucratic red tape, have recommended that the code be revised to make the license optional, and replaced with voluntary registration.[59] In general, it was difficult to monitor investors because global governance institutions recommended that the UIA's activities be focused on investment promotion rather than on regulation. In addition, although the agency had an Aftercare Department that was tasked with follow-up and monitoring of investment projects, it was not well-staffed or well-resourced enough to conduct rigorous auditing of approved investment projects; and even if it had been, there was no political incentive to do so given that global and state norms prioritized liberalization and the mobility of entrepreneurs, capital, goods, and migrant labor across borders. State officials have been under pressure to approve investment projects and provide evidence of Uganda's growth trajectory by meeting FDI targets and other abstract national development goals, prioritizing planned, or projected, rather than actual investment figures. Once again, the potentiality of investment, industrialization, and development—the nation's imagined future—is given precedence. And as the NRM's politicians and military elites nurture business connections, the state is fast becoming a "patronage state"—one that is invested in the lack of transparency surrounding the figure of "the foreign investor" and the content of "investment."

I had more access to observations of meetings where state agents initially, and informally, evaluated the intentions of foreign investors. Informal discernment practices identified so-called committed investors from opportunistic ones, or so-called investors from other kinds of businessmen engaged in commerce and trade. Agents discussed the importance of sorting out "real" (*kituuf*) investors from "fake" (*kiwaani*) investors as they screened potential investors. After one meeting, an agent laughed in exasperation, "Anneeth," he said, "*oyo mussajja tali* serious!" ("That man is not serious!"). Popular musician (and now political leader of the People Power Movement, the main political opposition of the NRM) Bobi Wine's famous song, "Kiwaani" now applied to foreign investors as well.

The privileged pathway for foreign investors was created by the Investment Code Act (1991), which initially authorized tax breaks and government incentives for almost all major investment projects. Since then, revisions have been made that allow incentives only for particular types of earmarked investments, negotiations that were not transparent to me. One official remarked to me, "I don't like it when investors don't want to hear what we have to say, but immediately ask about what the incentives are for them, right away, right at the beginning. How do we know if they are really interested in Uganda and Ugandans, how do we know if they will stay here, if their money will be re-invested here?" In one meeting, the official responded to the visitor's queries about the possibility of tax incentives by stating curtly, "Okay, the incentives are there. We are helping you to start your business here . . . but this is a place for business, we do not do politics here." Questions about tax incentives were becoming more sensitive as the UIA was under scrutiny because of the government privileges (especially taxation privileges) afforded to foreign investors compared with those afforded to "local," African or Ugandan businessmen and entrepreneurs.[60]

Certainly, the investment pipeline and failed investment projects revealed that "briefcase investments" and *kiwaani* investors were a serious issue. In some cases, a *kiwaani* investor would pool funds through their own networks and obtain an investment license without the intention to invest; they would instead operate a different business than originally stated, including trade in imported goods. While reputable industry men associated with high-level diplomatic trade and investment delegations were very welcome, state agents also described those who claimed to be foreign investors but for whom no capital for a "project" (meaning a factory or other industry) materialized; or for whom, if the project did appear, capital flight and the lack of Africanization in employment and skills transfer in the business remained significant challenges.

Generally, the NRM has maintained Africanization policies in certain sectors of economic activity, promoting trade, commerce, and the service industries for Ugandan (Black-identifying Africans) only, even as economic growth has increased and wage-labor jobs for Ugandans remain scarce. Yet liberalization, coupled with more aggressive neoliberal processes, has defanged protectionist policies, especially for African traders. While the rhetoric of Africanization is maintained, the question of what Africanization means substantively is unclear and continues to be a point of contention among opposition political groups. Employment practices "with a view to Africanization" are encouraged within policy frameworks; but in actuality, the extent to which Africans are employed, receive job-skills training, and can move into managerial and higher-level positions, especially in Asian-owned industry, firms, and businesses, is not monitored or assessed (and more research is necessary).

Although foreign investors can hire expatriate staff with specialized skills, it is frowned upon, and it is regulated through a complex and expensive tier of work permits and visa fees. In practice, businessmen, however, find ways to maneuver around these regulatory policies through patronage practices with state officials. As one official related to me, some Indian investors may agree to employ only a few specialized expatriate staff, but then use their own connections with immigration officers or front partnerships with Ugandan businessmen to facilitate the hiring of co-ethnic (and likely, caste-kin) noncitizen Indian nationals in their businesses. In my own conversations with members of the Indian diaspora business community that had settled in Uganda in the late 1990s and early 2000s, I found that the Ugandan Asian expulsion—although not experienced directly—was embedded in their consciousness with respect to assessing risk and strategy and establishing trust (amid their racial precarity) in their business practices. Many stated that hiring their own managerial staff (especially financial accounting staff) and other labor enhanced their ability to trust employees and maintain a sense of political and racial security as well as ensure the financial success of the enterprise. But these practices also reflected their preferences for maintaining racial (and caste) endogamy within their business operation and social distance from Africans, remaking race and class hierarchies and racialized economies in urban Uganda.[61]

The remaking of South Asian presence (both Ugandan Asian returnees and the new Indian diaspora) in the nation through the figure of the foreign investor led many urban Ugandans to question the racial re-"Indianization" of the national economy rather than the conditions and consequences of neoliberalism; the changing structures of empire, imperialism, and even sub-imperialism; or the relationships between neoliberalism, authoritarianism, and militarization. On one occasion, the increasing levels of Indian foreign investment and the presence of Indian foreign investors was conflated with Ugandan Asian returnees and their family firms. I was attending a panel and networking event hosted by the UIA that was held at the renowned Hotel Africana. After Kigozi presented on foreign investment opportunities and gave examples of successful businesses, a Ugandan businessman and audience member confronted the business privileges of Ugandan Asian family firms. Kigozi, in turn, challenged the audience member, arguing that Ugandan Asian businesses were multigenerational family businesses and thus were African, not foreign. She made claims for the political and racial inclusion of Ugandan Asian business families by re-racinating them, arguing that they were so culturally Ugandan and African that they were "tribal": they even spoke local languages from specific regions—their homelands— in Uganda. This exchange signaled to me that the presence of returnee Ugandan Asians, their political belonging, and their entitlements to land, property, and business and commercial enterprise in the nation, continued to be questioned. This is due not only to their racial status but to the new conditions of neoliberal Afro-Asianism and the state's agenda to attract Indian foreign investment.

Insecurities of Investment, Sources of Anti-Asianism, Specters of Indian Sub-imperialism, and Racial Expulsion

Despite the rhetoric of Afro-Asian and South-South cooperation in economic development then, general trends indicate that there is often a marked disparity between "planned" and "actualized" investment, with official GDP growth falling, and capital flight and limited job growth posing continuous challenges for Ugandans.[62] Beyond the general uptick in BRICS nations investment, and according to reports and estimates, "official" planned versus actualized investment ratios often hover between 30 and 50 percent or less, while the presence of Indian and Chinese merchants, managerial and service laborers, and sojourning migrants has grown. While India and China remain the top national-origin investors, Uganda, Eritrea, Sudan, the UAE, Pakistan, Lebanon, and Egypt are also now routinely top investors, revealing the importance of domestic (potentially naturalized citizens) and regional elites, in addition to BRICS nations, in the Ugandan economy.[63] State authorities continue to regulate "*kiwaani* investors," or foreign national traders, by increasing the fees for trading licenses and work permits, or even by denying permits and licenses to merchants and other migrants, bringing about a new regime of deportation of undocumented Indian and other South Asian nationals. This tendency is also amplified in relation to the racial and religious profiling of migrants in the context of the regional war on terror.[64] In fact, many of my long-term contacts claimed that the most committed investment in the nation had already occurred in the 1990s, when Ugandan Asian returnees repossessed their properties and reestablished their family firms. Nonetheless, the government continued to pursue policies that liberalize the economy with the goal of attracting increasing foreign investment. As one official explained to me, the presence of merchants, service workers, and sojourning migrants on the move was tolerated, "because in this country it is possible that they will eventually become 'serious' investors in the future."

"Newcomer" sojourners and migrants were also self-identifying as "investors," explaining that the government had invited them to develop the nation. The state-based racialized construction of the figure of the "Asian" as a foreign investor—becoming an "investor-citizen"—is thus the primary pathway to inclusion for those considered racially South Asian. Even so, this noncitizen racial incorporation of investor-citizens is precarious for migrants and sojourners, who are easily exploitable by more established Asian-owned businesses. They have few legal or political rights and protections, and they contend with everyday urban racial harassment, even the constant extraction of rent by state officials, as compared with those who enjoy class-based expatriate privileges and protections.

Despite the internal stratifications and variegated entitlements among those racialized as "Indian" or "Asian" then, and despite the fact that many middle-class urban Ugandans have embraced neoliberal governance that aims to shape citizens-subjects into entrepreneurial citizens, and despite liberalization policies that have welcomed foreign investment as a national development and job creation strategy, most urban Ugandans feel abandoned as they compete with noncitizen foreigners and expatriates who are settling long-term in the city.[65] Urban informal workers and petty traders in particular feel the loss of racial and economic entitlement and power with respect to those of South Asian heritage, especially as the government devalues "local" or Black African entrepreneurship and investment. Formally, African trade associations pressure the government to Africanize markets with policies that will protect them from Indian—and increasingly

Chinese—trade competition, focusing on increasing inflation and the competitive foreign undercutting of prices for commodities and even the cost of labor-power, which undermines the living wages of urban Ugandans. The cartoon shown in figure 4.2 reveals these late neoliberal-era racial and class tensions through stereotypical caricatures of "Ugandan" and "Asian" street vendors. A Ugandan street vendor, represented as native African and citizen, complains about being undercut by his foreign competitor, wondering at how and why an Indian (constructed as foreign and noncitizen) could be doing similar petty vending as he is (in contrast to the state's construction of foreigners and "Asians" as investors). The visual depiction of the Indian street vendor recalls the figure of the *muhindi* and stereotypical racial scripts of Indian merchants prior to their expulsion from the nation as well as the economic pressures in neoliberal India that have compelled South Asians to migrate. The migrant is assertive in his response that Ugandans do not have the exclusive right to conduct *kyeyo* (petty work or trade, "getting by," in Luganda).[66]

Government and foreign investor land grabs and high-profile failed investment projects; the privileged pathway of economic and other entitlements for noncitizen foreign investors involved in business; the *kiwaani* investor who is actually a merchant or low-wage service worker and temporary migrant or sojourner; the maintenance of South Asian racial (and ethnoreligious and caste) endogamy within businesses; the lack of attention paid to sensitive issues of Africanization (employment, skills-transfer, and job mobility) within Indian businesses in the post-expulsion context; and the circulation of patronage between key Ugandan Asian business tycoons and political and military elites in exchange for racialized security and protection—all this is resuscitating urban and societal-based memories of former president Idi Amin, the 1972 Asian expulsion, and an effective urban populist discourse that Asians economically and racially exploit Ugandans. This anti-Asian populist discourse is now reconfigured and aimed at the figure of the foreign investor as *kiwaani*, building on Africanization-era tropes of the opportunistic (and politically and socially) uncommitted *muhindi*.

I began to sense the more public, rather than private, nature of urban racial tensions, especially as I navigated the Kampala taxi parks and markets. The "post-memory generation" of Ugandan youths who were born into the NRM era and after the Amin regime and the 1972 Asian expulsion was resuscitating and mobilizing images of Idi Amin as a figure of Pan-Africanism and Black racial and economic empowerment. No longer made mythological or stereotypical through global media representations, and no longer haunting my dreams, Idi Amin now appeared emblazoned on *matatus* (privately

4.2 Cartoon representation of a Ugandan African-Indian business competition. From *The New Vision*, July 11, 2011.

owned minibuses), in murals and artwork, and in popular Luganda and Swahili songs. On social media, I found similar celebratory representations of Idi Amin. The same news articles that celebrated Ugandan Asian heritage or Indian diasporic investment in Uganda on Facebook also often included inflammatory anti-Asian commentary and the occasional Idi Amin meme, captioned, "Uganda's one true national leader," or "truly Pan-Africanist and cared for his people." Other memes shared excerpted quotes from some of Amin's most famous political speeches. This social-media-based project of reimagining Idi Amin in contemporary times was a memory project premised upon both remembering and forgetting—while Ugandan youth celebrated the strongman autocrat and the sense of Black racial dignity, pride, and political and economic empowerment that he bestowed upon them, they disappeared the military dictatorship, terror, and violence inflicted upon fellow Black Africans; the racism, nativism, and patriarchy inherent to the regime and Amin's version of anti-imperialism and cultural nationalism; the creation of the wealthy *mafutamingi* political class at the expense of the common urban Ugandan.

Some of my Ugandan Asian research contacts—again, fragmented, occupationally diverse, and with complicated feelings about each other's social and material investments and commitments—were extremely critical of state policies around foreign investment and the business practices of the "newcomers" from India and other South Asian nations. Although the new-comers were similarly racialized as "Asian," Ugandan Asians perceived them as *not* African in origin and lacking knowledge of the expulsion (especially Indian nation–based knowledge of the event); as harboring class, caste, and especially racist biases against Africans; and as not socially integrating or com-mitted to Africans, Ugandans, or Ugandan society. In private, they discussed with me small news items they had read in the local press about workplace abuses in Indian-owned shops and businesses and even the sexual harass-ment of African women in these establishments. Nervous about the image of "Asians" being created by newcomers, their fears and anxieties about the possible resurgence of anti-Asian sentiment and racial violence increased. Nusrat, whom I introduced in the previous chapter, remarked to me qui-etly one day, "You see, no one wants to learn from those of us who have experienced an expulsion." She worried about her own irrelevance and the irrelevance of the past to the current moment. But public political and so-cial critique was also risky business, as Ugandan Asian return was dependent upon the ruling party and its noncitizen racial inclusion of Ugandan Asians as well as foreign investors from India and other Asian nations. And both Ugandan Asians and "newcomers" were racialized similarly.

Perhaps, by rejecting the discourses of *kituuf* or *kiwaani* investors and of authentic Ugandan Asians or problematic Indian newcomers, it becomes possible to articulate a structural critique of changing imperial and sub-imperial formations and of racialized neoliberal capitalist arrangements—the ways that processes of neoliberal Afro-Asianism and transcontinental Afro-Asian governance engendered an urban-based Afro-Asian (multira-cial) political class, new racialized labor-capital arrangements, and more racialized inequality that were inflaming race and class tensions once again. My research at the UIA and other urban sites of "elite cosmopolitanisms" and neoliberal Afro-Asianisms compels a deeper interrogation of Indian nationalist, sub-imperialist, and even settler ambitions, as studied through the new overseas Indian diasporic capitalist class in East Africa. Their ambi-tions are related to the civilizational, racial, and caste-based sources of hier-archy and inequality that underpin capitalist arrangements transnationally, or racial-caste capitalism. Indian diasporic and capitalist ambition is also increasingly characterized by an exclusive Hindu nationalism, another point of consternation among Ugandan Asians—if less legible to most Africans—an issue that I explore more deeply in the next chapter.

5

Indian Ugandan, African Asian, or Both?

Community-Building, Community Citizenship, and Culture and Indigeneity

With a mix of anticipation and nervousness, I glanced at my notes and greeted fellow Ugandan Asian and other Indian diasporic community members before making my way to the stage that had been set up for the discussion. The first event of its kind, the community forum sponsored by the Asian African Association (AAA) in Kampala in 2013 would create space for dialogue about the 1972 Asian expulsion and contemporary race relations in urban Uganda. Established by Ugandan of Asian origin Mahmood Mamdani and other returnees, and in the aftermath of racial violence that targeted Asians in Kampala in 2007, Professor Mamdani had brought me on board to lead and coordinate AAA activities while I served as a research associate at the Makerere Institute of Social Research (MISR). Mamdani led the organization of the first forum, held exclusively with Ugandan Asians and other South Asians, asking us to reflect on three questions: (1) "If the objective of the expulsion was justice—the Africanization of the economy from which colonial power had excluded Africans on racial grounds—has that objective been achieved? Why or why not?" (2) "If the objective of the return of properties and opening of the door to South Asian immigrants was reconciliation, and if the point of reconciliation was development, to what extent has that objective been achieved?" (3) "To what extent have we not yet learned the lessons of the expulsion? To what extent is a second expulsion in the cards? And if it is, what should we do about it?"

Prior to the start of the forum, Amrita, a Ugandan Asian returnee and friend, had texted me, asking me to meet her in her car in the parking lot. She confided that she was feeling vulnerable about speaking publicly about her experiences of expulsion and return, and she worried about saying anything that might further harm an already precarious and minority community in Kampala. Reviewing her talking points together, I encouraged her to speak authentically about her perspectives and assured her that I would support her ideas in the larger conversation. Our brief encounter before the start of the forum clarified for me that public and especially critical discussion of the expulsion and its aftermaths—including the usual fraught and messy internal dynamics of minoritized communities made monolithic—had many Ugandan Asians feeling exposed and uncertain. This raised significant ethical questions about how to engage with the global critical event of expulsion among community members living in Uganda who were potentially vulnerable to racial violence.

As the community forum unfolded, it became apparent that most returnees felt that racial reconciliation between Ugandan Asians and the majoritarian African population had not been achieved despite the property repossession process. In addition to feelings of racial mistrust, interpersonal experiences of anti-Asian discrimination, and racial fear, some, like Amrita, also spoke about the mistrust among the small group of Ugandan Asians (*stayees* and returnees) who now resided in Kampala. She argued that racial reconciliation could not be achieved when internal community tensions persisted. Another key theme was the growing tension between Ugandan Asian returnees and so-called newcomers—the post-1990s Indian diaspora of Non-Resident Indians (NRIs), the businessmen, migrants, laborers, and their extended families who maintained strong connections with the Indian nation, many of whom had become leaders of the (now) resuscitated Indian Association of Uganda (IAU). In one telling exchange, a Ugandan Asian community leader accused the newcomers of prejudicial attitudes toward Africans and of inciting racial tensions. The chairman of the IAU retorted that the association was completely dedicated to fostering positive relationships between "the Indian community" (defined here as inclusive of Ugandan Asians) and Ugandans (defined here as Black Africans). Instead, he argued that it was certain high-profile Ugandan Asian family firms and businessmen who were the source of the racial tensions (see more below). In contrast to the returnees, he argued, it was the newcomers who were working in closer proximity to Africans and who were cultivating interracial harmony and respect.

In general, the tensions evident at the first community forum revealed competing claims surrounding constructions of the "Asian" or "Indian" community, its substantive complexity, and its internal boundaries and distinctions. The forum revealed competing claims over the source of reemerging urban racial tensions with Africans and the very terms and grounds of these tensions. The forum shed light upon the everyday practices of interracialism and social integration in the midst of feelings of racial minoritization and racial precarity. Finally, the continual construction and contestation over the substance and constituents of the category of "Asian" or "Indian" was also influenced by the ongoing state-based racialization of people of South Asian heritage in the nation as "Asian."

In this chapter, I examine the insecurities of expulsion in relation to the nexus of postcolonial state governance, community-building, and citizenship practices, with attention to the categories of community and culture and contestations surrounding social integration. In general, the "Indian" or the "Asian" merchant is a gendered racial formation and used ubiquitously in East Africa and in Uganda, shading into a singular category of a monolithic "Indian community" or "Asian community." I show that the postcolonial state construction of the "Indian/Asian community" (a legacy of racial and native rule) is an ongoing necessity for (1) the governance of Ugandan Asians, the Indian diaspora, and other South Asians; (2) the maintenance of "Asian" racial exclusion and the possibility of expulsion; and (3) the practice of "Asian" noncitizen racial incorporation.

I examine dissonances between state governance of the Asian social body and the extant complexity of "Asian" communities and their community-building practices. The state-based noncitizen incorporation of Ugandan Asians, the Indian diaspora, and other South Asians relies upon the institutionalization of the IAU. The IAU is increasingly necessary for making "community-citizenship" claims on the state, for internal racial community governance, and for providing welfare and security to community members. Community-building and citizenship practices can facilitate social integration and interracialism post-expulsion or, conversely, can reassert racial and communal endogamies, conjuring the specter of a socially distant "Asian community" in urban Uganda once again. Ugandan, African, Asian, African Asian, Indian, and South Asian categories, identities, subjectivities, and community-building practices are continually unfolding in relation to changing transcontinental, nation- and state-based logics of governance, sovereignty, and citizenship.

Remaking Asian or Indian Racial Community, State-Community Relations, Community-Citizenship Claims, and Community-Based Governance

My earliest encounters with South Asian community organizations were not with the AAA. Rajni Tailor, a longtime community leader and honorary member of the Buganda Lukiko and of Ugandan-Gujarati and Hindu heritage (mentioned in chapter 2), had assisted fellow Asians during the expulsion crisis in 1972 and managed to stay on during the Amin and Obote II years. He spearheaded the reconstitution of the IAU in the post–civil war and NRM-led reconstruction years. The IAU was originally part of the Central Council of Indian Associations in Uganda and was founded as the Indian Association of Kampala in 1908 and officially registered in 1922.[1] H. S. Morris observed that the Council was important despite the emergence of religious, sectarian, and caste-based associational life, and that the Council served those (especially vulnerable communities) who could not be served by communal-based organizations. It was represented by Westernized, elite Indian men and engaged the British colonial administration on matters pertaining to all communities racialized as "Asian" or "Indian" (in addition to the individual patrons, lawyers, and accountants that Ugandan Asians went to for assistance); helped charities, widows, and children; and received visiting delegations and celebrities from (pre-partition) India.[2] The 1947 partition of British India into India and Pakistan split a formerly united racial community of Indians in Uganda. In 1948, many Ugandan Asian Muslims (primarily Punjabi and Pakistani Sunni Muslims) withdrew from the Central Council and the IAU, forming instead a Muslim Association, with some communities, like the Khoja Ismailis, Sikhs, Goans, and other individuals left conflicted or ambivalent about the partition's impact on overseas Indians, especially in the context of Ugandan Asians' minority status in an African majoritarian nation.[3] Even as Ugandan Asians began to adopt new nationalist affiliations with the Indian and Pakistani nations, the community elites and leaders representing community organizations (and especially the dominant "umbrella" organization, the IAU) continued to play a critical role in political advocacy for Ugandan Asians with respect to political franchise and representation, commercial interests, and other rights and entitlements; this activity intensified in the independence-era and with respect to Africanization policies, anti-Asianism, and Amin's expulsion decree in 1972 (as addressed in chapter 1).

Tailor had deep knowledge of the IAU both before and after the expulsion, including a meticulously collected archive of local newspaper clippings on issues pertaining to people of South Asian heritage in Uganda, from property repossession to business and commercial activities, to the philanthropic work of community associations. His prominent role in civic life through his involvement in community organizations and social welfare activities, as well as his integration with African communities, allowed him to serve as a racial and cultural intermediary, building bridges between the Buganda Kingdom, the expelled and returnee Ugandan Asian community, and newcomer entrepreneurs and migrants from South Asia.

Many scholars of the overseas (pre-partition) Indian diaspora in East Africa have detailed the rich history of Indian civic and associational life. This research examines the varying ethnic, linguistic, religious, and even caste-based character of community associational life, with attention to the ways in which religious-based ethics became critical to the practice of philanthropy, and in turn, how philanthropy became central to citizenship claims for both racial and religious minorities in postindependence East African nations.[4] While scholars like Morris and Robert Gregory have attended to the emergence of Indian associational life—with focus on the religious, sectarian, and caste-based nature of such associations and their agency in building institutional community life and making East Africa home—scholars like Mamdani have examined the racialized governance of diverse (pre-partition) Indian communities as "Asian," or the racial governance of Subject Races like "Asians" or "Indians" via British indirect rule, and the practice of "decentralized despotism."[5]

However, there has been little analysis of the interactive nature of both colonial state-based racial governance and community-based governance. In fact, both the (post)colonial state and Ugandan Asian elites (usually men) co-constructed an imagined racial community constituency and discursive category of the "Asian or Indian community." State actors especially constructed an idea of a homogenous and monolithic "Asian or Indian community" (which in practice is internally diverse on the basis of ethnicity, language, religion, sectarian, and caste identities), devolving authority to male community elites. Racial community and other community association patriarchs helped establish governance over the lives of fellow "Asians" or their communal counterparts, while male heads of household governed the lives of women and children in domestic spaces. As such, women and children were disciplined and encouraged to respect male authority within what I describe as the "nested domains" of domestic, customary (communal-based), and race-based governance, even as women and communal-based associations also asserted their own forms of agency and competitive forms of authority with organizations like the IAU that were in dialogue with the colonial administration and state authority. At independence in 1962, formerly colonized subjects who were subject to racial and native rule—both men and women—were understood to be new, individual citizen-subjects with attendant rights, privileges, and duties in the nation and its nascent urban public sphere and civil society. The drift to authoritarian politics and the 1972 Asian expulsion resulted in the loss of Asian participation in formal politics (through political parties) and within other political, legal, and administrative bodies, including their participation in the nascent civil society and public sphere, whether via community associations or as individuals. Ugandan Asian women's expanding participation in the public sphere and civil society, and their challenge to the domains and norms of male authority, was especially affected by anti-Asianism and the expulsion (see more in chapter 6).

Given the "de-Indianization" of the state and economy in 1972 and the transformations in governance, sovereignty, and citizenship that I was tracing in urban Uganda, I did not expect that Ugandan Asians who had experienced expulsion and subsequently returned, or those who had remained, would be engaged in formal party politics or even affiliated with traditional political kingdoms and other institutions of political authority in the nation. Yet, in addition to Tailor, I met some Ugandan Asian–identifying individuals (all men) who were expanding the multiracial sphere of formal politics and citizenship by participating in local, city-based, district-level, and even national politics. Katongole Singh (Ugandan of Punjabi Sikh descent, and who practiced an integrated African Asian "big man" type persona) was an MP and party member of the NRM, despite the racial discrimination and anti-Asian xenophobia he experienced during his political campaign in 2011. Sanjay Tanna ran an independent campaign at the district level in his family's hometown of Tororo, in Eastern Uganda, where he also spoke the regional language and identified as *Mutooro*. Taken together, male "intermediary" figures like Tailor, Singh, and Tanna assert integrated "African Asian" and "Ugandan of Asian origin" identities and subjectivities—navigating domains of formal politics, traditional kingdoms, and community-based associational life—constructing racial and cultural bridges between African and South Asian urban worlds and using their platforms to advocate for and represent racial community concerns while maintaining social and ethical commitments to Black-identifying Africans.

I was more surprised by the many new communal organizations that reflected the new, post-expulsion-, postliberalization-era migration and settlement of the Indian diaspora, as well as South Asians from Pakistan, Bangladesh, Sri Lanka. I learned from Tailor and from Murtaza Dalal, a board member of the IAU, that in the early 1990s, a small group of *stayees*, returnees, and newcomer residents from South Asia created a formal association that would serve the interests of all those who shared South Asian heritage (and who, in Uganda, were racialized as "Asian"). These "community-builders" first formed the Asian Federation, which would be representative of the growing number of NRIs as well as Pakistani and other South Asian nationals. The Federation, however, soon fell apart due to the lack of coordinated leadership and tensions between members that reflected the geopolitical and nationalist tensions between postcolonial India and Pakistan—in short, an inclusive organization without communal politics was unable to emerge. Tailor and other Indian nationals stepped in to reestablish the IAU, which now serves as an umbrella group for a growing number of ethnic, linguistic, religious, sectarian, and caste-based organizations, some of which are contiguous with pre-1972 Ugandan Asian communities, while others are completely different (see the appendix). Therefore, while individuals like Tailor serve in advisory roles, the IAU is increasingly run by and reflects the post-1990s Indian diaspora in Uganda, which includes majority Hindu members but also a minority Muslim, Sikh, Jain, and Christian membership. Dalal and others emphasized that the organization does not discriminate against Pakistani nationals or Muslims—indeed, many Muslim-affiliated organizations, both Sunni and Shia, are affiliated with the IAU because of its outsized role in political advocacy for all racialized "Asians." But there is also a separate Pakistani Association that coordinates closely with the Pakistani Embassy in Uganda.

In this chapter, I focus my attention on the IAU and how it has become a significant political organization that advocates on behalf of the post-1972 Indian diaspora in Uganda and helps facilitate the institutionalization of numerous communal organizations that are critical for internal community governance, or what I describe as "community-based citizenship." I use "Indian diasporans" here to reflect the idea that most post-1990s entrepreneurs and laborers, migrants and sojourners, and their dependents (women and children) are noncitizens in the formal, legal-juridical sense (they are Indian citizens, defined as NRIs). Newcomer Indians retain strong ties to the (postcolonial) Indian nation through the construction of NRI identities and other affiliations with the Indian government and nationalism. They identify more with post-partition Indian nationalist identities than with more pluralistic prepartition East African Asian or African and Ugandan identities (although, over time, it is usually men who are socially integrating into Ugandan society, speaking African languages, and practicing ethical forms of citizenship in post-expulsion Uganda).

In fact, the majority of "Asians" in Uganda now are members of the postliberalization newcomer Indian diaspora community. Increasingly, they rely upon communal-based organizations and the IAU for social welfare and to make substantive citizenship claims for rights and entitlements upon various state actors and institutions. They make community-based, rather than normative liberal-style legal-juridical and individual citizenship–based claims on the basis of state recognition of formal citizens. Transcontinental Uganda is exemplary for the normalization, and not the exceptional nature, of its "postliberal" practices of governance, sovereignty, and citizenship. I refer to this "postliberal" mode of state-based governance as *heteropatriarchal racially nativist governance*, observing that, once again, it is shaped by male authority. I describe the nested, "Asian" racial community and South Asian communal-based nature of governance as *heteropatriarchal racially nativist communal governance*, noting that women and children continue to navigate male authority within communal and associational life.

"Re-Indianizing" Kampala? Facilitating Expatriate NRI Presence and the Normalization of Nonsocial Integration

If I began my study with a search for signs of South Asianness in post-expulsion Uganda (chapter 1), I found that during my follow-up research trips and between 2013 and 2015, when I had returned to Kampala, South Asianness was a growing feature of the city. The expansion of NRIs, or the post-1990s Indian diaspora (and other noncitizen South Asian nationals in Kampala), was reflected in the growth of new ethnic, religious, sectarian, and caste-based community associations; new financial investments in restaurants, hotels, and other service-sector related businesses (often serving other South Asians); more Indian merchants and wholesale and retail shops; two movie theaters in new malls that released Bollywood films in sync with their India-based releases; newcomers renting residences in repossessed Ugandan Asian properties in former Indian areas like Old Kampala; and the resurgence of devotional and spiritual cultures as residents attended old and newly built temples and mosques. According to community leaders and the Indian Embassy of Uganda, the number of Indian, Pakistani, Bangladeshi, and Sri Lankan "newcomers" was estimated to be between twenty-five and thirty thousand and growing in 2010, with no official census taken or available. In addition to the expelled Ugandan Asian population that was primarily of Gujarati and Punjabi ethnic origin, and subsequent chain migration from those regions, many new skilled professionals had arrived to work in Indian firms and factories, especially from Southern Indian states like Andrah Pradesh, Tamil Nadu, and Kerala.[6]

The facilitation of the residence and investments of NRIs and other South Asian nationals was related to the post-expulsion period of normalizing diplomatic relationships between Uganda and the Indian nation and the neoliberalization of the national economies, as discussed in the previous chapter. But (formal) noncitizen South Asian presence was also facilitated by the changing nature of the Indian nation-state's relationships to its overseas Indian diasporic populations. For example, Atal Bihari Vajpayee, BJP prime minister of India from 1998 to 2004, opposed the earlier Nehruvian policies that articulated a position of Afro-Asian solidarity and South-South cooperation, advising the overseas Indian diaspora to take on African national citizenship and socially integrate. Rather, Vajpayee argued that overseas Indian communities needed to maintain connections with India, building on ideas of a deterritorialized Indian nation-state wherever the global Indian diaspora resides, and based on essential notions of "Indianness" and the desire to attract diasporic investment capital back to the Indian nation.[7] Intensifying neoliberal policies; the capitalization of NRI and PIO diasporic identities under Manmohan Singh, the Indian National Congress prime minister from 2004 to 2014; and finally, the intensifying "commodification of people of Indian origin" and the advancement of the idea of an exclusively Hindu nation (Hindu *Rashtra*) and "the Hindutva claim on all Hindus as Indians," have coalesced into the development of an aggressive neoliberal Hindutva authoritarian project under the leadership of Narendra Modi, BJP prime minister from 2014 to the present.[8] While the political elites of New Delhi have tended to focus their energies on the Indian diaspora in Western liberal states, Modi and the BJP have zeroed in on South Africa and East Africa as key sites for developing the deterritorialized Indian nation vis-à-vis its overseas Indian diasporas. In fact, after Modi's visits to Kampala in 2007 and 2008, he returned for an official state visit to Kampala in 2018, the first Indian prime minister to address the Ugandan Parliament in an official speech. He unveiled a bust of India's independence-era activist and first statesman Sardar Vallabhbhai Patel as a gift to the Ugandan nation and a symbol of cooperative diplomatic, trade, and investment relations.[9]

The "floating" nature of the new Indian diaspora—not necessarily needing to, or compelled to, integrate political or socially within African polities and societies—is also related to the racially nativist and restrictive norms of citizenship constructed by the Ugandan state since the 1972 Asian expulsion, and especially in the 1990s (see chapter 3). In addition to their legal-juridical status as NRIs attached to the Indian nation, "newcomer" NRIs and expatriates can maintain long-term residence through the advent of temporary visas and work permits as well as through Certificates of Residence offered to those who have officially maintained residence for ten years or longer and who have contributed to the socioeconomic development of the nation (criteria oriented toward foreign investors and businessmen) or to those who have married a Ugandan citizen.[10]

I gained a sense of the day-to-day lives of newcomers through my research contacts engaged in business and industry in the IAU. I visited some of the temples in Nakasero, near the city center of Kampala, on the weekends, where professionals, labor-migrants, sojourners, and their dependents often gathered. There I met Seema, a young Bengali housewife who had had an interethnic and intercaste marriage to a managerial professional from Andhra Pradesh. Her husband, Jay, worked for Dairy Fresh, a subsidiary of a larger India-based agro-processing firm that produced milk and milk products in Uganda. Visiting her home after a religious program one Sunday, I gained a sense of how isolated and circumscribed her life was—limited to her home, the market, and religious temples, with little to no interaction with Ugandans. She lived with her husband and their three-year-old daughter in a flat in a guest house in the industrial area. The flat was provided by her husband's employer. Her husband worked long hours—seven days a week—with twelve-hour shifts. Sipping our cups of tea together, she explained that in addition to providing housing and paying for fees for work permits and visas, the company gave her family a monthly allowance for food and provisions, and that when they arrived, they did not need to pay for anything except for a few appliances. Gesturing to the TV across the room, she explained, "See, even the TV has cable and Indian channels." Uganda-based private company employers facilitated the nonresident status of new Indian managerial expatriates and their dependents in a manner that reconstructed a deterritorialized Indian life in urban Uganda. This offered them the comforts of expatriate life and made them feel racially safe and secure in the process.

Upon Jay's return from work, he shared with me more details about his plans for his family. He intended to stay on with his employer for a year or two, explaining that "this was the hard time of scrimping and saving," and that, ideally, he would like to move his family back to India. He observed that Ugandan and African culture was very different from Indian culture, although he did not elaborate upon these cultural differences. Here, "Indianness" and "Ugandanness" were often invested with essentialism, with the notion of culture often a stand-in for racial distinctions that were more difficult to discuss overtly. Although Seema's husband did not quite invest Indian "culture" with the sense of superior morality or even Indian (and Hindu) civilizational exceptionalism that I detected among others, this notion of "culture" did reproduce racial boundaries and distinctions, a sense of separateness that was reinforced by an uninterrupted "Indianness" constructed via Indian nation, urban Uganda, factory and home in the Industrial area, and market and temples in Nakasero. When I asked Jay more pointedly about his experiences in Uganda, especially given the history of fraught African-Asian racial tensions, he explained that his firm's objective was to support Ugandan dairy farmers, but that they (Indian-owned firms) also "had to respect Ugandans or else there would be problems." As always, as in many of these conversations, I sensed his uncertainty about whether Indian investments and Indian nationals were actually welcome—despite the policies of the current government to officially and symbolically welcome them. He expressed his concerns about how other Asians treated the Africans they worked with— he felt that people from South India, like his home state of Andrah Pradesh, were better trained, less arrogant, and more professional in their interactions with Ugandans in the workplace. He confided that he was embarrassed by the attitudes of many merchants in the city who unnecessarily verbally harassed or abused Ugandan urban workers or who talked to Ugandans in demeaning ways, making all people of Indian origin in the city vulnerable.

My conversations with Seema, Jay, and others revealed that many expatriate professional and managerial noncitizen Indians and their dependents viewed themselves as temporary guests who contributed to the socioeconomic development of the nation, but who disavowed any national, racial, or cultural connection to Uganda or the African continent. They identified as Indian nationals, temporarily in Uganda to save money and gain professional expertise in order to build a better life and future for their families after returning to India or moving elsewhere for further social standing and advancement. They had little formal or Indian nation–based knowledge of the earlier overseas Indian diasporas in Africa, the 1972 Asian expulsion, or even Gandhian history in Africa and Indian diasporic contributions to the Indian freedom struggle and African anticolonial struggles. They tended to reproduce Indian nation–centric imaginaries of expulsion exceptionalism, reinforcing racialized ideas of a liberal-democratic Indian nation and illiberal African nations. But they were also not untouched by the insecurities of expulsion, reflecting on Indian-African relationships, even though their interactions with Africans were limited. And while many noncitizen migrant professionals and workers possessed temporary contracts with clear plans for their return to India or further migration to another nation, over the course of my research, other sojourner migrants and unskilled laborers were residing in Kampala on a fairly permanent basis, even as they planned for and imagined other migration and settlement trajectories, whether or not they were actually possible.[11]

Developing my analysis of the "floating" Indian diaspora and their further "nonsocial integration" in Uganda, Aihwa Ong's conceptualization of "latitudinal citizenship" is useful for exploring "how markets stretch the bounds of governmentality" and the ways in which "the spatialities of market rights and deterritorialized ethnic power . . . constitute labor relations across national borders."[12] As I have indicated in the previous chapters, Uganda-based Indian firms and (some) notable Ugandan Asian–owned enterprises often employed Indian managerial and other skilled labor, handling the travel costs, visa fees, work permits, family dependent passes, and living accommodations and associated fees of those in their employ. I consider these transnational Indian firms and other Ugandan Asian family firms to be quasi-sovereign entities. Thus, the governance of "newcomer" NRIs and their families is forged through both historical experiences of political and racial insecurity and Indian neoliberal and corporate norms, including, but not always, the maintenance of ethnic and caste-based endogamy and exclusivity, made into racial endogamy and exclusivity. Ugandan Asian and transnational Indian firms thus uphold racial boundaries and the racialized aspects of society and the economy. NRIs negotiate racial privilege and racial insecurities. The heightened experience of racial exclusivity and racial consciousness is also a gendered phenomenon. Seema's racial alienation was exacerbated by her gendered location within the patriarchal family and a normalized deference to male authority within transnational Indian firms and within broader patriarchal society.

In general, long-term resident community and business elites, usually men, serve as patrons to newcomers, facilitating state-based and community-based governance, and heteropatriarchal racially nativist communal governance specifically. These patrons act as intermediaries be-tween the state and newcomers, and serve as intra-ethnic, religious, caste, and gender power brokers; they participate in the exploitation of labor and in the ideological disciplining of co-ethnics; and they facilitate the rise of racialized enclaves that are socially disconnected from the worlds of urban Ugandans and Black-identifying Africans. Given the tightly regulated net-works of racialized community governance, migrants look to employers and community leaders as patrons who can offer racial security and protection. Some newcomers invest their resources and energy in community institu-tions that can offer protection and social welfare. Unlike Ugandan Asians who stayed behind or who maintain the majority of their investments in Uganda, newcomers also invest their savings and capital back home and in the Indian nation.

A Transforming Indian Association: From Ugandan Asian to Indian Diasporic to "Ug-Indian" Community-Building

Tailor explained to me that it was important to reestablish the IAU because it institutionally empowered community leaders to begin formally repos-sessing numerous Asian community-owned properties that had been ex-propriated by the Amin government after the expulsion. While some *stayees* (chapter 2) managed to oversee Sikh and Hindu communal property in Kam-pala, Entebbe, and Jinja, most Asian Muslim communal property was real-located to African Muslim religious leaders and/or to members of Amin's inner circle; the rest was taken by military men and other tenants. Numerous Asian community properties were officially handed back to the IAU during the 1980s and 1990s. However, even if legal repossession had been granted for a property, military officials or other tenants and squatters continued to reside in community properties in more remote regions of the nation. As I noted earlier, property repossession did not align with the actual return migration and settlement of most Ugandan Asian exiles, who chose instead to remain in the UK, Canada, and elsewhere. Community leaders raised financial contributions from *stayees*, returnees, and new businesspeople to support the repossession of community properties. They explained that although the government officially supported communal property repos-session, corruption plagued government processes and that actual repos-session required offers of "goodwill," or patronage, and the application of other kinds of political pressure to evict existing tenants, especially those associated with the military, from communal property. In addition, some claims to communal property, including schools and sports facilities, were under internal legal dispute within specific religious communities.

I had a glimpse of the scale of the repossession efforts and the desires of resident communities of South Asian origin to reclaim their cultural and religious patrimony and heritage (and to maintain a sustained presence in them) during several road trips I took with community members to small towns outside of Buganda and Busoga. I traveled with members of both the Ugandan Asian Sikh community and the newcomer Indian Sikh migrant community during April Vaisakhi festivities in 2012. (Vaisakhi is the celebration of the birth of the Khalsa, or the establishment of the orthodox Sikh identity, religious order, and spiritual community as well as the traditional Punjabi spring harvest festival.) During these trips, I observed traditional *nagar kirtans* (ceremonial devotional singing on Vaisakhi), *ardaas* (prayers), and *langar* (communal meal), the cleansing of the *gurudwara* and the replacing of the Sikh *nishaan-sahib* (flag) from the *gurudwara* with a new one. On one road trip, we visited the historic Sikh *gurudwaray* in the eastern region, stopping in Mbale, then traveling north to Lira, and finally on to Gulu, where we visited empty *gurudwaray* that had no permanent resident priest or caretaker. Those *gurudwaray* had instead one or two long-term residents or migrants who had keys to the properties and maintained them during the year. The formal repossession and caretaking of communal properties, even without a resident religious community in town, was significant in that *stayees*, returnees, and newcomers could all establish local and territorial claims to community-based citizenship and urban racial and religious belonging, even as they were fragmented internally and working on building racialized religious community once again.

The IAU was critical to the facilitation of both the repossession and the caretaking of historical Asian community assets, and thus central to the remaking of Ugandan government-state Asian "racial" community relations and state-based (hetero)patriarchal racially nativist governance. It made community-based political claims—substantive claims for citizenship, including property repossession claims—upon the government, state institutions, and state actors, but this time under post–Asian expulsion and neoliberal conditions. Since the IAU leadership was composed exclusively of male-identifying community and business leaders, I highlight the patriarchal nature of male authority and governance central to the community organization. Male community leaders typically spoke for the interests of their community members, including women and children. In addition, Ugandan Asian and other long-term resident Indian diasporic women also revived the historic Indian Women's Association (IWA) in the early 1900s, while others were also very active in the International Women's Organization (IWO), which had multiracial African, South Asian, and European expatriate membership.

The gendered segregation of the IAU and the IWA reflected the social conservatism and traditional conventions of the historic Ugandan Asian community and the norms of community-building among the new Indian diaspora community. But they also reflected a gendered division of labor that sustains patriarchal norms of community governance and government-state-community relations: while IAU leaders interfaced with Ugandan state officials, business elites, and military and police officials; engaged in the labor of property repossession; forged diplomatic relationships; and negotiated substantive political and economic entitlements and claims for "Asians" in Uganda, the women's organizations focused on the "softer" and more feminine labor of philanthropic and social welfare activities geared toward African communities and the labor of preserving, producing, and representing "Indian culture," including religious and food festivals, bazaars, and other social events. Increasingly, both organizations were composed of, and reflected the interests of, the newcomer Indian diaspora, disseminating information on important religious holidays, festivals, and devotional gatherings at local temples (primarily for the ethnically diverse Hindu communities, inclusive of Punjabi Hindu Arya Samaji followers, devotees of Sanatan Dharma Swaminarayan Hinduism, BAPS Swaminarayan Sanstha, and other new Hindu religious movements like ISKCON and the Sathya Sai Baba organization); hosting entertainment and sports events taking place in the city; religious and spiritual missions and visitors from India (including meditation courses, yoga seminars and lectures by spiritual leaders); the reception of celebrities and musical guests from India; health and wellness-related events; publicizing death announcements; and sponsoring philanthropic missions and activities and other news and events of interest. Meetings and activities sponsored by both organizations were critical to Indian diasporic community formation and to building a sense of belonging. While individuals might seek patrons and social welfare from particular religious, communal, and sectarian organizations, the IAU served those who might not have this support.

Community organizations are not benign, apolitical groups. The IAU, while subject to state governance, is also a quasi-sovereign institution or political body that helps facilitate Indian diasporic community presence in the nation and the governance of those same settled communities. Over time, the mission of the IAU changed, reflecting the interests of a deterritorialized Indian nationalism, increasingly Hinduized and also shaped by Modi's BJP right-wing politics. As one of the chairmen explained to me, "The mission of the IAU is to serve and represent Indian minority interests in Uganda, [to] unify all communal organizations under the rubric of the IAU, and to build a strong partnership with the [Ugandan] government and nation by creating a successful Indian community that will contribute to the nation and to the broader NRM vision of building a prosperous Uganda." The IAU was invested in constructing a cohesive and monolithic racial "Indian community" as a positive, modernizing, and developmental force in the nation, in line with ideals of neoliberal-era nation-branding and South-South cooperation that I outlined in chapter 4. It was necessary that the figure of the "Asian" and the South Asian racial community be presented to the state and the majoritarian Black African public through deterritorialized Indian nationhood, using images of entrepreneurial success, philanthropy, and other social welfare activities geared toward social contributions to Africans and building positive relationships between Indians and Africans. Thus, "image-building" or "branding" an imagined and racialized construct of the "Asian" or "Indian community" was also a practice among community and business elites. It was further heightened in relation to the limits of racial reconciliation after the 1972 expulsion and the insecurities of expulsion.

In addition to the Indian government's and political elites' commodification of its overseas Indian diaspora, and the Indian diaspora in Uganda's own self-construction of community through the lens of neoliberal image-building, the IAU also participated in more familiar practices of fashioning essentialist and syndicated, or invented, ideas of "Indian culture" and "Indian tradition," especially at festivals that celebrated patriotic holidays such as "India Day" (January 26, the day on which Republic Day is celebrated in India), Indian Independence Day (August 15), and Ugandan Independence Day (October 9). Notions of Indian "culture" and "tradition" quickly became fixed and fossilized, often associated with a Hindu religious or civilizational exceptionalism, representative of the deterritorialized Indian nation or projected backward onto the Indian overseas community in pre-expulsion Uganda, erasing more conflicted histories of the 1947 partition, the 1972 Asian expulsion, and postcolonial nation-building in both India and Uganda. Indian "culture" and "tradition" were not seen as changing and moving, contested and fraught, shaped by encounter with (racial and religious) Others, especially African and African diasporic cultures, but quickly shaded into an Indian civilizational and even racial exceptionalism, exclusively owned. This self and community construction of exemplary Indian national culture was exemplified at IAU events. At one festival, IAU leaders commended "exemplary NRIs" and "Indian origin citizens" with "India Day Achiever Awards." Another award presented was the "Indian Community Ambassador Award," which celebrated an NRI, typically a recognized businessman or investor, who was "proud to be an Indian in Uganda" and who exemplified positive contributions by keeping the "corporate image high"—running a business that exemplified corporate social responsibility and philanthropy and that, thus, was beneficial for the larger Black-identifying African majoritarian population.

The emphasis on community-based practices of constructing a successful Indian diasporic community with a strong culture that contributed to the socioeconomic development of the Ugandan nation reflects a disinvestment in the logics and practices of a universally understood individual-based liberal citizenship and individual political participation in the formal institutions of civil society. Rather, this is a decidedly postliberal investment in community-based governance, community-based racial and political securitization, and the provisioning of social welfare through communal institutions. While many of the community-builders I spoke with—both Ugandan Asian returnees and Indian NRIs—identified with political liberalism in the sense that they had had exposure to living in what they imagined to be liberal democracies (such as the UK, Canada, and the Indian nation-state) and experience with liberal political institutions like citizenship, in Uganda, they focused their energies on investments in community-based associations. One community member explained to me that although it was important that there were some Ugandan Asians who served as public political figures since they advocated for others racialized as "Asian," community institutions like the IAU and business leaders with connections to the government served as patrons; they "provided security and safety for the entire 'Indian community.'" Notable here are the nonliberal domains of citizenship practice—government-state-racial community governance; internal racial community and communal-based governance; and patron-client relations between state officials and business elites essential to relations of protection and securing racialized South Asian presence.

In addition to well-heeled entrepreneurs and expatriates, more vulnerable migrants, sojourners, and dependents were incorporated into extant communal, ethnic, and religious-based networks that could help meet social welfare needs and provide immigration and citizenship support, labor opportunities, and crucial information about living arrangements and financial assistance. Over the course of successive research trips, I observed the remaking of ethnic, religious, sectarian, and caste-based community networks, and thus the resurgence of heteropatriarchal racial nativist communal governance, including the co-ethnic/religious/caste-based disciplining of new migrants by settled elites. The social reproduction of the community resulted in racial community endogamy. This racial community endogamy also helped to facilitate the noncitizen incorporation of vulnerable foreigners who would remain and settle in the city.

An array of schools, hospitals, and specialty medical clinics was being established by some entrepreneurial Ugandan Asian and Indian diasporic entrepreneurs, with the idea of serving South Asian communities as well as the Black African majoritarian population. With some exceptions, I found that almost all upwardly mobile NRI families patronized privately owned Ugandan Asian– or Indian-owned and affiliated institutions, rather than sending their children (now born and raised in Kampala) to public or African-run and African-owned schools or medical clinics (the Aga Khan educational and medical facilities were an exception, as they have always been multiracial and have always served both Asian and African communities). While some community members discussed the better standards and quality of private Indian-run institutions, it was also clear that they did not expect the state and its public institutions to provide social welfare services like health care and education to long-term resident NRIs and foreigners. Financial investments in Indian-owned and -run institutions were thus also expressions of both community racial endogamy and community-based racial securitization in a politically insecure environment, not unlike the Indian-owned private and gated housing communities in urban enclaves with walled compounds, security cameras, and security guards.

While many community leaders viewed the resurgence of Indian diasporic and other South Asians in Kampala as a positive development and a step toward healing the past, some viewed the reassertion of the Indian diasporic community as problematic and as a public expression of disinvestment in social integration with Africans (as, essentially, an investment in racial and communal segregation). This became clear to me one evening while attending a concert with Gurdeep, who had invited me along. The concert featured popular India-based Bollywood music artist Mika Singh and was sponsored by the IAU and several prominent Indian firms and businesses in the city. Together, we leaned back against a perimeter fence as we sang along to the Hindi-Urdu and Punjabi language lyrics to popular songs

"Subha Hona Na De" and "Mauja Hi Mauja," songs that we often heard in Kampala. As the hours passed, Gurdeep became more and more perplexed by the many thousands of concertgoers of South Asian origin; he had not expected there were so many NRIs residing in and around Kampala. "See, it's at events like these, you get to know how many Asians there really are in Uganda," he mused. As the night progressed, he was also increasingly disconcerted by the seemingly "Indian-only" nature of the concert. Shouting into my ear over the booming outdoor speakers, he complained, "You just can't have so many *desis* in one place like this and the only Africans you see around here are employed as the security guards and cleaners. How does this look? Newcomers don't have a sense of Ugandans and their feelings at all. They also love Bollywood, Indian music, films, and songs, so this should have been advertised to the general public. But then, they [the organizers] will start talking about crime, security, what-what." It was in this moment that the "post-memories" of the 1972 Asian expulsion became apparent to me, the ways in which Gurdeep was unsettled by the assertion of a very visible minority, racially precarious, and privileged Indian diaspora presence in the city and by his perceptions of the insensitivities of the programming leadership, amid lingering racial tensions. Leaving the concert and commiserating on our shared interests in the cosmopolitan nature of *bhangra* music, dancing, and DJ-ing, we brainstormed ideas for venues for musical programming that would appeal to a multiracial urban audience.

New urban Ugandan practices of Indian diasporic culture and community contained gendered and sexual dimensions as well. Related to syndicated, static, and essentialist ideas of Indian culture were the practice and performance of the ideal bourgeois Indian family and the modern Indian (NRI) diasporic woman. In 2009, the IWA hosted an inaugural Miss India Uganda talent and beauty competition in Kampala. While India's *Femina* beauty and fashion magazine and organization supported the event in African countries with large Indian diaspora populations—including in South Africa, Kenya, and Tanzania—many of my research contacts felt that the fact that the competition had arrived in Uganda would place both Uganda and its Indian diaspora "on the map." I attended the event one evening with a friend, noting the emphasis and production of Indian nationalism on display. As I anticipated, the ideal "Miss India Uganda" embodied an idealized notion of modern Indian heterosexual womanhood and femininity, marked by ideal North Indian beauty standards (light skin and long hair), the Indian sari as national dress, and an emphasis on strong Indian culture and traditionalism, morality, spirituality, and even domesticity. While one segment featured school-aged children wearing African-Indian fusion style dress, Indian womanhood was symbolized through the preservation of Indian fashion and style. While prominent female Ugandan (African) public figures were judges and helped cohost the event, arguing that it promoted intercultural understanding, some of them remarked upon the fact that African women were not also included in the event. The performance and show contrasted the kinds of fashion shows and performances I attended at the Aga Khan Schools in Old Kampala, where multiracialism intentionally informed the choreography of the events, with both African and Asian children wearing and expressing themselves in South Asian and African fashion, and where young Indian girls could express an African Asian girlhood or womanhood through Ugandan and African dress, as embodied by Sugra Visram (chapter 1).

Some community leaders described initiatives that more pointedly addressed the expulsion and its fallout as well as the substantive limits of racial reconciliation. Returnee Ugandan Asians and other Indian business leaders organized the Indo-Ugandan Friendship Society (IUFS), in which some Ugandan Asian *stayees* and returnees had developed workplace trainings to build positive race relations between Indian employers and Black African employees. Returnees who had experienced their expulsion in 1972 explained that the point was to educate newly arrived Indian entrepreneurs, merchants, and migrants about "professional workplace behavior"; it was a way to indirectly discuss caste and race-based prejudices and discriminatory behavior. Here, my interviewees mentioned that Indian employers also treated their employees poorly in India—intended, perhaps, to deflect from the racialized aspects of discrimination in Uganda but also, perhaps, to indicate the persistence of prejudices (caste, class, racial, religious) in Indian society.

The IAU and IWA, led by business families, also intensified philanthropic activities through highly publicized gifts to Ugandan schools and hospitals and other charitable causes. In addition to the traditional religious-based philanthropy, business, family firm, and corporate-based philanthropy had become an essential community-based citizenship and image-building practice that facilitated Indian-diasporic presence. The IAU raised funds for and organized regular medical missions of Indian doctors and specialists to Uganda to offer free medical services to vulnerable Ugandan children, youths, and senior citizens. They hosted frequent blood donation drives; led charitable fundraising drives to build hospital wings and schools; and promoted other initiatives that circulated private wealth back into African communities. The frequency of blood drives symbolized a kind of biological kinship on the basis of sharing "Indian" blood with "Africans," despite the maintenance of community-based religious, caste, or racial endogamy.

The IAU began to shift from a singularly "Indian" or even "Indian diaspora" community identity, articulating a new "Indian Ugandan," or "Indi-Ugandan," community identity. "Indi-Ugandan" became a community-citizenship claim, advertised in national newspaper pullouts and branded at IAU events. Reminiscent of the "Ug-Indian" identity that some youth of British Asian/Ugandan Asian heritage were constructing (see chapter 3), this identity affiliation was based on the primacy of an Indian diasporic identity, supplemented by a Ugandan identity. IAU informational material was released in local Ugandan newspapers, usually on the anniversary of Indian independence, celebrating "Indi-Uganda" and emphasizing South-South cooperation between the Indian and Ugandan nation. By 2015, India's Republic Day was being celebrated alongside the anniversary of the NRM/ NRA Liberation War and the NRM's takeover of Kampala in 1986. These new Global South–based postcolonial militarized nationalisms—both Ugandan and Indian—center an Indian diaspora that embodies Indian nationalism in Uganda while participating in and celebrating Ugandan nationalism and the current government.

The IAU's business-minded leadership also asserted community-based citizenship claims on the government, state ministries, and state officials. The Indian Business Forum (IBF) was created to advance the commercial interests of NRI business leaders. In recent years, the IAU and IBF have hosted town hall meetings with key governmental bodies, including the Department of Immigration and the new National Identification and Registration Authority (NIRA) to discuss the authorization of Certificates of Residence and other issues that impact Indian expatriates, including the fact that state officials continue to increase fees on work permits and visas in an effort to maintain Africanization policies and to enforce demographic limits on Indian enterprise, especially in commercial trade. The IAU worked closely with the Indian High Commission, which facilitated Overseas Indian Citizenship (OIC) cards and provided other legal support to NRIs, long-term resident passport holders with expired visas or work visas, those who did not have Certificates of Residence, and others. The IAU also organized meetings with the Ministry of Finance, Trade and Industries and the Uganda Revenue Authority to discuss amended tax laws and regulations affecting Indian businesses. And the IAU addressed other kinds of security issues that affected Indian merchants, including conflicts with African traders. Finally, in line with the Indian government's political class and the normalization of Hindu nationalism, the IBF began to host meetings with Gujarat-based businessmen, who provided information and presentations on capital loans from the Export-Import (EXIM) Bank of India, and the rights and privileges afforded to NRIs in East Africa. In addition to raising funds for humanitarian and other kinds of disaster relief in India then, the Indian diaspora is now increasingly at the center of a "soft" transnational Hindu nationalism, in which Uganda-based Indian diasporans seek support from, and in turn support, the Bharatiya Janata Party (BJP) government, especially through the existence of a Hindu right-wing religious infrastructure in Uganda and possible financial contributions to right-wing organizations.[13]

The efforts of community-builders to curate and manage perceptions of a racializd "Indian" or "Asian" racial community contributing to the socio-economic development of the Ugandan nation is belied by the fact that many newcomers to the nation are part of a growing transnational South Asian (Indian, Pakistani, Bangladeshi, etc.) proletariat, inclusive of sojourners on the move and even involuntarily trafficked labor-migrants. Sojourners, seeking high-wage jobs, are open to multiple migration trajectories and are not so easily assimilable to the image and practice of the Indi-Uganda identity, South-South cooperation, and Afro-Asian partnership that long-term resident community-builders invested in associational life want to see succeed. While some community leaders have expressed frustrations about Uganda's "open-door" policy to so-called foreign investors that has led to the increase of sojourning and temporary migrants, others expressed more optimism about creating a healthy and prosperous Indian diaspora community and positive race relations. One research contact explained, "Look, these are not the most productive members of Indian society that come here. Many of them could not hack it back there. Many of their ethics are different; for them, it's about making a quick buck, not about forming a relationship. There isn't that sense of being responsible to a community. But . . . this is just Uganda's growing pains. We laugh and call them 'N.A.S.A.' [at other times, I heard "rocket," "parachuter," or even "astronaut"] or 'S.O.B.' [straight off the boat]. They are doing just what our forefathers did three, four generations ago. It will take time, some of them will make it, and some of them won't. Things are coming up and only going to get better."

Reform-minded community-builders, especially *stayee* and returnee Ugandan Asians, believed that modeling leadership in community and entrepreneurship through social integration was critical to cultivating positive race relations post-expulsion; they function as intermediaries between new foreign residents and state officials and majoritarian Black African publics; they did the cultural and political work of facilitating new South Asian settlement and navigated roles as community and business leaders, community social workers, and philanthropists. Even here, there was a constant and careful management of the public image of "Asianness" and the imputed perceptions of the host Black African community and public, the continual fear of a surge in populist anti-Asian sentiment and violence. Community leaders were sensitive about accusations of "Indian" racial and cultural exclusivity and the lack of social integration with Ugandans and Africans, elevating ideals and practices of cooperation, friendship, and partnership between themselves and Ugandan political and business elites, a stand-in for communities, cultures, nations.

The Limits of Community Citizenship and Racial Securitization: The Mabira Forest Land Giveaway, Anti-Asian Populist Violence, and Indigenous Citizenship Claims

My research and the themes of racial securitization and racial community endogamy I was tracing were unfolding in the context of an episode of urban anti-Asian violence that had occurred while I was still in the US and preparing for research. In April 2007, the Ugandan Asian family firm, the Mehta Group, overseen by Mahendra Mehta and supported by President Museveni and the NRM, released a cabinet paper for debate to the Ugandan Parliament. The paper announced plans to expand the existing Sugar Corporation of Uganda Ltd. (SCOUL) estate, a subsidiary of the Mehta Group, by converting and privatizing national park land, Mabira Forest, into agricultural land for sugarcane cultivation. Holding 30 percent of the shares in the firm, the president, embodying the fusion of party, government, state, and private business interests, would no doubt benefit from the land giveaway, and he intended to move forward with the land concession.[14] Environmental activists, political opposition party members, and even internal dissenters within the NRM immediately contested the proposed land giveaway in Parliament and through political protest. Eventually, public opposition to the land concession grew to include urban Ugandans of all ethnic communities as well as many Ugandan Asian returnees and Indian diasporic (NRI) community leaders.

Political opposition members from the Forum for Democratic Change (FDC), environmental activists, and NGOs organized a public demonstration against the land concession and planned to march to the Parliament to publicly hand to the speaker of Parliament a signed petition resisting the land concession. The Buganda establishment and the *Kabaka* Ronald Mutebi II supported the demonstration—in fact, he even offered alternative land to the Mehta Group, which Mehta had rejected, with the support of Museveni. Kampala police provided a route for the protest march and, working with the UPDF (Uganda People's Defence Forces), securitized and militarized the protest immediately. Nonetheless, the procession quickly turned violent, with some demonstrators attacking passersby on the street who looked visibly "Asian" or Indian. Nearby shops of Indian merchants were vandalized. A motorist of Ugandan Asian descent in a car panicked and knocked over two Ugandan children while attempting to drive through a crowd, thus inciting more anger. A man of Gujarati origin on a motorbike was pelted with stones and killed. In the meantime, UPDF fired tear gas into the crowd, and security forces killed two Ugandan protesters. In media coverage of the protest, one could see that demonstrators had prepared protest signs with anti-Asian rhetoric, including slogans such as, "1 Tree Cut = 5 Asians Killed"; "All Asians Should Go"; "All Indians Back to Bombay!"; and "Mehta, Do You Want Another Amin?"

IAU leaders responded swiftly to the growing anti-Asian violence by communicating with their members to secure Indian places of business and community temples. Indian women in the marketplace were escorted by local police to the Central Police Station where they waited until it was safe for them to travel to their homes. One community leader described a phone tree that alerted merchants and shopkeepers that the city was locked down and to stay indoors. Community leaders, the security minister, the president, representatives from the Mehta Group, and other state officials met immediately to resolve the crisis and restore calm to the city. IAU leaders took the additional step of calling on Mehta and his spokespeople directly, expressing their disapproval of his bid to expand sugar operations at the expense of Ugandan majoritarian interests, undermining the IAU's efforts to build positive race relations between Africans and Asians. They publicly disassociated themselves from the Mehta Group's actions.[15] At this time, members of the Ugandan Asian community also mobilized and published a public statement in national newspapers, condemning the actions of Mehta, the Mehta Group, and the president as well as disaffiliating themselves from Mehta's ambitions.

In an escalation of state impunity, security forces arrested political opposition leaders, environmental activists, and organizers of the protest on the charge of inciting violence, despite the fact that all the official organizers condemned anti-Asian violence once it began, and despite the president's own involvement in the Mehta Group affair. In commentaries that the president himself published in the national press, Museveni scapegoated the political opposition as manipulating the land concession for their own political purposes; he also scapegoated "imperialist" and "foreign-funded" NGOS, which, he argued, were behind the organization of the protest, defending his position by arguing that the benefits of the land giveaway outweighed environmental harms.[16] In their official and public statements, the IAU, in keeping with their carefully calibrated relationship with state officials, condemned the Mehta Group and other rogue elements among the demonstrators, including the Kampala City Traders Association (KACITA), which had tense relationships with Indian merchants, for provoking anti-Asian sentiments. In the days that followed, the president eventually met with IAU leaders, assuring them of their security and even condemning anti-Asian violence on televised broadcasts and radio.[17] In the end, the land concession did not move forward. The IAU organized funeral arrangements for the young Indian migrant who was killed, raising funds to send his body back to Ahmedabad, Gujarat, for proper cremation and last rites among his family.

For Ugandan Asians in exile in the UK and Canada, for those following the news from abroad, and for Ugandan Asian returnees in Kampala, the events of April 2007 and African sources of anti-Asian racial hostility and violence were hauntingly familiar, consistent with their traumatic experiences of racial victimization and violence during their expulsion in 1972. Some Ugandan Asians and commentators of Indian origin have focused more on the persistence of anti-Asianism in post-expulsion Uganda—the enduring legacy of, and calls for Asian expulsion, the idea that all people of South Asian origin would always be regarded as foreign and potentially disenfranchised or subject to violence in the nation. For others, the event brought the so-called Asian minority question to the forefront of public debate again, eliciting more nuanced analysis of the internal complexities within the perceived monolithic "Indian" or "Asian" community and the substantive basis of their precarious citizenship, including the relationships of patronage and protection secured by the current government and business-oriented elites.[18] For urban Ugandans in general, the Mehta Group's collusion with the NRM only made more visible presidential and state-based violence, illiberalism, impunity, and repression; the "patronage state"; and the NRM's relationship to especially Ugandan Asian–owned capital.

The aftermath of the Mabira Forest land giveaway controversy revealed both the ways in which Ugandan Asians and the new Indian diaspora depended upon nonliberal practices of racial community securitization through the nurturing of relationships of security and protection with state officials; it illustrated as well the limits of such practices in protecting vulnerable members of the community from anti-Asian violence. In fact, these strategies made the "Asian community" complicit with the presidential ruling party's and the state and military's structural and physical violence against urban Ugandans—recall that two Ugandan demonstrators were also killed by security forces during the protest. Some of my Ugandan research contacts pointed out to me that the death of the NRI Indian trader seemed to be a larger public concern than the deaths of Ugandans, revealing the racial privileges and the substantive citizenship entitlements of the Asian racial minority in urban Uganda. Beyond the signs and symbols of South-South cooperation, the Mehta Group and Mabira Forest row revealed that post-expulsion racial reconciliation was a state- and elite-led project, more performative and symbolic than material and substantive.

Tellingly, the attempted land concession reinforced Ugandan Asian *stayees'*, returnees', and the new Indian diaspora's sense of racial precarity and political insecurity in the nation. In late 2007, a small section of the community was articulating a new legal-juridical citizenship claim, arguing for the inclusion of "Asians" within Schedule 3 of the 1995 Constitution of the Republic of Uganda, or recognizing "Asians" as indigenous and granting them "tribal recognition" through the category of *Bayindi* (Indian or Asian, in Luganda). Beyond the mobilization of the outmoded terminology of "tribe," claims to tribal, or "ethnic," recognition for racialized "Asians" or "Indians" could designate all people of South Asian descent as an ethnic collectivity with respect to existing indigenous groups such as the Ganda and Banyankole. In a town-hall meeting after the Mabira Forest violence fallout, community leaders addressed President Museveni and asked that they be recognized as an "official tribe" of Uganda, on par with their "Ugandan brothers and sisters." As an IAU leader explained to me, "We don't want any political favors . . . but if [the government] recognized us as a tribe . . . at least we will feel we are welcome, we will feel part of this country, more so than we do at the moment." He discussed the importance of disidentifying from the capitalist interests of the likes of Mehta and others, critiquing the NRM's crony capitalism and the quid-pro-quo and patronage relations between businessmen and state officials. While he recognized that relationships and advocacy with state officials were necessary to successful entrepreneurship, he stressed the importance of identifying with majoritarian Ugandan political interests, citing his own knowledge of environmental laws and regulations in India, and the fact that comparable laws in Uganda were being flouted by the president and Mehta. He also discussed the importance of social contributions to entrepreneurship and philanthropy as central to maintaining positive race relations between Asians and Africans. Here, there was a sense of the careful management of relationships with the president and the NRM, as well as the conflicts between the NRM, political opposition groups, and the growing anti-NRM sentiments of urban Ugandans. As he explained it, the claim to tribal recognition and legal-juridical citizenship was about attaining a sense of substantive political and racial belonging through categories of ethnicity and indigeneity, independent from the ruling party. If the Ugandan constitution had excluded South Asians from the nation on the basis of their race, could South Asians be included if they framed themselves as one of many "tribes" in the nation?

Later on, when I was affiliated with Makerere University in 2014, debates surrounding Schedule Three and the possibility of tribal recognition for all people of South Asian descent resurfaced among a small section of Kampala-based Ugandan Asian returnee and Indian business elites (they have also continued up to the publication of this book).[19] Kenyan Asian community and business leaders had recently been successfully recognized as an Indian "tribe" (*Wahindi*) in the Kenyan constitution, a novel strategy for attaining formal and substantive political inclusion. While many Kenyan Asians (both in Kenya and the diaspora) celebrated the move, others critiqued the Kenyatta government for exacerbating tribalism and ethnic and racial politics in the nation, while other Kenyan Asian critics suggested—with more than a touch of cynicism—that those who sought tribal recognition were primarily the business-oriented capitalist class of Kenyan Asians, those with close ties to the Kenyatta governments, who no doubt would acquire land and property to expand their business, and therefore state-based interests.[20] Back in Uganda, communities were divided over the idea—while some welcomed the possibility of formal inclusion in the nation, others ridiculed the idea of tribal recognition, arguing that South Asian–descendant communities are clearly immigrant communities and not indigenous to Africa; they maintained that this strategy would minimize the lived experiences of actual indigenous communities, which were also racialized as Black. The move would be seen as opportunistic and strategic, and as a way to expand settler ambitions through access to land ownership. Instead, Ugandan scholars like Mahmood Mamdani and Joseph Oloka-Onyango (see more below) argued that the best way forward was to continue to advocate for liberal constitutional reforms that created possibilities for the naturalization of those non-nationals who wanted to become Ugandan citizens (but without an assessment of how legal-juridical citizenship would map onto substantive belonging and racial and political security). In contrast to the president, many Ugandan government officials were hesitant to expand the domain of legal-juridical citizenship on a nonracial basis, given their concerns over both Ugandan Asian and Indian diasporic capitalist ambitions—including their ability to access entitlements such as land rights—noting that Asians could become citizens through existing jus sanguinis and jus solis definitions of citizenship, or even via intermarriage with Ugandans. In the end, the campaign for tribal recognition revealed the conundrums of a growing noncitizen South Asian population with varying degrees of economic and political power and contradictory forms of racial privilege and racial precarity—again, they had much more of a political presence than they might initially appear to have had as mere "economic citizens" essential to Ugandan nation and state-building.

While some Ugandan Asians and Indian diasporic community leaders were surprised by the resurgence and degree of anti-Asian hostilities and violence during the Mabira Forest row, I was less so. In my archival research I was continuing to trace populist urban Ugandan sentiments toward Idi Amin and the 1972 Asian expulsion. An earlier opportunity for Ugandans (across ethnic affiliations) to reflect upon the legacy of Idi Amin and expulsion had revealed itself in August 2003, when Amin died in exile in Jeddah, Saudi Arabia. Although he had fled Uganda in 1979, many of his descendants continued to navigate his legacy in the nation and had reflected more publicly upon his life in recent years (see more below). Upon his death, there was political controversy over whether his body should be allowed to be returned home for burial. Since the NRM leadership positioned itself as the singular and exceptional liberating force that brought political freedoms and economic development to the nation, it strategically participated in the Western liberal imaginary of Idi Amin as exceptionally illiberal, further constructing him as an enemy of the Ugandan nation and its people. Asserting his authority, Museveni ultimately decided that Amin's body would be returned to his family (who resided in Alur district in northern Uganda) for a village burial but that no formal and public state burial in his memory would be held.[21]

In the end, Amin's body was never returned to Uganda, and he was buried in exile in Saudi Arabia by family members. In my reading of press coverage during this era, I found that some commentators recalled Amin's more complicated legacy—as both a brutal dictator and also "a remarkable man."[22] For several weeks, op-eds in local newspapers discussed Amin's political and personal life, parsing fact from fiction, reproducing mythologies, discussing his foreign policy innovations and savvy negotiations with Western political leaders, and even reviewing popular media representations of him. It was clear to me: there was a reverence for the man-turned–military dictator, viewed as charismatic, personable, even fun-loving—in short, a national leader who could speak to and understand the struggles and challenges of everyday Ugandans. Some commentaries did fault Amin for the terror and violence he unleashed upon fellow Ugandans throughout the 1970s. Some were adamant that his body should not be allowed to return to Uganda, for he had killed many people, including members of their own families. But others suggested that his body be allowed to return for "the good things he did," including the expulsion of Asians and "the creation of business opportunities for Africans."[23] One commentator argued succinctly: "He was a good leader in his own right. He helped us move from the villages to the city. He motivated us to value work . . . people say he was a tyrant, but who is not a tyrant? People say that he was not educated, but what have educated leaders done for us?"[24]

Christopher Sembuya, a Kampala-based industrialist who had also benefited from the entrepreneurship opportunities made possible to Africans after the expulsion, published *The Other Side of Amin Dada* (2009). Finding the book in Kampala bookshops and sold by vendors in street corners, I purchased and read a copy. I later met Sembuya at his home, where he talked over his key points with me, specifically his problems with the NRM and its open-door policies to foreign investment that were leaving Black-identifying Ugandans behind. In his book, Sembuya examines the positive legacies of Amin's Economic War, focusing on the opportunities that Amin created for Ugandans like himself to enter commerce and, eventually, manufacturing and industry. In his analysis, he argues, "The declaration of the economic war was never to challenge or create racial divisions but rather to elevate the Ugandans." He further argues that his is not a "political book" meant to defend Amin's reign; instead, his work is meant to suggest that Amin's contribution was to be always "pro-Uganda" and "pro-Ugandans" ("Ugandans" defined as Black and African). (Throughout, Sembuya retains the common post-expulsion racial distinctions and categories of "Ugandan" and "Asian" in his text.) Overall, Sembuya selectively highlights the economic rather than the racially nativist aspects of Amin's version of Ugandan nationalism and Pan-Africanism. Using key historical examples, he describes Amin's freeing of Ganda political prisoners from Obote's UPC government prisons;

the return of *Kabaka* Sir Edward Muteesa II's body for a state funeral in Uganda in 1971; his support of Ugandans' entry into international competitive sports; and even his athleticism and participation in motor sports and the East African Safari Rally, which had been dominated by Europeans and Asians. He investigates Amin's hosting of the Organization of African Unity in Kampala in 1975, his promotion of Pan-Islamism and Uganda's membership in the Organization of Islamic Conference (OIC) in 1974, and the creation of state-owned and nationalist institutions such as the Uganda Airlines Cooperation and Uganda Railways Corporation, among other topics. In our conversation, Sembuya stressed that the book was not meant to stir up racial tensions between "Ugandans" and "Asians" but that he was offering a more balanced discussion of the legacies of Amin and the 1972 Asian expulsion. Based as he was in Kampala, Sembuya's book was unsettling the discourses and ideologies of expulsion exceptionalism that had invisibilized the experiences of Ugandans subject to European and Asian colonial and racial oppressions. His contemporary recasting and memorialization of Amin—always premised upon both remembering and forgetting—was now situated in relation to the growing political opposition and urban popular protest against Museveni, the NRM, and the tightening nexus of the state, Asian capital, and securitized and militarized governance.

On my way home that evening, I mused over the term *Aminism*, which I often heard as my research progressed. Referring to anti-Asianism, some of my Ugandan research contacts, typically educated and middle-class, had deployed Aminism negatively, as something that circulated among uneducated and poorer Ugandans. This view now struck me as paternalistic. Sembuya's book was articulating an empowering sense of Aminism, one that might offer agency, dignity, and pride to Black-identifying Ugandans who had been left behind by the structural violence of the global economy and by anti-Black African racism as well as by those who had been left behind by their political leadership, even as the book displaced the illiberal and racialist aspects of his governance. In the years since my conversation with Sembuya, many other Ugandan voices, like that of Idi Amin's son Jaffar Amin, have further unpacked Amin's legacy, as in his 2010 published account, *Idi Amin: Hero or Villain?*[25] Likewise in 2010, expelled Ugandan Asian Manzhoor Moghal published his own personal account of Amin, *Idi Amin: Lion of Africa*.[26] The fact that expelled Ugandan Asians themselves were complicating Idi Amin and his legacy is especially important, as they serve as a counterbalance to the discourses, ideologies, and representations of expulsion exceptionalism that are typically produced by exiled Ugandan Asians. They join a growing number of established scholarly works and public exhibitions on Idi Amin, that, following the late Ali Al'amin Mazrui, disrupt the global distortions and illiberal exceptionalism that surround the figure of Amin, while still holding his political governance to account.

Disavowing Indian-Uganda, Claiming Uganda: The Asian African Association and the Articulation of an Afro-Asian Identity

Circling back to the fraught tensions at the community forum with which I began this chapter, the political advocacy work of Mahmood Mamdani and other Ugandan Asians in the aftermath of the Mabira Forest crisis led to the formal creation of the Asian African Association (AAA) in Kampala in 2013, which I joined and whose meetings and activities I helped coordinate until 2015. Members included self-described "Ugandans of Asian origin," expatriate descendants of returnees, and other people of South Asian origin who were long-term residents and "committed to making futures in Uganda." In contrast to the primacy of the Indian nation in the IAU's conception of "Indi-Ugandan" identity, the category "Asian African"—Asians of African origin and the focus on being Ugandan of Asian origin—marked a more formal institutionalization of Afro-Asian subjectivities and identities, community, and citizenship. The growing presence of the Indian diaspora in Uganda and its close links to the Indian nation was in tension with the primary focus of Ugandan Asians who had returned after their expulsion and lived in Kampala on permanent or semi-permanent basis, and who were concerned with social and national integration with Africans and Ugandans. In general, the advent of the AAA paralleled similar initiatives by Kenyan Asians who were more strongly articulating Asian African modes of political, cultural, and racial belonging. The AAA's statement of purpose, authored by Mamdani, noted that the distinction between being a "South Asian who happens to live in Africa" as opposed to "Africans of South Asian origin" mattered, and that "Asian Africans" were not "permanent visitors"—that this was a ticket to "permanent insecurity" and "permanent irresponsibility."[27] As the main architect of AAA, Mamdani himself had long asserted a Ugandan of Asian origin identity and participated in Ugandan political commentary in print newspapers and in transformative intellectual initiatives at Makerere University. In this sense, the AAA was distinctive from the IAU and other South Asian community organizations because it elevated its membership as "Asian of African origin," incorporating lessons learned from the 1972 Asian expulsion. Here, the membership had few generational ties to India or South Asia and felt a sense of alienation from the post-1990s Indian diaspora presence in East Africa. Although there was some overlap between members who participated in both the AAA and IAU, and a few were more recent Indian entrepreneurs (NRIs), there was little space for a secondary Indian diasporic or South Asian identity affiliation in addition to the primacy of Asian African identity.

At our meetings, we discussed the weaknesses of the historical Ugandan Asian community (see chapter 1) that had made them vulnerable to expulsion. In addition, the AAA leadership constructed the organization as an independent body, free from government influence, such that members could take overt political positions and participate in political advocacy when required, as in the Mehta Group/Mabira Forest conflict. This was a critique of post-1990s Indian diaspora associational life that had become dependent upon institutionalized community-citizenship claims and upon relations of patronage, security, and protection with the NRM and state officials. In addition, the AAA leadership maintained that while philanthropy was important for demonstrating national and social commitment and recirculating wealth back into African communities, it did not reduce the social distance between Black-identifying Africans and South Asian heritage communities but instead sustained and fortified paternalistic and hierarchical relationalities.

Together, we established committees that developed educational, social, and cultural activities geared toward social integration and fostering harmonious race relations. Here, the work of the AAA paralleled that of Kenyan Asians who sought to remedy their marginalization from Kenyan Asian history, especially their contributions to anticolonial histories, including "published accounts of ordinary Asian families' migration and settlement histories, biographies of Kenyan Asian political figures, magazines such as *Awaaz*, and public exhibitions"[28] that recentered Kenyan Asians in dominant Kenyan national history. Likewise, the AAA promoted a culture of intellectual inquiry, disseminating Ugandan Asian histories and confronting contemporary challenges with planned educational forums and exhibitions of Ugandan Asian material culture and heritage.

My work with the AAA was significant because I helped to create bridges between the generation that had experienced expulsion and subsequently returned, the descendants of exiled Ugandan Asians who had grown up as transnationals and expatriates and then returned and who now lived permanently in the city, and other youths or children of post-expulsion and post-

1990s Indian migrants who had been born and brought up in Uganda, many of whom attended integrated schools, and some of whom spoke African and South Asian languages. My work with the youth committee brought together youths of different migration and diasporic histories, class statuses, and ethnic, religious, and caste backgrounds, all of whom shared commitments to nurturing an Asian African identity and were concerned about race relations as the Indian and other South Asian diaspora communities grew. This new generation of youths was more open to nurturing a secondary, South Asian or Indian diasporic identity in addition to a Ugandan Asian or Asian African one, and they were also shaped by a global South Asian diasporic consciousness, including affinities and connections to particular ethnic and religious communities and global popular culture that reflected both African diasporic and South Asian diasporic encounters. While the AAA youth group had many successes in organizing racially integrated events—sports and recreation, and even a multiracial comedy show with a well-known Ugandan comedian to unpack racial tensions and racial stereotypes—there were also clear challenges. Many AAA youth members remarked that they would not normally have socialized with each other because of the existing class-based, communal, and gendered divisions that kept them separated, and that maintaining leadership with political and intellectual analysis and sustainability would be obstacles in the future.

In accordance with its educational mission, the most significant contributions of the AAA were the public forums organized and moderated by Mamdani. The first forum on the 1972 Asian expulsion, discussed at the opening of the chapter, was an important step in disrupting political repressions and internal community silences, centering upon returnees' experiences of expulsion, return, and ongoing challenges, revealing tensions between old and new communities of South Asian heritage in urban Uganda. The second forum was publicly advertised in local newspapers, televised, and geared toward a multiracial crowd. Those of us affiliated with Makerere University—myself and Professors Mamdani, Sylvia Tamale, and Joseph Oloka-Onyango—argued that that the so-called Asian community was not necessarily safe from a future expulsion, particularly if community leaders and elites persisted in investing in the ruling party and government and patronage as a mode of securing racial and political protection. We made concrete recommendations, including divesting from state-based protection and racial community and communal parochialisms, and investing instead in models of racial and social integration and reforming existing business practices. Professor Oloka-Onyango reoriented the discussion back to the

NRM and its complicity in fomenting racial tensions through the continued mismanagement of the DAPCB (Departed Asians' Property Custodial Board), now located in the Ministry of Finance, which continues to maintain Asian property in its possession and has prevented the shutting down of the department (symbolizing a resolution of 1972) and the movement toward racial reconciliation. Aside from our short presentations, audience members made comments from the floor, ranging from the familiar terrain of returnees discussing their ninety-day experience of expulsion to the airing-out of racial grievances and expressions of racial stereotypes to other insightful suggestions for moving toward racial reconciliation and social integration using the experiences (both the possibilities and limitations) of nonracialism in postapartheid South Africa and of multiracialism and socialism in Tanzania as examples. Some commentators spoke of other key events of political violence in Ugandan postcolonial history for which there has been no sense of resolution or justice, deparochializing the violence of the expulsion and using it to open up into other unresolved histories of violence impacting other Ugandan ethnic communities.

The AAA forums were beginning to dissipate the repressive political culture of silence surrounding expulsion and the limits of property repossession as a mode of reconciliation, and despite the fears expressed by some community members about feeling vulnerable and exposed, about potentially becoming targets of anti-Asian violence once again, and about dealing with their own traumatic wounds of the past. But the forums also disrupted normative scripts of expulsion exceptionalism and created spaces for Ugandans of Asian and Black African descent and newcomers to reflect on the past together. The pedagogical practices of Ugandan intellectuals continue to be significant—Mamdani, for example, consistently writes op-eds in national newspapers that reflect on Asian presence. He asserts a Ugandan and African identity that now mostly resides in exile and that is now outnumbered in Uganda by the new Indian diasporic presence. But most Ugandan Asian exiles and their descendants are not present in Kampala. Here was also a deep loss—the missing voices of other African and Asian intellectuals, artists, and cultural workers who might also establish other models for being "Asian African" in post-expulsion Uganda.

In contrast to universalized Western liberal expectations that the arrival of nationhood, capitalist modernity, and modern political institutions in postcolonial societies would lead to the demise of collectivities on the basis of racial, ethnic, religious, sectarian, and caste-based norms, postcolonial Uganda continues to be characterized by the making of racial, cultural, and ethnic difference; of populist desires to purify the nation of racial and cultural Others; of persistent everyday racialized tensions and resurging events of racial violence. My research traces continuities between the racialized dynamics of capitalist accumulation, or the "Asian" nature of racial-caste capitalism, as well as between the enduring logics of state-based racial and native rule, or heteropatriarchal racially nativist governance, and internal racial community governance, or heteropatriarchal racially nativist communal governance. After the expulsion, postliberal domains of citizenship-making and citizenship claims involve institutionalized community-based citizenship claims on the state on the basis of relations of patronage, protection, and racial security; articulations of an "Indi-Uganda" identity; intensifying public image-building practices revolving around philanthropy and even claims to indigeneity or tribal citizenship to expand the legal-juridical terrain of racial, political, and substantive inclusion. In addition, new, more autonomous community organizations like the AAA claim an "Asian African" identity and expand the domain of racial and political citizenship for "Asians of African origin" through urban-based pedagogical narratives that place Ugandan Asians, their expulsion, and lessons learned within nationalist discourse. Here, I am not suggesting that there are no investments in ideals of liberal, legal-juridical citizenship, and direct political participation in formal politics; instead, I suggest that the dominant nonliberal terrains of citizenship practices as well as the claims to tribal recognition that I map in this chapter reveal the normalization of racial nonreconciliation after the 1972 Asian expulsion, despite the promise of socioeconomic national development and Global South–based elite visions of South-South cooperation and Afro-Asianism in urban Uganda. Community identifications with the race and class-based oppressions and with the political and economic oppressions that most urban Ugandans experience might offer political and racial security for all.

Of Gendered Insecurities

Contingent and Ambivalent Feminist Afro–South Asian
Intimacies and Solidarities

In contemporary urban Uganda, the representational figure of the Asian
or Indian woman is foundational to nationalist and majoritarian African
constructions of the racialized and minoritized "Asian" or "Indian" community. The Asian community is often constructed through the gendered
racial formation of the Asian or Indian merchant-figure or entrepreneurial
businessman. Moreover, since the colonial era, trans–Indian Ocean patriarchal kinship and marriage networks have been central to the migration and
mobility of South Asian women to East Africa. As discussed in chapter 1,
Asian women negotiated the colonial and postcolonial state, community,
and family patriarchies even as they remained central to the material and
social reproduction of the Asian or Indian family; they both preserved and
defined the religious, sectarian, and caste-based boundaries of the family
and community and were central to defining the racialized boundaries of
Indian or "Asian" racial community in relation to urban Black African
majoritarian communities. In the decolonization era, both African and
Asian women played critical roles in anticolonial nationalism, even as they
came into tension with the patriarchal nature of nationalisms. Ultimately,
the figure of the Asian woman, or the patriarchal representations of the figure of the Asian woman, became essential to debates on Africanization, the
social and political integration of Asians in the new Ugandan nation, and
the possibilities and limitations of multiracialism. An especially pernicious

component of President Idi Amin's racially nativist nationalism and anti-Asian populist discourse was his observation that Asians refused to socially integrate with Africans and maintained social distance, as evidenced by the lack of interracial marriages between Africans and Asians, and especially between Asian women and African men.[1] If the lead-up to the 1972 Asian expulsion was characterized by Ugandan Asians' racialized political insecurities, these insecurities were also deeply informed by gendered and sexual anxieties about the status of Asian women in the nation. Idi Amin's vision of national belonging relied upon the normalization of interracial intimacies or, more specifically, on a heteropatriarchal and heterosexual racially exogamous citizenship based on affinal kinship ties—marriage alliances—between African men and Asian women. Throughout my research, I found that traditionally hypogamous interracial marriage alliances (especially between Asian men and African women) continued to be an important practice and even public performance of national citizenship and a key strategy to attain legal-juridical and substantive citizenship employed by Ugandan Asians and post-1990s South Asian noncitizens who had settled in the nation. The issue of interracial intimacies and interracial marriage alliances between African men and Asian women continued to be sensitive and a taboo subject, a lingering component of expulsion-era anti-Asian populist discourse.[2]

I was able to access these more subtle racialized gendered and sexual domains of the insecurities of expulsion by building on the research I had conducted while working with Kampala-based internationally funded NGOs on gender violence in Ugandan Asian and South Asian communities in 2003–4; my work included attending to the varying experiences and vulnerabilities of Ugandan Asian returnees and Indian diasporic migrant women who had arrived via transnational marriage networks from the late 1990s onward.[3] In this chapter, I map Ugandan Asian women's displacement via their expulsion and their return settlement experiences, showcasing complexity in Ugandan Asian women's religious, sectarian, caste, and class status and their experiences; these women have been followed by more recent migration streams of vulnerable noncitizen Indian diasporic women who are negotiating the structures of the postcolonial state-based heteropatriarchal nativist and communal forms of governance I traced in the previous chapter. I focus on several prominent and publicized cases of gender-based violence in the Ugandan national press, examining women's interlocking experiences of domestic, communal, state-based, and transnational patriarchies and their encounters with Ugandan women and feminist activists and other nonstate actors such as NGOs and community-based organizations (CBOs) that have offered them significant sources of safety and welfare, revealing the signifi-cance of transnational global gender governance on women's everyday lives.

For the first time since 1972, publicized cases in the national press are bringing African majoritarian attention to a growing and increasingly vis-ible South Asian presence in the nation, and they are resuscitating old and shaping new discourses surrounding "Asian" or "Indian" womanhood, "Asian" or "Indian" culture, and even discourses about interracial intima-cies, intermarriage, and citizenship. Ugandan Asian and Indian diasporic women's negotiations of patriarchal formations are also engendering novel interracial Afro–South Asian feminist practices, strategies, and tactics in the context of heightening militarized state repression, securitization, neolib-eral authoritarianism, and heteropatriarchal state violence targeting Ugan-dan feminist and women's activists, gender-queer, and queer-identifying urban Ugandans. In contrast to the rhetoric and performances of an elite cosmopolitan-based South-South cooperation and the persistence of racial and class divides and inequalities in urban Uganda, the urban and communal worlds of Ugandan Asian and Indian migrant women became an unexpected site for examining interracial encounters and the possibili-ties and limitations of cross-racial feminist solidarities. Finally, I note that by focusing on high-profile cases of gender-based violence that affected Asian women, my aim is not to exceptionalize them or to minimize Black-identifying African women's experiences of multiple heteropatriarchies or gender-based violence; rather, the cases I explore reveal the gendered and sexualized dimensions of the insecurities of expulsion and the possibilities and limitations of interracial Afro-Asian universalisms, amid the contradic-tions and tensions of geopolitical Ugandan-Indian diplomatic and economic cooperation and the fallout of the 1972 expulsion.

Gendering Racial Community: Migrations, Displacements, Return Migrations, and New South-South Migrations

In chapter 1, I introduced a discussion of trans-Indian Oceanic and trans-national migration, marriage, and kinship. In fact, the arrival of Indian women from British India to East Africa and the Uganda Protectorate in the colonial era contributed to the embourgeoisement of overseas Indian com-munities and reinforced communal, or religious, sectarian, and caste bound-aries. The patriarchal safeguarding of the sexual purity and *izzat* of women of the endogamous community shored up both moral and racial distinctions between "Asians" and "Africans," or racial Asianness and Blackness.[4] Richa

Nagar argues that the intersection of Victorian-era European racism, patriarchies, and gender ideologies, applied to colonized subjects (both Asian and African) and to various religious, ethnic, and caste communities internal to Asian and African racial groups, supplemented by existing South Asian traditions of caste endogamy and Brahmanical patriarchy, helped to normalize gendered racial formations that constructed Indian women in East Africa as either the embodiment of purity and virtue or as excessively religious and orthodox. By contrast, European racial discourses and South Asian subcontinental racial and caste discourses (in line with sexual ideologies ascribed to low-caste, Dalit, or even *adivasi* women) perceived racialized Black African women as transgressive and immoral, or even "as the oversexualized 'Other' who was readily available to quench the [sexual desires] of Asian men."[5] Given Asian men's cross-racial intimacies with urban African women—from marriage alliances to concubinage and long-term intimate companion relationships to access to African women in the urban sex work economy—patriarchal community elites and Asian women who were confined to domestic spaces often considered African women as real and symbolic moral threats to the integrity and religious and caste-based purity of the Indian patrilocal marriage, family, and racial community. These same ideologies buttressed the imputed superior racial and moral purity and prestige of the middle-class Indian woman in the colonial and, later, postcolonial era.

As Felicity Hand writes, "The ideology governing gender relations continued to be based on the necessity to control and safeguard women's sexual purity and men's honor and social status being heavily dependent on it. This translated into an excessive enclosure of the various Asian groups within their own communities for fear that their daughters and wives would be led astray by African men."[6] African men were themselves constructed through gendered racial formations and related ideologies, according to which Asian men inhabited a moral, if emasculated, heterosexuality as compared with Black-identifying African men, who were constructed through European and South Asian racial ideas as hypermasculine and hypersexual. In short, the South Asian racial meanings ascribed to Blackness and Africanness were connected to ideas of gendered and sexual immorality and impurity, as alien and outside of the racially endogamous Indian family, home, and community. According to the prevailing racial, gendered, and sexual logics, further heightened by racial and native rule and the labor-capital relations shaped by racial-caste capitalism, Asian men who had marriage alliances with African women and multiracial (referred to as "half-caste") children were typically relegated to the margins of their respective Asian communities.

Drawing on African and Indian postcolonial scholarship and studies of the gendered nature of racial and native rule and anticolonial nationalism,[7] we can conclude that Indian or Asian men in postcolonial Uganda came to be associated with "the outer face" of the racially defined "Asian" or "Indian" community, serving as intermediaries between the state, the masculinist nature of civil society, and the communal (religious, sectarian, and caste-based) and domestic spheres of urban life. Indian women came to be associated with the domestic sphere of the Indian family and home and constituted the substantive "inside" of communal and domestic life. They symbolized, drawing on Partha Chatterjee, the "spiritual inner essence,"[8] of the overseas Indian community, as opposed to their more Westernized and Europeanized male counterparts. Indian women were usually also understood as the preservers and reproducers of syndicated and essentialized ideas of Indian culture, religion, and community.

Nonetheless, women also asserted agency as they negotiated heteropatriarchal racially nativist communal governance (see also chapter 5), both reproducing and challenging the racial and patriarchal structures they encountered. Indian women were thus structurally, materially, and symbolically distanced from Africans, and especially from Black African men. I underscore the nested and interlocking domains of racialized, communal (religious-, sectarian-, and caste-based), and gendered oppressions that Indian women navigated (and likewise, the nested heteropatriarchal racial and customary oppressions that their [female] African counterparts negotiated). While there was class diversity internal to the racial Indian community, for the middle-class urban Indian woman, her interactions with African men and women were circumscribed and typically hierarchical—such as in the master–domestic servant relationship, for example. For many Africans, who also participated in European and Orientalist racial myths and ideologies surrounding South Asians, the figure of the Indian or Asian woman was thus one of excessive closure, representative of Indian alterity, exoticism, and cultural difference, or even a figure of curiosity and mystique.[9]

At independence in 1962, however, Ugandan Asian women were also beginning to imagine themselves as individual citizen-subjects on equal terms with African subjects in the nation, and some women invested in a multiracial future in Uganda, participating in a growing public sphere of elite and multiracial women's associations and gender-based organizing geared toward the liberal reform of the highly patriarchal customary laws that governed everyday women's lives (see also chapter 1).[10] Even as more privileged and educated women were experimenting with individualized liberal and juridically recognized rights, namely, in the promulgation of the Ugandan constitution, women continued to navigate both state-based or civil and customary governance. Moving outside of the domestic realm to join politics, voluntary associations or other vocations, Ugandan Asian women continued to negotiate patriarchal demands, including gendered and sexual ideologies and norms of *izzat* as applied to Asian women. Modern womanhood continued to be based on the politics of honor and respectability, emphasizing the importance of women's virtue across African and Asian communities; of maintaining proper heterosexual and reproductive roles as wife and mother; of the upkeep of the domestic home in addition to and despite new interracial (and for Asian women, potentially immoral) encounters with the public sphere and broader society; and of investment in the overall civilizational progress and uplift of the racial community, all in the service of modern nation-building, development, Africanization, and multiracialism.[11]

Idi Amin's racially nativist and nationalist anti-Asian discourse was constructed via a gendered and heteropatriarchal discourse surrounding Asian women and the presumed sexual inaccessibility of Indian women to African men. Here, the idea of (African male–Asian women hypergamous) interracial marriage alliances as a means of social and racial integration for Asians reached its height prior to the expulsion, in addition to other accusations and forms of ideological propaganda deployed against the Asian community. Ugandan Asian community leaders—all men—prepared responses to Amin's accusations and participated in tense exchanges with Amin about social integration and interracial marriage in their presentations at the 1971 Asian Conference and in a series of op-eds published in national newspapers prior to the expulsion announcement.[12] In general, however, it was both African and Indian men who discussed and debated the status of "the Asian/Indian women" and female sexual honor in a male-led public sphere, without the participation of Asian women.[13] Notably, in the persistent urban discourses about interracial marriage, racial endogamy is typically explained away through naturalized community and caste-based endogamies, and as a mode of preserving religious, sectarian, and caste-based "Indian"/"Asian" culture, even as Africans view it as racial (and not necessarily religious, sectarian, or caste-based) endogamy and the lack of interracial marriages as an upholding of racial distinctions and boundaries.

6.1   Uganda Council of Women Congress, August 21, 1961. Image quality related to photo film damage in archives. Courtesy of the Uganda Broadcasting Corporation, Kampala.

In the aftermath of the expulsion, and the typical harassment and violence that Asian women experienced as they fled the nation with their children and families (see chapter 1), the few women who remained or who returned during the Amin years were under the tight patriarchal protection and control of their male kin. But my research also corroborated the findings of Akbar Keshodkar, who researched the experiences of Asian and Arab women who managed to stay on after the 1964 Zanzibar Revolution and the expulsion of their communities.[14] After 1972, it was mainly mixed-racial heritage Afro-Asian women like Rani (chapter 2) who managed to stay on, with the majority of Asian women displaced abroad as refugees or as dependent, or estranged, partners of their husbands' national citizenship status, with other Asian and mixed racial heritage women resettled with kinfolk elsewhere in East Africa as the political situation worsened for Ugandan Asians. Many of the women who stayed on delayed marriages or remained unmarried, as they were unable to find suitable intra-racial community marriage partners—marrying hypogamously for women, which would mean marrying African men, would be a violation of community-based rules of racial, religious, and caste purity, while remaining unmarried allowed women to retain their *izzat* and status in the community, especially as racial hierarchies shifted in the Amin era. By contrast, it was the Ugandan Asian men who stayed on who typically engaged in hypogamous, or interracial, interreligious marriages, as in the many Punjabi Sikh and Afro-Asian men who, from my data, married Black African, Afro-Asian and even Arab Muslim women from the Swahili Coast after 1972.

In the aftermath of civil war and the accession of the National Resistance Movement (NRM), Ugandan women (Black-identifying Africans) became central to the national reconstruction process, gaining employment in public service and government positions, earning a presence in entrepreneurship and in the marketplace, and constituting a growing urban workforce. Some Ugandan Asian women, like Nusrat (chapter 3), returned with their male kin during the property repossession and repatriation process of the late 1980s and early 1990s. Many Ugandan Asian women who returned had joined the workforce in Western liberal nation-states in the intervening years since their expulsion. They developed more independent lives and careers, in addition to the traditional roles of motherhood and managing households. They now put these skills and experiences to practical use as they joined family firms and other small businesses, navigating transnational mobilities and residences, and domestic and workplace obligations. As my research unfolded, Ugandan Asian women returnees and their descendants (including female British and Canadian South Asians of Ugandan heritage) were just beginning to interface with the new post-1990s Indian diaspora in Kampala, including Indian migrant women and their children, across different religious, sectarian, caste, and class backgrounds. Post-1990s Indian diasporic and migrant women are the legal or undocumented dependents of the noncitizen professional class of businessmen and entrepreneurs, merchants, and even sojourning migrant laborers. Many were young wives and mothers, raising a new generation of children in Kampala. Upwardly mobile housewives were active in community organizations. Some migrant women traded goods informally or offered cosmetic services, while young women educated in Kampala joined the workforce, primarily performing secretarial and accounting work in Indian firms and small businesses (which

6.2   An exceptional marriage? After the expulsion, Amin attended the marriage celebration of a Ugandan military official and his Indian bride in Gulu in June 1977, with the Indian and Pakistani ambassadors in attendance. From Adam Seftel, comp., *Uganda: The Rise and Fall of Idi Amin: From the Pages of Drum* (Lanseria: Bailey's African Photo Archives, 1994).

was considered to be work that maintained unmarried women's respectability). Women in this latter group, whom I met at various community events and functions, were very anxious about how to shape their futures in Uganda and East Africa.

Young South Asian (Khoja Ismaili, Punjabi Sikh and Hindu, Gujarati Hindu, Sunni Muslim) women born in Museveni's Uganda to working-class families were brought up attending racially integrated secondary schools and were all struggling with interlocking domains of family/domestic, communal (religious), societal, and state-based patriarchies and patriarchal gendered expectations during a time of tremendous change in urban Uganda, with post-1972 racialized anxieties expressed through highly moralized gendered and sexual domains.

Zubeda, an Ismaili Muslim woman and longtime resident of Kampala, shared with me her recollection of Ugandan Asian women's return migration and the arrival of more Indian migrant women during the early years of the NRM. She herself was born in India but had settled in Kampala in 1986 after her marriage to a Ugandan Asian (Ismaili) returnee who had successfully repossessed his property in the early 1990s. Over a meal at the food court at Garden City, a popular mall frequented by many expatriates and migrants in Kampala, she described the gradual communal reconstruction of the Ismaili Khoja Shia Muslim community, focusing on women's experiences.

In 1991 we officially opened our mosque . . . the *jamatkhana* was repossessed. So that is when our numbers increased. In 1994, we were very few. We were six women, and probably thirty men. We were married to Ugandan Asians. Okay, let me say three of us were married to Ugandan Asians, and three of them were returnees, after the exodus . . . and then we used to get together, so we had that part of our social life. We also mingled with other communities . . . like the Sikh community, the Hindus, and the other Muslims. We were close to each other. We knew, actually at the time, most of us knew what was going on in another woman's life. Because we were very few, we were isolated, and the situation was so bad . . . so you had to help each other. In many cases, people were afraid to help each other, because, before this time, there was no, how do I say . . . there were no elders around, and we didn't have the government backing us. In this sense there was no protection. You felt unsafe, isolated and alone. So it was like a lost community in itself.

She continued her narrative.

Actually in 1986 when Museveni took over, things changed rapidly . . . women, let me say, Ugandan women got their voice in getting education . . . and I think this president gave women a lot of prominence as far as economic growth was concerned. He promoted the rights of women in all spheres. Then the laws started. People started recognizing the laws for women, the rights of women . . . that is when you could think that yes, we are safe . . . we can talk to someone, and we can get protection. Like before it was . . . oh, you don't talk about it [violence or abuse in relationships with men or in the home] . . . and even if you talked about it, nobody would hear you, and even if they heard you . . . they don't want to deal with it, or they wouldn't like to help you if you were an Asian or a Ugandan woman. The political situation was so bad, and each one cared for her own family, the safety of her own family. Women could not look out for each other at this time. The economic situation was so bad . . . there was no security, isn't it, at the same time? So it was only when Museveni took over in 1986, then it took them a little while to evolve . . . to come out . . . then Asian women started coming here in numbers. The repossession had started and Museveni supported the Asians, so women started to feel that they could get some support here also.

Property repossession and the formal and public backing of Ugandan Asian return by Museveni and the NRM compelled more gendered migration and the reconstruction of the Indian family and community life. This, in turn, as Zubeda and other women active in Asian community affairs described, also led to the reinstitutionalization of women's associations. Several women recalled their active engagement with the Indian Women's Association (IWA) in Uganda as early as 1996. In addition to returnee Ugandan Asian women and new migrant Indian women, some multiracial Afro-Asian women whose families had stayed on and had retained a foothold in Uganda were able to take on prominent roles in the national reconstruction process, participating in NRM party politics or in public service in government institutions. Others pursued higher education, as being of mixed-racial heritage afforded them opportunity, status, and prestige after the expulsion, especially if they remained unmarried or delayed marriage. These women served as important state-government-community intermediaries as they navigated both African and Asian spaces. They enjoyed more public visibility, mobility, and opportunities in shaping independent lives for themselves than other women who still felt limited by community norms surrounding *izzat*, including returnee and new migrant Indian women.

A key consequence of the expulsion, then, was the loss of displaced Ugandan Asian women in exile, including women's rights activists who worked to reform the patriarchal nature of state and customary power through legal and civil society–based advocacy. Building on the interventions of African and South Asian postcolonial and transnational feminist scholars,[15] the analytic of postcolonial *heteropatriarchal racially nativist communal governance* underscores the specificity of heteropatriarchal governance that vulnerable women of South Asian descent contend with in contemporary Uganda. Heteropatriarchal structures of governance were remade in relation to NRM governance and the racialized noncitizen incorporation of Ugandan Asian returnees and post-1990s Indian diasporic and other South Asian migration. South-South, or trans–Indian Ocean, marriage alliances, mobility, and migration; patriarchal and patrilocal kinship and marriage systems; racial boundaries and distinctions were remade; and patriarchal communal governance over the lives of women was reasserted.

The "re-Indianization" of Kampala and other urban spaces is related to the racialized and gendered remapping of urban space. According to the entwined logics of racial community endogamy, religious and caste purity, and class consciousness, morally sanctioned and racialized South Asian spaces include the home, communal spaces such as temples and mosques, schools with other South Asians, and sites of employment. For family patriarchs, the locus of patriarchal control rests upon the unmarried young woman and racialized and patriarchal anxieties surrounding women's agency, autonomy, and mobility—especially mobility beyond the morally sanctioned spaces of family and community. Here, the notion of *izzat* and its association with women's sexual purity, morality, and respectability seemed heightened, as it reflected not only the *izzat* of the family patriarch but of the family itself; the religious, sectarian, and caste-based community; and the racial community's honor. Women's bodies and their comportment—including their choices of Western fashion and dress—became important sites of regulation; so too did their interactions with men. Many women's capacity to assert autonomy in dating and sexual agency was completely restricted until it was time for (in most cases) traditionally arranged marriages sanctioned by patriarchal family and community. These observations were especially relevant for new post-1990s migrants, whereby the diaspora community took on more conservative aspects in relation to women's autonomy in a racially alien urban environment.

As I formed relationships with returnees and post-1990s migrants and their families, the high school– and college-going daughters in many of these families would seek me out for advice and guidance as they shouldered family and communal patriarchies. Transitioning into postsecondary education, they were balancing gendered expectations and norms in a newly forming Indian diaspora community with their own desires for educational and job opportunities; and they were beginning to plan for marriage and having their own families. Some women described how their male kinfolk (brothers and cousins) were tasked with monitoring their movements, especially their interactions with communal, caste, and racial outsiders. Unrestricted mobilities might lead to intimate encounters and dating, the violation of sexual and moral purity expectations, and the possibility of transgressive interfaith or intercaste marriages, typically described as "love marriages," or the even greater taboo of interracial intimacies between South Asian women and Black African men. Although young South Asian men were shaped by and reproduced these patriarchies, they also contended with and challenged patriarchal norms surrounding their marriage prospects. Nonetheless, in a patriarchal society, it was often considered permissible and normal for young men to date African or mixed-racial heritage women, but to not settle with them in marriage.

An Indian Association of Uganda (IAU) leader explained to me that one of the most difficult challenges with Ugandan Asian returnees, the newcomer Indian diaspora, and other South Asians reestablishing themselves after the expulsion was the difficulty in finding suitable marriage prospects and alliances for the younger generation of marriageable age, especially given that there were often gender imbalances within specific religious, sectarian, and caste communities. One unexpected outcome of the expulsion, then, was the disruption in conventional marriage norms guided by strict endogamy. During my fieldwork I noted increasing numbers of intercaste and interfaith marriages between individuals who had grown up in and who intended to stay in Uganda. Although interfaith, intercaste, and interracial alliances between Ugandan Asian and Indian men and other mixed-racial heritage, Arab, and African women occurred in the early colonial period and in the aftermath of the expulsion due to the lack of Asian women in the nation, they were hypogamous and considered socially acceptable. By contrast, there were very few marriage alliances between Asian women and Ugandan men (I knew of two cases, one a woman of South Indian origin who had met her Ganda husband in India and was raising her family in Kampala; the other a woman who had been cast out from her kin-community because of her marriage with an African man). Moreover, despite the sensitivity surrounding interracial liaisons, some community leaders upheld examples of interracial marriages (of Ugandan Asian men and African women) as examples of Asian integration. Overall—and despite the fact that youths (both men and women) desired more conversations about topics such as dating, relationships, marriage, agency, and consent—there was little open discussion or education to lead youth on these issues. Community-based patriarchal and racial anxieties persisted surrounding the question of the social reproduction of the "Asian" racial community after the expulsion, especially through the strategy of marriage endogamy and in a context where suitable marriage alliances were not always available.

Young women reproduced patriarchal notions of racial, community, and caste purity and honor, even as they also transgressed these ideas and practices. Women's lives prior to marriage were clearly a risky business, requiring skillful negotiation of autonomous desires and patriarchal pressures, heightened in the racially alien and racially insecure environment of Uganda. In this sense, many women actually looked forward to the next major life transition of finding a life partner and marriage. Although marriage would entail new kinds of patriarchal pressure, it would also afford women access to entitlements and privileges, such as being able to work in a business or for an employer and participating in social engagements with Black African friends in socially acceptable and respectable ways.

Some young women were more adamant about resisting patriarchal forces by delaying their marriages, family planning, and domestic responsibilities in order to pursue higher education and professional careers. Here, there were additional racialized and patriarchal anxieties centered on sending women to majoritarian Black African universities for higher education. Despite the excellent and international reputation of Makerere University, I knew of only one Punjabi Sikh woman from a more modest socioeconomic background who attended the institution for her BA, although this might change as more South Asian youths in Uganda join the university (many also attend the Aga Khan University regionally in East Africa). Most post-1990s Indian migrants sent their sons and daughters to universities abroad in India, Singapore, or Malaysia, with women especially sent to universities under the care of kin abroad. Those young women who remained behind in Kampala often pursued postsecondary accounting or computer training courses, or other business and marketing associate degrees, at private educational institutions in Kampala.

In accord with the patriarchal kinship norms of many Indian-owned family firms, wholesale and retail shops, and other workplaces, it was usually young men who were expected to take over and run family businesses, with women typically involved in accounting and other managerial work. Many urban African women served as receptionists, secretaries, and assistants to Indian bosses and managers. Indian-owned workplaces were thus important sites of racial and gendered sovereignty and cross-racial encounter in which men are able to assert class, racial, and patriarchal power over Indian and African women. It was generally considered morally improper for unmarried Indian or other South Asian women to seek autonomous employment without kinship or other community-based connections to an Indian-owned business, much less African-owned ones. The young Indian women I spoke with were very aware of the double standards placed upon them compared with their male counterparts as well as the differing racial and gendered constructions that shaped their relationships to African women. In some cases, they reproduced these gendered and racialized expectations and ideologies; and at other times they resisted and challenged these expectations.

Women who transgressed patriarchal family and community norms of purity and respectability by participating in premarital dating or by choosing more autonomous paths for education and employment could be constructed as "bad," "dirty," or shameful women—those without respect. They could be subject to malicious gossip, harassment, and ostracization, impacting the honor of their family and even their sisters and other womenfolk. The ramifications of transgressive behavior were even more severe for mixed-racial heritage Afro-Indian women, who were always already constructed as "impure" with respect to existing Ugandan Asian and North Indian–centric notions of racial and caste purity, as guided by Brahminism, casteism, and colorism. I often discussed these issues with twenty-four-year-old Joti, whom I first met at a youth-hosted *karoga*-style party on a lakefront beach in Entebbe; I later got to know her and her family during regular visits to the Singh Saba Sikh *gurudwara* in Kampala and their family home. Joti came from a modest class background and identified racially and culturally as a Ugandan and Indian Punjabi and Gujarati woman, although others in the Punjabi community often pointed out her "half-caste" status to me and noted that her darker-skinned appearance and curly hair was due to her biracial (half-Punjabi Sikh and half-Ugandan) mother, who was also part of the community. Like others from multiracial communities, she spoke a scintillating fusion of English, Punjabi, Gujarati, Luganda, and Swahili when she interacted with different racial and ethnic communities, spoke on her mobile, or engaged with coworkers.

Joti's formidable social skill set and fluency in African languages meant that she never had problems finding employment in Indian firms after college, and at the time she worked as a site manager for an Indian property management and construction firm (later she would work with many Ugandan colleagues as a sales and marketing agent for a well-known paint manufacturing company). During one of our meetings at the Hotel Equatorial in the city center near her office, Joti helped me outline the normative racial, gendered, and sexual ideologies that I was mapping in my research, contrasting the virtuousness and respectability of racially "pure" Indian women with other "half-caste" women like Joti, who were often seen as beautiful and desirable but also as less virtuous. In our discussion about dating and marriage prospects she explained that mixed-racial heritage women could "go with anyone"; "with *bazungu, bahindi, baganda*" (whites, Indians, Africans); yet, "they did not hold the same respect as Indian women and were not brought up with the same values." Women like Joti, who had Indian fathers, had been raised as Indian and were expected to marry into the Indian community, preserving their and their families' honor, as well as their racial, religious, and community honor and prestige. Even as Joti reproduced these normative notions of Indian racial community endogamy and race-based *izzat*, she deemphasized her Black and African heritage. She also surprised me by recalling a deeply painful experience of racist discrimination that she experienced by an elite and dominant caste Ugandan Asian woman of Gujarati heritage for whom she had previously worked, and who had addressed her in a derogatory and insulting way due to her African heritage, calling her "half-caste" and thus excluding her to her face. Although Joti also explained to me that she was proud of both her Indian and her Ugandan and African indigenous heritage, I was beginning to make sense of not only East African patterns of Brahmanical up-casteing, or Sanskritization among different (and even dominant-caste) South Asian communities, but also what I describe as "racial up-casteing." Racial up-casteing in the East African and Ugandan context describes the ways in which individuals from multiracial Afro-Asian communities often value and emphasize their South Asian and Indian racial identities as compared with racial Blackness and indigenous African ancestry, maintaining South Asian racial endogamy in their choice of marriage partners. In Joti's case, although she wished to marry a South Asian partner, she also experienced racial discrimination from South Asians who constructed hierarchical boundaries between themselves and those with mixed-racial ancestry.

In general, I was struck by the fact that many of the young South Asian women I spent time with declared their deep commitments to and love for Uganda and Ugandans, desiring to marry and settle down in Kampala and remain near their families and friends. However, compared with their male counterparts, who would take on family businesses and who could bring female partners for marriage from South Asia if necessary, the traditional patriarchal, patrilocal, and endogamous marriage expectations placed upon young women and the relatively limited selection of partners available in Kampala might ultimately prevent them from settling in Uganda, and they might just have to leave. Their families would likely search for marriage partners for them in Kenya and Tanzania, in South Asia (India and Pakistan), or even *bhaar* (which signifies the West [the UK or Canada]). Most women did not want to marry partners in India or Pakistan, locations that they imagined to be much more socially conservative and traditional, observing that East African society was a more "open" and "free" society. In a few cases, some women, born and brought up in Uganda, did end up leaving East Africa after their marriages to join their husbands in India, or pursued other migration trajectories to Canada and elsewhere.

The Joshi-Sharma Case: Media Circulations and Interpretations

The context and analysis I lay out above is essential as it allows us to understand other kinds of patriarchal violence, especially domestic violence and other forms of gender-based violence, that have affected Indian migrant women in the context of community rebuilding efforts and the reassertion of patriarchal and communal modes of governance in the post-1972 racially nativist and politically and racially insecure environment of Uganda. Here, I revisit my earlier research on a highly publicized case of domestic violence and the femicide of a migrant Indian woman that took place during the property repossession period of the 1990s. In contrast to the more recent, early 2000s-era, first-generation South Asian women born and raised in Kampala who fretted about possibly leaving Uganda due to the lack of marriage prospects and the resurrection of transnational marriage practices, Renu Joshi had arrived in Kampala as a spousal dependent and migrant following her marriage to an Indian entrepreneur.

Domestic violence that results in femicide is colloquially referred to as "wife-murder" by Ugandans; it is also understood via the international liberal human rights rubric of "violence against women" that has accompanied gender-based human rights governance in Africa and the Global South.[16] Joshi's case, both tragic and revealing, was discussed widely in the media during the 1990s and constituted a more public moment of making sense of the so-called Asian question after 1972, including the gendered domains of racial and cultural difference in urban Uganda. Her tragic death also occurred in the midst of a powerful Ugandan women's movement that was active and growing in the context of a number of processes that accompanied structural adjustment and neoliberal transformation: international donor-aid funding, the making of the developmental state, the normalization of international humanitarian interventions and human rights governance, and the NGO-ization of civil society. Joshi's death revealed the importance of African women's participation in gender rights communities and women's rights activism in urban Uganda. Indian and other South Asian migrant women increasingly encountered and made use of quasi-sovereign and internationally funded entities such as women's rights NGOs and community-based organizations that had the capacity to intervene on behalf of vulnerable women and in domestic disputes within South Asian communities.

The post–Liberation War reconstruction and liberalization period led to extensive donor interest in funding Western ideal–type organizational formations of civil society; this was especially the case with internationally funded domestic NGOs that were organized around global governance agendas. Mahmood Mamdani has critiqued the ways in which Ugandan civil society had become "NGO-ized" by organizations that filled the gaps left by the privatized and militarized state apparatus but whose members received charity rather than rights and whose leaders were primarily accountable to donors.[17] Adam Branch and Zachariah Mamphilly have elaborated upon this argument, arguing that civil society took on a "self-proclaimed 'non-political character,'"[18] especially as the institutionalization of NGOs led to the depoliticization of Ugandan citizen-subjects and impeded social justice movements, and as government and state interests influenced or actively repressed the autonomy of NGOs and vice versa. Further deconstructing any discrete binaries between the state and NGOs, Aihwa Ong has observed, "It is widely assumed that NGOs, as actors in the global public sphere, operate as watch-dogs of human rights vis-à-vis the state . . . but in practice NGOs, both local and transnational, have had to engage the nation-state in a variety of practical ways shaped by a nexus of variables."[19] The complex web of women's and gender rights activists and professionals who worked in NGOs in urban Uganda negotiated this same kind of complexity with state and national projects, managing relationships with state ministries and officials and international organizations and their donors, becoming part of the state as much as they labored to reform its institutions and policies. Moreover, state co-optation of women's political and social activism has proceeded through neoliberal-era (global and international) "gender-mainstreaming" and the incorporation of women's rights agendas into government institutions. As Ugandan women—both professionalized and subaltern—work out the differences between gender-based activism and feminism according to varying class, ethnic, and religious positionalities, more dissident feminist, gender-queer, and queer mobilizations continue to resist militarized and state-based violence and oppression as well as the depoliticized nature of the transnational NGO-state nexus.[20] Here, I explore some of the unintended consequences of the fragmented sovereignties that linked supposedly discrete entities like the state in Africa, international organizations, and NGOs by exploring the interface between Ugandan gender rights NGOs and the everyday lives of noncitizen migrant South Asian women. I end with an examination of interracial women's mobilizations.

Although Joshi's murder took place in late December 1998, it played out in media coverage of criminal trial proceedings and public commentary in English-language and Luganda-language print media and radio until the early 2000s and again in 2012.[21] Print media, rumor, and community "gossip" supplement each other as different forms of circulating urban knowledge, traversing racialized communities, and remaining critical to the study of race and citizenship.[22] Joshi's story continues to be told today (in 2024), given the escalating militarized state violence and ongoing patriarchal backlash against women and LGBT communities. At the time of the murder, many of the more elite or middle-class Ugandan Asian women and the more recently arrived South Asian women community leaders who were active in voluntary work with charitable organizations in the city became involved in the case. They shared with me their own accounts of the case and of their political mobilization, usually while assessing their own life histories and confrontations with family, community, and state patriarchies, past and present. In contrast to the ways in which Ugandan Asian men spoke of racial violence and the expulsion as the defining rupture of their life, women often pointed to other experiences of gender discrimination and abuse as impacting their interpersonal relationships and life possibilities, including aspects of marriage and family life. In my analysis I weave together this delicate urban landscape of racial and gendered anxieties, rumor, and hearsay; interviews with Ugandan, Ugandan Asian, and other South Asian women activists involved in the case; archival research; and media analysis to offer a narrative of the case, a brief analysis of its discussion in print media, and a contextualized analysis of intimate partner violence impacting women like Joshi. Offering a coherent narrative of the Joshi femicide is important because of the ensuing spectacular, even exceptionalized, visual representations and the typically Orientalizing and essentializing ideas of Asian womanhood, community, and culture that accompanied the majoritarian urban African interpretations of her case (especially since sensational pictures of Joshi's body after her death were published in Ugandan print media).

Joshi's husband was a local businessman and the owner of Sharma Supermarket in Old Kampala; he was of Punjabi Hindu and dominant caste-origin

(Brahmin).[23] Sharma and his wife, Renu Joshi, lived with their two small children, Sharma's brother, and two other, likely noncitizen, migrant dependents, referred to in news reports as male Indian "houseboys" or domestic servants, Raju Kamaru and Babu Rajukumar.[24] They resided in a rented house that was divided into two apartments, with Ugandan (African) neighbors on the other side of a dividing wall. According to news reports, their neighbor, Mrs. Twine, heard a woman's cries and the cries and shouts of children for their mother in the early morning of Christmas Eve. According to transcripts of court proceedings, the next morning the neighbors noticed that a mattress was covering an outdoor window to the Sharma residence, visible from a shared hallway of the building.[25]

Early in the morning, Sharma called community leaders and a doctor to report that Joshi was ill. He explained that she had taken medicine for malaria or possibly some sleeping pills the night before and had passed away during the night.[26] Sharma attempted to move forward quickly with traditional Hindu cremation rites, so that the bruises on Joshi's body as she lay under the bedcovers would not be discovered by community members. Sharma had summoned another prominent local businessman (possibly his patron) to bribe Old Kampala police to not bring him in for questioning. Sharma's contact and others in their community network also attempted to summon a doctor with the intention to falsify a medical report and state that Joshi had passed away from hypertension due to sleeping pills.[27] Despite these attempted cover-ups, other community leaders, including IAU members who arrived at the scene, discovered extensive bruises and what appeared to be electrical burns on Joshi's body. They joined local African neighbors and residents and cried foul as more police arrived on the scene. One of the houseboys, also a witness, was found in the apartment—bruised, beaten, and unconscious—and was immediately taken to the hospital. Both Sharma and his brother, Kumar, were arrested by Old Kampala police and detained. Six days after Joshi's death, both were charged with murder.[28] In the interim, Ugandan Asian and IAU community leaders organized a (foreign) Kenyan Asian pathologist to carry out a second postmortem on Joshi's body. The commander of police handling the case, suspecting another possible attempt at a "community cover-up," argued that a pathologist from Makerere Hospital (herewith implying an African pathologist) was more than qualified to carry out an official postmortem on Joshi's body in the city mortuary.[29] Some community representatives explained to me that the request for the second postmortem by an Asian doctor was about ensuring privacy for the family and deflecting negative public attention from the "Asian" or

"Indian" community in the midst of the news coverage about the case and their ongoing feelings of racial insecurity. In the end, the official postmortem report confirmed that Joshi had been brutally beaten and tortured; she had been electrocuted with live wires, which led to her death.

As the news about the femicide began to circulate in the media, women leaders in the Indian Women's Association (IWA) began to consult with each other in the hope of preventing anyone else internal to the community from attempting to bribe authorities or assisting the perpetrators in fleeing the country. The women from the IWA approached prominent Uganda women's rights activist, then-member of Parliament (MP) Winnie Byanyima. Byanyima, the spouse of Forum for Democratic Change (FDC) political opposition leader Kizza Besigye, and other Ugandan women's activists had extensive connections with NGOs and other civil society organizations, academics at Makerere University, and journalists. Collectively, Byanyima and other prominent Ugandan academics and activists attended the official postmortem of Joshi's body with a group of Ugandan Asian and Indian women community leaders to offer them support and to serve as witnesses.[30] Next, the now multiracial group of African and Asian women coordinated with others: the International Women's Organization (IWO), the Ugandan Women's Efforts to Save Orphans (UWESO), the newly formed Asian Women's Support Group, and other NGOs that worked on gender-based violence issues in African communities such as Hope Against Rape, the Ugandan Association of Women Lawyers (FIDA Uganda), and Action for Development (ACFODE). They mobilized professors and graduate students at the School of Women and Gender Studies at Makerere University.[31] Together, the activists, academics, community leaders, and other prominent Ugandan Asian and Indian women attended Joshi's cremation and funeral. They used the funeral as an opportunity to break the silence surrounding speaking out about the epidemic of domestic violence in Uganda and across both African and South Asian communities, creating awareness of gender-based violence as a societal issue that afflicted all women. In their press release and in media write-ups, they educated the public about the warning signs of abuse and the importance of reporting them to relevant authorities as well as about developing support systems for vulnerable women, which might have saved Joshi's life.[32] Next, the group of multiracial women attended the judicial criminal court proceedings where Sharma and his brother were arraigned and eventually charged with murder and subsequently detained without bail until trial. Finally, women attended the criminal court trial proceedings in large groups, participating in powerful "silent demonstrations" in order to seek justice on Joshi's behalf and to intimidate anyone involved in the potential corruption or mishandling of the case proceedings.[33]

Because of women's mobilizations—and despite the fact that two key witnesses, the two Indian migrants (houseboys), in the case had disappeared, likely bribed or bullied into leaving the country—Sharma and his brother were charged, prosecuted, pronounced guilty, and ultimately imprisoned for the murder.[34] Fearing he would also flee Uganda, women's groups lobbied the court when Kumar appealed and applied for bail several months later.[35] Although Sharma was initially given the death penalty for his crimes, his sentence was reduced to a life sentence in Luzira, a notoriously harsh and inhumane prison. Sharma and Kumar lost their appeal in 2002, although Kumar was later released. In 2012, President Museveni pardoned Sharma and set him free, which in keeping with the existing patterns of state-based backlash against women's and gay rights mobilizations, unleashed furor among human rights activists.[36]

Importantly, according to my research in press archives, while Ugandan media routinely publishes reports of violence against African women, the Joshi-Sharma case has received the most media attention by far. This was partly due to the strategy of Ugandan women activists who, in contrast to Indian community leaders, wanted to publicize and draw as much media attention to the case to ensure racialized and gendered accountability and justice for Joshi's death. But the media attention paid to Joshi's victimization was also related to her racial and gendered status as "Indian" or "Asian" and to persistent Orientalist and essentialist meanings attached to the figure of the "Asian woman"—little understood by many urban Africans, but central to the fabric of Ugandan society. The brutal details of the case, including the publication of photographs of the victim's body in local newspapers, further sensationalized and exceptionalized the case. Finally, Joshi was considered to have come from an upper-caste, respectable, and upwardly mobile background. For many Ugandans, the mediatization of Joshi's bruised, burned, and deceased body—partially unclothed and under a cotton sheet—seemed suddenly to render visible and accessible the inner life and private struggles of an Asian woman, one of those whose bodily integrity, purity, and honor seemed to have always been excessively safeguarded and regulated.

The case and its mass-mediatization offered an alternative perspective, an intimate glimpse of extant gendered struggles within a seemingly monolithic racialized "Indian or Asian community" that was gendered male and that was also just reasserting its (both old and new) presence in the city. In their published op-eds, urban Ugandan commentators often mobilized singular representations of the "Asian community" as "secretive," "above the law," "closed," "inaccessible," or as having special connections to the government. These assertions reflected the truths of patron-client relations between state officials and patrons and wealthy community clients as well as the challenges of racial community endogamy. But they also generated reductive stereotypes of completely victimized Asian women without agency or autonomy in an excessively patriarchal and misogynistic Asian culture. The commentaries also provided an occasion to comment on the limits of state-based institutions of accountability, and rightly criticized the attempts of wealthy and powerful businessmen to participate in a cover-up by protecting the perpetrators, bribing the police, and bullying and threatening witnesses. One editorial entitled "Asian Women in Danger" discussed the need to protect Asian women from community elites.[37] Its author also blamed the "Asian community" as a whole, noting that "the death of Joshi points to a blind spot in the application of the law in the country. There is a whole class of people who are not closely scrutinized by the law—expatriates and the Asian community. Somehow the assumption is that these people's lives are governed by their own 'peculiar culture' . . . these people have made crime and atrocity a private affair."[38]

Hence, the case and its mass-mediatization were also central to constructing African-based understandings and ideas of Indian or Asian racial and cultural difference. This cultural difference was viewed as alien, excessive, patriarchal, even pathological. These interpretations mirrored what scholar Uma Narayan has described as the "death by culture"[39] explanations for dowry deaths in India: Joshi's murder was exceptionalized as a uniquely Indian cultural phenomenon, despite the extremely high rates of domestic violence and intimate partner violence, including femicide, across Ugandan and African communities. And if the figure of the Indian woman had historically been constructed by Ugandan nationalists as intimately inaccessible to African men—if one of the criteria for inclusion and membership, of multiracialism or interracialism, in the nation continues to be defined on the basis of "sexual kinship," or African male–Indian woman affinal kinship ties and cross-racial exogamy—Joshi's case was a public, pedagogical tale of the dangers of intracommunity Indian racial, religious, and caste endogamy; it was a warning of what might befall Indian women who became "communal property/sexual property"[40]—or, in urban Uganda, the "racial property"—of Indian men.

In discussing Joshi's case with academic colleagues at Makerere University, I was better able to understand the urban worlds that Ugandan Asian,

Indian migrant, and other South Asian women victims and survivors of domestic violence experienced. I had little sense of whether the femicide was an honor-related atrocity, if it was abuse that had escalated into femicide, or if it was related to both. But what was significant was that the 1972 Asian expulsion, the normalization of racially nativist nationalism and noncitizen South Asian incorporation, and the heteropatriarchal racially nativist logics of state and communal governance had all contracted the political domain of especially (noncitizen, legally and substantively) women's access to rights and entitlements, leaving them vulnerable and in a profoundly unequal terrain of citizenship in relation to their male counterparts. Joshi's legal status as a dependent of her husband—an entrepreneur—in a neoliberalizing market economy left her vulnerable to communal disciplinary violence and domestic-based patriarchal violence that escalated to femicide. The relative alienation and vulnerability of migrant women within transnational patrilocal and patriarchal marriage and kinship systems—without access to their own kinship networks and support systems—also contributed to Joshi's precarity. The racialized and patriarchal policing of migrant women's urban mobility and interactions with Africans; South Asian sources of racialism on the basis of religious and caste endogamy, with women's bodies and behaviors seen as the locus of patriarchal control and honor; and anti–Black African racism—all of these factors exacerbated Joshi's vulnerability to compounding emotional, psychological, and physical abuse, torture, and neglect that ended in her death. Here, one Ugandan woman academic colleague bemoaned the fact that many Indians' communal self-segregationist tendencies left Joshi and other women like her vulnerable to violence; she maintained that if Joshi had had the support of other women, including the support of African women, she would still be alive.

Significant here also is community elites' post-1972 careful monitoring and regulation of an imputed African majoritarian gaze upon the "Asian or Indian racial community" and the respectability politics that were upheld by community leaders—those who felt politically and racially precarious and fearful that the more negative, shameful, and unsavory aspects of internal community life, including South Asian sources of anti-Black African racism and gender-based violence, would be exposed for public criticism and inspire anti-Asianism and calls for anti-Asian violence and expulsion. The desire to maintain an image of the "Asian" racial community as contributing to national development and prosperity, then, relied upon the repression of the internal complexities and oppressions within the racial community, including gender-based discrimination, and was always inflected by class and caste and other social factors. The Ugandan woman academics and activists I spoke with also discussed the militaristic and patriarchal nature of state institutions, the masculinist architecture and patron-client networks that linked security and policing, judicial and carceral institutions and systems to wealthy businessmen and politicians. Feminist activists did not merely complain about "corruption"; they spoke of the systemic nature of webs of patronage and protection cultivated among male-led institutions as reproducing structures of institutional, community, and family-based patriarchal violence. Finally, the lack of internal reform efforts within Ugandan Asian and Indian migrant communities to combat patriarchy, sexism, and misogyny, coupled with the militarized political culture of urban Uganda and the normalization of African heteropatriarchies, all contributed to a society in which women remained vulnerable to gender-based violence and femicide.

Experiments in Cross-Racial Feminist Organizing: Commonalities and Tensions

African, Ugandan Asian, and newcomer communities of Indian diasporic and South Asian heritage expressed shock and disbelief at the brutality of violence that Joshi experienced. There were two general interpretations of her death: one that framed the violence as an exceptional problem of an incommensurable, essentialized, and alien Indian culture; and the other that framed the violence as a universal problem that affected all women, that cut across indigenous African and South Asian communities, and that could be understood within human rights discourses and universal liberal citizenship claims. In regard to the latter, Byanyima and other Ugandan women activists helped educate and organize elite and middle-class Ugandan Asian and Indian diasporic women about domestic violence, galvanizing feminist consciousness-raising and feminist political organizing among them. They argued that the violence that Joshi experienced was an issue that existed across communities, regardless of racial or cultural origin and difference; it was an endemic problem of patriarchal gender violence. In addition, mobilizing universal liberal human rights frameworks, they articulated moral and affective claims for Joshi's posthumous racial, gendered, and cultural inclusion and belonging on the basis of ideas of universal women's rights. Their ideas emerged from the United Nations and the Committee on the Elimination of Discrimination Against Women (CEDAW; instituted in 1981) and especially in the aftermath of the Fourth World Conference on Women at Beijing in 1995, at which point Ugandan women and gender-based activists and organizations made stronger international governance-based claims for women's rights to live free from violence, engaging state-based, legal, and institutional strategies for the criminalization of gender-based violence and the enforcement of forms of accountability and justice. In the Joshi case, activists argued that even if noncitizen migrant women were not protected by Ugandan constitutional law, they should be protected from gender-based violence on the basis of universal human and gender rights, such that all residents of Uganda, no matter their citizenship status, were subject to criminal laws.[41] While activists did not make additional demands to formalize women's (legal) noncitizen status in the nation or develop pathways for legal citizenship, their rhetoric appealed to broader moral and substantive claims about noncitizen South Asian women's rights to bodily integrity and to live free from violence.

Thus, their political demands for justice for Joshi's murder appealed to women's innate right to live free from violence and abuse, regardless of migration history, race, culture, ethnicity, national origin, or citizenship status. Ugandan activists experimented with international and nation-based liberal and nonliberal imaginaries of citizenship for South Asian women's bodily integrity and inclusion in the nation, advancing ideas of a multiracial pluralism and histories of Afro-Asian connection in their discussion of women's health and flourishing in broader Ugandan society. Finally, their calls for justice for Joshi overlapped with the larger Ugandan women's movement and with political demands on the state to reform customary laws that continued to govern African women, namely, the controversy over a tabled parliamentary bill called the Domestic Relations Bill.[42] For Ugandan women activists, the Joshi-Sharma case intersected with debates about the prevalence of gender-based violence in African societies and the need to reform constitutional laws to protect women from customary laws (often referred to as "culture") and patriarchal customary-based (ethnic) violence, and with emphasis on essentialist notions of Indian "culture."[43] These political strategies were in concert with international feminist perspectives on violence against women that were current at that time, ones that located the source of gender-based violence within "cultural institutions" rather than in the interlocking domains of patriarchal oppression emerging from colonial and postcolonial institutionalized state and societal violence, market fundamentalism, transnational migration, and communal or customary-based patriarchies. Their activist strategies primarily coalesced around state and institutional-based reforms and feminist consciousness-raising in Ugandan society generally.

While Ugandan women activists located the Joshi case within their activist imperatives, women of South Asian origin, both Ugandan Asian returnees and new Indian migrant housewives, were not necessarily conscious or aware of this international and national context of Ugandan women's political organizing and activism. Two Ugandan Asian–Gujarati women had initially mobilized on their own, encouraging women in their networks to talk to each other about the case and the injustices involved in its handling. They also worked closely with Byanyima, supporting her efforts to draw public attention to the case. One of the Ugandan Asian women organizers persuaded her husband to take photos of Joshi's body at one of the postmortems as evidence of her abuse (she presented these same photos to me during one of our meetings to demonstrate that they had helped break the silence and sense of community complicity surrounding Joshi's case at the time). Both women expressed their sorrow and dismay at Joshi's tragic death and at the community management of the case in a local Hindi-language radio program called *Aap Ki Pasand* (your choice/desire). As one of the women described to me, "We were disgusted, especially when, after her death, Sharma kept trying to say that she [Joshi] was a very bad woman." Before organizing the radio program, they held a closed meeting with fellow expatriate Ugandan Asian women. Together, they established the Asian Women's Support Group and a mobile phone hotline number for any woman of South Asian descent who was experiencing domestic problems; they offered moral and emotional support to each other and returned to the courthouse during Sharma's booking and trial, despite the intimidation and threats that they faced by his defenders and powerful men in the community. Thus, beyond the existing knowledge that Ugandan women activists already possessed surrounding state-based legal strategies, media engagement, and consciousness-raising, Ugandan Asian and newcomer South Asian women were also learning about organizing and feminist consciousness-raising strategies in their community networks.

Feminist organizing was not without its tensions. A daughter of one of the expatriate Ugandan Asian housewives in Kampala explained to me that the initial Asian Women's Support Group meeting was controversial. Some women did not support any community sensitization efforts for fear of attracting more visibility to the case. They were frightened by the public attention afforded the case and its relationship to negative ideas of "the Asian community." They pushed back against the participation of Ugandan women activists in the communal and domestic affairs of South Asian women—especially since they feared it would bring "undue attention" and shame to the reputation of community at a time when Ugandan Asians were already feeling racially precarious and in light of the efforts of the post-1990s South Asian community-builders to put forth a positive image of the Asian racial community. Unspoken and unsaid here was the idea that any public discussion of "Asianness" in Kampala seeded possibilities of anti-Asian violence and calls for racial community expulsion. Some women were thus inclined to remain quiet in order to protect their individual honor, their families, and racial community interests.

Therefore, while some Asian women worked closely with Ugandan women activists, they were challenged by fellow women who also became gatekeepers. Some Ugandan Asian women chose to distance themselves from the case and declined to participate in the silent demonstrations at Sharma's trial—although they were privately following and discussing the news. A few women mentioned to me that they did this because they had received advice from their husbands to avoid involving themselves in the affairs of other families. They feared retribution for their actions, stating that "one could never be too careful." Some women chose not to learn about and participate in cross-racial feminist organizing that would place them at odds with a sense of racial loyalty and community preservation. This was the case, even if they were empathetic to Joshi's plight. For example, some women privately expressed their concerns about a political and societal culture of rampant intracommunity gender violence and misogyny. Others expressed feelings of remorse and guilt, explaining that Joshi had gone to the local Hindu and Sikh religious temples and had asked others for help, but that religious leaders and women had failed to intervene and save her life.

One of the most sensitive issues was the publication of photographs of Joshi's deceased body in national newspapers. Not only did the photos showcase the internal aspects of imputed "Asian racial community" life, but many felt that the mass-mediatization of the photos was disrespectful to Joshi's posthumous sense of privacy and a violation of *izzat* as well as of the honor of the family. Joshi's body was also a symbolic representation of Indian women at large—the publication of the images of her body in a victimized state violated norms of women's racialized religious and caste-based purity and honor. Historically, Indian women's proper and respectable bodily comportment, especially in public, was essential to maintaining moralized and racialized community boundaries and distinctions. The Ugandan African majoritarian community's ability to access images of Joshi's body seemed symbolically to transgress the moral construction of virtuous Indian womanhood, rendering the larger Indian racial community precarious.

Other women argued that there was no grand or systemic problem of domestic violence in the racial community, but that Joshi's murder was a tragic aberration. They argued that Sharma must have been pathological or "half-insane," likening the case to those often deemed in juridical terms as "crimes of passion." They asserted that the case did not represent the "Asian community" or, by implication, "Indian" culture or race at large, nor did it represent the way that women were treated, particularly the Ugandan Asian community in Kampala. They were concerned about the media emphasis on Indian women as passive victims of selective and reductive representations of racially arrogant, misogynistic, and criminal-minded Indian men in Uganda. A section of elite women argued that this was a problem among uneducated and "illiterate" newcomers, thus distancing themselves from post-1990s Indian migrants and those from Pakistan and elsewhere. These comments point to identity, class, and migrant history divisions among the racialized Asian community; returnees tended to understand themselves to be Westernized and liberal moderns as opposed to those South Asian newcomers they constructed as "traditional" or "backward." Overall, some women downplayed the structural and contextual nature of gender violence and the many interlocking factors that had led to Joshi's death, including the relationship between her case and other vulnerable populations, including Ugandan women and young Indian and African girls and women. They maintained an elite respectability politics that shored up racial and community loyalties and downplayed classed, racial, and gendered vulnerabilities among new migrants, echoing what Anannya Bhattacharjee has described as "the habit of ex-nomination"[44] among the Indian immigrant bourgeoisie in the United States.

Although some culturally sensitive workshops within women's organizations and conversations among youth are beginning to address violence against women, the noncitizen (legal and substantive) status of South Asian migrants and their reliance upon endogamous religious, caste, and kinship networks and domestic and communal patriarchal governance means that victimized women primarily interface with their own family members and community elders, who tend to reproduce patriarchal norms and practices, urging women to accommodate abuse or return to their families and continue to endure harmful behavior. Transnational NGOs and other organizations oriented toward African women victims and survivors of violence and African women's activists and feminist leadership are becoming crucial sources of support for South Asian women seeking assistance. For example, my research at Kampala-based NGOs revealed that many Indian and

Pakistani migrant women have started to file police reports, visit Ugandan hospitals and medical clinics due to injuries, and are referred to caseworkers at legal aid and other gender-based NGOs.

Ultimately, Joshi's tragic and untimely death provoked important societal discussions about the status and well-being of migrant noncitizen South Asian women and the larger issue of Asian noncitizen incorporation in post-1972 Uganda. African women's activists, who were connected to internationally funded NGOs and other organizations, mobilized human and gender rights discourses to make claims for the moral inclusion and right of noncitizen and racialized migrant women to belong in urban Uganda and to live free from violence in the nation. Their claims were couched in moral registers of valuing humanity and women in general and the bodily integrity of migrant South Asian women in particular, placing the struggles of South Asian women in conversation with the struggles of African women in Uganda. Ugandan activists also mobilized the figure of the migrant Indian woman, embodied by Joshi's life story and untimely death, to represent the plight of all women living with domestic violence. Joshi's story elicited a sense of moral and affective obligation among all Ugandans, including feelings of responsibility and accountability for the welfare and bodily integrity of all women, regardless of racial and cultural origin. Moving past the rhetoric of liberal inclusion and legal-juridical citizenship and its attendant rights and privileges, universal gender rights and human rights discourses offered new strategies and discourses for the substantive (racial and cultural) inclusion of South Asian migrant women in the aftermath of the expulsion. Finally, even if some Ugandan Asian and other South Asian women leaders were elitist and paternalistic in their approach to activism and organizing, for the first time since the expulsion, women came together politically across racial, cultural, class, and migration histories; it was a creative, if untimely, example of Afro–South Asian feminist political consciousness-raising and activism, establishing urban visions of racial and gendered inclusion in which all women might live free from violence.

Yet, the responses to the case also exposed the internal frictions among elite Ugandan Asian women and the tensions between women of African indigenous and South Asian heritage (both Ugandan Asian and newcomer South Asian women) in their feminist strategies. Despite renewed interest in Afro-Asian connections and Afro-Asian solidarity practices within Global South contexts, feminist and queer scholars caution against the romanticization of these coalition-building practices, highlighting instead the power relations and hierarchies within and between differentially positioned groups—and even the occlusion of these power differentials within activist representations and scholarly writing.[45] I found that this contingent moment of urban cross-racial feminist activism was not necessarily reciprocal across racial communities. Joshi's death compelled Ugandan Asian women and other community leaders of South Asian heritage to participate in a growing urban feminist consciousness and in organizing sensibilities. However, these same women are not engaged in a range of other gender-based struggles that Ugandan women have been part of since the NRM came to power, including basic proletarian "bread and butter" struggles, and especially pro-democracy, antimilitarization and anticorruption campaigns led by Ugandan women. Instead, their reciprocity has often been limited to benevolent voluntary work within existing multiracial organizations or to charitable activities structured by their racial and class consciousness and their rather parochial expatriate and communal worlds. Ugandan women's activists often view these practices as paternalistic and elitist, as maintaining racial distinctions rather than working to dismantle them by nurturing interracial intimacies with African women on their terms. Contextualizing these practices in the challenging aftermaths of the 1972 Asian expulsion—and in light of the contradictory experiences of both racialized and gendered inclusion and exclusion, privilege and precarity, among Ugandan Asian and South Asian migrant women—allows us to better analyze the complexities of even fleeting and contingent moments of cross-racial and gendered feminist organizing, as in the Joshi-Sharma case. Certainly, stratifications and hierarchies continue to persist in spite of, and perhaps as a result of, horizontal-based interracial solidarities and alignments, and all amid the abstract and professed claims to liberal and universal citizenship, the state and capitalist project of South-South cooperation, and elite cosmopolitan appeals to Afro-Asianism in urban and transcontinental Uganda.

The Tanmeet Kaur Case: Race, Culture, Custom, and Difference

While some Ugandan Asian and Indian women community leaders condemned community-based patriarchal violence and supported African women's activists struggles to reform customary laws and gendered communal governance, others mobilized reactive claims that reaffirmed the significance of customary laws and the uniqueness of an essentialized, rather than a dynamic and changing, "Asian culture" and "religion," reasserting instead formations of heteropatriarchal racially nativist communal governance. In 2006, the father of twenty-two-year-old Tanmeet Kaur (of Punjabi Sikh heritage) pulled her out of an educational institution, expecting her to stay home until her parents successfully arranged her marriage. A Ugandan friend (of African indigenous descent), in support of Tanmeet's wishes to remain unmarried, located a job for her in a shop in the city center. Her parents then refused to allow Tanmeet to work. Tanmeet ran away from home, and she and her Ugandan friend asked for assistance at FIDA Uganda (the Uganda Association of Women Lawyers), where they provided an account of Tanmeet's physical and psychological abuse since childhood, in addition to being forced to leave school involuntarily and endure marital pressure.[46] They described how she had been pulled out of several other schools, most recently due to accusations that she was having an affair with another (unclear whether Asian or African) student. Claiming that she feared the involvement of the Indian Women's Association (IWA) in her case, Tanmeet began to reside temporarily at the home of a prominent Ugandan woman activist. Eventually, FIDA began to pursue a formal arbitration process, with IWA representatives, between Tanmeet and her family. All parties eventually settled upon an agreement whereby Tanmeet would be sent to a boarding school near Kampala, away from her family, where she would complete her education. Women from the IWA raised funds for Tanmeet to support her school fees so that the parents would not be liable for the expenses.[47]

Once again, this case was heavily mediatized in the national press. A series of op-eds by both Ugandan and Ugandan Asian–identifying women debated whether international human rights and nation-based gender-rights laws or traditional culturally specific frameworks of customary governance—usually derived from the colonial era—should have more prominence for Tanmeet. One angry editorialist observed that she was not a minor and should be able to "take her own decisions."[48] This was written in response to reports that Tanmeet's father and other Indian women leaders had claimed that "Indian culture [is] not up for debate," and that "being in Uganda does not mean we should disrespect our Indian laws."[49] Prominent women's activist Jackie Asiimwe responded to the editorial by stating, "Ugandan laws affect both citizens and non-citizens . . . according to the 1995 Constitution and Marriage Act, forcing anyone into marriage is a crime, and anyone can be deported"; Asiimwe thus emphasized that despite the non-citizen incorporation of "Asians" in the nation, the laws applied equally to indigenous communities and to migrants and to foreigners alike, and that noncitizens' political status was contingent.[50] Asiimwe continued, "There is a need to advocate for a clear family law in order to protect women . . . this case reveals the gaps in our legal regime . . . [it is] unfortunate that the Domestic Relations Bill has not passed."

In debating Tanmeet's case and whether a reformed universal family law framework could be applied to migrant noncitizen women or even to the Uganda-born children of newcomer South Asian migrants in Kampala, activists had the opportunity to advocate for the proposed 2003 Domestic Relations Bill (DRB). The DRB—which was intended to criminalize the actions of perpetrators of gender violence to a greater extent than before and to provide protections to women of all communities in Uganda, regardless of their citizenship status or racial, ethnic, and religious affiliation—was tabled by the Parliament in 2008. Activists had framed the DRB according to global governance norms surrounding universal women's human rights and gender rights, including the reform of customary laws that applied to African women, especially traditions surrounding polygamy, female genital mutilation, and marriage and divorce. In this case, Ugandan activists mobilized the global governance language of gender rights discourse to suggest that both African and Indian women, regardless of citizenship status or nationality, have the right to live free from violence. These discourses were couched in moral and affective claims surrounding women's universal experience of patriarchal violence, victimization, and suffering and aimed to bring the domain of women's governance from the realm of customary law into the purview of civil law. According to feminist activists, state-based legal reforms would help to inaugurate the deeper societal and cultural shifts in which women's autonomy, health, and safety would be respected, especially through an interrogation of "culture" and "tradition" that aligned with the customary domains of ethnicity and religion.

But state officials and prominent Indian community leaders have also aggressively resisted the DRB, and for different reasons. State officials—including parliamentary representatives—argued that practices like polygamy are "cultural" or "religious" (as sanctioned by Islamic law) and inherent to what they constructed as essentialist African traditions and cultures. Their defense of tradition was motivated by their potential loss of patriarchal entitlements and other grievances surrounding women's growing entitlements, which created a national and media-based backlash against Ugandan gender activists. By contrast, representatives of the "Indian" or "Asian" community argued that the bill, although posited as universal, did not address the specificity of traditional customs such as marriage practices that applied to Hindu, Sikh, and Muslim communities. A prominent lawyer argued that "Asian women" were not oppressed in the way that they had been depicted in the media, but that traditionally, "women must respect their parents."[51] She argued, "Parents who choose partners for their daughters mean well, and usually pick a man based on his family history. . . . Tanmeet is too young to take decisions on her own."[52] She further argued that the DRB was problematic because it would ostensibly retract the Customary Marriage Act, the Hindu Marriage and Divorce Act, and the Marriage and Divorce of Mohammedans Act (colonial-era customary laws that applied to Asian communities). In short, she argued, the DRB "does not define what custom is," and the reform or even abolishment of customary governance and their replacement with a universal family law would not attend to the domain of "cultural" and religious (and, by extension, also racial) difference. Customary law, by contrast, recognizes the specificity of different religious communities' marriage rites and traditional norms surrounding issues of marriage and divorce, polygamy, dowry, funerary rites, and so on.

Ultimately, Indian community leaders argued that customary law should be preserved but reformed to better align with the concerns of particular communities' specific versions of the family law that DRB proponents have argued for. For many African women lawyers and activists, this position was nonetheless viewed as preserving a sense of Indian racial and cultural difference. Once again, what is seen from one side as the preservation and reproduction of Indian culture and tradition in a racially antagonistic environment after 1972 is viewed from the other side as the assertion of Indian racial and cultural difference. Here, the preservation of religious, sectarian, and caste-based—and therefore racial and community-based— endogamy is essential for community elites and patriarchs. This project, in itself, relies upon essentialist notions of culture and tradition that are made static rather than remaining dynamic and changing in relationship to encounters with Africans, African ethnicity, Blackness, and Ugandanness. This assertion of racial and cultural difference, of course, poses obstacles to Ugandan women activists' work to advocate for the universal right for all women to live free from gender violence or to have recourse to legal protections that could protect them from community patriarchs and intracommunity violence. The desire to preserve an invented and fixed construct of "Asian" culture, custom, or tradition, despite the fact that culture, custom, and tradition are not monolithic and have never been unchanging, reveals desires to preserve "Asianness" and "Asian community" through domains of gender and custom, especially after 1972.

Understandably, Ugandan women's activists and lawyers considered this assertion of Asian/Indian difference via culture, custom, and tradition to be a challenge to their objectives, even as Ugandan women continued to be significant mediators between vulnerable South Asian women and sources of patriarchal authority. Lawyers at FIDA explained that they were aware that community leaders wanted to be discreet about these cases and could even perpetuate patriarchal norms and normalize abusive and coercive behavior; thus, FIDA took on a "watchdog" presence over Indian community organizations when a case emerged under their purview. Vulnerable women like Tanmeet usually had little access to resources or other sources of support beyond their immediate kinship networks. Over time, South Asian victims and survivors of violence began more frequently and directly approaching prominent Ugandan women's activists and NGOs, forging relationships of safety, welfare, and even practices of accountability and justice with Ugandan women and nonstate institutions.

One consequence of the Tanmeet Kaur case was that community desires to preserve legal custom compelled Ugandan women activists to construct their own ideas of racial "Asianness" and "South Asianness" and the "Asian racial community"—as wanting to remain culturally separate, as having self-segregating and inward-looking tendencies; and these communal tendencies invariably also reasserted patriarchal authority, putting vulnerable women in harm's way. While the IWA and Ugandan-Asian community leaders recognized the importance of FIDA in helping to address cases of domestic violence, as in the Joshi-Sharma case, they also viewed Ugandan women's activists and lawyers as insensitive to privacy issues, a product of Ugandan Asians' post-expulsion sense of racialized precarity and desires to project a positive image of a monolithic "Asian racial community" as integrating and contributing socially and economically to the nation.

In general, the Joshi and Kaur cases allowed Ugandan women's activists to advocate on the behalf of gender rights for all women of both indigenous African and South Asian descent. The same newspapers in which I found images of Joshi's victimized body contained educational notices about gender-based violence, editorials denouncing violence against women, and political advocacy messaging for the DRB to the Ugandan Parliament.[53] In public commentary, activists used the evidence of family and domestic violence within an abstract "Asian racial community" to argue that violence against women is a universal problem, raising societal consciousness and promoting education about gender-based violence and ways to intervene to support women as well as advocating for state and legal-based strategies of reform, accountability, and justice.

But there are some limitations to these approaches. Gender-based organizations, although not exclusively, mobilize Western-based legal-juridical and carceral solutions in seeking justice from perpetrators; they experiment less with other forms of intracommunity or family-based forms of safety and mediation, transitional justice, and reconciliation. Nor is there as much focus on the varying needs of different communities in a plural society like Uganda, whereby notions of "African" and "Asian or Indian" women are made discrete and essential, and whereby educational and consciousness-raising initiatives are not contextualized in relation to stratifications and interlocking social factors of race, ethnicity, class, religion, caste, and so on. Their approaches still tend to reify notions of "tradition" and "culture" in their analysis of and interventions into violence against women, underemphasizing the deeply historical and structural, overlapping state, institutional, communal-based sources of patriarchy that women struggle against. This is also the case as debates over existing customary law and the DRB continue amid the growing presence of transnational religious organizations from the United States and violent state-based antifeminist, homophobic, and trans-phobic backlash.[54] Despite the often-shared structural experience of patriarchal violence that racialized African and South Asian women contend with in urban Uganda, and as transnational South-South connections intensify, there has been little attention paid to the experiences of racially diverse urban women and the ways in which the unresolved aftermaths of the 1972 Asian expulsion continue to make it difficult to forge common solidarities and resistances.

Centering Contingent and Ambivalent Afro–South Asian Feminist Solidarities

The Renu Joshi and Navpreet Kaur cases, along with the experiences of many women with whom I interacted, allowed me to construct an understanding of the modalities of postcolonial and heteropatriarchal nativist and communal governance that more vulnerable South Asian women contend with in post-expulsion Uganda. This gendered experience of ambivalent racial inclusion and exclusion poses empirical contrasts to the gendered racial formation of a monolithic and singular "Asian racial community," or even of the discursive construct of "Asian" in East Africa. The demise of the Ugandan Asian community in 1972 ended Asian women's participation in politics and the public sphere, while state and community-based masculinist and patriarchal structures of community- and citizenship-building were normalized. The figure of the "Asian" woman—and especially a postcolonial discourse on cross-racial marriage exogamy between Asian women and African men as a litmus test for national citizenship—has continued to circulate in a national and public imaginary since 1972. This imaginary shapes majoritarian and populist notions of Asian women as victims of a closed and inaccessible "Asian" or "Indian" culture that is constructed as excessively patriarchal and territorial over Asian women. Unfortunately, Ugandan Asian and Indian community leaders, often concerned about attracting negative attention to a precarious and fragmented racial community, and thus masking internal conflicts and violence in the post-expulsion era, pose challenges to women's safety and autonomy as well as to gender-based activism surrounding domestic and family violence.

While some Ugandan, Ugandan Asian, and other Indian women activists were able to strategize and work well together in advocating for vulnerable women, others had strained relationships with each other. Women from both communities acknowledged the deeply rooted divides that they would have to overcome in order to work together to improve the lives of all urban Asian women. Moreover, activist responses did not proceed smoothly at all. They were instead rather contingent and short-lived in relation to specific needs, and typically strategic solidarities—and they were uneven, not always reciprocal, riven with concerns over class-consciousness, respectability politics, and cross-racial and internal racial community tensions, including fears of racial visibility and anti-Asian violence from the majoritarian Ugandan community. It is not clear to me if my analysis of feminist mobilizations will be important for the women who were involved, if lessons will be learned for posterity's sake, or mobilized in the future for more sustained feminist activist strategies, or if they will even be contextualized historically and in relation to the ruptures of 1972. Nonetheless, the responses to both cases challenge us to think across imperial, postcolonial, diasporic, and Global South formations and consider interracial, class-based, and feminist-based solidarities in new ways. By more consciously working past abstract and aspirational projects of Afro-Asianism and South-South cooperation, we can gain a better sense of women's experience and the extant, often tense and ambivalent nature of these racial and gendered alliances in practice. Finally, the multiple claims about, and the actual domains of, gender, culture, community, and custom remain constitutive of the insecurities of expulsion.

Conclusion

Toward a Transcontinental Anthropology
of Afro–South Asian Entanglement

After I wrote my memoir of childhood, *Dreams in a Time of War* (2006),
I looked back and saw how much India had become an equally important
thread in my life. I had not planned to bring out the Indian theme in my life,
but there it was, staring at me right from the pages of my narrative. . . . The
links between Asia and Africa and South America have always been present,
but in our times they have been made invisible by the fact that Europe is still
the central mediator of Afro-Asian-Latino discourse.

Ngũgĩ wa Thiong'o, "What Is Asia to Me? Looking East from Africa"

Theirs was a diasporic nostalgia, which has shaped the politics of an earlier
generation who felt they were neither here nor there. Thirty years later, we
might return to these stories: to radically reimagine a politics of alliance
against authoritarianism, a located politics against supremacy, a different way
of being here and there.

Durba Mitra, "'Mississippi Masala' @30: Revisiting a Film Classic
in Authoritarian Times"

The insecurities of expulsion—the effects of the expulsion, its global and
Uganda-based representations, interpretations, memories, and affective
resonances, and the practices and performances of citizenship fashioned
in its aftermath—followed me into my first postdoctoral position at

Makerere University. They especially haunted me as I ambled up and down the dramatic and sprawling campus hill on my walks, day after day, contemplating my embodied racial and gendered South Asianness and its possible significations at the iconic university. The colonial government had founded Makerere College as a small technical training school in 1922; in 1950 they refounded it as a university with degrees granted by the University of London, thus ensuring European influence at the university in the midst of anticolonial nationalism. After independence, African leaders renamed it as the University of East Africa; the institution ultimately reclaimed part of its original name and became Makerere University in 1970.[1] As I strolled on campus in the evenings, I noted how the left branch of the campus's main road veered past the law school and guest house, winding up the hill through an older side of the campus, past student dorms, becoming first chinked and then potholed, reflecting the persistent and troubled political histories of the 1960s, 1970s, and 1980s. The right branch of the main road was well-paved and smooth, descending down the hill and then veering back up and to the right, tracing a path past the gleaming and more recently constructed business school and the Department of Women and Gender Studies buildings, continuing toward the main library and the colonial-era architecture of the administration building. Here, campus infrastructures reflected the entwined and layered processes of state, neocolonial, and structural violence, the presence of private contractors and international agencies' donor-aid funding, the neoliberal edges of the African university. Reflecting on these contradictory sides of the campus, I argue that a more contemporary critique of the global and structural processes of neoliberal developmentalism that shape Makerere University has sidelined the impacts of postcolonial processes of Ugandan nation-building, citizenship, and race-making—including the processes of Africanization and racial expulsion—on higher education. The 1972 Asian expulsion, a critical rupture in the nation, has forged the *African postcolonial nativist university*. This has implications for Africa-based and global knowledge production and the decolonization of African universities.

In *Insecurities of Expulsion*, I have argued that anthropological studies of citizenship have typically remained in the remit of nation-states defined as Western, liberal secular, and democratic. These studies of citizenship have typically examined processes of inclusion and exclusion and the making of formal and legal-juridical and substantive citizens and noncitizens; or they have focused on the deportation or expulsion of racialized minorities with less racial and cultural power than the majoritarian white European and

North American host societies. In contrast, I shift our lens to the politics of nation-building, citizenship, racial exclusion and inclusion, and racial expulsion in postcolonial Uganda, examining the making and unmaking of racial privilege and entitlements across co-colonized Subject Race and native subjects–turned-citizens in the postcolony. I demonstrate that an anthropological approach to race and citizenship in postcolonial Uganda cannot be primarily or exclusively understood through methodological nationalism or colonial determinism; instead, it requires critical engagements with shifting ideas, practices, and processes of empire and imperialism, postcolonial nation-building, diaspora, sub-imperialist ambition, transnationalism, and geopolitics. These are the processes that I explore through the lens of transcontinental Uganda. I demonstrate that the anthropology of citizenship is also necessarily an anthropology of governance and sovereignty; I examine the interactive elements of the liberal, illiberal, and nonliberal domains of political practice. I offer a critical and contextualized feminist engagement with shifting domains of empire, race, labor, and capitalism; race, religion, and caste; and gender and sexuality, showcasing how communities of Ugandan Asian and South Asian heritage continue to negotiate accrued imperial and colonial racial and class privileges, racial/civilizational power, and postcolonial privileges relative to many of their non-elite Black African counterparts, navigating both racial privilege and racial precarity after the 1972 expulsion event. In doing so, this book offers a more complicated picture of inclusion and exclusion in postcolonial Uganda than the dominant citizen and subject framework that is typically applied to relationships between native majorities and racial minorities in the African postcolony/nation.[2] While this latter framework emphasizes the enduring legacy of colonial institutions and the inherited "substantive" structures of racial and native governance in postcolonial societies (indeed, the overall limits of settler or quasi-settler incorporation in postcolonial Uganda), I deploy instead both historical and ethnographic approaches to account for the always-changing, transcontinental nature of nation-building, state formation, sovereignty, governance, and citizenship- and race-making.

In doing so, in this book, I more specifically engage with the 1972 Asian expulsion as a global critical event. This framing challenges the dominant "global," or Western liberal, and racialist ideas, discourses, and representations of the expulsion, referred to as *expulsion exceptionalism*, which produces and normalizes Black African race essentialisms and exceptional African illiberalisms. Among South Asians, the South Asian diaspora, and the exiled Ugandan Asian community, expulsion exceptionalism builds upon South Asian sources of racialism to construct ideas of the exceptional racial victimhood of Ugandan Asians at the hands of military dictator Idi Amin. More generally, expulsion exceptionalism relies upon racialized representations of Black African political leaders and their political governance as exceptionally illiberal and excessive in relation to the exceptionally civilized liberal democratic Western nations (the Global North), or even a normative construction of the Indian liberal secular nation and democracy. Expulsion exceptionalist discourse, representations, and memories elevate the experiences of Ugandan Asians as opposed to Black-identifying Ugandans; they also typically obscure and invisibilize the historical and structural processes that led to postcolonial racial antagonisms, the rise of Amin and his government, and the expulsion decree. When more critical histories are mobilized, they can assume forms of colonial determinism, obscuring the ongoing agency of South Asians and South Asian diasporas in producing and reproducing civilizational and racial difference and hierarchies in relation to Black Africans, including propagating anti-Black African racisms and anti-Blackness. Crucially, I argue that ideas about race, racial formations, and racial practices have multiple origins. While both Africans and South Asians fought against their civilizational and racial subordination from Europeans, producing their own sense of race consciousness, including forms of Black and African diasporic, South Asian, and Afro-Asian identities, subjectivities, and solidarities, they were also implicated within European civilizational and race hierarchies differently and experienced racism differently. South Asian sources of civilizational and racial practice, especially those that derive from religious and caste-based ideologies and practice, continue to inform Black African and African diasporic and South Asian and South Asian diasporic encounters, producing a more complicated accounting of racial practice in transcontinental Uganda.

In *Insecurities of Expulsion*, I resignify the 1972 Asian expulsion as a *global critical event*, demonstrating that although unique, it is neither an exceptional nor a provincial event. The nation was never fully "de-Indianized" in 1972; instead, even as the majority Ugandan Asian community was exiled abroad, Afro–South Asian racial entanglements persisted in urban Uganda in the ensuing years. Ugandan Asian and postcolonial South Asian labor, capital, migration, and mobility continued to be intrinsic to the production of *transcontinental Uganda* (signifying the political territory's connections to other "postimperial" and postcolonial nation-states and to the Indian Ocean and Black Atlantic worlds, both transnational and transoceanic connectivities). Tracking the impacts of the expulsion, the transnationally circulating representations of and affects surrounding the expulsion, its differential meanings and memorializations, and the practices of citizenship that have emerged in its aftermath, I assemble these registers of the ongoing event into what I conceptualize as the *insecurities of expulsion*. I show that since the expulsion, Ugandan political leaders and state projects maintain a logic and practice of racially nativist nationalism. African national identity and membership is constructed upon the basis of exclusivist biological and phenotypical definitions of racial Blackness and constructions of African indigeneity and autochthonous relationships to land; it is accompanied by a nationalist, continent-based, and global race consciousness wrought through histories of African self-determination, Black internationalism, and Pan-Africanism. Liberalization-era Ugandan Asian repatriation and property repossession was forged via a normalized politics of racial non-reconciliation that has allowed racialized political insecurities among those racialized as "Asian," racial antagonisms, and even racial resentments to persist. The National Resistance Movement (NRM) has participated in the noncitizen racial incorporation of Ugandan Asians and other Indian diasporic and South Asian entrepreneurs and migrants who are constructed as economic citizens. These economic citizens are increasingly understood as *investor-citizens* rather than as political, racial, or cultural citizens. Moreover, noncitizen racial incorporation is strategic for Ugandan political leaders and state actors as they continue to negotiate Western imperialism, form new geopolitical connections with other Global South nations, and establish state projects of neoliberal authoritarianism, militarization, securitization, and repression.

As I outline in the first three chapters, then, the expulsion event is not resolved but persists as a global critical event; and examined through the experiences of Ugandan Asian exiles, stayees and returnees and their urban African counterparts, it remains essential to Ugandan nation-building, race-making, and citizenship. In addition to the persistent presence of racial estrangements; the articulation of race essentialisms and racial binaries; competing racialized sovereignties; state and majoritarian practices of racial nativism and populist anti-Asianism; and South Asian sources of anti-Black African racism and anti-Blackness, there are also more capacious social constructions, performances, and practices of African and Black identities; practices of Afro–South Asian intimacies; cross-racial intermarriages; creative practices of kinship, conviviality, and neighborliness; and strategic, performative, and ambivalent interracial solidarities. Ugandan Asians (in urban Uganda and displaced abroad), Indian diasporans, and other South Asian migrants practice and perform an array of citizenship claims and strategies as they memorialize or represent expulsion; negotiate their varied racial, gendered, and class privileges and precarities; and construct and manage representations of self and racial community for imputed African majoritarian publics. As Afro–South Asian racial entanglements have intensified in urban Uganda, the new postcolonial Indian diaspora has become the dominant South Asian–origin community in post-expulsion Uganda. And as the depredations of the ruling party have intensified in urban Uganda, the visibility of South Asians on the urban scene has created openings for reassessing the past and former president Idi Amin's anti-Asian accusations against the Ugandan Asians. I explore three domains of African populist anti-Asianism—economic and racial exploitation of Africans, social integration, and interracial marriage alliances—in the final three chapters on the UIA and the search for Indian foreign direct investment; Indian diasporic and African Asian community-building, responses to the Mehta-Mabira Forest crisis and the resurgence of anti-Asian populist violence in 2007, and the everyday lives of Ugandan Asian returnees and Indian migrant women and their daughters, including African and Asian women's feminist activist mobilizations surrounding domestic violence cases internal to the racial community.

The challenges of *decolonizing citizenship*, of determining and practicing the ethical substance of citizenship across postcolonial identities, has primarily been understood in relation to the African postcolonial state and the territorial dimensions of the postcolony/nation.[3] Instead, in *Insecurities of Expulsion*, I show that articulating a project of decolonizing citizenship—indeed, of arriving at Afro-Asian interracialisms and universalisms with the goal of achieving anti-racist multiracial or nonracial polities—requires transcontinental analysis, or careful and close readings of the conceptual and ideological work of theories of diaspora, imperialism, nationalism, postcolonialism, and transnationalism; of the unequal global mobilities of critical events and their significations and occlusions; of the durability of racialisms; and of the need for attendant analytics of labor-capital relations, religion and caste, gender and sexuality. The theoretical concept of the insecurities of expulsion can thus be mobilized as a framework for knowledge production, reorienting anthropologies of citizenship into decolonizing directions within and beyond the assumed liberal geographies of the Global North and the assumed construct of the nation-state. Here, the practice of decolonizing citizenship centers the possibilities and limitations of racial reconciliation and the meaning and practice of integration, assessing the possibilities and limitations of Afro–South Asian interracialisms and universalisms.

In fact, the insecurities of expulsion also haunted the very production of this text—studying the 1972 Asian expulsion as a critical global event and making legible the insecurities of expulsion required a foundational confrontation with dominant knowledge formations, or the very constitution of disciplinary agendas, area studies, and particular intellectual traditions within discipline and area. These dominant knowledge formations are characterized by traditional white-Black or white-Asian racial binaries and constrained the possibility of research on Afro–South Asian worlds. I first began this project by assessing testimonials and writings produced on the 1972 Asian expulsion in diasporic locations in Western nation-states, states that became critical to the study of displaced migration trajectories of postcolonial scholars who constructed the field of South Asian diaspora studies. Building on these insights, I became attentive to the experiences of displaced and even deracinated East African Asians in Europe and North America (as they experienced racial discrimination) and African Asians within larger South Asian diasporas. I paid attention to their practices of anti-Black racial prejudice and the ways they challenged these prejudices; their ongoing entanglements with Africa, the African diaspora, and Blackness as well as Black and Afro–South Asian expressions of consciousness, identity, and community. Second, I found that area-based studies paradigms of South Asian studies and African studies, particularly in the US academy, were always already constituted by an either/or racial and ethnic politics (race for South Africa, ethnicity for the rest of Africa),[4] or an exclusively religious (communal) and caste-based politics in South Asian studies, both of which rendered the 1972 Asian expulsion in Uganda challenging to study. The politics of race and white racial supremacy in US-based universities obstructed prior intellectual affinities between what would become institutionalized as African studies, African diaspora studies (referring primarily to descendants of the transatlantic slave trade), and Black studies, those intellectual formations that had previously engaged with Pan-Africanism, Black internationalism, and even Afro-Asianism, especially Afro-Dalit global solidarities.[5] Third, although the study of Afro-Asianism and African diasporic/Black–South Asian diasporic connections has been undertaken in various disciplines—including at the Birmingham School of cultural studies in the UK or in the "interdisciplines"[6] of ethnic studies and Asian American studies in the United States—these critical knowledge formations could also be constrained by nationalist imaginaries that made imperial and settler-colonial entanglements less accessible. Finally, growing scholarly commitments to Indian Ocean studies among historians were central to my training, offered more critical approaches to area studies that reengaged global Afro-Asianisms and Afro–South Asian connections less directly mediated by "the West," or the Global North. But I also found that studies of premodern and precolonial Afro–South Asian connections were often not in dialogue with the transcontinental Afro–South Asian circulations (and the connections between Indian Ocean and Black Atlantic histories and presents) that I was ultimately invested in.

In 2013, I arrived at the Makerere Institute of Research (MISR), at that time under the directorship of Mahmood Mamdani, to participate in the development of a rigorous course of doctoral study geared toward African doctoral students amid conversations about the conditions and context of research and knowledge production at Makerere and in the African university generally.[7] With a PhD program now attached to the research institute and more innovative funding streams, there was at the time an opening to wrest research and knowledge production away from primarily NGO-consultancy work that prioritized the uncritical developmental aims of external donors. My own as well as others' arrival at the institute offered possibilities for research and scholarship on the expulsion, its aftermaths, and persistent Afro–South Asian entanglements in the very university that had been impacted by the expulsion of Ugandan intellectuals of Asian origin. Indeed, the university was not only reflective but constitutive of the practice of racially nativist nationalism, which had become consequential for research agendas and knowledge production. Here, the same scholarly frames I contended with as I prepared for my fieldwork—not only the emphasis on the African ethnicity paradigm after the 1972 Asian expulsion without attention to transnational racial formations in Africa[8] but also the predominance of intellectual formations of colonial determinism—challenged my ability to make legible more contemporary Afro–South Asian entanglements, especially the presence of the Indian nation and its diasporas in Uganda. As a corrective, I energetically added scholarship on Africa, African Asians, and the Indian Ocean, South Asia, and South Asia diasporas to our library collection. I revised course syllabi to introduce old and new scholarship on Afro–South Asian connections to African students who had not been exposed to these more complex racial histories of East Africa. I integrated gendered and feminist approaches to the study of South Asian diasporas on the African continent, including studies of old and new Indian and South Asian diasporas in Africa and old and new African diasporas in India and in South Asia, reflecting Indian Ocean and geopolitical connections across geographies and area studies–based knowledge formations. Finally, I introduced scholarship that placed Indian Ocean and Black Atlantic histories in conversation with each other, a thematic that became increasingly important to our discussions of African societies prior to European colonization as well as modern histories of slavery and indenture, and to our study of colonial (racial and caste-based) capitalism and global and transoceanic abolitionist and anticolonial movements.

Yet I continued to grapple with the structural and epistemological limitations of the research institute and the postcolonial racially nativist African university. While it was certainly convenient to idealize Global South and African research institutes for challenging dominant Western and Eurocentric knowledge productions in African universities, how exactly would I confront the overwhelming structural logic of racial nativism that was constitutive of the university and nation? And what about the ambivalent forms of embodied racial and gendered exclusion and racial and gendered privilege that I embodied? How would I avoid exceptionalizing the expulsion and obscuring accrued imperial and racial South Asian privilege, on the one hand, and avoid devolving into reactionary and racially exclusionary nativist nationalisms and chauvinisms, on the other hand? This was another crucial, if tricky, landscape of identity politics that required careful and ethical reflection and awareness. Ultimately, in my graduate seminar, I worked to center Black African experience and their histories and struggles for political and self-determination alongside Afro–South Asian solidarities in political and intellectual struggle. Just as I was completing my tenure at MISR and at Makerere University in 2015, the #Ghandimustfall (*sic*) movements that began in Ghana exemplified a significant, if under-appreciated, episode that revealed lingering Afro–South Asian tensions in an African continent–wide perspective.

Tracing University and Student Movements: Gandhi Must Fall, from Africa to the UK to the United States

By 2013, the South African university student–led #Rhodes Must Fall (RMF) movement—initiated by the students at the University of Cape Town toppling a statue of Cecil Rhodes, the European imperialist architect of the apartheid project—drew renewed attention to the persistence of colonial and racial legacies at South African universities and the exclusion of Black African students from higher education. RMF was the foundational basis for the

#Fees Must Fall (FMF) movement, which articulated connections between Black African racial exclusion from higher education and their economic exclusion, offering a more trenchant analysis of the neoliberal restructuring of South African public higher education. Statuary politics and the ensuing African university and student movements compelled a growing body of activist and scholarly reflections on the material and epistemic decolonization of the African university. These works foreground the negotiations and tensions between and among Black, white, Indian, and Colored student communities with respect to the limitations of postapartheid nonracialism, racial neoliberalism, and feminist and queer movements.[9]

Across the Atlantic, activists and students founded and joined the Movement for Black Lives, or #BlackLivesMatter (BLM), in the United States, in response to the acceleration of militarized police brutality against Black American communities. The massive protests in 2014–15 in Ferguson, Missouri, in response to the police killing of Michael Brown—just prior to the accession of Donald Trump as president in 2017—compelled anti-Black racist and abolitionist student activism in universities and new directions in Black and African diaspora studies. These disciplines continue to center the afterlives of white supremacy, transatlantic plantation slavery, settler colonialism, policing, and incarceration on the US scene, building on insights from the Black radical tradition, Black feminism, and Afro-pessimism to understand the foundational conceits of anti-Black racism and anti-Blackness in the seemingly liberal-democratic nation. Taken together, activist and scholarly critique have worked to dismantle US university-based scripts of Obama-era postracialism and the disciplining effects of (post–civil rights era affirmative action) diversity, equity, and inclusion (DEI) models that continue to exclude Black American and African diasporic students from universities, enabling trenchant critiques of the neoliberal, militarized, and anti-Black university and abolitionist futures. As I traveled between East Africa and the United States, it became clear that BLM circulated globally and virtually through the internet and social media, especially in Africa and even among African diasporic people in South Asia. The movement spoke to the common condition of the denigration and oppression of Black, African, and African diasporic communities globally, shaping common identifications through the embodied experience of Blackness and requiring new analytics of global Blackness in relation to formations of structural (neoliberal capitalist) violence and state violence.

I was also keeping track of developing dynamics across the Indian Ocean and in the Indian nation. The accession of the Narendra Modi–led Bharatiya

Janata Party (BJP) government in 2014 led to the normalization of, if already existing, authoritarian and populist Hindu supremacist nationalist impulses, the unraveling of existing liberal democratic institutions in the judiciary and legislature, the accelerated neoliberalization of domestic-based markets and society, and the repression and attacks on academic freedom, free speech, rights of protest, and dissent. While prior to BJP rule, many regions and communities in India had long borne the impacts of the illiberal politics constitutive of the liberal-democratic-secular political center, the effects of Modi, the BJP, and the ruling class's neoliberal and Hindu supremacist policies continue to be disproportionately felt by the class- and caste-oppressed—Muslims and other religious minorities who are understood as racially foreign to the nation via the construction and indigenization of Aryan, Brahmanical, Hindu, and other dominant caste identities and Dharmic identities—as opposed to the supposedly foreign Abrahamic (Islamic and Christian) religions. Political violence and oppression have led to long-standing social suffering in Kashmir and the Punjab, as predominantly Muslim Kashmiris and Sikhs in the Punjab are variously constructed as insiders and outsiders of the Indian nation in the context of 1980s–2000s militancy, insurgency, and counter-insurgency operations and ongoing settler occupations.[10]

At the same time, in 2014, the question of race—pertaining to phenotypical Blackness, Africans, and the African diaspora—and not only religion or caste, emerged on the Indian national public scene and within transnational Indian diasporic networks, especially social media. In the intervening decades since the liberalization of India's economy and its growing Global South intimacies with African nations, new generations of urban African migrants, workers, professionals, and students have settled in India. Unsurprisingly, and despite, the rhetoric of South-South cooperation, Africans of many different national origins are referred to in derogatory ways as "Nigerians" and are stereotypically associated with criminal networks and especially the drug trade (primarily men) and prostitution (primarily women). In 2017, a spate of ugly violent and racist attacks and slurs against Ugandan and Congolese college students by Indian students at Indian universities (from New Delhi, Uttar Pradhesh, and the Punjab) circulated in the news and on social media.[11] In Kampala, where I was based at the time, members of the African Asian Association (AAA) met to discuss the cases and their relevance for Ugandan, Ugandan Asian, and new Indian diasporic communities in Kampala, even as the NRM remained silent about the racial attacks on Ugandans in India. The Indian government, for its part, also denied the existence of racism in India—one commentator even argued that India has its own "Blacks," in reference to phenotypically darker-skinned South Indians who had been defined by ethno-linguists and later racialized as Dravidian, and potentially in relation to India's Adivasi (tribal, indigenous) and Siddi (Afro-Asian) communities.[12] In fact, the position of the government of India on the nonexistence of racism in India also seemed consistent with its opposition to the admission of Dalits to the UN Conference Against Racism in 2001, and, despite the work of scholars and researchers, its denial of connections between religious ideology, casteism, colorism, and racism.[13]

Critical commentators like Renu Modi and Rhea D'Silva continue to observe that the racial attacks on Africans in India contradict "meta-narratives of ascendant African and Indian political and economic relations."[14] Anti-Black racism in India has compelled more scholarly and popular engagement with the transnational and global study of the intimacies between race and caste, reviving earlier scholarly traditions on race/caste analogy, Afro-Dalit connections, and global solidarities.[15] Some commentators, like Arundhati Roy—who have continued to emphasize the enduring impacts of caste hierarchy and caste discrimination in Indian society despite legal and societal reforms that ban caste discrimination and that have introduced caste-based reservations—have further argued that India is a deeply racist society.[16] Feminist scholars have deepened epistemological critiques of South Asian studies and associated disciplines of study like South Asian religion, deploying feminist theories and methodologies to understand the intersections of religion, caste, and race central to the production of knowledge.[17] Progressive Indian students have continued to participate in antifascist protests and demonstrations in major urban centers like New Delhi, drawing out lines of connection between Hindu supremacy and fascism, Brahmanical Hinduism, caste violence, colorism, and prejudice against Black and African diasporic communities in India, while South Asian diaspora students, scholars, and activists in Global North contexts are tracing connections between racial and caste abolition in universities and broader society.[18]

When I joined the University of California, Merced, in the Californian Central Valley in 2015, I was struck by the contradictory ways in which the US-based BLM movement had circulated to and transformed social movements and protest in Africa and South Asia, and conversely, how African and Indian political and university student–based movements were not legible in the US settler-imperialist state. Moreover, intensifying transnational political, economic, and social intimacies between Africa and South Asia were not as accessible in the United States, under institutional conditions in which area and disciplinary formations of African and South

Asian studies and Black and African diasporic and South Asian diasporic studies are separated and compartmentalized. Our conversations felt circumscribed by imperial and colonial hegemonies and by national borders and boundaries, despite the fact that parallel issues of neoliberalism, militarized repression, racial injustices, and decolonization were occurring transnationally, and despite the top-down administrative discourse urging university leaders and faculty to work to diversify and internationalize the UC system. So, even though most of my American undergraduate students had an intuitive sense of the United States' declining global position and image in shifting geopolitical times, they had little to no knowledge of how to think about the divides and connections between the Global North and the Global South, the intensification of South-South connections, or the driving impulses behind university and student movements occurring in South Africa and India.

As statues of slaveholders and Confederate army officers began to fall in the United States, I framed my lectures around the falling imperialists in South Africa and in European metropoles. Connecting these university and student movements—and despite our location within the constraints of American settler-colonial and imperial power, wrought through liberal nationalist exceptionalism—we discussed the significance of statues and monuments and their role in memorializing, remembering, and forgetting contested and painful histories. After the statues monumentalizing slaveholders, Confederates, and imperialists fell, what would replace them? And how would the painful histories that they commemorated be preserved and made accessible for reparative presents and futures? What practices of ethical identity-formation, community, and citizenship would be constructed and practiced amid the anger, pain, and violence of protest and rebellion? What were the limitations of practices of apology, commemoration, reparations, reconciliation, and justice thus far?

In 2015, a colleague forwarded to me a social media tweet regarding the first #Ghandimustfall (*sic*; hereafter GMF) protest at the University of Ghana, in Accra, after which I began to follow additional Africa-based protests and their demands to remove statues of Mohandas K. Gandhi. These protests were led by African academics and students activists in Ghana, and they quickly spread to South Africa and Malawi.[19] Anti-Gandhianism was an expression of an African continent–based understanding of what has been articulated as the more complicated life story of "the South African Gandhi,"[20] focusing on Gandhi's often cited use of the derogatory term *kaffir* to refer to Black Africans and his participation in other practices of upholding the civilizational and racial hierarchies of British empire with respect to Africans in colonized South Africa. Here, African activists who wanted to topple Gandhi monuments did not necessarily have access to, nor were they persuaded by, Indian nation-based popular histories of Gandhi as a pioneer of nonviolent civil disobedience campaigns critical to the dismantling of empire; nor were they privy to other global representations of Gandhi as a radical figure of spiritual and political resistance. Nor did they necessarily have access to a scholarly engagement with other historiographies of Gandhi in South Africa that have challenged exclusively Indian nationalist hagiographies of Gandhi, placing his life itinerary within interconnected geographies of Afro–South Asia and the Indian Ocean.[21] Here, Gandhi was not understood as a figure representing anticolonial solidarity between African and Indian nations or South-South cooperation. Indeed, Gandhi seemed to represent a stand-in for a transhistorical and ambivalently received "Indian" or Asian racial presence in Africa.

As GMF unfolded in Africa and on social media, it garnered considerable attention and generated varied public and scholarly commentary. Some, from the vantage of South Asian studies and Indian national history, including those who have deeply studied Gandhian thought and practice, have dismissed the protests as reactionary and misguided. They have minimally observed that Gandhi has continually been subject to parallel critique in the South Asian academy and Indian public sphere with respect to caste and gender politics.[22] Others have argued that Africans and others impassioned by GMF are incorrectly imposing the language, categories, and practices of contemporary antiracism upon a Gandhi negotiating the historical racial contexts of late nineteenth and early twentieth century. This is a distortion that sidelines the innovations of Gandhian thought and praxis at the time, his eventual political maturation in anticolonial struggle in British India, and his later evolution into a global and transnational symbol and resource for the nonviolent civil disobedience campaigns of Black Americans during the civil rights struggle in the United States and the antiapartheid struggle in South Africa.[23] They have found especially problematic the globally circulating use of "anti-Blackness" among Africans, which originated in the philosophy of Afro-pessimism and became normalized during the BLM movement. Anti-Blackness is now understood as a global phenomenon encompassing the experiences of Black Africans in Africa.[24] Others have argued persuasively that Gandhi monuments and statues serve as a metaphor for both racial tensions with the older Indian diaspora in Africa and tensions with the new Indian diasporic presence in places like Ghana and South Africa.[25] Finally, some have argued that from the perspective of Africans, the defacing or toppling of Gandhi statues is not naive or reactionary but reveals a significant engagement with the contradictions of Gandhi and Gandhian philosophy (as understood in Africa) and insidious South Asian sources of civilizational racism, Brahmanical casteism, colorism, and other practices of discrimination directed toward Black African and African diasporic people; practices that are often difficult and uncomfortable for dominant-caste and privileged South Asians—especially within the academy—to contend with.[26] From this perspective, when young Africans and South Asian students and activists deploy the flippant phrase "Gandhi was anti-Black," they are articulating more critical positions on Gandhi in relation to their present, and often interconnected, transcontinental struggles with racism and casteism.

In their commentary on GMF, Neilesh Bose, Renu Modi, Shobana Shankar, and Meera Venkatachalam have maintained that attention should be paid to the differences between what we know about "the historical Gandhi" and the "images of Gandhi" that circulate globally; they argue that both are in dialogical relationship with each other, constructing competing and contested knowledge formations.[27] In African nations, the statuary monumentalization of Gandhi has symbolized different things for different communities at different times: mid-twentieth-century anticolonial solidarity between Africans and Indians; performances of Cold War Third Worldism, nonalignment, Afro-Asian political diplomacy; and more recently, the cementing of geopolitical ties and South-South cooperation between the Indian nation and African nations that are already part of or attempting to gain entry into BRICS, a project embraced by African political leaders and elites enticed by lucrative trade, investment, and diplomatic agreements with the Indian government. The Modi-led BJP government and political class has continued to participate in the monumentalization of Gandhi in African nations, but also now embraces a range of Indian political figures: from Sardar Vallabhbhai Patel to Vinayak Sarvarkar (the architect of the Hindu right-wing political parties that were involved in the assassination of Gandhi), alongside other anticolonial figures, from Bhagat Singh to B. R. Ambedkar to Subhas Chandra Bose.[28] In doing so, Modi and the BJP are crafting a nationalist and state project based on an assemblage of neoliberal capitalist, militarist, nationalist, populist authoritarian, illiberal, Hindu supremacist, and heteropatriarchal processes; while skillfully capturing both radical and complicated political figures, histories, and symbols of anticolonial nationalism and liberal democracy to advance their agenda.

Visiting Kampala again in the summer of 2017, I followed the reception of both India-based racist attacks on African students and GMF in Uganda. Ugandan Asians and community leaders in the Indian diaspora community were variously sympathetic to the motivation behind the protests and anxious about potential implications, revealing their political and racial vulnerabilities in the post-expulsion context and their knowledge of internal community practices of civilizational and racial arrogance with respect to Africans. Indian political diplomats and Indian businessmen and entrepreneurs, largely pro-Modi and BJP, continued to construct positive relationships between Africans and a transhistorical "Indian community" while minimizing the 1972 Asian expulsion as a minor episode. The NRM continued its reception of Indian investment and cultivated political and economic ties with the Indian government, strategic for its own nation-state building project, building regional power, asserting geopolitical resistance to the West, and mobilizing its own revisionist histories of national liberation and Pan-Africanist unity.

In fact, in 2018, ten years after I attended the first Vibrant Gujarat conference in Kampala, Prime Minister Narendra Modi visited the Ugandan Parliament to strengthen bilateral relationships between the Museveni and Modi governments. This was the first parliamentary visit of an Indian Prime Minister since the NRM had come to power. In his address to Ugandan Parliamentarians, Modi evoked both Indian Ocean and Afro-Asian histories, highlighting "the ancient bonds of solidarity and friendship between our people." Although Museveni, in his own address, artfully pushed back on some of the Indian paternalism to Africans in Modi's speech, the visit successfully cemented Ugandan-Indian diplomatic and trade relations, with Modi pledging to build a Gandhi Heritage and Convention Center at the source of the Nile River in Jinja, where a bust of Gandhi already stood.[29] For their part, Modi and the BJP constructed a modern, strong, and industrializing idea of the Indian nation, uplifting its internal diversity (and even African presence) in strategic ways—yet simultaneously invisibilizing critical orientations to the 1947 partition, communal violence, the exclusion of religious minorities, insidious systems of gendered and caste violence, and the marginalization of indigenous communities, African-descendant people like the Siddis, and postcolonial African migrants in India. In their speeches, both Museveni and Modi downplayed the global critical event of the 1972 Asian expulsion. Recently, however, this shifted when Museveni issued the first official state apology for the 1972 Asian expulsion at the now late neoliberal–era revived Non-Aligned Movement (NAM) conference hosted by the Ugandan government in Kampala in January 2024.[30] It is telling that the apology was geared toward the Indian nation and the Indian diaspora and its business class rather than the expelled Ugandan Asians who have not risen to the prominence of becoming valuable investors in the nation.

But racial tensions and racialized insecurities persist, the underbelly of the abstract and performative celebration of the resurgence of African-Indian political and economic ties. In this sense, GMF protests bring attention to the more contemporary entanglement between African elites, the Indian nation, and other South Asian nations. Here, we can surmise that GMF was also about the persistent racial and economic exclusion of Black Africans globally, structurally, and in urban Africa, this time at the hands of both African and Indian postcolonial elites alike. Even if some (primarily South Asian and Global South–based) scholars had reservations about the global uptake of US-based racial categories in Africa-based protest movements, GMF opened up a significant Africa-based reading of the transcontinental dynamics of capitalism, racism, Brahminism, casteism, and colorism. And GMF led to even more critical engagements by African scholars on the possibilities and limitations of Afro-Asianism, Pan-Africanism, Black internationalism, the Black radical tradition, and Afro-pessimism in formulating responses to South Asian sources of racism.[31] India-based Dalits and others who have long identified with Black global struggles for self-determination supported GMF because they felt the protests drew attention to India's own internal color, caste-based, and religious minority discriminations, enabling new openings for the monumentalization of anti-caste activists like B. R. Ambedkar on the African continent.[32] Ultimately, the GMF protests compelled a dialogue between student and university movements and scholarly criticism, fashioning an African continental and social media–based conversation on Black, African, and African diasporic struggle against South Asian sources of racial oppression, making visible the fault lines and occlusions in equivalent formulations of "Africa–South Asia" or "Africa-India," and revealing the limitations of racial solidarities. Finally, the GMF protests showcased the intellectual labor that remains in terms of epistemic decolonization—that Africa–South Asia has been insufficiently and unevenly engaged with across African, Indian, and Western-based (Global North– and South-based) universities; that African university students do not necessarily read what is being read in the South Asian academy, and vice versa; that the South Asian academy must do more to engage with African and African diasporic intellectual traditions. The US academy, it seems, increasingly parochializes itself in relation to Africa–South Asia, even as its university and student movements impact those in Africa and its diasporas.

GMF did not peter out on the African continent. In 2019, and after I had arrived at the University of California, Irvine, I received a Facebook invitation to attend an anti-Gandhi protest that was organized by Sikh, Kashmiri, and Dalit South Asian American undergraduate student activists on Indian independence day (August 15) at the UC Berkeley campus. Following commentary and checking out photos posted on the page, I saw that Black American students and others had joined the protest in solidarity, and to demonstrate their allied criticisms of Gandhian commemoration and popular Indian nationalist Gandhian hagiography. This protest was not engaged with scholarly criticism or scholarly debate but was a public demonstration intended to express dismay at, first, the ways in which Modi and the BJP government have mobilized Gandhi on patriotic and nationalist grounds to posture about Indian liberal secular democracy (especially to Western governments) via celebrations of Indian independence (often obscuring partition and communal violence); and second, the ways in which student activists traced formations of illiberalism even prior to the ascendancy of the Hindu right in India and in relation to the liberal-secular Congress Party. They were especially voicing dissent at the Indian government's revocation of Article 370 of the Indian Constitution (which had previously granted autonomous status to Jammu and Kashmir); the Indian military's occupation of Kashmir, and the long-standing human rights abuses and injustices that members of the Sikh community had experienced in the aftermath of 1984 and throughout the 1990s in the Punjab; and they were expressing solidarity with the victims of caste-based discrimination (experienced by many students in the UC system). These same networks of student activist dissent were revived in relation to the 2019 Citizenship Act in India that created differentiated and religious-based (Dharmic and Abrahamic) lines of inclusion and exclusion for minorities in the Indian nation and that especially targeted Muslim communities. They were revived again during the New Delhi–based Shaheen Bagh protests of 2019–20, and the Farmers Agitations in New Delhi in 2020–21, the latter two protests primarily Muslim and Sikh-led resistance to the BJP. Remarkably, just as many students of South Asian heritage had participated in solidarity struggles with Black students during earlier BLM agitations, Black students now joined Indian students in their critiques of Indian fascism, neoliberal exploitation, religious minority oppression, and authoritarian repression. Here, earlier histories of Afro–South Asian transnational solidarities were being revived—but also reworked—through new cross-racial, religious, and caste-based alliances in the United States. Despite diasporic displacements, national boundaries, and differentiated privileges, students were making incipient, if global, connections between global white and Brahmanical supremacy, racisms, casteisms, anti-Black racism, and anti-Blackness (even now, scholarship and activism on the lingering practices of Brahmanism, casteism, and anti-Blackness within diasporic Sikh and Kashmiri communities continues). In 2020 in the UK, BLM activists participated in a GMF protest at Parliament Square just after the police murder of George Floyd.[33] And so, GMF traveled to the United States and the UK, from Africa and to the Black African diaspora, building upon African perceptions of racial dynamics between Africans and Indians in African nations and in India.

For many of my colleagues in the scholarly community, GMF protests and their participants are not legible; they are perceived as suspicious and even as illegitimate. In the United States and US academy, Mohandas Gandhi is also, of course, central to Black political thought and to the political and spiritual praxis of Dr. Martin Luther King and other key political figures of the civil rights movement, which is itself informed by a history of transnational Afro-Dalit solidarity and struggle. Yet, the arrival of GMF in African and South Asian diasporic contexts in the United States and the UK reveals the persistent racial reckonings still needed internally within South Asian communities as well as the internal hierarchies and exclusions within supposedly homogenous racial South Asian communities. It has made visible the interconnected terrains of political and social struggle and the dynamic social formations of critique, solidarity, and resistance that will be required to counter sources of inequality, supremacy, chauvinism, and elite capture.

Toward an Anthropology of Transcontinental Afro–South Asian Entanglement and Afro–South Asian Study

The GMF movements, like the 1972 Asian expulsion, are global critical events, ones that are neither parochial nor exceptional but challenging and uncomfortable moments—those that visibilize a *transcontinental anthropology of Afro–South Asian entanglement* and what I call *Afro–South Asian study*. On the African continent, more research that centers Black African experiences and encounters with "South Asianness" and "Indianisms"[34]— focusing on specific African and South Asian (ethnic, religious, caste-based) communities—will be paramount. Important, too, will be the shift away from exclusively secular-based understandings of political solidarities toward the study of other practices of intimacy and conviviality, the centering of gendered and sexual formations, shared ethical orientations derived from religion and spirituality, and shared cultural economies, cultural productions, and aesthetics. Across the Indian Ocean and in South Asia, more attention to longue-durée histories of old and new African diaspora communities on the South Asian subcontinent, including a centering of the experiences of Afro-Siddi communities in Gujarat, contemporary Pakistan, and Sri Lanka, or the experiences of more recently arrived African migrants, workers, and students in urban India and other South Asian contexts, will compel South-South dialogue on Afro–South Asian encounter. South-South, trans–Indian Ocean connections must also be in dialogue with the Black Atlantic world, drawing transatlantic connections to African, African Asian, and South Asian diasporas in the Global North and back to Africa and the Global South again. This approach does not lose sight of the West or the Global North, empire and neo-colonialism, and Eurocentrism and white supremacy in mediating Afro–South Asian encounters; but it emphasizes the changing postcolonial nationalisms and even sub-imperial dynamics that also mediate Afro–South Asian entanglements. It highlights the need to contend with dynamic and transcontinental formations and processes of capitalism and labor-capital relations; race, ethnicity, religion, and caste; and gender and sexuality; interrogating anticolonial, postcolonial, and decolonial theories and methods in our studies.

Following Black American internationalist and feminist anthropologists like Faye V. Harrison who advocate for "the decolonizing tradition,"[35] I argue that ethnographic research can transform the priorities of research and knowledge production in academic institutions often already constrained by imperialist and nationalist ambitions in the Global North, or the structural inequalities and unequal access to resources and power in the Global South. While African universities and other institutions in the Global South are constrained by neocolonial developmentalism and the racial legacies of colonialism, anthropologists working in the US academy who focus on Africa and the Global South are positioned within more privileged institutions and networks. They challenge the liberal nationalist conceit of universities by visibilizing imperialist and settler-colonial machinations and confronting the compartmentalizing and illegibility of globally entangled knowledge formations, histories, and presents.

In the United States, the aggressive neoliberalization and privatization of academic institutions and generational and demographic shifts mean that a "majority minority" now characterizes the state of California and the University of California public university system where I currently work. At the same time, threats to the epistemic liberal "baseline" of the university system, including free speech and academic freedom as well as militarized police repression, white supremacy, ethno-religious nativist nationalisms, and heteropatriarchies, render faculty and students committed to decolonizing the university and knowledge production precarious. Racial and religious minoritized feminist intellectuals like myself, who came of age in the United States as our parents negotiated violent ethno-racial, religious, and gendered nationalisms in India and Africa, had reasonable, if differentiated, expectations surrounding the potential securities, privileges, and entitlements of relocating to Western liberal democratic societies. Instead, the material and ideological decline of US empire and its legitimacy, coupled with the changing geopolitical alliances in our multipolar world, have upended these expectations and traditional conventions surrounding the intellectual possibilities of networks of knowledge production globally. Even with their own constraints, the advent of anticolonial-oriented research institutes and scholarly networks in Africa and other Global South locations that center transcontinental connection might very well be the future of the university—further de-exceptionalizing and de-provincializing knowledge production in the Global North.

To be sure, we need political solidarities, anti-racist feminist interracialisms and nonracialisms, and critical research and scholarly collaborations to build the world we want. But we must also continually assess, dismantle, and rebuild these relationalities-in-the making. In this book, I have shifted away from a politics of exceptionalism, nostalgia or racial victimization, race essentialism or primordial racial conflict, and interracial redemption or romanticization. I have produced instead a multilayered analysis of the 1972 Asian expulsion and the ambivalent and uneasy politics of racial reconciliation, examining knowledge formations and the transcontinental implications of expulsion. In our current predicament, and in vigilant assessment of the ethics of knowledge production, I thus argue that *Insecurities of Expulsion* is also entangled with the boundaries and edges of disciplines and area studies, with knowledge- and university-making; with identity-, community- and citizenship-making; with world-making—of Afro–South Asian universals and futures, made tangible, possible.

Fifty Years On

The year 2020—the pandemic, urban rebellion in the wake of the police murder of George Floyd, and the ensuing quarantines and militarized lockdowns—was a turbulent time. Inviting me to speak on numerous Zoom webinars at US and India-based universities, my hosts asked me to reflect on BLM and on social and political movements in the United States, with a focus on the South Asian diaspora and community complicities with anti-Black racisms and anti-Blackness. That same year, the rise in anti-Asian xenophobic violence elicited more invitations from university initiatives and community organizations to discuss and analyze anti-Asian hate crimes and responses. These interventions built upon my earlier work on post-9/11 Islamoracism and its impacts upon the American Punjabi Sikh community, which has borne disproportionate levels of violence as white racial nativist nationalism intensifies.[1] The complicated dynamics of late neoliberal capitalist and racist US society, the contradictory mobilities of political figures like Kamala Harris (Black and South Asian descent) and Nikki Haley (Punjabi and Sikh heritage) in the Democratic and Republican parties, respectively, the Black American billionaire political class, the phenomenon of South Asian American "neoliberal Hindutva democrats"[2]—these shifting terrains of Black–South Asian intimacies and entanglements compelled me to question the nationalist borders that framed our discussions.

The ways in which the figures of the Asian police officer and the Arab merchant became implicated in the conditions and context of Floyd's murder and within systems of racial capitalism, Black American racist policing, and the incarceration of Black men recalled for me the persistent figure of the Asian merchant in the urban context. The Asian merchant figure was constructed as a stranger, unassimilable, and exploitative of the imputed Black "native" population, typically implicated in anti-Black racist violence, and analyzed especially through the lens of Black-Asian (specifically, Black-Korean) conflict in the United States.[3] Black-Asian racial conflict (Asian sources of anti-Black racism and Black sources of anti-Asianism) was a critical theme both prior to the 1992 police beating of Rodney King and during the LA uprising that followed the court verdict that offered no justice to King, his family, or Black Americans.[4] Black-Asian racial conflict is also depicted powerfully in relation to labor and capital in New York City in Spike Lee's 1989 film, *Do the Right Thing*.[5] While these earlier analyses of race relations in the US were less engaged with US imperialist and settler histories, the need for imperial and transnational analyses of militarization and policing, racism, and neoliberal capital with respect to race relations in the US continues to be necessary. In the months that followed Floyd's racist murder, it suddenly seemed to me that the 1972 expulsion of Ugandan Asians by military dictator Idi Amin—a rather obscure historical event of African nativist and populist anti-Asian violence entwined with imperial and neocolonial racial and capitalist forces that generated and intensified racial hierarchies and antagonisms between Africans and Asians, and that continued to exceed its colonial context—was now becoming relevant to the lived and complex realities that my undergraduate students were navigating in the United States.

Ugandan Asian expulsion and its aftermaths tend to be more relevant in what is constructed as the "postimperial" UK, where racial reckonings, especially surrounding themes of race, immigration, and empire, persist. The majority British East African Asian diasporic population and their descendants live in the UK, and many have now moved into the professional classes and even the British political class. In the context of the rise of the British populist right and the 2016 referendum on Brexit, it is telling that former UK home secretary Priti Patel (in the Boris Johnson government), former home secretary Suella Braverman (Sunak government), and former prime minister Rishi Sunak, all key figures in the Tory conservative party, are all of East African Asian, and even Ugandan Asian heritage (of Gujarati Hindu, Punjabi Hindu, Goan Christian, and Tamil Hindu descent, respectively). This showcases the significance of East African Asian/South Asian conservativism, model minority racism, and even religious and dominant caste ties to Modi's overseas Hindu nationalism within the British political class.[6] Braverman and Sunak, in particular, were at the helm of a UK investment scheme with President Paul Kagame and the government of Rwanda to deport and re-settle undocumented migrants from diverse national origins in the UK to Kigali, schemes that continue to be taken up by other right-wing European political movements and parties.[7] Imperial entanglements, it seems, have come full circle, with the children of those who were racially exiled from Africa now at the helm of machinations to expel less fortunate Others from the imperial homeland. The politics of race and class—and of race, religion, and caste—within the British Asian and especially East African Asian dias-pora communities are central to the ongoing practice of empire and right-wing populisms and fascisms made multiracial.

In contrast, other British Asian and North American–based youths of East African Asian descent are showcasing their antiracist and Left-progressive analysis of these developments.[8] Some British Asian youths are invested in continuing to learn about their East African heritage and reckon with their parents' and grandparents' experiences of expulsion or exile from Uganda and East Africa with respect to multiracial Britain.[9] The UK, unlike the United States, has an important historical tradition of political Blackness, multiracial-Left trade union organizing and antifascist mobilization, experimenting with Black British identities and even with Black feminist organizing.[10] More recent criticisms of anti-Black racism and anti-Blackness, Hindu nationalist sentiments, and Islamophobia within British Asian communities map the possibilities and limits of coalitional politics and the lived substance of solidarities in the UK. Therein remain critical resources for a multiracial, anti-caste, and plural multireligious Left to respond to the predations of state, race, and capital on the British scene.

Fall 2022 marked the fifty-year commemoration of the 1972 Asian expul-sion. Amid the official commemorations and events taking place, the retiree generation of Ugandan Asian exiles continues to process their experiences of expulsion, retaining a stake in their African Asian identities, refusing to for-get, offering more detailed insights and complexity into the lead-up to their forced exile from Uganda that eventful year. I attended some of the com-memoration events and conferences taking place virtually (online) and in person in the UK, especially those organized by the British Ugandan Asians at Fifty (or the BUA@50 project), supported by the British Asian and Indian Overseas Trust and other government and Ugandan Asian family donors.[11]

In addition, Faisal Devji organized a scholarly conference supported by the Asian Studies Centre at Oxford University, followed by others at UK universities and colleges as the fifty-year commemoration approached.[12] Gaurav Desai and James Ocita organized a panel at the virtual African Studies Association in 2021 and a special issue, "Fifty Years after the Asian Expulsions," in the *Journal of the African Literature Association*.[13] Back in Kampala, a small and underattended event was sponsored by the Ruparelia Group, with very little Ugandan Asian diasporic engagement, and Mahmood Mamdani held a public lecture at Makerere University in 2022 in collaboration with Ugandan colleagues.[14] At the Ugandan Asian community level, the global Ismailia Jamat organized Zoom webinar panel discussions to commemorate the expulsion; and another panel reflected on the emergence of the Ismaili diaspora in North America, which enlisted less visible Ugandan Asian intellectuals and professionals such as Mohamed Keshavjee, Jalal Jaffer, Mobina Jaffer, Arafat Jamal, and many others to speak about the expulsion and its legacies, fifty years later.[15] Despite the fact that many of us addressed the 1972 expulsion and its legacies in global news outlets,[16] there remained a sense that commemoration events and academic reassessments of the 1972 Asian expulsion were rather sparse and muted. It was clear that the global pandemic had impacted the now elderly community of Ugandan Asian exiles most deeply affected by the event; that there were different approaches to commemoration among community members, those with business interests, and academics and scholars; and that many events engage the past rather than illuminating connections between 1972 as a global critical event and possible futures for Afro–South Asian relationalities. Significantly, there was very little scholarly and public conversation in Uganda (aside from Museveni's most recent practice of reconciliation in the form of apology with respect to aligning with strategic Indian government and business interests). But there was also little to no conversation on the expulsion in scholarly, intellectual, and artistic venues in African and Indian universities or within other African and Indian national contexts.

The extent to which expulsion memorialization and commemoration occurs is significant, for such events reveal the investments of the exiled generation in shaping a dialogue surrounding their experiences and their ongoing attachments to an African Asian identity. But the content of and participation in these events matter as well. Memorialization is premised on both remembering and forgetting, with selective narrations of events and of the historical processes that shape them. As I have traced in this book, community-based commemoration events and the dominant social memory of the event often reproduce "expulsion exceptionalism"—singular narratives of Asian racial victimization at the hands of the reductive and uncomplicated figure of President Idi Amin, in which binaries between a liberal West and illiberal Africa (read through the specific context of Uganda) continue to circulate vis-à-vis a racist commonsense made universal. In the UK, expulsion commemorations—especially those sponsored by the British government—advance the racial stereotyping of the Ugandan Asian diaspora as a successfully assimilated refugee and business community, positioning them within white supremacist racial hierarchies and at odds with British Black and African diaspora communities (those of Black African and Caribbean heritage and their descendants).

While it is important to commemorate the pain and violence that many disenfranchised Ugandan Asians experienced upon their expulsion, and while nostalgia and emotional sentiments for pre-expulsion Ugandan Asian life are legitimate feelings, Black African perspectives are often strategically unseen, and British government, Ugandan government, Indian government, and elite community practices are uncritically embraced, often for politically expedient reasons. Rather, Ugandan Asians and their descendants continue to be entangled in relationships of empire, race, and capital with their Black African counterparts and across multiple geographies and contemporary nation-state territories. The fact is that many commemoration events are constituted by the experience of racial estrangement and exile. New nationalist identities, which themselves require a forgetting of entanglements with Africa, Africans, and Blackness, make it difficult to attend to the practice of interracialism, antiracism, and related movements against oppression and exploitation across transcontinental geographies.

Back in Kampala, discussions of expulsion continue to be refracted through the NRM's strategic investments in geopolitical and economic ties with the Indian government. The sparse community-based commemoration events are also in danger of being shaped by the political agendas of the NRM, business elites, and the BJP-led government's relationships to the Indian diaspora in Africa. As the NRM has entered a heightened stage of securitized and militarized political repression, neoliberal capitalist exploitation, and brutality against its citizens, Ugandans continue to resist the regime—especially in the aftermath of the latest round of election-related violence in 2021 that has targeted Robert Kyagulani Ssentamu's (Bobi Wine's) People Power, Our Power Movement and resulted in the deaths, injuries, and mass arrests and detentions of thousands of Ugandans.[17] Many Ugandan Asians, displaced or returned, remain out of step with the political context and political sentiments of Ugandans in general. As one British Asian friend of Ugandan heritage explained, "It used to be that there was a general sense of anti-Asian sentiment, but now you see that most of the resistance is against the government, with anti-Asian sentiments mixed up in it." Indeed, since at least 2020, it is also Black-identifying Ugandan youths, in both Uganda and the diaspora, who have been at the forefront of making BLM transnational and African, leading antimilitarization and anti-police-brutality campaigns in Uganda and Kenya, typically without the participation or allyship of Ugandans of South Asian heritage or the Indian diaspora in Africa.[18]

Without sustained dialogue between and among intellectuals, activists, and community leaders, the space for critical conversations and perspectives on the expulsion and its aftermaths will close—and so, too, will the possibilities for transracial solidarities in diasporic spaces that can engage with contemporary struggles in post-expulsion Uganda. However, new publications, memoirs, and archival projects are joining the existing testimonies and analyses of those expelled during the 1970s. I have been pleased to discover that it has been mostly exiled Ugandan Asian and African Asian women who are at the forefront of new podcasting and archiving projects, and who are also thinking about expulsion and its futures. Dolar Vasani's and Yasmin Jamal's podcasts are excellent examples of archiving projects from Ugandan Asian woman of Hindu and Muslim heritage that engage the complexity of the expulsion event.[19] Bharti Dhir's 2021 memoir, *Worth*, follows in a tradition of East African Asian women writing of their displacements from Africa, from the works of Yasmin Alibhai-Brown to Sophia Mustafa to Jameela Siddiqi. Detailing her experiences as a biracial Afro-Asian woman and adoptee in a Ugandan Punjabi Sikh family, Dhir recounts her traumatic experiences of expulsion and migration to the UK, of anti-Black racism in South Asian communities, of identifying as Black British, and traversing African and South Asian communities. These writing practices are about building community and retracing paths to relationship and connection, and of inhabiting expansive categories and conditions of Blackness. Indeed, the care-work of Afro-Asian and Asian women of Ugandan heritage challenges conventional expulsion discourse and even the racially compartmentalized, patriarchal, and masculinist nature of state projects, elite community voices, and scholarly analysis. New voices disrupt expulsion exceptionalism, revealing the uneasy imperial, postcolonial, geopolitical, and diasporic Black and Afro–South Asian entanglements that belie any easy path to reconciliation or resolution, as suggested by property-ownership, commemorative events, political monuments or statues, or presidential apology.

Active South Asian Community Associations and
Institutions in Uganda since the Early 1990s

Indian Association Uganda (IAU), Kampala and Jinja Branch

Jammu Kashmir Dogra Association Uganda
Muslim Sunni Association
Pakistani Association Uganda

Indian Association Uganda Affiliates

Aga Khan National Council (Ismaili Muslims Charitable Trust)
Andhra Cultural Association
The Art of Living Uganda
Arya Samaj Uganda
BAPS Swaminarayan Santha
Bengali Association
Bhatia Samaj / Kutchi Bhatia Samaj
Brahma Kumaris
Brahma Kumari Raja Yoga Centre
Dawodi Bohora Jamaat Corporation
East India Cultural Association Ltd.
Goan Association
Hindu Swayamsevak Sangh
Indian Business Forum Uganda
Indian Catholic Community

Indian Community Kayunga

Indian Women's Association (IWA), Kampala and Jinja

ISKCON Uganda

Jain International Trade Organization (JITO)

Jain Samaj

Kalashree

Karnarataka Sangha

Kerala Samagam Uganda

Khoja Shia Ithnasheri Jamat

Lohana Community of Kampala

Maharashtra Mandal Kampala

Memon Community

Narayan Seva Sansthan (NSS) Uganda

North Gujarat Association

North Indian Cultural Association

Odisha Association Uganda Limited

Patidar Samaj

Patidar Shishu Kunj

Punjabi Cultural Society

Rajasthani Association

Ramgharia Sikh Society Kampala

Ramgharia Sikh Sports Club

Saurashtra Hindu Samaj

Shiradi Sai Baba Temple

Shree Brahmbatt Samaj

Shree Govardhan Nathji Pustimargi Haveli

Shree Halari Visa Oshwal Community Uganda

Shree Jain Samaj Uganda

Shree Kachchhi Leva Patel Samaj

Shree Kutch Satsang Swaminarayan Temple

Shree Limbach Samaj Uganda

Shree Sanatan Dharma Mandal (SSDM)

Shree Sthanakwasi Jain Sangh

Shri Akhil Uganda Brahma Samaj

Sikh Association Uganda

Sikh Youth Federation of Uganda

Sindhi Community of Uganda

SMVS Shree Swaminarayan Mandir

The Social Service League (Seva Samiti)

Surat Group District
Tamil Sangam Mandal
Tamizh Sangam
Telangana Association
Uganda Brahma Samaj
World Malayalee Council
Youth League

Pre-1972 Religious and Community Institutions (Kampala)

Allidina Visram Mosque
Ismaili Jamatkhana, Kampala
Nakasero Mosque
Ramgharia Sikh Society, Kampala
Ramgharia Sikh Sports Club, Kampala
Shree Kutch Satsang Swaminarayan Mandir, Kampala
Shree Sanatan Dharma Mandal (SSDM) Mandir, Kampala
Singh Sabha Sikh Gurudwara, Kampala

New Religious Institutions (Kampala)

Entebbe Mandhir (Brahmin)
Kampala Shirdi Sai Baba Center
Kololo Jamatkhana (Khoja Ismaili)
Kololo Jamia Masjid
Naguru Sikh Gurudwara (Ramgharia)
Old Kampala Mosque (Sunni)

Preface. From Diasporic to Transcontinental Entanglement

1   Du Bois, *Souls of Black Folk*, 11.

2   Ballantyne, *Between Colonialism and Diaspora*.

3   Hall, "New Ethnicities."

4   See also Prashad, *Karma of Brown Folk*, for a landmark text on Black–South Asian relationalities in the United States.

5   Macharia, "On Being Area-Studied."

6   Gilroy, *Black Atlantic*.

7   In this book, I trace transcontinental (both global and regional) racial formations, and thus am invested in critical engagement with two intellectual traditions, the Black Radical Tradition (and its dialogue with Pan-Africanism and Black Internationalism) and Afro-pessimism, which I indicate through my use of both "anti-Black racism" and "anti-Blackness."

Introduction. Expulsion as Closure, Expulsion as Opening

1   Herzfeld, *Cultural Intimacy*.

2   Partridge, *Hypersexuality and Headscarves*; Vora, *Impossible Citizens*.

3   Mamdani, *Citizen and Subject*.

4   Plascencia, *Disenchanting Citizenship*.

5   Rosa and Bonilla, "Deprovincializing Trump."

6   D. Thomas, "Crisis, Epochal Shifts," 550.

7   I use both "the West/non-West" and "Global North/Global South" in this book, primarily as a reflection of the scholarship relevant to my study. These terms generally indicate material, geopolitical, and racial divisions and inequalities according to histories of empire's and colonialism's racialized geographies. I use them to map epistemological inequalities as well.

8   Partridge, *Hypersexuality and Headscarves*, 19–22.

9   Comaroff and Comaroff, in *Theory from the South*, among others, have made this argument.

10   See Lalani, *Ugandan Asian Expulsion*, for a compilation of media coverage on the expulsion; see Seftel, *Uganda*, for media coverage of the Amin government in the South African periodical *Drum*. Scholarship on the 1972 Asian expulsion is extensive and rich, peaking in the late 1970s, and I attend to it selectively in this book.

11   M. Nair, *Mississippi Masala*; Macdonald, *The Last King of Scotland*.

12   Some influential expulsion memoirs are Mamdani's *From Citizen to Refugee*, and Alibhai-Brown's *No Place like Home*. Novels by exiled Ugandan Asian authors like Gulshan Ahmed, Yusuf Dawood, Jameela Siddiqi, and Peter Nazareth, among others, speak to themes of migration, identity, displacement, individual and collective trauma, and memory. Younger Black African Ugandan writers like Moses Isegawa and Goretti Kyomuhendo are also reflecting on Asianness and expulsion from the perspective of their particular ethnic communities and histories.

13   For scholarly analysis of East African Asian literature, see Ojwang, *Reading Migration and Culture*; G. Desai, *Commerce with the Universe*; Ocita, "Diasporic Imaginaries."

14   Bhachu, *Twice Migrants*; Brah, *Cartographies of Diaspora*; Muhammedi, *Gifts from Amin*; Parmar, *Reading Cultural Representations*; Fulford, *The Exiled*.

15   See the Uganda Collection in the Archives and Special Collections of the Carleton University Library.

16   Bhachu, *Twice Migrants*, which focuses on the displaced East African Ramgarhia Sikh community in Britain.

17   Popat, *A British Subject*. See especially Lord (Baron) Dolar Popat's debate to mark the fortieth anniversary expulsion of the Ugandan Asians in the UK Parliament. Hansard, House of Lords, "Ugandan Asians."

18   Brah, *Cartographies of Diaspora*; Centre for Contemporary Cultural Studies, *The Empire Strikes Back*; R. Gupta, *From Homemakers to Jailbreakers*.

19   Former Tanzanian president Julius Nyerere experimented with a conditional inclusion for the Indian minority on the basis of their acclimation

to socialist policies and nonracialism. A more gradual Africanization took place in Kenyatta's Kenya, in which Indians lost commercial and business opportunities through state-based trade and commercial restrictions, leading to the Kenyan Asian exodus between 1968 and 1969, and their subsequent resettlement in the United Kingdom. In postapartheid South Africa, Indians were integrated as citizens in line with an official policy of nonracialism and inclusive notions of "Blackness" that encompassed African, Colored, and Indian communities.

20   Taylor, "Race and Nation."

21   I. Patel, We're Here.

22   Taylor, "Asians and Africans in Urban Ugandan Life."

23   In Nair, Mississippi Masala, we see the complexity of expulsion and its aftermaths as we follow the migration trajectories of Jay, an exiled Gujarati lawyer of Ugandan origin, his wife Kinnu and their daughter Meena as they migrate to Greenwood, Mississippi, and negotiate dynamics of US-based state, racial, class, gender, and sexual power. In a notable scene, Jay sues the government of Uganda over his expulsion and eventually returns to repossess his property and connect with his childhood African friend Okello; likewise, the interracial romance between Meena (growing up South Asian American of Ugandan heritage) and Demetrius (of Black American heritage) offers insight into lingering Afro–South Asian intimacies in Uganda and its diaspora.

24   Leopold and other scholars argue that there is no factual evidence to support written accounts of Amin that describe practices of cannibalism and other ritual practices. He attributes them to Western propaganda, anti-Black African racism, and stereotypes among Southern communities like the Ganda about the Kakwa people and West Nile region of Uganda in particular. Leopold, Idi Amin, 1. See also Leopold, Inside West Nile; D. Peterson and Taylor, "Rethinking the State in Idi Amin's Uganda"; Mazrui, "Between Development and Decay"; Moghal, Idi Amin.

25   Bonee, "Caesar Augustus and the Flight of the Asians"; Chivers, "Is Expulsion Rational?"; Read, "Some Legal Aspects of the Expulsion."

26   Ghai, "The Bugandan Trade Boycott"; Ghai, "The Asian Minorities"; Jamal, "Asians in Uganda"; Mazrui, "Casualties of an Underdeveloped Class Structure"; Mamdani, Politics and Class Formation; Tandon, "The Expulsions from Uganda"; Tandon and Raphael, The New Position of East Africa's Asians.

27   Mamdani, Imperialism and Fascism; Mamdani, Citizen and Subject; Mamdani, When Victims Become Killers.

28   A more expansive reading of expulsions and exile during this era reveals the existence of many diverse displaced populations, both Black African

and South Asian. There is no comparative research on multiracial Ugandan exiles and their trajectories in the intervening years since Amin, Obote II, and the short-term governments that followed.

29 Fulford, *The Exiled*.

30 Taylor, "Asians and Africans," 1–40.

31 Amin also expelled the Israelis and the British European administrative and capitalist class just prior to the 1972 expulsion decree aimed at Asians. Mamdani, *Imperialism and Fascism in Uganda*. According to A. B. K. Kasozi, at least one million Ugandans were killed in the period between 1964 and 1985, and he estimates that the number killed during the Amin regime were between 50,000 and 300,000, with increasing levels of terror and violence during the Obote II period. Kasozi, *The Social Origins of Violence in Uganda*. Mark Leopold notes that most informed scholars agree Obote was responsible for more deaths than Amin over a shorter period of time. Leopold argues that unlike Obote's second period in power, "Amin did not specifically direct mass violence towards civilians from particular tribes, and Obote's earlier expulsions of Kenyan and Rwandan workers are not remembered alongside Amin's targeting of the Asian, although the Kenyans and Rwandans were greater in number." Leopold, *Idi Amin*, 3.

32 Adida, *Immigrant Exclusion*.

33 Sassen, *Expulsions*.

34 Das, *Critical Events*.

35 Das, *Critical Events*, 5–6.

36 I have been unable to locate research that places in dialogue the partition of British India and the Ugandan Asian expulsion and larger Asian exodus from East Africa, although there are clear parallels in terms of nation-building, displacement, state bureaucracy, and the transfer of property and assets. Some communities were affected by both events (the partition and the Asian expulsion). Reading both critical events together offers possibilities for engaging with race, religion, caste, class, gender, and sexuality across these geographies.

37 See Das, *Life and Words*. I build on the "ethnography of events" that questions the dichotomy of "structure" and "event," arguing "for studies which explore the dynamic relationship between moments of disruption and moments of calm." Tarlo, *Unsettling Memories*, 6.

38 Tarlo, *Unsettling Memories*, 6.

39 Das, *Life and Words*, 223.

40 Das, *Critical Events*, 5–6. Taylor, in "Asians and Africans in Ugandan Urban Life," drawing on Sinha, *Specters of Mother India*, has also argued that the 1972 Asian expulsion was a "global public event" (264).

41 Fanon, *Wretched of the Earth*.

42 Das, *Life and Words*, 9.

43 Das, *Life and Words*, 7.

44 Ong, *Neoliberalism as Exception*, 6.

45 Mamdani, *Citizen and Subject*, 9.

46 Uganda studies scholarship is dominated by statist political science approaches. See, for example, Collier and Reinikka, *Uganda's Recovery*; H. Hansen and Twaddle, *Developing Uganda*; and H. Hansen and Twaddle, *Changing Uganda*. The state is typically understood as a weak or quasi-state, while the NRM government is typologized as an authoritarian regime, a personalist regime, or more recently, a "hybrid regime," given its mix of liberal democratic and illiberal traits. See Tripp, *Museveni's Uganda*. Other themes include ethnic conflict, neopatrimonial politics, or the thwarting of constitutional norms and the failure of transparent, free, and fair presidential elections.

47 Note the "imagined geography" of post-partition India as a liberal democratic nation, as opposed to other nations in South Asia and to African nations. Rana, *Terrifying Muslims*.

48 I use *postliberal* to indicate a critical undertaking of the universality of liberal political formations. See also Comaroff and Comaroff, *Theory from the South*, with the caveat that Africa cannot be construed via South African exceptionalism.

49 See Bernal, *Nation as Network*; Clarke, "Notes on Cultural Citizenship"; Diouf, "Engaging Post-colonial Cultures"; Englund, *Prisoners of Freedom*; Malkki, *Purity and Exile*; Nyamnjoh, *Insiders and Outsiders*; Nyamnjoh, "From Bounded to Flexible Citizenship"; Geschiere, *Perils of Belonging*; Geschiere and Nyamnjoh, "Capitalism and Autochthony."

50 Mamdani, *Citizen and Subject*.

51 Foucault, *History of Sexuality*, vol. 1; Foucault, *Birth of Biopolitics*; Foucault, *Security, Territory, Population*; Mbembe, "Necropolitics." I follow Foucault in the study of "governmentality" as an array of knowledges and practices that are concerned with the systematic and pragmatic guidance and regulation of everyday conduct, or the strategies that individuals in their freedom can use in dealing with each other. My analysis is informed by discussions of biopower, biopolitics, and racism and by the distinctions in the biological field over the management, cultivation, and protection of life as opposed to those who must die.

52 T. B. Hansen and Stepputat, *Sovereign Bodies*. I build on anthropological scholarship that has critiqued notions of sovereignty rooted in European/Western intellectual genealogies that are themselves responding to normative

conceptions of nation-state sovereignty in an international world order. Anthropologists studying the global South stress ethnographic attention to the multiple forms of governance, sovereignty, and citizenship in (by normative definition) nonliberal, non-Western nation-states, including the transnational formations of sovereignty and power that constitute "the state" and attendant projects of nationalism.

53 Ross, "The Agamben Effect"; Robinson, *On Racial Capitalism*.

54 Vora, *Impossible Citizens*, 16.

55 Partridge, *Hypersexuality and Headscarves*, 22.

56 Wimmer and Schiller, "Methodological Nationalism."

57 I am departing here from culturalist/racist framings of corruption that locate these practices within perceived "closed" national economies. I am engaged instead with those who are studying the category of corruption and its shifting practices and meanings over time and space to upend liberal global imaginaries. See Akhil Gupta, "Blurred Boundaries."

58 Branch, *Displacing Human Rights*; Finnstrom, *Living with Bad Surroundings*; Epstein, *Another Fine Mess*.

59 Hundle, Szeman, and Hoare, "What Is the Transnational?"

60 Goldberg, *The Threat of Race*.

61 Mudimbe, *The Invention of Africa*; Mbembe, *Critique of Black Reason*; Grovogui, "Come to Africa."

62 Pierre, *Predicament of Blackness*.

63 The Chicago school of sociology normalized the "race relations" and "racial conflict" frameworks that circulated in African universities and in East African scholarship in the 1960s and 1970s. The legacy of race relations frameworks includes the use of essentializing racial categories, the masking of European and white supremacy, and the use of colonial discourses such as "the Asian question" or "the Native question." Race relations, racial conflict, and "minority question" frameworks police the possibilities of studying race via dynamic global and local racial formations and as mediated by global white supremacy.

64 Aiyar, *Indians in Kenya*; Brennan, *Taifa*; Glassman, *War of Words, War of Stones*; and Taylor, "Asians and Africans in Ugandan Urban Life." I build on studies of race, religion, and caste formation in the Indian Ocean world; see Jayawardene, "Racialized Casteism."

65 Herbert, "Oral Histories of Ugandan Asians in Britain"; see also Modi and Pandurang, "Women as an Invisible Constituency."

66 With few exceptions, see the feminist scholarship by Richa Nagar on East Africa, especially Tanzania.

67　Aiyar, *Indians in Kenya*; Aminzade, *Race, Nation, Citizenship*; Bertz, *Diaspora and Nation*; Brennan, *Taifa*; Oonk, *Settled Strangers*; Soske, *Internal Frontiers*; Taylor, "Asians and Africans in Ugandan Urban Life."

68　Shukla, "Locations for South Asian Diasporas"; Vora, *Impossible Citizens*; Axel, *The Nation's Tortured Body*.

69　Niranjana, *Mobilizing India*; Rana, *Terrifying Muslims*; T. Hansen, *Melancholia for Freedom*.

70　Bhachu, *Twice Migrants*; Brah, *Cartographies of Diaspora*; Joseph, *Nomadic Identities*; Parmar, *Reading Cultural Representations*.

71　Hall, "Negotiating Caribbean Identities."

72　C. Lee, *Making a World after Empire*, 4.

73　Mazrui, "Afrabia"; Zeleza, "Rewriting the African Diaspora."

74　Lowe, *Intimacies of Four Continents*; Lewis, "Afro-Asian Worlds"; Desai, *Commerce with the Universe*.

75　Burton, *Africa in the Indian Imagination*; Shankar, *An Uneasy Embrace*. Burton reminds us of the persistence of civilizational and racial hierarchies and that "there are good reasons for [these] histories of difference, resentment, and suspicion in the Afro-Indian context, among them racialized capitalist relations, colonial-era racial histories, and entrenched practices of racial endogamy" (*Africa in the Indian Imagination*, 3).

76　Shryrock, *Off Stage, on Display*.

77　In fact, the meanings behind "Asian" are shifting with respect to a growing East Asian, especially Chinese, presence.

78　Jeyifo, "The Nature of Things."

Chapter 1. Becoming a Racial Exile, Becoming a Black Nation

1　Obbo, "Village Strangers," 239.

2　Mankekar and Gupta, "The Missed Period."

3　Morrison, *Beloved*, 43.

4　Morrison, *Beloved*, 86.

5　Reid, *Political Power*, 135–73.

6　Kasozi, *Social Origins*, 27–28.

7　Mamdani, *Politics and Class Formation*, 17–18.

8　Thapar, "Theory of Aryan Race."

9　Ranger, "The Invention of Tradition Revisited"; Dirks, *Castes of Mind*; Mamdani, *Politics and Class Formation*; Mamdani, *Citizen and Subject*.

European travelers, anthropologists, and colonists compared the civilizational development of the centralized kingdoms of the South in relation to the suppose lack of civilization in the North. The fact that the modern nation-state is called Uganda, which encompasses regions and people beyond the traditional kingdom and territory of Buganda, continues to be politically controversial.

10 Reid, *Political Power*, 149–73.

11 Mangat, *History of the Asians*. Over the period from 1896 to 1902, a total of 31,983 Indian indentured laborers constructed the Uganda Railway. Mangat, *History of the Asians*, 31–32; Metcalf, *Imperial Connections*, 200. Of the indentured individuals, 10 to 15 percent would renew their contracts or return to East Africa on fresh indentures after their three-year contracts had ended. See Mangat, *History of the Asians*, 37.

12 Growing economic opportunities in British East Africa attracted between ten and twenty thousand free, or passenger, Indian immigrants; this number increased substantially during the interwar years. Gregory, *Quest for Equality*, 304.

13 Jamal, "Asians in Uganda."

14 Mangat, *History of the Asians*, 27–28.

15 Mamdani, *Politics and Class Formation*, 1–14, 18–39.

16 Mamdani, *Politics and Class Formation*, 40–44.

17 Mamdani, *Politics and Class Formation*, 71.

18 Hunt, *A Colonial Lexicon*, 7–8.

19 Mamdani, *Politics and Class Formation*, 65–119, 147–88.

20 Mamdani, *Politics and Class Formation*.

21 Hegel, *Philosophy of History*.

22 Mamdani, *Citizen and Subject*, 16–23.

23 Mamdani, *Citizen and Subject*, 17.

24 Mamdani, *Define and Rule*.

25 Mamdani, *Citizen and Subject*; Mamdani, "Beyond Settler and Native."

26 For Furnivall, "plural society is in the strictest sense a medley, for they [ethnic groups] mix but do not combine. Each group holds its own religion, its own culture and language, its own ideas and ways. As individuals they meet, but only in the market-place . . . with different sections of the community living side by side, but separately, within the same political unit." Furnivall, *Colonial Policy and Practice*, 304–5, as cited in Guan, "Furnivall's Plural Society."

27 Pierre, *Predicaments of Blackness*.

28 Mamdani, *Citizen and Subject*.

29   Mama, "Sheroes and Villains"; Hundle, "Postcolonial Patriarchal Nativism."

30   Hundle, "Postcolonial Patriarchal Nativism."

31   Mamdani, *Citizen and Subject*; Pierre, *Predicaments of Blackness*.

32   Ambedkar, *Annihilation of Caste*.

33   Dirks, *Castes of Mind*.

34   Thapar, "The Theory of Aryan Race."

35   Patton, "Cosmic Men and Fluid Exchanges"; see also T. B. Hansen, *Melancholia for Freedom*, 123–27, for an excellent discussion of South Asian sources of racial practice deriving from religion and caste.

36   Morris, *Indians in Uganda*, 16.

37   Morris, *Indians in Uganda*, 17.

38   Morris, *Indians in Uganda*, 17.

39   Morris, *Indians in Uganda*, 91–103.

40   Srinivas, *Caste in Modern India*; Morris, *Indians in Uganda*, 91–103.

41   Morris, *Indians in Uganda*, 43, 77–90.

42   Yengde, "Caste among the Indian Diaspora," 65–66.

43   Amiji, "Asian Communities"; Barot, "Varna, Nât-Jât and Atak"; Penumala, "Hindu Diaspora."

44   Nagar, "Communal Discourses, Marriage," 125.

45   I draw on Verne Dusenbery's notion of *izzat*, a "multivocalic term defying simple translation . . . it is central to a whole complex of emotionally charged values including honor, respect, reputation, shame, prestige, and status." Dusenbery, "On the Moral Sensitivities of Sikhs," 242–43. This definition of *izzat* draws on the Punjabi and Sikh context but can be generalized to Ugandan Asian contexts as well.

46   Bharati, *Asians in East Africa*, 157.

47   Southall and Gutkind, *Townsmen in the Making*, 40–41, 78–79.

48   Kyomuhendo and McIntosh, *Women, Work and Domestic Virtue*, 77.

49   Southall and Gutkind, in *Townsmen in the Making*, argue that it was strategic for some Indian men, mostly Muslims and Goans, to marry African women in order to acquire stable housing in Buganda, given the existing restrictions on nonnative Indians from owning property on *mailo* land.

50   Leonard, *Making Ethnic Choices*.

51   Robinson, *On Racial Capitalism*.

52   See Chhabria, "Where Does Caste Fit?," for an important engagement with Black Atlantic thinkers and Black Marxists W. E. B. Du Bois, Cedric Robinson, and Oliver Cromwell Cox. Cox's *Caste, Class, and Race* is significant for its early conceptualization of race and caste analogy, race and caste

intimacies, and its explorations of race, capitalism, and class as systems of domination and exploitation.

53 Morris, *Indians in Uganda*.

54 N. K. Mehta, *Dream Half-Expressed*; Madhvani and Foden, *Tide of Fortune*.

55 Modi and Taylor, "Indian Diaspora in Africa," 914.

56 Modi and Taylor, "Indian Diaspora in Africa," 914.

57 Oonk, *Settled Strangers*.

58 Hansen, *Melancholia of Freedom*; Soske, *Internal Frontiers*.

59 Grovogui, *Sovereigns, Quasi-sovereigns, and Africans*; Mamdani, "Beyond Settler and Native."

60 Morris, *Indians in Uganda*, 133–46.

61 Tabaire, "Press and Political Repression." Beyond postcolonial era repression and criminalization of Asian political activity, I have begun to locate corroborating material indicating the political surveillance of Asians for further research, recently made available at the Uganda National Archives and Records Center in Kampala.

62 Thompson, as cited in Twaddle, Was the Expulsion Inevitable?," in *Expulsion of a Minority*, 7.

63 Askew, *Performing the Nation*; Ivaska, *Cultured States*; Joseph, *Nomadic Identities*.

64 Twaddle, "Was the Expulsion Inevitable?," in Twaddle, *Expulsion of a Minority*, 7.

65 Nkrumah, *Neo-colonialism*.

66 Mamdani, *Citizen and Subject*.

67 Anderson, *Imagined Communities*.

68 Manby, *Struggles for Citizenship in Africa*, 5.

69 Oloka-Onyango, "From Expulsion to Exclusion."

70 Mamdani, "Beyond Settler and Native"; Ahluwalia, "When Does a Settler Become a Native?"

71 Anirudha Gupta, "India and the Asians in East Africa."

72 Mamdani, *Politics and Class Formation*, 258–60.

73 Mamdani, *Politics and Class Formation*, 266–74.

74 Mamdani, *Politics and Class Formation*, 278–81.

75 Mamdani documents, "By 1970, out of a total of 76,600 Asians resident in Uganda, 30,000 were Uganda citizens, while some 12,000 had applied for citizenship under the 1962 constitution and reapplied under the 1967 constitution; but their applications had not been processed." Mamdani, *Politics and Class Formation*, 279.

76 Mamdani, *Politics and Class Formation*, 273.

77 Mamdani, *Politics and Class Formation in Uganda*, 279. In the same year, Obote expelled Kenyan Jaluo workers in response to trade union activism.

78 Twaddle, "Was the Expulsion Inevitable?," in Twaddle, *Expulsion of a Minority*, 8.

79 Moghal, *Idi Amin*.

80 Mazrui, "The Social Origins of Ugandan Presidents."

81 Moghal, *Idi Amin*.

82 Kasozi, *Social Origins of Violence in Uganda*, 13.

83 Kasozi, *Social Origins of Violence in Uganda*, 112–16.

84 Moghal, *Idi Amin*.

85 Amin, "Speech by His Excellency"; Taylor, "Race and Nation"; H. Patel, "General Amin."

86 Mamdani, *Imperialism and Fascism*.

87 Taylor, "Race and Nation"; Moghal, *Idi Amin*.

88 Moghal, *Idi Amin*.

89 Kara, "Vanishing Mediators."

90 Keshodkar, "Marriage as the Means to Promote 'Asian-ness,'" 230; and Amory, "Politics of Identity," 134, as cited in Keshodkar, "Marriage as the Means to Promote 'Asian-ness.'"

91 Government of Uganda, *Immigration (etc.) (Amendment) Decree*, Decree 30, October 5, 1972.

92 Read, "Some Legal Aspects of the Expulsion." Enoch Powell's infamous "Rivers of Blood" speech was a response to the migration of formerly colonized subjects to Great Britain.

93 Humphrey and Ward, "Passports and Politics"; Read, "Some Legal Aspects."

94 Anirudha Gupta, "India and the Asians in East Africa."

95 Yadav, *India-Uganda Relations*, 130–31. There were also numerous diplomatic attempts by Indian officials to secure compensation for lost assets of exiles.

96 Accounts vary on the number expelled, according to citizenship status and time of out-migration or displacement, and they continue to be updated. According to A. B. K. Kasozi, who wrote the first comprehensive account of violence in postcolonial Uganda, "of the accounted for Ugandan Asian refugees, 27,200 British passport holders went to Britain; 6,000 stateless refugees went to Canada; 4,500 Indian nationals went to India; and 2,500 went to Kenya. The United States, Pakistan, Malawi, and West Germany took 1,000 refugees each. Smaller numbers of refugees went to Australia (500), Austria (100), Sweden (300), Mauritius (100), and New Zealand (200). A total of 3,600 Ugandan Asians were placed into refugee camps

before their resettlement in different countries, and 20,000 of an estimated 75,000 Asians remain unaccounted for." Kasozi, *Social Origins of Violence in Uganda*, 119. See also Brown, *Ugandan Asians*.

97 The Indian government and Ugandan Asian family firms played a role in the resettlement of refugee Ugandan Asians in Ahmedabad, Gujarat. S. Nair, "Despite Dislocations." There is little research on the migration and settlement of other South Asian nationals to post-partition Pakistan and Bangladesh.

98 See Indian Overseas Trust, "British Ugandan Asians at 50," for more information.

99 Moghal, *Idi Amin*.

100 Adams and Bristow, "Ugandan Asian Experiences"; Hundle, "Politics of (In)security."

101 Moghal, in *Idi Amin*, notes that Makerere University Students Union published a letter of condemnation against the decree.

102 Mazrui, "Between Development and Decay," 55.

103 Twaddle, "Was the Expulsion Inevitable?," in Twaddle, *Expulsion of a Minority*, 1–14.

104 Taylor, "Race and Nation."

Chapter 2. Exceptions to the Expulsion

1 The term *half-caste* has its origins in British colonial administrations as a derogatory racial category associated with the moral condemnation of miscegenation and individuals whose ancestry comprised multiple ethnic/racial groups. Aspinall, "Social Evolution of the Term 'Half-Caste' in Britain." It persists in postcolonial East Africa, can be used as a self-descriptor, and also marks ideas of Indian racial/caste purity among South Asians in East Africa.

2 See also Ojwang, "The Half-Caste and the Dream."

3 Mamdani, *Imperialism and Fascism*, 54.

4 Younger generations of Ugandans critical of the current ruling party, the NRM, likewise contend with state violence, militarism, and surveillance, including the navigation of intrafamilial and generational tensions.

5 This is not a culturalist claim and is not exclusive to Uganda but common to citizens of societies confronted by different kinds of state projects. Even in liberal democratic states, political repression can take on many different expressions.

6 Theroux, "Hating the Asians."

7 In the aftermath of war in Northern Uganda, Sverker Finnstrom argues, "rumors are part and parcel of war . . . rumors verbalize a wartime

ontology of stress and uncertainty." Finnstrom, *Living with Bad Surroundings*, 68.

8   See Abraham, "Seguranca/Security in Brazil", 21–39; and Williams, *Marxism and Literature*, 128–35.

9   Decker, *In Idi Amin's Shadow*, 17–19.

10   "Asians Milked the Cow: They Did Not Feed It—Gen. Amin," *Uganda Argus*, August 7, 1972.

11   K. Peterson, *Speculative Markets*, 6.

12   "Only 800 Stateless Asians Left as Amin Deadline Expires," *Times* (London), November 9, 1972. Interviewees quoted figures of Ugandan Asian nationals who remained.

13   There is no further research on the DAPCB and the property expropriation and allocation process during this period. The signifier "departed" obscures the forced and involuntary nature of Ugandan Asian expulsion.

14   After the collapse of the East African Community (EAC) in 1977, Kenya began to dominate formal trade in the region.

15   Asiimwe, "From Monopoly Marketing"; Decker, *In Idi Amin's Shadow*; Taylor, "Asians and Africans."

16   Based on my interviews, by 1976, there were between twenty and thirty Punjabi Sikh families in construction who worked as laborers for the Amin government and other private companies. A prominent figure was Ram Singh, the chief engineer of the Ministry of Defense, who secured labor contacts for others from India. He passed away in California in 2011.

17   Tandon, *Technical Assistance Administration in East Africa*. Syed Abidi observes, "[The] intelligentsia of Uganda ran away from the country, creating a serious gap in the civil service, judiciary, and education sector. Amin was forced to bring planeloads of teachers, accountants, magistrates, pharmacists, and medical doctors from Bangladesh and Pakistan in 1974." Indian Association of Uganda, *Namaste* (newsletter), vol. 1, 2005.

18   Yadav, *India-Uganda Relations*, 130–31. Indian state officials had traveled to Uganda to discuss matters related to the expulsion of Indian citizens resettled in India. Amin also showed interest in developing bilateral relations with Prime Ministers Morarji Desai and Indira Gandhi.

19   Stoler, *Carnal Knowledge*.

20   Mamdani, *Citizen and Subject*.

21   Mazrui, *Soldiers and Kinsmen*.

22   Decker, *In Idi Amin's Shadow*.

23   Leopold, "Sex, Violence and History," 321.

24   De Certeau, *Practice of Everyday Life*, xvii–xx.

25　D. Peterson and Taylor, "Rethinking the State."

26　While Foucauldian biopolitics foregrounds the management and fostering of life with respect to labor productivity and economic rationality, Mbembe's "necropolitics" refers to the relational subjugation of the colonized to death. In *On the Postcolony*, Mbembe argues that colonial governance is a racialized endeavor of "commandement," based on a foundation of racial violence. In *Citizen and Subject*, Mamdani's discussion of indirect rule as the basis of "decentralized despotism" demonstrates that state governance is racialized, and that postcolonial violence is meted upon racial populations differently.

27　T. B. Hansen and Stepputat, *Sovereign Bodies*, 20.

28　Mbembe, *On the Postcolony*.

29　Karamoja is a rural and more isolated region of northeastern Uganda, ethnic home of the Karamajong, a nomadic, cattle-keeping society. Idi Amin threatened that those who dared to remain after the deadline would be sent to live in camps in Karamoja, and that there would be a head count of remaining Asians. "Asians to be Counted-Person by Person," *Uganda Argus*, November 7, 1972. Amin stressed Asians' lack of an ethnic homeland; he maintained that they thus had no political claim to indigeneity and autochthony to the land and to territorial Uganda. Further, the threat revealed the circulating post–World War II imaginaries of the technology of the concentration camp: the "decivilizing" or dehumanization of "civilized" urban Asians by shifting them to a site deemed primitive and without civilization.

30　Das, "The Signature of the State."

31　Obbo, "Village Strangers," 229.

32　Holly Hanson has also studied the relationships between violence and love in traditional African political authority, arguing that "in the Ganda practice of power, visible expressions of love and affection created relationships of mutual obligation between people with authority and those they ruled." Hanson, *Landed Obligation*, 1.

33　Obbo, "Village Strangers," 232

34　Obbo, "Village Strangers," 240.

35　Chatterjee, *Politics of the Governed*.

36　Two well-known cases are the late Amirali Karmali of the Mukwano Group and Mohammed Hussein of the Rafiki Group.

37　Mamdani, *Imperialism and Fascism*, 54.

38　Harding, "Representing Fundamentalism."

39　In 1979, Amin followed army mutineers and invaded Tanzania. The Tanzanian army and two Ugandan exile groups, led by Obote and Yoweri

Museveni's guerilla group FRONASA, banded together to oust Amin. The exile groups had convened the Moshi Conference earlier that year to form the UNLF (Uganda National Liberation Front). The UNLF developed a National Consultative Council (NCC) that was inclusive of different political groups and associations invested in democratic rule. Yusuf Lule, the former president of Makerere University, became the first chairman of the NCC and the first president of Uganda after the fall of Amin.

Chapter 3. Insecurities of Repatriation

1   Constructs of war and peace and security and insecurity continually shifted, depending upon an individual's contexts, locations, experiences, and memories of state terror and violence, civil war, and times of political transition. Indeed, we now know that the NRM's production of security (always premised upon an imagined "insecurity" or security threat) for citizens in the southern and prosperous regions of Uganda also relied upon violent counterinsurgency in the north, with Buganda becoming a key site of repressive state and military violence in response to political and popular protest against the NRM. Another context for the securitization of the city was the July 2010 Al-Shabaab terrorist bombings in Kampala in retaliation for Ugandan support for AMISOM (African Union Mission in Somalia), which set the stage for the NRM and Ugandan military's continued counterterrorism interventions in the region and the repression of Muslim "Others" in Uganda, including South Asian Pakistanis.

2   Among Ugandan Asians and other South Asians who had arrived in Uganda after the expulsion, Besigye and the FDC were widely perceived as being anti-Asian. I was able to find a few sources of anti-Asian rhetoric among the FDC in the Ugandan press but there was no official position on Ugandan Asian return. At the time, the FDC political platform was primarily concerned with NRM-based family nepotism, patronage, and corruption as well as with labor rights and fair-trade policies, and Ugandan Asian capital was implicated in NRM governance.

3   Taylor, "Asians and Africans," 320. Former president and professor Yousuf Lule did not have an opportunity to consider the repatriation of Ugandan Asians after the expulsion. Former president Godfrey Binasia was not interested in Ugandan Asian repatriation. See "Uganda, Idi Amin," TV Eye, December 13, 1979, uploaded to YouTube, September 4, 2016, https://www.youtube.com/watch?v=y-zi2OgOoIE&list=PLLEb8279wQqQ7G1KzvFKquut-NU7koeYz&index=3&t=626s.

4   Ahluwalia, *Plantations and the Politics of Sugar*. The sugar industry was rehabilitated on the basis of a joint venture between the government and firms, creating an alliance between the UPC and Ugandan Asian capital

through public-private partnerships. Some urban Ugandans speculate that the Mehta and Madhvani family firms were compensated twice for their losses during the Amin regime, once through property repossession and again through international donor aid agencies. I was unable to confirm this through research. Indian officials in Prime Minister Indira Gandhi's government attempted to negotiate with Idi Amin's government for compensation for expelled Indian nationals exiled to India several times after 1972. See J. Mehta, "Negotiating Compensation."

5 Some returnees discussed the ease of obtaining Ugandan passports through relationships with state and government officials; others talked about men who married Ugandan women and were then able to access property and land entitlements; still others noted that citizenship retractions for Asians were common during this period.

6 The systematic violence and atrocities perpetrated by the UNLA in the Luwero Triangle during the 1981–86 Bush War is also constitutive of the NRM's logics of violence, militarization, and securitization. See Kasozi, *Social Origins of Violence in Uganda*.

7 Kassimir, "Reading Museveni."

8 D. Peterson, "A History of the Heritage Economy."

9 Muhamadi Matovu, "Museveni Uses *Bazzukulu* Phrase to Patronise—Nicholas Opiyo," *Nile Post*, July 22, 2024, https://nilepost.co.ug/index.php /news/208467/museveni-uses.

10 Museveni, *What Is Africa's Problem?*; Museveni, *Sowing the Mustard Seed*, 183–86.

11 Prashad, *The Darker Nations*; Prashad, *The Poorer Nations*.

12 Himbara and Sultan, "Reconstructing the Ugandan State and Economy"; H. Hansen and Twaddle, *Changing Uganda*; H. Hansen and Twaddle, *Developing Uganda*.

13 For more context, see Mujagu, *Uganda's Age of Reforms*; Mujagu and Oloka-Onyango, *No-Party Democracy*; Oloka-Onyango, "Constitutional Transition."

14 The NRM mobilized the anti-imperialist rhetoric of "African solutions to African problems" in its political discourse, despite the persistence of imperialist and neocolonial relationships with the United States and the UK. See Halsteen, "Taking Rights Talk Seriously," 113–15.

15 A student of postcolonial thinkers at the University of Dar es Salaam, Museveni's writings about the structural obstacles that the revolutionary national bourgeoisie must confront in order to plan their own economies and societies have given way to complicities with these same structures. See also Fanon, *Wretched of the Earth*.

16   Richard Reid, in "Ghosts in the Academy," argues that the NRM elevates
      selective aspects of its own history such as the Liberation War and that
      claims that complicate Ugandan history or that threaten the NRM's political
      authority are silenced. Reid's analysis misses how neoliberal universalisms
      and their imbrication with authoritarianism and repression also prevent
      critical engagement with history and historical claims.

17   Quinn, "Constraints."

18   Mamdani, *Citizen and Subject.*

19   Carrasco, "Challenges and Tribulations."

20   See especially Lord (Baron) Dolar Popat's debate to mark the fortieth
      anniversary of the expulsion of the Ugandan Asians, which was central
      to reinforcing Ugandan Asian refugee and immigrant exceptionalism
      in both in-person and virtual sites of commemoration. UK Parliament
      Hansard, House of Lords, "Ugandan Asians," Vol. 741, December 6, 2012,
      https://hansard.parliament.uk/lords/2012-12-06/debates/12120659000796
      /UgandanAsians.

21   Oonk, *Settled Strangers,* 9.

22   "Herculean Task of Winning Back Investors," *New Vision,* November 10,
      1997.

23   T. B. Hansen, *Saffron Wave.*

24   Van der Veer, "Virtual India."

25   Van der Veer, "Virtual India."

26   Mankekar, *Unsettling India.*

27   "India Forgives Uganda over 1972 Expulsions," *New Vision,* October 6,
      1997.

28   "India Forgives Uganda over 1972 Expulsions."

29   Abidi, "Return of Asians."

30   Mamdani, "Ugandan Asian Expulsion."

31   There is no existing comprehensive research on Ugandan Asian experi-
      ences of the property repossession process.

32   Kassam, "The Asian Minority."

33   This research is based on interviews with key experts and government of-
      ficials and my work consulting the *New Vision,* *Weekly Topic,* and the *Star*
      between 1990 and 1997 at the Centre for Basic Research (CBR) in Kampala.

34   Based on an interview with a former DAPCB employee, with respect to a
      total of about 9,000 Asian properties, the DAPCB handed over 4,063 prop-
      erties to their original Ugandan Asian owners between 1983 and 1997. The
      government sold an additional 1,500 properties; while around 2,000 remain
      unclaimed. The Indian Association of Uganda has also filed several legal

claims with the DAPCB to repossess community properties. See also Liam
Taylor, "Expelled Uganda Asians Fight for Seized Properties Fifty Years On,"
Gulf Times, December 6, 2022, https://www.gulf-times.com/article/651062
/opinion/expelled-uganda-asians-fight-for-seized-properties-50-years-on.

35 Oloka-Onyango, "From Expulsion to Exclusion"; Ng'weno and Aloo, "Irony
of Citizenship."

36 I am referring here to scholarship on citizenship, neoliberal globalization,
and transnationalism. See Rose, *Powers of Freedom*; Sassen, "Repositioning
of Citizenship"; Ong, *Flexible Citizenship*; Ong, *Neoliberalism as Exception*.

37 Ong, *Flexible Citizenship*.

38 Oloka-Onyango, "From Expulsion to Exclusion," 2–4.

39 Oloka-Onyango, "From Expulsion to Exclusion," 4–10.

40 Certificates of Residence are available in renewable five- and ten-year
terms as well as on a lifetime basis. Becoming a lifetime resident requires
a history of at least ten years of continuous residence and work permits
held in the country and an application that vouches for the character of
the individual seeking residency, including details of their contributions to
socioeconomic development of the nation. Directorate of Citizenship and
Immigration Control, "Certificate of Residence," accessed November 14,
2024, https://www.immigration.go.ug/services/certificate-residence.

41 The Ugandan national ID was established in 2015 and is tied to employment,
voter registration, accessing passports and bank accounts, purchasing health
and insurance policies, land ownership, pension and social security transactions, and taxes, among other public services. Oloka-Onyango, "From
Expulsion to Exclusion," 14. It follows the Kenyan model of registering
and surveilling citizens in order to collect biometric data in relation to
presumed security threats, especially those who are now imagined to be
African, Arab, and South Asian Muslim "Others" in East Africa.

42 Oloka-Onyango, "From Expulsion to Exclusion," 2.

43 Mamdani, *Citizen and Subject*.

44 Oloka-Onyango, "From Expulsion to Exclusion," 15–18.

45 In the 1990s, family firms moved into manufacturing, agricultural processing, banking and foreign exchange dealings, insurance, tourism, the
hotel and restaurant industry, pharmaceuticals, and printing and publishing sectors. Abidi, "Return of Asians," 54–56.

46 T. B. Hansen and Stepputat, *Sovereign Bodies*, 1–5.

47 N. K. Mehta, *Dream Half Expressed*. After expulsion, some family firm
members were in legal battles over generational succession, assets, wealth,
and inheritance. Madhvani and Foden, *Tide of Fortune*, 157–63.

48 Abidi, "Return of Asians."

49 "Sudhir Ruparelia: 2015 Africa's 50 Richest Net Worth," *Forbes*, November 18, 2015, http://www.forbes.com/profile/sudhir-ruparelia.

50 Mamdani, "Ugandan Asian Expulsion."

51 Tangri and Mwenda, "Corruption and Cronyism"; Tangri and Mwenda, "Change and Continuity."

52 The government instituted an open trade licensing system in the 1980s, reversing previous Africanization policies in the trade sector. Rubongoya, *Regime Hegemony in Museveni's Uganda*.

53 Nagar, "Saboteurs? Or Saviors?"

54 I was not able to carry out more intensive research on post-expulsion merchant networks; note, however, that the same traditional *baniya* (upper-caste Hindu) and Shia Muslim communities participated in established trade, in addition to other communities who engaged in petty trade but did not traditionally do so.

55 Officials from the Ministry of Trade, Internal Affairs, the Indian and Chinese embassies, and the Kampala City Council Authority (KCCA) interface with and regulate the presence and activities of Indian and Chinese nationals and traders.

56 In the context of post-expulsion return, conversations about hiring practices, job mobility, and knowledge and skills transfer to Africans were very sensitive and will need further research.

57 Goldberg, *Threat of Race*, 315–17.

58 Christian and Namaganda, "Good Mzungu?"

59 Applicants must provide proof of former citizenship, residency, or other documents attesting to the fact that they had once owned property in the country. The dual citizenship law is available only to East African Asians who have become permanent residents of the country, enabling entitlements like the legal ownership of *mailo* (freehold land).

60 See Article 12 of the 1995 Constitution of the Republic of Uganda.

61 Bissell, "Engaging Colonial Nostalgia."

62 Rasch, "Postcolonial Nostalgia," 148–49. Her analysis resonates with scholarship on whiteness and settler-turned-postcolonial citizen communities, especially in East and Southern Africa. See also Crapanzano, *Waiting*; and Besteman, *Transforming Cape Town*.

63 On "post-memory," see Hirsch, "Family Pictures."

64 McIntosh, *Unsettled*.

65 Ong, *Buddha Is Hiding*, 3.

66 Indian Overseas Trust, "Fortieth Anniversary Commemoration," accessed November 8, 2024, http://www.asiansfromuganda.org.uk/40th _anniversary_commemoration.php.

67 UK Parliament Hansard, House of Lords, "Ugandan Asians."

68 Parmar, "Memorialising 40 Years."

69 Facebook groups in 2012 included Ugandan Asians who left Uganda in 1972 and their descendents; VivaUganda!—Uganda Asian Expulsion—Aftermath, Beforemath etc.; Uganda Reunion; UGANDANS AT HEART (UAH) COMMUNITY; Commemoration of 1972 Uganda Asian Expulsion (2013 Commemoration England).

70 Aziz Islamshah, "Aga Khan Visits East Africa for Golden Jubilee Visit," AKDN, October 15, 2007, https://www.akdn.org/press-release/aga-khan -visits-east-africa-first-golden-jubilee-visit. Ismailimail, "Uganda: Celebrating Fifty Years under His Highness Karim Aga Khan," July 10, 2007, https://ismailimail.blog/2007/07/10/uganda-celebrating-50-years-under -his-highness-karim-aga-khan.

71 Taylor, "Asians and Africans," 313–14.

Chapter 4. Insecurities of Foreign Direct Investment

1 Gandhi, "Hindutva and the Shared Scripts."

2 Government of India, Ministry of External Affairs, *Declaration on the New Asian-African Strategic Partnership*, April 24, 2005. Following the 2005 Afro-Asian Conference, the 2006 China-Africa Summit, the 2008 India-Africa Summit, and 2009 China-Africa Summit ushered in an era of cooperation between African and Asian nations (note the dissonance and inequality between Africa as a continent and India and China as nations in some of these "bilateral" summits).

3 "History of the EAC," East African Community, accessed August 8, 2024, https://www.eac.int/eac-history. A new Ministry of East African Commerce was established in 2007.

4 Ewout Frankema and Marlous van Waijenburg, "Africa Rising? A Historical Perspective," Africa Is a Country, October 17, 2018, https://africasacountry .com/2018/10/africa-rising-a-historical-perspective.

5 "India-Uganda Relations on the Right Track," *New Vision*, August 15, 2003.

6 Zakaria, *Post-American World*.

7 On "Afro-pessimism," see Diawara, *In Search of Africa*.

8 I conducted research for almost eight months at the UIA from 2009 to 2010, with follow-up visits in 2013–15 and 2017 and online. I observed meetings, helped to prepare for and attended investment promotion events, and participated in city tours with state officials and investors.

9   The code provides guidelines for UIA operations, investor appraisal, and the allocation and terms of investment licenses; it also addresses the issues of investor incentives and investor protection.

10   "Asian Tigers" refers to the four developed Asian economies that underwent rapid industrialization and high growth rates, especially between the 1950s and the onset of the Asian financial crisis in 1997. Ann Pitcher suggests that more developed African economies, such as South Africa and Mauritius, followed the Asian Tiger economies and shifted to the IPA model between the mid-1980s and early 1990s. The World Bank offered a template that was then "tweaked" by the development economists and state officials of less developed African economies. Personal communication, January 4, 2012.

11   United Nations, *An Investment Guide to Uganda*, 52.

12   United Nations, *An Investment Guide to Uganda*, 52.

13   Government of Uganda, *Investment Code Act, Cap. 92.*

14   United Nations, *An Investment Guide to Uganda*, 31.

15   National planning refers to the policy priorities of the Ministry of Financial Planning and Economic Development (MoFPED), the Ministry for National Development, and the National Vision documents produced by the NRM government. The latter include the Poverty Eradication Action Plan (2007), the National Development Plan (2009), the National Vision Framework (2009), and the Comprehensive National Development Planning Framework (2009).

16   Mamdani, *Citizen and Subject.*

17   Cooper, "Recurrent Crises."

18   Wiegratz, Martiniello, and Greco, *Uganda.*

19   Comaroff and Comaroff, *Millennial Capitalism*; Comaroff and Comaroff, *Theory from the South*; J. Ferguson, "Seeing like an Oil Company"; J. Ferguson, *Global Shadows.*

20   D. A. Thomas and Clarke, "Globalization and Race."

21   Mahajan, *Africa Rising.*

22   Wiegratz, Martiniello, and Greco, *Uganda*, 2. Mbeki's speech on the African Renaissance was the framing architecture of economic policy in the 1990s and 2000s. It was accompanied by Barack Obama's inaugural speech on Africa-US relations that celebrated his Kenyan heritage in a neoliberalized Pan-Africanist discourse. Thabo Mbeki, "The African Renaissance, South Africa and the World," United Nations University, April 9, 1998, http://archive.unu.edu/unupress/mbeki.html.

23   Cheru and Obi, *Rise of China and India*; Gudavarthy, "Globalisation and Regionalisation."

24 Bond and Garcia, *BRICS*.

25 Tripp and Kwesiga, *Women's Movement in Uganda*.

26 Kigozi retired from her position of Executive Director at the UIA in 2012, but she continues to advocate for women's and girls' empowerment in Uganda.

27 On "radical rudeness," see Tamale, "Nudity, Protest, and the Law in Uganda."

28 "Government Offers Shs4b to Shimoni Investor," *Daily Monitor*, April 6, 2009; "Shimoni Land Saga Rages On," *Daily Monitor*, April 6, 2009; "Investor Reaps Shs30b from Government," *Daily Monitor*, November 9, 2009.

29 "Uganda CHOGM Ministers Face Fraud Charges," BBC, October 11, 2011.

30 Ogwang and Vanclay, "Resource-Financed Infrastructure."

31 The database is used to track information on visitors—the name of their company, place of origin, sector of interest, reason for visit, investment license, and so on—whether or not the investor actually decides to apply for a license and set up a business. It also contains information on licensed foreign investors, the status of their investment "project," and logistics. Quarterly and annual reports from this data then generate statistics indicating "real" versus "planned" investment, which are critical for policy development.

32 Ong, *Neoliberalism as Exception*.

33 Ferguson, *Anti-politics Machine*.

34 The government "created a network with all relevant government agencies to provide services to investors" (United Nations, *An Investment Guide to Uganda*, 52). Client charters were prepared for twenty-three organizations in Uganda that deal regularly with investors (United Nations Conference on Trade and Development [UNCTAD], *Report on the Implementation of the Investment Policy Review*, 2). A "client charter" is a "brief schedule of procedures, costs, and time involved in securing a service from such an agency. The charters are placed on public notice boards where investors and the general public can easily access them for needed information. The intention is to reduce red tape, corruption, and other malpractices in dealing with investors" (United Nations, *An Investment Guide to Uganda*, 52).

35 United Nations, *An Investment Guide to Uganda*, 55.

36 United Nations, *An Investment Guide to Uganda*, 55.

37 Kaur, *Brand New Nation*. Ravinder Kaur examines these late neoliberal capitalist nationalist desires in relation to the Indian nation-state context.

38 Reflecting the liberalization of Ugandan and Indian economies and intensifying South-South cooperation in the 1990s, planned investment statistics compiled by the United Nations (*An Investment Guide to Uganda*, 15) from 1999 to 2002 reveal that Indian FDI outranked US FDI and was exceeded

only by the UK. See also planned investment figures, Uganda Investment Authority, "Investment Abstract Fiscal Year 2011/2012." General trends of estimated planned and actual investment can be assessed from the investment reports compiled at the Uganda Investment Authority website (https://www.ugandainvest.go.ug/) and compared against other sources, including reports compiled by UNCTAD, the World Bank, the IMF, and the Reserve Bank of India.

39 Bharatiya Janta Party, "PM Shri Narenda Modi Addresses Parliament of Uganda," YouTube, July 25, 2018, https://www.youtube.com/watch?v=HTxw1PevYzo.

40 Museveni has attended the "India-Africa Forum Summit," first held in 2008 in New Delhi (also held in Addis Ababa in 2011 and in New Delhi in 2015); the "Vibrant Gujarat" conference, which began in 2003 and is a biennial conference; and the CII-Exim Bank Conclave "India-Africa Project Partnership," which began in 2005 and is an annual event. See "Third Africa-India Forum Summit," October 29, 2015, https://www.mea.gov.in; "Partners in Progress: Towards a Dynamic and Transformative Development Agenda," accessed October 5, 2024, https://www.mea.gov.in/uploads/publicationdocs/25981_framework.pdf; "Vibrant Gujarat Global Summit—2024," accessed August 8, 2024, https://www.vibrantgujarat.com/; Confederation of Indian Industry (CII), "India Africa Business Conclave," accessed August 8, 2024, https://www.ciieximafricaconclave.com.

41 UNCTAD, *Report on the Implementation of the Investment Policy Review*, 1.

42 Foucault, *Security, Territory, Population*.

43 Harvey, *New Imperialism*.

44 Note that this research was primarily carried out between 2009 and 2010, and it is possible that in the context of intense political opposition, political protest, and repression, agents may be discussing the government differently, more overtly, or not at all.

45 Field notes on a meeting between the Chinese Economic Council and Dr. Maggie Kigozi, UIA Offices, Kampala, March 17, 2010.

46 Al-Bulushi, "#SomeoneTellCNN."

47 J. Ferguson, *Global Shadows*, 6–7.

48 The Ugandan diaspora "Home Is Best" Investment Summit that I attended in December 2010 is an example.

49 Ong, *Neoliberalism as Exception*.

50 Ong, *Neoliberalism as Exception*, 78.

51 UNCTAD, *Report on the Implementation of the Investment Policy Review*, 16.

52 UIA, "Status of Industrial and Business Parks and Agricultural Lands in Uganda—July 2021," accessed October 7, 2024, https://www.ugandainvest

.go.ug/wp-content/uploads/2021/10/Industrial-and-business-parks-in
-Uganda-July-2021.pdf.

53   Finnstrom, *Living with Bad Surroundings.*

54   David Rupiny, "Development of Infrastructure Network in Namanve Industrial Park Kicks Off," UIA: Uganda Investment Authority, January 13,
2020, https://www.ugandainvest.go.ug/development-of-infrastructure
-network-in-namanve-industrial-park-kicks-off.

55   Government of Uganda, *Investment Code Act, Cap. 92.*

56   Government of Uganda, *Investment Code Act, Cap. 92.*

57   Capital must be deposited in the Bank of Uganda, and it can be distributed
over time, although private banks are used as well.

58   Policy frameworks do not provide for a minimum capital requirement in
order to obtain an investment license, but the UIA "has applied a 'silent'
threshold of US$100,000 for foreign investors and US$50,000 for local investors." UNCTAD, *Report on the Implementation of the Investment Policy
Review*, 5.

59   UNCTAD, *Report on the Implementation of the Investment Policy Review*, 3.

60   See Tangri and Mwenda, "Corruption and Cronyism," for an analysis of
crony capitalism between the NRM and foreign businessmen. In practice,
it was very difficult to understand how tax breaks and incentives worked
based on both official policy and private negotiations with government
officials outside of the UIA. Some officials discussed how the issue of tax
incentives was becoming more contentious as they tried to create stan-
dardized practices but experienced "meddling" from state ministers and
other government officials.

61   Officials mentioned that Indian and Chinese businessmen were the most
apt to maintain racially endogamous businesses. Some explained that Indian entrepreneurs made strategic use of cost-cutting practices that they
had learned in the competitive "business climate" of India. I was not able
to carry out further empirical research on these issues at the time of my
fieldwork, but I noted that they were controversial claims and a source
of racial tension.

62   Based on my assessment of Uganda Investment Authority reports and
memos between 2007 and 2019; see note 38. GDP growth in Uganda fell
from 6.4% to 2.9% in 2020 due to the global COVID-19 pandemic, and it
slowly recovered to 3.3% in 2021 and has continued growing. UIA, "State of
Investment Memo," December 2022, https://www.ugandainvest.go.ug/wp
-content/uploads/2023/06/State-of-Investment-Memo-WEB-Final.pdf.

63   "Uganda Investments Slow Down," *Daily Monitor*, November 23, 2011,
https://www.monitor.co.ug/uganda/news/national/uganda-investments
-slow-down-1503966.

64   Traders do not need to obtain an investment license, but they are required by law to obtain a trading license and incorporate and register a company.

65   According to the UN, Uganda's poverty rate hovers at 40 percent of the total population.

66   "Uganda: Govt Warns Foreign Investors of Doing Small Businesses," *New Vision*, November 23, 2011, https://allafrica.com/stories/201111240218.htm, accessed December 17, 2012.

Chapter 5. Indian Ugandan, African Asian, or Both?

1   Morris, *Indians in Uganda*, 107.

2   Morris, *Indians in Uganda*, 108–10.

3   Morris, *Indians in Uganda*, 110–11.

4   Gregory, *Rise and Fall of Philanthropy*.

5   Mamdani, *Citizen and Subject*.

6   Community leaders have petitioned the Ministry of Internal Affairs to conduct a census of Indian origin nationals without success and are mobilizing resources for their own census. With Uganda's total population at approximately 46 million (as of 2021), people of South Asian descent are a micro-minority, but a visible racial presence in Kampala and other small towns in Uganda.

7   Modi and Taylor, "Indian Diaspora in Africa," 918.

8   Modi and Taylor, "Indian Diaspora in Africa," 918–19.

9   "Visit of Prime Minister to Uganda," Ministry of External Affairs, Government of India, July 25, 2018, https://www.mea.gov.in/press-releases.htm?dtl /30151/Visit+of+Prime+Minister+to+Uganda+July+2425+2018; Press Trust of India, "PM Modi Unveils Sadar Patel's Statue at Community Event in Uganda," NDTV, July 25, 2018, https://www.ndtv.com/india-news/pm-modi -unveils-sardar-patels-statue-at-community-event-in-uganda-1889573.

10   Ministry of Internal Affairs, "Certificate of Residence," Directorate of Citizenship and Immigration Control of Uganda, accessed November 21, 2024, https://www.immigration.go.ug/services/certificate-residence.

11   In the context of neoliberal globalization, the aftermath of 9/11, and the mobility of precarious labor migrants from South Asia, there is increased migrant mobility and migrant trafficking of South Asians, especially to the Middle East and Gulf States (Rana, *Terrifying Muslims*). While the study of labor migration from India and Pakistan and the migrant trafficking economy were outside the purview of my research, I learned of cases in which South Asia–based traffickers and Uganda-based employers exploited migrants by providing fake travel documents or by withholding travel

documents from them. Community leaders have applied pressure on the Indian High Commission to impose stricter policies to curb trafficking (the High Commission, for its part, has worked to assist Indian nationals with travel documentation, or assisted Ugandan state officials with deportations). Community leaders serve as improvisational social workers by assisting trafficked labor migrants, finding them housing, lending them money, or hiring them for odd jobs to earn money to get back to India. Migrants are exposed to a high degree of violence and exploitation.

12   Ong, *Neoliberalism as Exception*, 121.

13   See the appendix for a list of community organizations. The Hindu right wing and the Indian diaspora in East Africa, both old and new communities, require further research.

14   See S. Nair, "Despite Dislocations," for further discussion on the reverberations of the 1972 Asian expulsion and Ugandan Asian exile history in Gujarat, India.

15   Chris Obore, "Indians Attack Mehta, Tell Him to Go to DR Congo, Sudan," *Sunday Monitor*, April 15, 2007; Taha Mohammed, "It's Not in the Interest of Mehta to Take Mabira," *New Vision*, April 17, 2007.

16   Vision Reporters, "M7 Speaks Out on Violence," *New Vision*, April 14, 2007; Museveni, Yoweri, "Why I Support Mabira Give-Away to Mehta," *New Vision*, April 20, 2007.

17   Jan Ajwang, "Racism Will Affect Investment, Says UIA Boss," *Sunday Monitor*, April 15, 2007.

18   Mahmood Mamdani, "The Asian Question Again: A Reflection," *Sunday Vision*, April 29, 2007.

19   New Vision TV, "Indians Want to Become a Ugandan Tribe", YouTube, July 27, 2017, https://www.youtube.com/watch?v=lj7cTYP3Df8; Immaculate Nabadda, "Interview: Dr. Sudhir Says Its Time to Recognize Uganda's Asian Community as a Tribe," *Trumpet News*, October 10, 2024, https://trumpetnews.co.ug/2024/10/10/interview-dr-sudhir-says-its-time-to-recognize-ugandas-asian-community-as-a-tribe/.

20   Hilary Kimuyu, "Kenya: Asians Now Recognized as Kenya's 44th Tribe," *The Nation*, July 24, 2017; Kimiko de Freytas-Tamura, "Asian Kenyans Seek to Be Declared a 'Tribe' of their Own," *New York Times*, May 25, 2017; Zain Verjee, "Kenya's 44th Tribe: Why I'm Finally a First Class Citizen of My Country", CNN, August 7, 2017.

21   "Amin's Body Can Return—Museveni," *New Vision*, July 23, 2003.

22   "Amin Buried in Saudi Arabia," *Sunday Vision*, August 17, 2003.

23   "Dead or Alive; Amin Should Return," *The Monitor*, July 22, 2003.

24   "Should Amin be Allowed to Return?," *New Vision*, July 23, 2003.

25 Amin and Akulia, *Idi Amin.*

26 In addition to Mark Leopold's scholarship, see D. Peterson and Vokes, *Unseen Archive.* A photographic exhibition of images of Idi Amin was held in Kampala in 2019, expanding possibilities for public reflection on the 1970s. Derek Peterson and Richard Vogel, "Thousands of Recently Discovered Photographs Document Life in Uganda during Idi Amin's Reign," *The Conversation,* June 25, 2019.

27 African Asian Association (AAA), Statement of Purpose, Internal document, January 5, 2013.

28 Dickinson, "Chronicling Kenyan Asian Diasporic Histories", 740–41. An Asian African Heritage Exhibition was held in Kenya in 2005–6, with a permanent exhibition launched in the Nairobi National Museum in 2022. See Tirop, "Reconciling National and Community Identity." See the published works of Zarina Patel for Kenyan Asian autobiographies, and www.awaazmagazine.com for more information about the contributions of *Awaaz* to Kenyan Asian and Kenyan national history.

Chapter 6. Of Gendered Insecurities

1 Amin, "Speech by His Excellency."

2 In a third AAA public forum that I co-organized and that addressed themes of citizenship, social integration, and interethnic and interracial marriage, the panel and audience discussion was rather limited in its ability to discuss the heteropatriarchal, gendered, and sexual dimensions of interracial alliances (unequal hypergamous and hypogamous marriage alliances across race and gender positions) that I map in this chapter; thus, what is imputed to be the ordinary and normalized nature of religious, sectarian, and caste-based endogamy continues to be the politicization of perceived racial endogamy among African communities. The intimacies between race and caste, and their gendered and sexual domains, also require further analysis.

3 I worked with Raising Voices in the early 2000s; it is an organization that offers award-winning domestic violence prevention tools and training for indigenous African communities. My research assisted them with potential advocacy efforts for South Asian women. See the Raising Voices website at http://raisingvoices.org.

4 I draw on Ann Stoler, who in *Carnal Knowledge and Imperial Power* argues that the arrival of white women in settler colonies in Asia and Africa "coincided with the embourgeoisement of colonial communities and with a significant sharpening of racial categories . . . white women needed to be maintained at elevated standards of living, in insulated social spaces cushioned with the cultural artifacts of 'being European'" (19).

5   Nagar, "Communal Discourses," 127.

6   Hand, "Impossible Burdens," 107.

7   Chatterjee, *Nation and Its Fragments*; Sangari and Vaid, *Recasting Women*.

8   Chatterjee, *Nation and Its Fragments*, 116–57.

9   The circulation of Bollywood films in East Africa also constructed ideals of moral and virtuous South Asian womanhood during this time. See Fair, *Pastimes and Politics*.

10 Tripp, "Women's Mobilization"; Tripp and Kwesiga, *Women's Movement*.

11 Kyomuhendo and McIntosh, *Women, Work and Domestic Virtue*; Musisi, "Gender and the Cultural Construction."

12 Moghal, *Idi Amin*; Taylor, "Race and Nation."

13 Hundle, "The Politics of (In)security."

14 Keshodkar, "Marriage as the Means."

15 Mama, "Sheroes and Villains"; Marks, *Divided Sisterhood*; Nagar, "Communal Discourses"; Alexander and Mohanty, *Feminist Genealogies*; Grewal and Kaplan, *Scattered Hegemonies*; Mohanty, *Feminism without Borders*.

16 Following Burrill, Roberts, and Thornberry's *Domestic Violence and the Law*, I use the term "domestic violence" to "indicate overwhelmingly controlling and punitive behavior—whether physical, psychological, or emotional—directed by one member of a household toward another as a means of establishing control and dominance. Such punitive actions very often take the form of gender-based violence, but not always. 'Domestic,' in this sense, indicates a realm of shared living space oriented around relationships within households" (iv).

17 Mamdani, "Pluralism"; Mamdani, "Politics of Democratic Reform."

18 Branch and Mamphilly, *Africa Uprising*.

19 Ong, *Neoliberalism as Exception*, 199.

20 Hundle, "Militarization and Miniskirts."

21 In 2012, a presidential pardon released Sharma from prison, prompting public discussions about the shadowy connections between the NRM and "the Asian business community" and wealthy tycoons.

22 See Taylor's "Asians and Africans in Ugandan Urban Life" for a discussion about the press and rumor, referred to as "Radio Katwe." In Luganda, some urban Ugandans used the phrase *okola kukee* to refer to wife-beating (*kukee* referring to the perpetrator).

23 Some community members argued that Sharma was well-connected with business tycoons in the community and that his shop was a front for other illegal activities.

24   "Sex Twist in Asian Wife's Murder," *The Crusader*, January 3, 1998, 1–2.

25   Kooky Sharma and Anor v. Uganda (2002) UGSC 18 (April 15, 2002); Criminal Appeal No. 44 of 2000, https://ulii.org/akn/ug/judgment/ugsc /2002/18/eng@2002-04-15.

26   I read two differing accounts, one that Joshi took sleeping pills, another that says she took malarial medicines, which caused her death.

27   D. J. Weddi, "Corpse Shocks City: Asian Community Blocks Cremation, Electric Shocks Suspected," *Sunday Vision*, December 28, 1997; D. J. Weddi, "Police Block Cremation," *New Vision*, December 27, 1997.

28   "Indian Murdered Wife, Says Police," *The Monitor*, December 30, 1997.

29   D. J. Weddi, "MUK Don to Examine Asian Women's Corpse," *New Vision*, December 29, 1997.

30   D. J. Weddi and G. Kamali "Autopsy Confirms Asian Wife Murder," *New Vision*, December 30, 1997.

31   Makerere University professors Joy Kwesiga, Florence Bainanga, and Ruth Mukama as well as Jackie Asiimwe-Mwesigye, another prominent women's rights activist, mobilized in response to Joshi's murder.

32   "When 'Investors' Tried to Cover Up a Murder," *Sunday Monitor*, January 4, 1998.

33   "Kooky Inquiries Complete," *New Vision*, January 10, 1998; D. J. Weddi and G. Kamali, "Renu Joshi Murder: Women Set for Demo," *New Vision*, January 9, 1998.

34   H. Tumwine and G. Kamali, "Kooky Case: Second Asian Gone Missing," *New Vision*, January 21, 1998; "Indian Witness Refuses Bribe," *New Vision*, January 16, 1998.

35   "Women Group Lobbies against Kumar Bail," *New Vision*, July 31, 1998.

36   "President Museveni Pardons Sharma Kooky," *New Vision*, March 27, 2012.

37   D. J. Weddi, "Asian Women in Danger," *The Monitor*, December 30, 1997.

38   Weddi, "Asian Women in Danger."

39   Narayan, "Cross-Cultural Connections."

40   Bachetta, "Communal Property/Sexual Property."

41   "This Death Must Not Be Forgotten," *New Vision*, December 30, 1997; W. Byanyima, "When 'Investors' Tried to Cover up a Murder," *Sunday Monitor*, January 4, 1998.

42   See von Struensee, "The Domestic Relations Bill in Uganda."

43   A. Kamugasa, "It Is Time to Say No," *New Vision*, January 6, 1998.

44   Bhattacharjee, "Habit of Ex-nomination."

45   Burton, *Africa in the Indian Imagination*; S. Roy, "Women's Movements."

46   Alice Emasu and Elvis Basudde, "I Am in Trouble for Rejecting Marriage," *New Vision*, January 19, 2006; Agnes Assimwe, "Indian Women Intervene in Forced Marriage Case," *The Monitor*, March 10, 2006.

47   Assimwe, "Indian Women Intervene in Forced Marriage Case."

48   "Come on, Deepa, Be More Serious," *The Monitor*, January 20, 2006.

49   Emasu and Basudde, "I Am in Trouble for Rejecting Marriage"; Assimwe, "Indian Women Intervene in Forced Marriage Case."

50   Alice Emasu, "Indian Dowry Woes: Test for Law-Makers," *New Vision*, January 31, 2006.

51   "Does the Proposed Family Law Solve Any Dowry Problems?," *The Monitor*, February 5, 2006.

52   Assimwe, "Indian Women Intervene in Forced Marriage Case."

53   "Domestic Violence Not Family Matter," *The Monitor*, December 2, 1998; "The Renu Joshi Murder, Justice Has Been Done," *New Vision*, January 25, 1997; "This Death Must Not Be Forgotten," *New Vision*, December 30, 1997.

54   Hundle, "Militarization and Miniskirts."

Conclusion. Toward a Transcontinental Anthropology of Afro–South Asian Entanglement

1   Sicherman, "Makerere's Myths."

2   Mamdani, *Citizen and Subject*.

3   Mamdani, "Beyond Settler and Native."

4   Pierre, *Predicament of Blackness*.

5   Pierre, *Predicament of Blackness*; my emphasis on Afro-Asian and Afro-Dalit studies.

6   R. Ferguson, *Reorder of Things*.

7   Kwesiga and Ahikire, "Student Access and Equity"; Mamdani, *Scholars in the Marketplace*; Mamdani, "Importance of Research in the University."

8   Pierre, "Race in Africa Today"; Tembo and Topolski, "Exploring the Entanglement of Race and Religion."

9   Booysen, *Fees Must Fall*; Ramaru, "Feminist Reflections"; Nyamnjoh, *#RhodesMustFall*; Nyamnjoh, *Decolonizing the Academy*.

10   Kaul, "India's Obsession with Kashmir"; Mahmood, "'Khalistan' as Political Critique."

11   Maya Prabhu, "African Victims of Racism in India Share Their Stories," *Al-Jazeera*, May 3, 2017, https://www.aljazeera.com/features/2017/5/3/african-victims-of-racism-in-india-share-their-stories; Nnamdi Ezeugo Lawrence, "Let's Talk about Racism: I Am Tired of Being a Black Man in

India," *Hindustan Times*, May 23, 2017, https://www.hindustantimes.com/india-news/let-s-talk-about-racism-kallu-was-the-first-word-this-african-man-learnt-in-india/story-fo4HSkREMwyIBh3GlO3DDM.html.

12   "Tarun Vijay Lands in Trouble with 'Black People' Remarks, Later Apologises on Twitter," *The Hindu*, April 7, 2017, https://www.thehindu.com/news/national/if-we-were-racist-why-would-we-live-with-south-indians-tarun-vijay/article17866698.ece.

13   See also Shankar, *An Uneasy Embrace*, for further discussion.

14   Modi and D'Silva, "Liminal Spaces."

15   Yengde, *Caste Matters*; Wilkerson, *Caste*; and see many other useful critical commentaries by Wilkerson, especially her US-centrism and departures from Trinidadian American sociologist Oliver Cox Cromwell's earlier global engagements with race, caste, and capital.

16   "Indian Racism toward Black People Is Almost Worse than White People's Racism: An Interview with Arundhati Roy," *Dalit Camera*, June 8, 2020, https://mronline.org/2020/06/13/indian-racism-towards-black-people-is-almost-worse-than-white-peoples-racism-an-interview-with-arundhati-roy.

17   S. Thomas, "Studying Race."

18   Pathania, *University as Site of Resistance*; Soundararajan, *Trauma of Caste*.

19   Michael Safi, "Statue of Racist Gandhi Removed from University of Ghana," *The Guardian*, December 14, 2018, https://www.theguardian.com/world/2018/dec/14/racist-gandhi-statue-removed-from-university-of-ghana.

20   A. Desai and Vahed, *The South African Gandhi*.

21   Hofmeyr, *Gandhi's Printing Press*; Hofmeyr, "Gandhi in Africa."

22   Roy, "The Doctor and the Saint."

23   Pankaj Mishra, "Gandhi for a Post-truth Age," *New Yorker*, October 22, 2018, https://www.newyorker.com/magazine/2018/10/22/gandhi-for-the-post-truth-age. There is a large scholarly literature on Gandhi, especially related to Indian nationalist historiography and hagiography, which I do not cite extensively here, but that is sidelined or made irrelevant in the GMF's interpretation of Gandhi.

24   Personal communication, summer 2018.

25   Dilip Menon, "Was Mohandas Gandhi a Racist?," *Africa Is a Country*, March 10, 2017, https://africasacountry.com/2017/03/was-mohandas-gandhi-a-racist.

26   Shankar, *An Uneasy Embrace*.

27   N. Bose, "India and Africa in Parallax."

28   Pavan Kulkarni, "How Did Savarkar, a Staunch Supporter of British Colonialism, Come to Be Known as Veer?," *The Wire*, August 15, 2022. https://

thewire.in/history/veer-savarkar-the-staunchest-advocate-of-loyalty-to
-the-english-government.

29 Anneeth Kaur Hundle, "On Blue Economies: Afro-Asianism, Imperial
    Entanglements, Geopolitics," *American Anthropologist*, August 4, 2022,
    https://www.americananthropologist.org/geopolitical-lives/hundle.

30 Kallol Bhattacherjee, "Expulsion of Indians from Uganda by Idi Amin Was
    a Mistake: Museveni," *The Hindu*, January 21, 2024, https://www.thehindu
    .com/news/international/expulsion-of-indians-from-uganda-by-idi-amin
    -was-a-mistake-museveni/article67763086.ece.

31 Chigumadzi, "Who Is Afraid of Race?"

32 Zachariah Mamphilly, "Africa Holds up a Mirror to India: An Interview
    with Shobana Shankar," *Africa Is a Country*, September 14, 2022.

33 Amit Roy, "Gandhi Statue Defiled in London," *The Telegraph*, September 6,
    2020, https://www.telegraphindia.com/world/gandhi-statue-defiled-in
    -london/cid/1779732.

34 Shankar, *An Uneasy Embrace*.

35 Harrison, *Decolonizing Anthropology*.

Postscript. Fifty Years On

1   Singh, "Death of Islamophobia"; Hundle, "After Wisconsin."

2   Shambuka, "Neoliberalizing Racial Justice."

3   Kim, *Bitter Fruit*.

4   Gooding-Williams, *Reading Rodney King*.

5   Lee, *Do the Right Thing*.

6   Neha Shah, "How Did British Indians Become so Prominent in the Con-
    servative Party?," *Guardian*, February 27, 2020, https://www.theguardian
    .com/commentisfree/2020/feb/27/how-did-british-indians-become-so
    -prominent-in-the-conservative-party.

7   Philbert Girinema, "UK Interior Minister Visits Rwanda to Expand De-
    portation Plan," *Reuters*, March 18, 2023, https://www.reuters.com/world
    /uk/uk-interior-minister-visit-rwanda-discuss-migration-partnership
    -2023–03–17.

8   Will Shoki, "Roti and Roses: A Feature with Zohran Kwame Mamdani,"
    Africa Is a Country, January 30, 2020, https://africasacountry.com/2020
    /01/roti-and-roses.

9   Shrai Popat, "My Family's Anti-Blackness and Boris Johnson's Cabinet,"
    The Juggernaut, February 26, 2020, https://www.thejuggernaut.com/anti
    -blackness-boris-johnson-cabinet.

10 Ambikaipaker, *Political Blackness*.

11   See British Ugandan Asians at 50, https://www.bua50.org, for more information.

12   See "Expulsion: Uganda's Asians and the Remaking of Nationality," Oxford Talks, St. Anthony's College, May 20, 2022, https://talks.ox.ac.uk/talks/id/cc30d753-80e7-45c6-a5f9-b8c050161801.

13   See Hundle, "Fifty Years On."

14   See "Dr. Mahmood Mamdani's Lecture: A Critical Look at the Forced Expulsion of Uganda Asians 50 Years Ago," *Ismailimail* (blog), September 27, 2022, https://ismailimail.blog/2022/09/27/video-dr-mahmood-mamdanis-lecture-a-critical-look-at-the-forced-expulsion-of-uganda-asians-50-years-ago.

15   See "Panel Discussion to Commemorate 50th Anniversary of Uganda Asian Expulsion," *Ismailimail* (blog), October 5, 2022, https://ismailimail.blog/2022/10/05/event-panel-discussion-to-commemorate-50th-anniversary-of-uganda-asian-expulsion; and "First Female East Asian Senator (Canada) Describes Her Uganda Expulsion Experience," *Ismailimail* (blog), April 13, 2023, https://ismailimail.blog/2023/04/13/video-first-female-east-asian-senator-canada-describes-her-uganda-expulsion-experience.

16   Liam Taylor, "Fifty Years after Expulsion: Asians Are Thriving Again in Uganda but Insecurities Still Linger," *Economist*, November 17, 2022, https://www.economist.com/middle-east-and-africa/2022/11/17/fifty-years-after-expulsion-asians-are-thriving-again-in-uganda.

17   Human Rights Watch, "Uganda: Elections Marred by Violence," January 21, 2021, https://www.hrw.org/news/2021/01/21/uganda-elections-marred-violence.

18   Kelsey Neilsen and Caleb Okerere, "We Were Arrested in Uganda for Protesting for Black Lives," *Mail and Guardian*, July 2, 2020, https://mg.co.za/africa/2020-07-02-we-were-arrested-in-uganda-while-protesting-for-black-lives.

19   Dolar Vasani, "Uganda Remembers: If We Don't Tell Our Stories, No One Will," *Daily Maverick*, January 10, 2022, https://www.dailymaverick.co.za/article/2022-01-10-uganda-remembers-if-we-dont-tell-our-stories-someone-else-will; Dolar Vasani, "Expulsion @ 50," https://podcasts.apple.com/gb/podcast/expulsion-50/id1548728020. See also Yasmin Jamal, "Ugandan Asian Migration: Forced to Flee," accessed November 22, 2024, https://open.spotify.com/show/192UVeFHlEWU19ZiGu1tUZ.

Internet Archives and Government Documents

Carleton University Library, Archives and Special Collections. The Uganda Collection. https://carleton.ca/uganda-collection.

Government of India, Ministry of External Affairs. *Declaration on the New Asian-African Strategic Partnership*. April 24, 2005. https://www.mea.gov.in/bilateral-documents.htm?dtl/6608/Declaration.

Government of Uganda. *The Constitution of the Republic of Uganda*. Entebbe: Government Printer, 1967.

Government of Uganda. *The Constitution of the Republic of Uganda*. Entebbe: Uganda Print and Publication Corporation, 1995.

Government of Uganda. *Declaration of Assets (Non-citizen Asians) Decree*. Decree 27, 1972.

Government of Uganda. *Draft Constitution of the Republic of Uganda*. Kampala: Uganda Constitutional Commission, 1993.

Government of Uganda. *Expropriated Properties Act, Cap. 87*. Kampala: Government Printer, 1983.

Government of Uganda. *Immigration (Cancellation of Entry Permits and Certificates of Residence) Decree*. Decree 17, 1972.

Government of Uganda. *Immigration (etc.) (Amendment) Decree*. Decree 30, October 5, 1972.

Government of Uganda. *Investment Code Act*. Kampala: Government Printer, 2019.

Government of Uganda. *Investment Code Act, Cap. 92*. Kampala: Government Printer, 1991.

Government of Uganda. *Investment Code, Statute No. 1*. Kampala: Government Printer, 1991.

Government of Uganda. *Land Act*. Kampala: Government Printer, 1998.

Government of Uganda. *Poverty Eradication Action Plan (2004/5–07/8)*. Kampala: Ministry of Finance, Planning and Economic Development, 2004.

Government of Uganda. *Public Finance Management Act, 2015*. UPPC, Entebbe, 2015.

Government of Uganda. *The Trade (Licensing Act)*. Entebbe: Government Printer, 1969.

Government of Uganda. *The Uganda Citizenship and Immigration Control (Amendment) Act, No. 5*. Kampala: Government Printer, 2009.

Government of Uganda. *Uganda Independence Act*. UPPC, Entebbe, 1962.

Government of Uganda, Ministry of Trade, Industry and Cooperatives. *Uganda Micro, Small and Medium Enterprise (MSME) Policy*. June 2015.

Indian Overseas Trust. "British Ugandan Asians at 50." Accessed November 8, 2024. https://www.bua50.org.

Indian Overseas Trust. "Fortieth Anniversary Commemoration." Accessed November 8, 2024. http://www.asiansfromuganda.org.uk/40th_anniversary_commemoration.php.

National Archives, Kew, Richmond, UK. "Marking the 50th Anniversary of the Arrival of Ugandan Asians." 2022. https://www.nationalarchives.gov.uk/education/outreach/projects/migration-histories/marking-the-50th-anniversary-of-the-arrival-of-ugandan-asians-in-britain-2022.

National Resistance Movement. "Manifesto, 2021–2026: Securing Your Future." https://www.nrm.ug/manifesto-2021-2026.

Uganda Investment Authority. "Investment Abstract Fiscal Year 2011/2012." Accessed October 5, 2024. https://www.ugandainvest.go.ug/wp-content/uploads/2016/02/Investment-Statistical-Abstract-2011-20122.pdf.

Uganda National Planning Authority. *The Comprehensive National Development Planning Framework (CNDPH) [Draft]*. Kampala: National Planning Authority, 2009.

Uganda National Planning Authority. *National Development Plan (2010/11–2014/15): Growth, Employment and Prosperity for Socio-economic Transformation*. Kampala: National Planning Authority, 2010.

Uganda National Planning Authority. *National Vision Framework [Draft]*. Kampala: National Planning Authority, 2009.

Uganda National Planning Authority. *Second National Development Plan (NDPII) 2015/16–2019/20*. Kampala: National Planning Authority, 2015.

UK Parliament Hansard, House of Lords. "In Focus: Ugandan Asians Fifty Years since Their Expulsion." Vol. 824, October 27, 2022. https://lordslibrary.parliament.uk/ugandan-asians-50-years-since-their-expulsion-from-uganda.

UK Parliament Hansard, House of Lords. "Ugandan Asians." Vol. 741, December 6, 2012. https://hansard.parliament.uk/lords/2012-12-06/debates/12120659000796/UgandanAsians.

United Nations. *An Investment Guide to Uganda*. New York: United Nations, 2004.

United Nations Conference on Trade and Development (UNCTAD). *Report on the Implementation of the Investment Policy Review: Uganda*. New York: United Nations, 2007.

Articles, Books, and Other Publications

Abidi, Syed A. H. "The Return of Asians to Uganda." *Africa Quarterly* 36, no. 3 (1996): 45–58.

Abraham, Itty. "Seguranca/Security in Brazil and the United States." In *Words in Motion: Toward a Global Lexicon*, edited by Carol Gluck and Anna Lowenhaupt Tsing, 21–39. Durham, NC: Duke University Press, 2009.

Adams, Bert, and Michael Bristow. "Ugandan Asian Expulsion Experiences: Rumor and Reality." *Journal of Asian and African Studies* 14, nos. 3–4 (1979): 191–203.

Adida, Claira. *Immigrant Exclusion and Insecurity in Africa: Coethnic Strangers*. Cambridge: Cambridge University Press, 2014.

Ahluwalia, D. P. S. *Plantations and the Politics of Sugar in Uganda*. Kampala: Fountain, 1995.

Ahluwalia, Pal. "When Does a Settler Become a Native? Citizens and Identity in a Settler Society." *Pretexts: Literary and Cultural Studies* 10, no. 1 (2001): 63–73.

Aiyar, Sana. *Indians in Kenya: The Politics of Diaspora*. Cambridge, MA: Harvard University Press, 2015.

Al-Bulushi, Samar. "#SomeoneTellCNN: Cosmopolitan Militarism in the East African Warscape." *Cultural Dynamics* 31, no. 4 (2019): 1–27.

Alexander, M. J., and C. T. Mohanty, eds. *Feminist Genealogies, Colonial Legacies, Democratic Futures*. New York: Routledge, 1997.

Alibhai-Brown, Yasmin. *No Place like Home: An Autobiography*. London: Virago, 1997.

Ambedkar, B. R. *Annihilation of Caste*. 1936. London: Verso, 2014.

Ambikaipaker, Mohan. *Political Blackness in Multiracial Britain*. Philadelphia: University of Pennsylvania Press, 2018.

Amiji, Hatim. "The Asian Communities." In *Islam in Africa*, vol. 4, edited by James Kritzeck and I. M. Lewis, 141–75. New York: Van Nostrand-Reinhold, 1969.

Amin, Idi. "Speech by His Excellency the President of Uganda, General Amin, to the Asian Conference Held on 8th December, 1971, in the Uganda International Conference Centre." *East Africa Journal* 9 (1972): 2–5.

Amin, Jaffer, and M. Akulia. *Idi Amin: Hero or Villain? His Son Jaffer Amin and Other People Speak*. N.p.: Millennium Global, 2010.

Aminzade, Ron. *Race, Nation, and Citizenship in Post-colonial Africa: The Case of Tanzania*. Cambridge: Cambridge University Press, 2013.

Amory, D. "The Politics of Identity of Zanzibar." PhD diss., Stanford University, 1994.

Anderson, Benedict. *Imagined Communities: Reflection on the Origins and Spread of Nationalism*. London: Verso, 1991.

Asiimwe, Godfrey. "From Monopoly Marketing to Coffee Magendo: Responses to Policy Recklessness and Extraction in Uganda, 1971–79." *Journal of Eastern African Studies* 7, no. 1 (2013): 104–24.

Askew, Kelly. *Performing the Nation: Swahili Music and Cultural Politics in Tanzania.* Chicago: University of Chicago Press, 2002.

Aspinall, Peter. "The Social Evolution of the Term 'Half-Caste' in Britain: The Paradox of Its Use as Both Derogatory Racial Category and Self-Descriptor." *Historical Sociology* 26, no. 4 (2013): 503–26.

Axel, Brian. *The Nation's Tortured Body: Violence, Representation, and the Formation of a Sikh "Diaspora."* Durham, NC: Duke University Press, 2001.

Bachetta, Paola. "Communal Property/Sexual Property: On Representations of Muslim Women in a Hindu Nationalist Discourse." In *Forging Identities: Gender, Communities and the State in India,* edited by Zoya Hassan, 188–225. Boulder, CO: Westview, 2018.

Ballantyne, Tony. *Between Colonialism and Diaspora: Sikh Cultural Formations in an Imperial World.* Durham, NC: Duke University Press, 2006.

Barot, Rohit. "Varna, Nât-Jât and Atak among Kampala Hindus." *New Community* 3, nos. 1–2 (1974): 59–66.

Bernal, Victoria. *Nation as Network: Diaspora, Cyberspace, and Citizenship.* Chicago: University of Chicago Press, 2014.

Bertz, Ned. *Diaspora and Nation in the Indian Ocean: Transnational Histories of Race and Urban Space in Tanzania.* Athens: Ohio University Press, 2015.

Besteman, Catherine. *Transforming Cape Town.* Berkeley: University of California Press, 2008.

Bhachu, Parminder. *Twice Migrants: East African Sikh Settlers in Britain.* London: Tavistock, 1985.

Bharati, Agehananda. *The Asians in East Africa: Jayhind and Uhuru.* Chicago: Nelson-Hall, 1972.

Bhattacharjee, Ananya. "The Habit of Ex-nomination: Nation, Woman, and the Indian Immigrant Bourgeoisie." *Public Culture* 5, no. 1 (1992): 19–44. https://doi.org/10.1215/08992363-5-1-19.

Bissell, William. "Engaging Colonial Nostalgia." *Cultural Anthropology* 20, no. 2 (2005): 215–48.

Bond, Patrick, and Ana Garcia. *BRICS: An Anti-capitalist Critique.* Haymarket, 2015.

Bonee, John L. "Caesar Augustus and the Flight of the Asians: The International Legal Implications of the Asian Expulsion from Uganda in 1972." *International Lawyer* 8, no. 1 (1974): 136–59. https://www.jstor.org/stable/40704859.

Booysen, Susan. *Fees Must Fall: Student Revolt, Decolonisation and Governance in South Africa.* Johannesburg: Wits University Press, 2016.

Bose, Neilesh. "India and Africa in Parallax: In Conversation with Renu Modi, Shobana Shankar, and Meera Venkatachalam." *Borderlines,* June 15, 2021.

Bose, Sugata. *A Hundred Horizons: The Indian Ocean in the Age of Global Empire.* Cambridge, MA: Harvard University Press, 2009.

Brah, Avtar. *Cartographies of Diaspora: Contesting Identities*. London: Routledge, 1996.

Branch, Adam. *Displacing Human Rights: War and Intervention in Northern Uganda*. Oxford: Oxford University Press, 2011.

Branch, Adam, and Zachariah Mamphilly. *Africa Uprising: Popular Protest and Political Change*. London: Zed, 2015.

Brennan, James. *Taifa: Making Nation and Race in Urban Tanzania*. Athens: Ohio University Press, 2012.

Brown, Thomas. "Ugandan Asians: 50 Years since Their Expulsion from Uganda." House of Lords Library, August 31, 2022. https://lordslibrary.parliament.uk /ugandan-asians-50-years-since-their-expulsion-from-uganda.

Burrill, Emily, Richard L. Roberts, and Elizabeth Thornberry, eds. *Domestic Violence and the Law in Colonial and Postcolonial Africa*. Athens: Ohio University Press, 2010.

Burton, Antoinette. *Africa in the Indian Imagination*. Durham, NC: Duke University Press, 2012.

Campbell, Horace. *Four Essays on Neo-colonialism in Uganda: The Military Dictatorship of Idi Amin*. Toronto: Afro-Carib, 1975.

Carrasco, Milton. "The Challenges and Tribulations of Our Migrations: Migrant's Perspective." In *Uganda South Asians Exodus: Kololian Perspectives*, edited by Narendra Wagle, Peter Nazareth, Zulema de Souza, and Bina Mehta, 22–27. Toronto: Centre for South Asian Studies, University of Toronto, 2002.

Centre for Contemporary Cultural Studies. *The Empire Strikes Back: Race and Racism in 70s Britain*. London: Routledge, 1982. https://doi.org/10.4324/9780203639948.

Chatterjee, Partha. *The Nation and Its Fragments: Colonial and Postcolonial Histories*. Princeton, NJ: Princeton University Press, 1993.

Chatterjee, Partha. *The Politics of the Governed: Reflections on Popular Politics in Most of the World*. New York: Columbia University Press, 2004.

Cheru, Fantu, and Cyril Obi. *The Rise of China and India in Africa: Challenges, Opportunities, and Critical Interventions*. London: Zed, 2010.

Chhabria, Sheetal. "Where Does Caste Fit in a Global History of Racial Capitalism?" *Historical Materialism* 31, nos. 2–3 (2023), accessed November 8, 2024. https:// www.historicalmaterialism.org/article/where-does-caste-fit-in-a-global-history -of-racial-capitalism.

Chigumadzi, Panashe. "Who Is Afraid of Race?" *Boston Review*, March 10, 2021. https://www.bostonreview.net/articles/who-is-afraid-of-race.

Chivers, T. S. "Is Expulsion Rational? Dealing with Unwanted Minorities as Issues of Rationality." *Ethnic and Racial Studies* 8, no. 8 (1985): 81–89.

Christian, Michelle, and Assumpta Namaganda. "Good Mzungu? Whiteness and White Supremacy in Postcolonial Uganda." *Identities* 30, no. 2 (2022): 217–36.

Clarke, Kamari. "Notes on Cultural Citizenship in the Black Atlantic World." *Cultural Anthropology* 28, no. 3 (2013): 464–74.

Collier, Paul, and Ritva Reinikka. *Uganda's Recovery: The Role of Farms, Firms, and Government*. Kampala: Fountain, 2001.

Comaroff, Jean, and John Comaroff. *Millennial Capitalism and the Culture of Neo-liberalism*. Durham, NC: Duke University Press, 2001.

Comaroff, Jean, and John Comaroff. *Theory from the South, or How Euro-America Is Evolving toward Africa*. Chicago: University of Chicago Press, 2012.

Cooper, Frederick. "The Recurrent Crises of the Gatekeeper State." In *Africa since 1940: The Past of the Present*, 156–90. New York: Cambridge University Press, 2002.

Cox, Oliver C. *Caste, Class, and Race: A Study in Social Dynamics*. New York: Monthly Review Press, 1959.

Crapanzano, Vincent. *Waiting: The Whites of South Africa*. New York: Harper Collins, 1985.

Das, Veena. *Critical Events: An Anthropological Perspective on Contemporary India*. Oxford: Oxford University Press, 1995.

Das, Veena. *Life and Words: Violence and the Descent into the Ordinary*. Berkeley: University of California Press, 2007.

Das, Veena. "The Signature of the State." In *Anthropology at the Margins of the State*, edited by Veena Das and Deborah Poole, 225–52. Sante Fe: School of American Research, 2004.

de Certeau, Michel. *The Practice of Everyday Life*. Berkeley: University of California Press, 1984.

Decker, Alicia. *In Idi Amin's Shadow: Women, Gender, and Militarism in Uganda*. Athens: Ohio University Press, 2014.

Desai, Ashwin, and Goolam Vahed. *The South African Gandhi: Stretcher-Bearer of Empire*. Stanford, CA: Stanford University Press, 2015.

Desai, Gaurav. *Commerce with the Universe: Africa, India, and the Afrasian Imaginary*. New York: Columbia University Press, 2013.

Dhir, Bharti. *Worth: An Inspiring True Story of Abandonment, Exile, Inner Strength and Belonging*. London: Hay House, 2021.

Diawara, Manthia. *In Search of Africa*. Cambridge, MA: Harvard University Press, 2010.

Dickinson, Jen. "Chronicling Kenyan Asian Diasporic Histories: 'Newcomers', 'Established' Migrants, and the Post-colonial Practices of Time-Work." *Population, Space and Place* 22, no. 8 (2016): 736–49.

Diouf, Mamadou. "Engaging Post-colonial Cultures: African Youth and Public Space." *African Studies Review* 46, no. 1 (2003): 1–12.

Dirks, Nicholas. *Castes of Mind: Colonialism in the Making of Colonial India*. Princeton, NJ: Princeton University Press, 2001.

Du Bois, W. E. B. *The Souls of Black Folk*. 1903. New York: Gramercy, 1994.

Dusenbery, Verne A. "On the Moral Sensitivities of Sikhs in North America." In *Divine Passions: The Social Construction of Emotion in North America*, edited by Owen M. Lynch, 239–61. Delhi: Oxford University Press, 1990.

Englund, Harri. *Prisoners of Freedom: Human Rights and the African Poor*. Berkeley: University of California Press, 2006.

Epstein, Helen. *Another Fine Mess: America, Uganda, and the War on Terror.* New York: Columbia Global Reports, 2017.

Fair, Laura. *Pastimes and Politics: Culture, Community and Identity in Post-abolition Urban Zanzibar, 1890–1945.* Athens: Ohio University Press, 2001.

Fanon, Frantz. *The Wretched of the Earth.* 1961. Grove, 2005.

Ferguson, James. *The Anti-politics Machine: Development, Depoliticization, and Bureaucratic Power in Lesotho.* Minneapolis: University of Minnesota Press, 1994.

Ferguson, James. *Global Shadows: Africa in the Neoliberal World Order.* Durham, NC: Duke University Press, 2006.

Ferguson, James. "Seeing like an Oil Company: Space, Security, and Global Capital in Neoliberal Africa." *American Anthropologist* 107, no. 3 (2005): 377–82.

Ferguson, Roderick. *The Reorder of Things: The University and Its Pedagogies of Minority Difference.* Minneapolis: University of Minnesota Press, 2012.

Finnstrom, Sverker. *Living with Bad Surroundings: War, History, and Everyday Moments in Northern Uganda.* Durham, NC: Duke University Press, 2008.

Foucault, Michel. *The Birth of Biopolitics: Lectures at the College de France 1977–78.* New York: Picador, 2008.

Foucault, Michel. *The History of Sexuality: An Introduction.* Vol. 1. New York: Vintage, 1985.

Foucault, Michel. *Security, Territory, Population: Lectures at the College de France 1977–78.* New York: Picador, 2009.

Fulford, Lucy. *The Exiled: Empire, Immigration and the Ugandan Asian Exodus.* London: Coronet, 2023.

Furnivall, J. S. *Colonial Policy and Practice: A Comparative Study of Burma and Netherlands India.* 1948. Reprint, New York: New York University Press, 1956.

Gandhi, Supriya. "Hindutva and the Shared Scripts of the Global Right." *The Immanent Frame,* October 12, 2022. https://tif.ssrc.org/2022/10/12/hindutva-and-the-shared-scripts-of-the-global-right.

Geschiere, Peter. *The Perils of Belonging: Autochthony, Citizenship, and Exclusion in Africa and Europe.* Chicago: University of Chicago Press, 2009.

Geschiere, Peter, and Francis Nyamnjoh. "Capitalism and Autochthony: The Seesaw of Mobility and Belonging." *Public Culture* 12, no. 2 (2010): 423–52.

Ghai, Dharam. *The Asian Minorities in East and Central Africa (up to 1971).* Report no. 4. Minority Rights Group, 1971. https://minorityrights.org/resources/the-asian-minorities-of-east-and-central-africa-up-to-1971.

Ghai, Dharam. "The Bugandan Trade Boycott: A Study in Tribal, Political and Economic Nationalism." In *Protest and Power in Black Africa,* edited by Robert Rotberg and Ali Mazrui, 755–70. New York: Oxford University Press, 1970.

Gilroy, Paul. *The Black Atlantic: Modernity and Double-Consciousness.* Cambridge, MA: Harvard University Press, 1993.

Glassman, Jonathan. *War of Words, War of Stones: Racial Thought and Colonial Violence in Zanzibar.* Bloomington: Indiana University Press, 2011.

Goldberg, David. *The Threat of Race: Reflections on Racial Neoliberalism*. Hoboken, NJ: Blackwell, 2009.

Gooding-Williams, Robert, ed. *Reading Rodney King, Reading Urban Uprising*. New York: Routledge, 1993.

Gregory, Robert. *Quest for Equality: Asian Politics in East Africa, 1900–1967*. Orient Longman, 1993.

Gregory, Robert. *The Rise and Fall of Philanthropy in East Africa: The Asian Contribution*. New York: Routledge, 2017.

Grewal, Inderpal, and Caren Kaplan. *Scattered Hegemonies: Postmodernity and Transnational Feminist Perspectives*. Minneapolis: University of Minnesota Press, 1994.

Grovogui, Siba. "Come to Africa: A Hermeneutics of Race in International Theory." *Alternatives: Global, Local, Political* 26, no. 4 (2001): 425–88.

Grovogui, Siba. *Sovereigns, Quasi-sovereigns, and Africans: Race and Self-Determination in International Law*. Minneapolis: University of Minnesota Press, 1996.

Guan, Lee Hock. "Furnivall's Plural Society and Leach's Political Systems of Highland Burma." *Sojourn: Journal of Social Issues in Southeast Asia* 24, no. 1 (2009): 32–46.

Gudavarthy, Ajay. "Globalisation and Regionalisation: Mapping the New Continental Drift." *Economic and Political Weekly* 44, no. 24 (2009): 93–100.

Gupta, Akhil. "Blurred Boundaries: The Discourse of Corruption, the Culture of Politics, and the Imagined State." *American Ethnologist* 22, no. 2 (1995): 375–402.

Gupta, Anirudha. "India and the Asians in East Africa." In *Expulsion of a Minority: Essays on Uganda Asians*, edited by Michael Twaddle, 125–39. London: Althone, 1975.

Gupta, Rahila, ed. *From Homebreakers to Jailbreakers: Southall Black Sisters*. Oxford: Zed, 2003.

Hall, Stuart. "Negotiating Caribbean Identities." *New Left Review* 209, no. 1 (1995). https://newleftreview.org/issues/i209/articles/stuart-hall-negotiating-caribbean-identities.

Hall, Stuart. "New Ethnicities." In *Stuart Hall: Critical Dialogues in Cultural Studies*, edited by D. Morley and K. Chen, 441–49. 1988. Reprint, London: Routledge, 1996.

Halsteen, Ulrik. "Taking Rights Talk Seriously: Reflections on Ugandan Political Discourse." In *Rights and the Politics of Recognition in Africa*, edited by Harri Englund and Francis Nyamnjoh, 103–24. Oxford: Zed, 2004.

Hand, Felicity. "Impossible Burdens: East African Asian Women's Memoirs." *Research in African Literatures* 42, no. 3 (2011): 100–116.

Hansen, Holger Bernt. *Ethnicity and Military Rule in Uganda*. Research report no. 43. Uppsala: Scandinavian Institute for African Studies, 1977.

Hansen, Holger Bernt, and Michael Twaddle, eds. *Changing Uganda*. London: James Curry, 1991.

Hansen, Holger Bernt, and Michael Twaddle, eds. *Developing Uganda*. Oxford: James Curry, 1998.

Hansen, Thomas Blom. *Melancholia for Freedom: Social Life in an Indian Township in South Africa*. Princeton, NJ: Princeton University Press, 2012.

Hansen, Thomas Blom. *The Saffron Wave: Democracy and Hindu Nationalism in Modern India*. Princeton, NJ: Princeton University Press, 1999.

Hansen, Thomas Blom, and Finn Stepputat. *Sovereign Bodies: Citizens, Migrants, and States in the Postcolonial World*. Princeton, NJ: Princeton University Press, 2005.

Hanson, Holly. *Landed Obligation: The Practice of Power in Buganda*. Portsmouth, NH: Heinemann, 2003.

Harding, Susan. "Representing Fundamentalism: The Problem of the Repugnant Cultural Other." *Social Research* 58, no. 2 (1991): 373–93.

Harrison, Faye. *Decolonizing Anthropology: Moving Further toward an Anthropology of Liberation*. Arlington, VA: American Anthropological Association, 1991.

Harvey, David. *The New Imperialism*. Oxford: Oxford University Press, 2003.

Hegel, G. W. F. *The Philosophy of History*. 1830–31. New York: Dover, 1956.

Herbert, Joanna. "Oral Histories of Ugandan Asians in Britain: Gendered Identities in the Diaspora." *Contemporary South Asia* 17, no. 1 (2009): 21–32.

Herzfeld, Michael. *Cultural Intimacy: Social Poetics in a Nation-State*. London: Routledge, 1997.

Himbara, David, and Dawood Sultan. "Reconstructing the Ugandan State and Economy: The Challenge of an International Bantustan." *Review of African Political Economy* 22, no. 63 (1995): 85–93.

Hirsch, Marianne. "Family Pictures: *Maus*, Mourning, and Post-memory." *Discourse: Journal for Theoretical Studies in Media and Culture* 15, no. 2 (1992): 3–29.

Hofmeyr, Isabel. "Gandhi in Africa." *Public Books*, June 1, 2014. https://www.publicbooks.org/gandhi-in-africa.

Hofmeyr, Isabel. *Gandhi's Printing Press: Experiments in Slow Reading*. Cambridge, MA: Harvard University Press, 2013.

Humphrey, Derek, and Michael Ward. *Passports and Politics*. Harmondsworth: Penguin, 1974.

Hundle, Anneeth Kaur. "After Wisconsin: Registers of Sikh Precarity in the Alien-Nation." *Sikh Formations: Religion, Culture, Theory* 8, no. 3 (2012): 287–91.

Hundle, Anneeth Kaur. "Exceptions to the Expulsion: Violence, Security and Community among Ugandan Asians, 1972–79." *Journal of Eastern African Studies* 7, no. 1 (2013): 164–82.

Hundle, Anneeth Kaur. "Fifty Years On: The 1972 Asian Expulsion as Global Critical Event, or the Insecurities of Expulsion." *Journal of the African Literature Association* 16, no. 3 (2022): 407–24. https://www.tandfonline.com/toc/rala20/16/3.

Hundle, Anneeth Kaur. "Insecurities of Expulsion: Emergent Citizenship Practices and Political Practice in Contemporary Uganda." *Comparative Studies in South Asia, Africa and the Middle East* 39, no. 1 (2019): 8–23.

Hundle, Anneeth Kaur. "Of Militarization and Miniskirts: Sovereignty and Sexuality in Urban Uganda." *Los Angeles Review of Books*, December 14, 2014. https://lareviewofbooks.org/article/of-militarization-and-miniskirts-sovereignty-and-sexuality-in-urban-uganda.

Hundle, Anneeth Kaur. "The Politics of (In)security: Reconstructing African-Asian Relations, Citizenship and Community in Post-expulsion Uganda." PhD diss., University of Michigan, 2013.

Hundle, Anneeth Kaur. "Postcolonial Patriarchal Nativism, Domestic Violence and Transnational Feminist Research in Uganda." *Feminist Review* 121, no. 1 (2019): 37–52.

Hundle, Anneeth Kaur, Ioana Szeman, and Joanna Pares Hoare. "What Is the Transnational in Transnational Feminist Research?" *Feminist Review* 121, no. 1 (2019): 3–8.

Hunt, Nancy Rose. *A Colonial Lexicon: Of Birth Ritual, Medicalization, and Mobility in the Congo*. Durham, NC: Duke University Press, 1999.

Ivaska, Andrew. *Cultured States: Youth, Gender, and Modern Style in 1960s Dar es Salaam*. Durham, NC: Duke University Press, 2011.

Jamal, Vali. "Asians in Uganda, 1880–1972: Inequality and Expulsion." *Economic History Review* 29, no. 4 (1976): 602–16.

Jamal, Vali. "Uganda Asians: We Contributed, We Contribute." Unpublished manuscript, 2021.

Jayawardene, Sureshi. "Racialized Casteism: Exposing the Relationship between Race, Caste, and Colorism through the Experiences of Africana People in India and Sri Lanka." *Journal of African American Studies* 20 (2016): 323–45. https://link.springer.com/article/10.1007/s12111-016-9333-5.

Jeyifo, Boyodun. 1990. "The Nature of Things: Arrested Decolonization and Critical Theory." *Research in African Literatures* 21, no. 1 (1990): 33–48.

Joseph, May. *Nomadic Identities: The Performance of Citizenship*. Minneapolis: University of Minnesota Press, 1999.

Kabwegyere, Tarsis. *The Politics of State Formation and Destruction in Uganda*. 1975. Kampala: Fountain, 1995.

Kara, Taushif. "Vanishing Mediators, or Multiculturalism Expelled." *Public Culture* 36, no. 3 (2024), in press.

Kasozi, A. B. K. *The Social Origins of Violence in Uganda*. Kampala: Fountain, 1994.

Kassam, Mumtaz. "The Asian Minority in Uganda." In *Uganda South Asians Exodus: Kololian Perspectives*, edited by Narendra Wagle, Peter Nazareth, Zulema de Souza, and Bina Mehta, 12–21. Toronto: Centre for South Asian Studies, University of Toronto, 2002.

Kassimir, Ronald. "Reading Museveni: Structure, Agency and Pedagogy in Ugandan Politics." *Canadian Journal of African Studies* 33, nos. 2–3 (1999): 649–73. https://doi.org/10.2307/486282.

Kaul, Nitasha. "India's Obsession with Kashmir: Democracy, Gender, (Anti-)nationalism." *Feminist Review* 119, no. 1 (2018): 126–43. https://doi.org/10.1057/s41305-018-0123-x.

Kaur, Ravinder. *Brand New Nation: Capitalist Dreams and Nationalist Designs in Twenty-First Century India.* Stanford, CA: Stanford University Press, 2020.

Keshodkar, Akbar. "Marriage as the Means to Preserve 'Asian-ness': The Post-revolutionary Experience of Asians of Zanzibar." *Journal of Asian and African Studies* 45, no. 2 (2010): 226–40.

Kim, Claire. *Bitter Fruit: The Politics of Black-Korean Conflict in New York City.* New Haven, CT: Yale University Press, 2000.

Kim, Claire. "The Racial Triangulation of Asian Americans." *Politics and Society* 27, no. 1 (1999): 105–38.

Kwesiga, Joy, and Josephine Ahikire. "On Student Access and Equity in a Reforming University: Makerere in the 1990s and Beyond." *Journal of Higher Education in Africa* 4, no. 2 (2006): 1–46.

Kyomuhendo, Grace Bantebya, and Marjorie McIntosh, eds. *Women, Work and Domestic Virtue in Uganda, 1900–2003.* Oxford: James Curry, 2006.

Lalani, Z. *Ugandan Asian Expulsion: 90 Days and beyond through the Eyes of the International Press.* Tampa, FL: Expulsion, 1997.

Lee, Christopher. *Making a World after Empire: The Bandung Moment and Its Political Afterlives.* Athens: Ohio University Press, 2010.

Lee, Spike, dir. *Do the Right Thing.* Universal Pictures, 1989.

Leonard, Karen. *Making Ethnic Choices: California's Punjabi Mexican Americans.* Philadelphia: Temple University Press, 1992.

Leopold, Mark. *Idi Amin: The Story of Africa's Icon of Evil.* New Haven, CT: Yale University Press, 2021.

Leopold, Mark. *Inside West Nile: Violence, History and Representation on an African Frontier.* Kampala: Fountain, 2005.

Leopold, Mark. "Sex, Violence and History in the Lives of Idi Amin: Postcolonial Masculinity as Masquerade." *Journal of Postcolonial Writing* 45, no. 3 (2009): 321–30.

Lewis, Krishna. "Afro-Asian Worlds: Introduction." *Transition* 119 (2016): 17–21.

Lowe, Lisa. *The Intimacies of Four Continents.* Durham, NC: Duke University Press, 2015.

Macdonald, Kevin, dir. *The Last King of Scotland.* DNA Films and Film 4; distributed by Fox Searchlight Pictures, 2006.

Macharia, Keguro. "On Being Area-Studied: A Litany of Complaint." *GLQ: A Journal of Lesbian and Gay Studies* 22, no. 2 (2016): 183–90.

Madhvani, Manubhai, and Gilles Foden. *Tide of Fortune: A Family Tale.* Noida: Random House India, 2009.

Mahajan, Vijay. *Africa Rising: How 900 Million African Consumers Offer More than You Think.* Upper Saddle River, NJ: Pearson Education, 2009.

Mahmood, Cynthia Kepley. "'Khalistan' as Political Critique." In *The Oxford Handbook of Sikh Studies,* edited by Pashaura Singh and Louis Fenech, 371–80. Oxford: Oxford University Press, 2014.

Malkki, Lisa. *Purity and Exile: Violence, Memory, and National Cosmology among Hutu Refugees in Tanzania.* Chicago: University of Chicago Press, 1995.

Mama, Amina. 1996. "Sheroes and Villains: Conceptualizing Colonial and Contemporary Violence against Women in Africa." In *Feminist Genealogies, Colonial Legacies, Democratic Futures*, edited by Jacqui Alexander and Chandra Mohanty, 46–62. New York: Routledge, 1997.

Mamdani, Mahmood. "Beyond Settler and Native as Political Identities: Overcoming the Political Legacy of Colonialism." *Comparative Studies of Society and History* 43, no. 4 (2001): 651–64.

Mamdani, Mahmood. *Citizen and Subject: Contemporary Africa and the Legacy of Late Colonialism*. Princeton, NJ: Princeton University Press, 1996.

Mamdani, Mahmood. *Define and Rule: Native as Political Identity*. Cambridge, MA: Harvard University Press, 2021.

Mamdani, Mahmood. *From Citizen to Refugee: Uganda Asians Come to Britain*. London: Frances Pinter, 1973.

Mamdani, Mahmood. *Imperialism and Fascism in Uganda*. Trenton, NJ: Africa World, 1984.

Mamdani, Mahmood. "The Importance of Research in a University." MISR Working Paper, no. 3. Makerere University, Kampala, 2011.

Mamdani, Mahmood. "Pluralism and the Right of Association." In *Uganda: Studies in Living Conditions, Popular Movements, and Constitutionalism*, edited by Mahmood Mamdani and Joseph Oloka-Onyango, 555–56. Vienna: JEP and Centre for Basic Research, 1994.

Mamdani, Mahmood. *Politics and Class Formation in Uganda*. New York: Monthly Review Press, 1976.

Mamdani, Mahmood "The Politics of Democratic Reform in Contemporary Uganda." *East African Journal of Peace and Human Rights* 2, no. 1 (1996): 91–101.

Mamdani, Mahmood. *Scholars in the Marketplace: The Dilemmas of Neo-liberal Reform at Makerere University, 1989–2005*. Dakar, Senegal: CODESRIA, 2007.

Mamdani, Mahmood. "The Ugandan Asian Expulsion: 20 Years After." *Journal of Refugee Studies* 6, no. 3 (1993): 265–73.

Mamdani, Mahmood. *When Victims Become Killers: Colonialism: Nativism, and the Genocide in Rwanda*. Princeton, NJ: Princeton University Press, 2002.

Manby, Bronwen. *Struggles for Citizenship in Africa*. London: Zed, 2009.

Mangat, J. S. *A History of the Asians in East Africa c. 1886 to 1945*. Oxford: Clarendon, 1969.

Mankekar, Purnima. *Unsettling India: Affect, Temporality, Transnationality*. Durham, NC: Duke University Press, 2015.

Mankekar, Purnima, and Akhil Gupta. "The Missed Period." *American Ethnologist* 46, no. 4 (2019): 417–28.

Marks, Shula. *Divided Sisterhood: Race, Class and Gender in the South African Nursing Profession*. London: Palgrave Macmillan, 1994.

Marx, Karl. "On the Jewish Question." In *The Marx-Engels Reader*. 2nd ed. Edited by Robert Tucker. New York: Norton, 1978.

Mazrui, Ali Al'amin. "Afrabia: Africa and Arabs in the New World Order." *Ufahamu: A Journal of African Studies* 20, no. 3 (1992): 51–62. https://escholarship.org/uc/item/9896d35t.

Mazrui, Ali Al'amin. *The Africans: A Triple Heritage.* Boston: Little, Brown, 1987.

Mazrui, Ali Al'amin. "Between Development and Decay: Anarchy, Tyranny and Progress under Idi Amin." *Third World Quarterly* 20, no. 1 (1980): 44–58.

Mazrui, Ali Al'amin. "Casualties of an Underdeveloped Class Structure: The Expulsion of Luo Workers and Asian Bourgeoisie in Uganda." In *Strangers in African Societies,* edited by William A. Shack and Elliott P. Skinner, 261–78. Berkeley: University of California Press, 1979.

Mazrui, Ali Al'amin. "The Social Origins of Ugandan Presidents: From King to Peasant Warrior." *Canadian Journal of African Studies* 8, no. 1 (1974): 3–23.

Mazrui, Ali Al'amin. *Soldiers and Kinsmen in Uganda: The Making of a Military Ethnocracy.* Beverly Hills: Sage, 1975.

Mbembe, Achille. *Critique of Black Reason.* Durham, NC: Duke University Press, 2017.

Mbembe, Achille. "Necropolitics." *Public Culture* 15, no. 1 (2003): 11–40.

Mbembe, Achille. *On the Postcolony.* Berkeley: University of California Press, 2001.

McIntosh, Janet. *Unsettled: Denial and Belonging among White Kenyans.* Berkeley: University of California Press, 2016.

Mehta, Jagat. "Negotiating Compensation for Indians with Idi Amin's Government." *India International Centre Quarterly Monsoon* 28, no. 3 (2001): 25–46.

Mehta, Nanji Kalidas. *Dream Half-Expressed: An Autobiography.* Bombay: Vakils, Feffer and Simons, 1966.

Metcalf, Thomas. *Imperial Connections: India in the Indian Ocean Arena, 1860–1920.* Berkeley: University of California Press, 2007.

Mitra, Durba. "'Mississippi Masala' @30: Revisiting a Film Classic in Authoritarian Times." *Public Books,* February 3, 2022. https://www.publicbooks.org/mississippi-masala-at-30-revisiting-a-film-classic-in-authoritarian-times.

Modi, Renu, and Rhea D'Silva. "Liminal Spaces: Racism against Africans in India." *Economic and Political Weekly* 15, no. 41 (2016): 18–20.

Modi, Renu, and Mala Pandurang. "Women as an Invisible Constituency: A Gendered Reading of the Life Narratives of Nanji Kalidas Mehta and Muljibhai Madhvani." *South Asian Diaspora* 9, no. 2 (2017): 179–92.

Modi, Renu, and Ian Taylor. "The Indian Diaspora in Africa: Commodification of Hindu Rashtra." *Globalizations* 14, no. 6 (2017): 911–29.

Moghal, Manzoor. *Idi Amin: Lion of Africa.* Central Milton Keynes: Authorhouse, 2010.

Mohanty, Chandra. *Feminism without Borders: Decolonizing Theory, Practicing Solidarity.* Durham, NC: Duke University Press, 2003.

Morris, H. S. *The Indians in Uganda: Caste and Sect in a Plural Society.* London: Weidenfeld and Nicholson, 1968.

Morrison, Toni. *Beloved.* 1987. New York: Vintage, 2004.

Morrison, Toni. "On the Backs of Blacks." *Time*, December 2, 1993.

Mudimbe, V. Y. *The Invention of Africa: Gnosis, Philosophy, and the Order of Knowledge*. Bloomington: Indiana University Press, 1988.

Muhammedi, Shezan. *Gifts from Amin: Ugandan Asian Refugees in Canada*. Winnipeg: University of Manitoba Press, 2022.

Mujagu, Justus, ed. *Uganda's Age of Reforms: A Critical Overview*. Kampala: Fountain, 1996.

Mujagu, Justus, and J. Oloka-Onyango. *No-Party Democracy in Uganda: Myths and Realities*. Kampala: Fountain, 2000.

Museveni, Yoweri. *Sowing the Mustard Seed: The Struggle for Freedom and Democracy in Uganda*. 1997. London: Macmillan, 2007.

Museveni, Yoweri. *What Is Africa's Problem?* Minneapolis: University of Minnesota Press, 2000.

Musisi, Nakanyike. "Gender and the Cultural Construction of 'Bad Women.'" In *"Wicked" Women and the Reconfiguration of Gender in Africa*, edited by Dorothy Louise Hodgson and Sheryl A. McCurdy, 171–86. Portsmouth, NH: Heinemann, 2001.

Nagar, Richa. "Communal Discourses, Marriage, and the Politics of Gendered Social Boundaries among South Asian Immigrants in Tanzania." *Gender, Place, and Culture: A Journal of Feminist Geography* 5, no. 2. (1998): 117–39.

Nagar, Richa. "Saboteurs? Or Saviors? The Position of Tanzanian Asians." *Samar: South Asian Magazine for Action and Reflection* 13 (2001): 14–19.

Nair, Mira, dir. *Mississippi Masala*. Studio Canal Souss and Tristar Pictures, 1991.

Nair, Savita. "Despite Dislocations: Uganda's Indians Remaking Home." *Africa* 88, no. 3 (2018): 492–517.

Narayan, Uma. "Cross-Cultural Connections, Border-Crossings and 'Death by Culture': Thinking about Dowry Murders in India and Domestic Violence Murders in the US." In *Dislocating Cultures: Identities, Traditions, and Third World Feminism*, 81–117. New York: Routledge, 1997.

Ngũgĩ wa Thiong'o. "What Is Asia to Me? Looking East from Africa." *World Literature Today* 86, no. 4 (2012): 14–18. https://doi.org/10.1353/wlt.2012.0059.

Ng'weno, Bettina, and L. Obura Aloo. "Irony of Citizenship: Descent, National Belonging, and Constitutions in the Postcolonial African State." *Law and Society Review* 53, no. 1 (2019): 141–72. https://doi.org/10.1111/lasr.12395.

Niranjana, Tejaswini. *Mobilizing India: Women, Music, and Migration between India and Trinidad*. Durham, NC: Duke University Press, 2006.

Nkrumah, Kwame. *Neo-colonialism: The Last Stage of Imperialism*. London: Panaf, 1956.

Nyamnjoh, Francis. *Decolonizing the Academy: The Case for Convivial Scholarship*. Basel: Basler Afrika Bibliographien, 2020.

Nyamnjoh, Francis. "From Bounded to Flexible Citizenship: Lessons from Africa." *Citizenship Studies* 11, no. 1 (2007): 1–11.

Nyamnjoh, Francis. *Insiders and Outsiders: Citizenship and Xenophobia in Contemporary South Africa*. Zed, 2006.

Nyamnjoh, Francis. *#RhodesMustFall: Nibbling at Resilient Colonialism in South Africa*. Oxford: African Books Collective, 2016.

Obbo, Christine. "Village Strangers in Buganda Society." In *Strangers in African Societies*, edited by William Shack and Elliott Skinner, 227–41. Berkeley: University of California Press, 1979.

Ocita, James. "Diasporic Imaginaries: Memory and Negotiation of Belonging in East African and South African Indian Narratives." PhD diss., Stellenbosch University, 2013.

Ojwang, Dan. "The Half-Caste and the Dream of Secularism and Freedom: Insights from East African Asian Writing." *Scrutiny2* 13, no. 2 (2009): 16–35.

Ojwang, Dan. *Reading Migration and Culture: The World of East African Indian Literature*. Basingstoke: Palgrave Macmillan, 2013.

Ogwang, Dan, and Frank Vanclay. "Resource-Financed Infrastructure: Thoughts on Four Chinese-Financed Projects in Uganda." *Sustainability* 13, no. 6 (2021): 3259. https://doi.org/10.3390/su13063259.

Oloka-Onyango, Joseph. "Constitutional Transition in Museveni's Uganda: New Horizons or Another False Start?" *Journal of African Law* 39, no. 2 (1995): 156–72.

Oloka-Onyango, Joseph. "From Expulsion to Exclusion: Revisiting Race, Citizenship and the Ethnicity Conundrum in Contemporary Uganda." *Mawazo* 12 (2017): 1–20.

Ong Aihwa. *Buddha Is Hiding: Refugees, Citizenship, the New America*. Berkeley: University of California Press, 1993.

Ong, Aihwa. *Flexible Citizenship: The Cultural Logic of Transnationality*. Durham, NC: Duke University Press, 1999.

Ong, Aihwa. *Neoliberalism as Exception: Mutations in Citizenship and Sovereignty*. Durham, NC: Duke University Press, 2006.

Oonk, Gijsbert. *Settled Strangers: Asian Business Elites in East Africa, 1800–2000*. New Delhi: Sage, 2013.

Orme, Jenni. "Reaching Out—Ugandan Asians 40 Years On." *National Archives* (blog), October 22, 2012. https://www.nationalarchives.gov.uk/education/outreach/projects/migration-histories/ugandan-asians-40-years-on.

Pailey, Robtel Neaji. "Women, Equality, and Citizenship in Contemporary Africa." *Oxford Research Encyclopedia of Politics*, April 26, 2019. https://oxfordre.com/politics/view/10.1093/acrefore/9780190228637.001.0001/acrefore-9780190228637-e-852.

Parmar, Maya. "Memorialising 40 Years since Idi Amin's Expulsion: Digital Memory Mania to the Right to Be Forgotten." *South Asian Popular Culture* 12, no. 1 (2014): 1–14.

Parmar, Maya. *Reading Cultural Representations of the Double Diaspora: Britain, East Africa, Gujarat*. Cham: Palgrave Macmillan, 2019.

Partridge, Damani. *Hypersexuality and Headscarves: Race, Sex, and Citizenship in the New Germany*. Bloomington: Indiana University Press, 2012.

Patel, Hasu. "General Amin and the Indian Exodus from Uganda." *Issue: A Journal of Opinion* 2, no. 4 (1972): 12–22.

Patel, Ian Sanjay. *We're Here Because You Were There: Immigration and the End of Empire*. London: Verso, 2021.

Patel, Sharad, dir. *Amin: The Rise and Fall*. International Film Marketing, 1981.

Pathania, Gaurav. *The University as a Site of Resistance: Identity and Politics*. New Delhi: Oxford University Press, 2019.

Patton, Laurie. "Cosmic Men and Fluid Exchanges: Myths of Arya, Varna, and Jati in the Hindu Tradition." In *Religion and the Creation of Race and Ethnicity: An Introduction*, edited by Craig Prentiss, 181–96. New York: New York University Press, 2003.

Penumala, Pratap Kumar. "Hindu Diaspora and Hinduisms in Africa, with Special Focus on South Africa." In *Hindu Diasporas*, edited by Knut Jacobsen, 125–45. Oxford: Oxford University Press, 2023.

Peterson, Derek. "A History of the Heritage Economy in Museveni's Uganda." *Journal of Eastern African Studies* 10, no. 4 (2016): 789–806.

Peterson, Derek, and Edgar Taylor. "Rethinking the State in Idi Amin's Uganda: The Politics of Exhortation." *Journal of Eastern African Studies* 7 (2013): 58–82.

Peterson, Derek, and Richard Vokes. *The Unseen Archive of Idi Amin: Photographs from the Uganda Broadcasting Corporation*. Munich: Prestel, 2021.

Peterson, Kristin. *Speculative Markets: Drug Circuits and Derivative Life in Nigeria*. Durham, NC: Duke University Press, 2014.

Pierre, Jemima. *The Predicament of Blackness: Postcolonial Ghana and the Politics of Race*. Chicago: University of Chicago Press, 2012.

Pierre, Jemima. "Race in Africa Today: A Commentary." *Cultural Anthropology* 28, no. 3 (2013): 547–51.

Plascencia, Luis. *Disenchanting Citizenship: Mexican Migrants and the Boundaries of Belonging*. New Brunswick, NJ: Rutgers University Press, 2012.

Prashad, Vijay. *The Darker Nations: A People's History of the Third World*. New York: New Press, 2007.

Prashad, Vijay. *Everybody Was Kung-Fu Fighting: Afro-Asian Connections and the Myth of Cultural Purity*. Boston: Beacon, 2002.

Prashad, Vijay. *The Karma of Brown Folk*. Minneapolis: University of Minnesota Press, 2000.

Prashad, Vijay. *The Poorer Nations: A Possible History of the Global South*. London: Verso, 2014.

Quinn, Joanna R. "Constraints: The Un-doing of the Ugandan Truth Commission." *Human Rights Quarterly* 26, no. 2 (2004): 401–27.

Ramaru, Kealeboga. "Feminist Reflections on the Rhodes Must Fall Movement." *Feminist Africa*, no. 22 (2017): 89–96.

Rana, Junaid. *Terrifying Muslims: Race and Labor in the South Asian Diaspora*. Durham, NC: Duke University Press, 2011.

Ranger, Terence. "The Invention of Tradition Revisited." In *Interventions and Boundaries: Historical and Anthropological Approaches to the Study of Ethnicity and Nationalism*, edited by Preben Kaarsholm and Jan Hultin. Roskilde, Denmark:

International Development Studies, Roskilde University, 1994. https://ojs.ruc.dk /index.php/ocpa/issue/view/774.

Rasch, Astrid. "Postcolonial Nostalgia: The Ambiguities of White Memoirs of Zimbabwe." *History and Memory* 30, no. 2 (2018): 147–80.

Read, James. "Some Legal Aspects of the Expulsion." In *Expulsion of a Minority: Essays on Uganda Asians*, edited by Michael Twaddle, 193–209. London: Althone, 1975.

Reid, Richard. "Ghosts in the Academy: Historians and Historical Consciousness in the Making of Modern Uganda." *Comparative Studies of Society and History* 56, no. 2 (2014): 351–80.

Reid, Richard. *Political Power in Pre-Colonial Buganda: Economy, Society and Warfare in the Nineteenth Century*. Oxford: James Currey, 2002.

Robinson, Cedric. *On Racial Capitalism, Black Internationalism, and Cultures of Resistance*. London: Pluto, 2019.

Rosa, Jonathan, and Yarimar Bonilla. "Deprovincializing Trump, Decolonizing Diversity, and Unsettling Anthropology." *American Ethnologist* 44, no. 2 (2017): 201–8.

Rose, Nicholas. *Powers of Freedom: Reforming Political Thought*. Cambridge: Cambridge University Press, 1999.

Ross, A. "The Agamben Effect." *South Atlantic Quarterly* 107, no. 1 (2008): 1–13.

Roy, Arundhati. "The Doctor and the Saint." Introduction to B. R. Ambedkar, *Annihilation of Caste: The Annotated Critical Edition*. London: Verso, 2014.

Roy, Srila. "Women's Movements in the Global South: Towards a Scalar Analysis." *International Journal of Politics, Culture, and Society* 29, no. 3 (2016): 289–306.

Rubongoya, Joshua. *Regime Hegemony in Museveni's Uganda: Pax Musevenica*. New York: Palgrave Macmillan, 2007.

Said, Edward. *Culture and Imperialism*. London: Vintage, 1993.

Salvadori, Cynthia. *We Came in Dhows*. Nairobi: PaperChase Kenya, 1996.

Sangari, Kumkum, and Sudesh Vaid, eds. *Recasting Women: Essays in Indian Colonial History*. New Brunswick, NJ: Rutgers University Press, 1990.

Sassen, Saskia. *Expulsions: Brutality and Complexity in the Global Economy*. Cambridge, MA: Belknap Press of Harvard University Press, 2014.

Sassen, Saskia. "The Repositioning of Citizenship: Emergent Subjects and Spaces for Politics." *New Centennial Review* 3, no. 2 (2003): 41–46.

Seftel, Adam, ed. *Uganda: The Rise and Fall of Idi Amin*. Lanseria, South Africa: Bailey's African Photo Archives Production, 1994.

Sembuya, Christopher C. *Amin Dada: The Other Side of Amin Dada*. Kampala: Sest Holdings, 2009.

Shambuka. "Neoliberalizing Racial Justice: Caste, Race, and Diaspora Hindutva Democrats." *Peace and Change* 46, no. 4 (2021): 384–402. https://doi.org/10 .1111/pech.12492.

Shankar, Shobana. *An Uneasy Embrace: Africa, India and the Spectre of Race*. Oxford: Oxford University Press, 2021.

Shryock, Andrew, ed. *Off Stage, on Display: Intimacy and Ethnography in the Age of Public Culture*. Palo Alto, CA: Stanford University Press, 2004.

Shukla, Sandhya. "Locations for South Asian Diasporas." *Annual Review of Anthropology* 30 (2001): 551–72.

Sicherman, Carol. "Makerere's Myths, Makerere's History: A Retrospect." *Journal of Higher Education in Africa/Revue de l'enseignement supérieur en Afrique* 6, no. 1 (2008): 11–39.

Singh, Jaideep. "The Death of Islamophobia: The Rise of Islamo-Racism." *The Race Files* (blog), February 23, 2016. https://www.racefiles.com/2016/02/23/the-death -of-islamophobia-the-rise-of-islamo-racism.

Sinha, Mrinhalini. *Specters of Mother India: The Global Restructuring of an Empire*. Durham, NC: Duke University Press, 2006.

Soske, Jon. *Internal Frontiers: African Nationalism and the Indian Diaspora in Twentieth-Century South Africa*. Athens: Ohio University Press, 2017.

Soundararajan, Thenmozhi. *The Trauma of Caste: A Dalit Feminist Meditation on Survivorship, Healing, and Abolition*. Berkeley, CA: North Atlantic, 2022.

Southall, Aidan. "General Amin and the Coup: Great Man or Historical Inevitability?" *Journal of Modern African Studies* 13 (1975): 85–105.

Southall, Aidan W., and Peter C. W. Gutkind. *Townsmen in the Making: Kampala and Its Suburbs*. Kampala: East African Institute of Social Research, 1957.

Srinivas, Mysore N. *Caste in Modern India and Other Essays*. Bombay: Media Publishers, 1962.

Stoler, Ann Laura. *Carnal Knowledge and Imperial Power: Race and the Intimate in Colonial Rule*. Berkeley: University of California Press, 2002.

Stoler, Ann Laura. *Race and the Education of Desire: Foucault's History of Sexuality and the Colonial Order of Things*. Durham, NC: Duke University Press, 1995.

Tabaire, Bernard. "The Press and Political Repression in Uganda: Back to the Future?" *Journal of Eastern African Studies* 1, no. 2 (2007): 193–211.

Tamale, Sylvia. "Nudity, Protest, and the Law in Uganda." *Feminist Africa* 22 (2017): 52–86.

Tandon, Yash. "The Expulsions from Uganda: Asians' Role in East Africa." *Patterns of Prejudice* 6, no. 6 (1972): 1–8.

Tandon, Yash. *Technical Assistance Administration in East Africa*. Stockholm: Almqvist and Wiksell, 1973.

Tandon, Yash, and Arnold Raphael. *The New Position of East Africa's Asians: Problems of a Displaced Minority*. London: Minority Rights Group, 1984.

Tangri, Roger, and Andrew Mwenda. "Change and Continuity in the Politics of Government-Business Relations in Museveni's Uganda." *Journal of Eastern African Studies* 13, no. 4 (2019): 678–97.

Tangri, Roger, and Andrew Mwenda. "Corruption and Cronyism in Uganda's Privatization in the 1990s." *African Affairs* 100 (2001): 117–33.

Tarlo, Emma. *Unsettling Memories: Narratives of the Emergency in Delhi*. Berkeley: University of California Press, 2003.

Taylor, Edgar Curtis. "Asians and Africans in Ugandan Urban Life, 1959–1972." PhD diss., University of Michigan, 2016.

Taylor, Edgar Curtis. "Claiming Kabale: Racial Thought and Urban Governance in Uganda." *Journal of Eastern African Studies* 7, no. 1 (2013): 143–63.

Taylor, Edgar Curtis. "Race and Nation in Ugandan Public Discourse: Debates over the Status of Indians in Ugandan Nationalism in 1971." MA thesis, Makerere University, 2008.

Tembo, Josias, and Anya Topolski. "Exploring the Entanglement of Race and Religion in Africa." *Social Dynamics* 48, no. 3 (2022): 377–88.

Thapar, Romila. "The Theory of Aryan Race and India: History and Politics." *Social Scientist* 24, nos. 1–3 (1996): 3–29.

Theroux, Paul, "Hating the Asians." *Transition* 33 (1967): 46–51.

Thomas, Deborah. "Crisis, Epochal Shifts, and Conceptual Disenchantment." *American Anthropologist* 121, no. 3 (2019): 549–53.

Thomas, Deborah A., and M. Kamari Clarke. "Globalization and Race: Structures of Inequality, New Sovereignties, and Citizenship in a Neoliberal Era." *Annual Review of Anthropology* 42 (2013): 305–25.

Thomas, Sonja. "Studying Race in the Field of South Asian Religions." *Religion Compass* 15, no. 4 (2021): e12394.

Thompson, Gardener. "The Ismailis in Uganda." In *Expulsion of a Minority: Essays on Ugandan Asians,* edited by Michael Twaddle, 30–52. London: Althone, 1975.

Tinker, Hugh. *A New System of Slavery: The Export of Indian Labor Overseas, 1830–1920.* Oxford: Oxford University Press, 1974.

Tirop, Chepchirchir. "Reconciling National and Community Identity in Kenya through the Asian African Heritage Exhibit." *Eastern African Literary and Cultural Studies* 9, no. 2 (2023): 111–31.

Tripp, Aili Mari. *Museveni's Uganda: Paradoxes of Power in a Hybrid Regime.* Boulder, CO: Lynne Reiner, 2010.

Tripp, Aili Mari. "Women's Mobilization in Uganda: Nonracial Ideologies in European-African-Asian Encounters, 1945–1962." *International Journal of African Historical Studies* 34, no. 3 (2001): 543–64.

Tripp, Aili Mari, and Joy Kwesiga, eds. *The Women's Movement in Uganda: History, Challenges, and Prospects.* Kampala: Fountain, 2002.

Twaddle, Michael, ed. *Expulsion of a Minority: Essays on Uganda Asians.* London: Althone, 1975.

van der Veer, Peter. "Virtual India: Indian IT Labor and the Nation-State." In *Sovereign Bodies: Citizens, Migrants, and States in the Postcolonial World,* edited by Thomas Blom Hansen and Finn Stepputat, 276–90. Princeton, NJ: Princeton University Press, 2005.

von Struensee, S. "The Domestic Relations Bill in Uganda: Potentially Addressing Polygamy, Bride Price, Cohabitation, Marital Rape, Widow Inheritance and Female Genital Mutilation." Working paper, 2004. SSRN, posted April 17, 2005. https://ssrn.com/abstract=623501.

Vora, Neha. *Impossible Citizens: Dubai's Indian Diaspora*. Durham, NC: Duke University Press, 2013.

Wiegratz, Jorg, Guiliano Martiniello, and Elisa Greco, eds. *Uganda: The Dynamics of Neoliberal Transformation*. London: Zed, 2018.

Wilkerson, Isabel. *Caste: The Origins of Our Discontents*. New York: Random House, 2020.

Williams, Raymond. *Marxism and Literature*. Oxford: Oxford University Press, 1977.

Wimmer, Andreas, and Nina Glick Schiller. "Methodological Nationalism, the Social Sciences, and the Study of Migration: An Essay in Historical Epistemology." *International Migration Review* 37, no. 3 (2003): 576–610. https://doi.org/10.1111/j.1747-7379.2003.tb00151.x.

Yadav, S. N. *India-Uganda Relations: A New Model for South-South Cooperation*. New Delhi: Global Vision, 2017.

Yengde, Suraj. "Caste among the Indian Diaspora in Africa." *Economic and Political Weekly* 50, no. 37 (September 12, 2015). https://www.epw.in/journal/2015/37/notes/caste-among-indian-diaspora-africa.html.

Yengde, Suraj. *Caste Matters*. New Delhi: India Viking, 2019.

Zakaria, Fareed. *The Post-American World*. New York: W. W. Norton, 2009.

Zeleza, Paul Tiyambe. "Rewriting the African Diaspora: Beyond the Black Atlantic." *African Affairs* 101, no. 414 (2005): 35–68. https://www.jstor.org/stable/3518632.

African Union Mission in Somalia (AMISOM), 325n1

African women: Amin, I., regulating, 123–24; Indian men marrying, 319n49; interracial intimacies between Indian men, 57, 124

African women activists, NGOs connected to, 271

Africa-US relations, 331n22

Afro-Asian Conference (1955), 61, 174, 175, 179

Afro-Asian governance, 180, 187–92

Afro-Asianism, 34

Afro-Asian women, 252

Afro-pessimism, 311n7

Afro–South Asian entanglements, 31; Asian expulsion and, xx; expulsion exceptionalism surrounding, 94; transcontinental, 40, 297–99

Afro–South Asian feminist solidarities, 277–78

Afro–South Asian friendship, promotion of, 153

Afro–South Asian racial violence, in transcontinental Uganda, xxi–xxii

Afro–South Asian study, 297–99

Afro–South Asian tensions, GMF revealing, 287

Aga Khan, Karim, 4, 55, 78, 81, 140, 168

Aga Khan Development Network (AKDN), 140, 149

Alibhai-Brown, Yasmin, 312n12

alienation, 45

Ambedkar, B. R., 53, 295

American West, Punjabi Sikh migration to, xvi

Amin, Idi, 82, 83, 84, 85, 250, 324n29; African Muslim population elevated by, 77; African women regulated under, 123–24; Asian Conference convened by, 78, 107; Asian expulsion by, 4, 302; Asianness expunged by, 106; British officials carrying, 108; cannibalism and, 15, 313n24; denizenship under, 101–11; entrepreneurial culture under, 105–6; in exile, 72, 127, 234; expulsion exceptionalism and, 109–10; FRONASA ousting, 324n39; gendered and

heteropatriarchal discourse of, 247; illiberalism of, 196; legacy of, 234–35; liberalization reversing, 152–53; Mazrui, Ali A., on, 3; media coverage of, 312n10; mixed racial heritage opposed by, 93; OAU presided over by, 83; Obote overthrown by, 75–76; patronage to, 104–5; photographic exhibition of images of, 337n26; Punjabi Sikh families working for, 323n13; rumor and myth around, 97; Singh, L., fascinated by, 122–23; South Asian immigration allowed by, 105; Ugandan youths resuscitating, 204–5; UNLF ousting, 127; UNLIT ousting, 127; UPC overthrown by, 75–76

Amin, Jaffar, 236

Amin government, Ugandan Asian men and, 126

Aminism, 236–37

Amin regime: Black Africans elevated during, 136; racial denizenship during, 125; Ugandans killed during, 314n31

AMISOM (African Union Mission in Somalia), 325n1

anthropology: of Africa, 178; of citizenship, 8–10, 281; of expulsion, 5–6; feminist, 29; of neoliberal globalization, 178; of transcontinental Afro–South Asian entanglements, 40, 297–99

anti-Asianism, 202–6

anti-Asian populism, 63–70, 204, 284

anti-Asian rhetoric, FDC associated with, 225n2

anti-Asian violence: Asian expulsion compared with, 231; IAU responding to, 230; Mabira Forest controversy and, 229–32, 237; refugees fearing, 161

anti-Blackness, 292, 311n7

anti-Black racism, xvi, 290, 311n7

anticolonial consciousness, in Indian diaspora, 67–68

anticolonial nationalisms, 63–70

anticolonial solidarity, 178–79

anti-Gandhi protest, at University of California, 296

anti-imperialist rhetoric, of NRM, 326n6

archiving projects, by Ugandan Asian women, 306

the army, Ugandan Asian cultivating relationships with, 121

arrested decolonization, 40

Article 370, of Indian Constitution, 296

Asian African Association (AAA), 237–38, 239–40

Asian African category, Indi-Ugandan identity contrasted with, 237

Asian African Heritage Exhibition, 337n28

Asian business community, NRM connected to, 338n21

Asian community, 264; domestic violence and, 270; expulsion risked by, 239; remaking, 210–14; South, 56, 284. *See also* Ugandan Asian community

Asian Conference, Amin, I., convening, 78, *107*

Asian domestic wealth, Black African ownership receiving, 103–4

Asian exodus, from East Africa, 314n36

Asian expulsion (1972), xiii, 10–15, 86–87, 299, 314n36; Afro–South Asian entanglements and, xx; by Amin, I., 4, 302; anti-Asian violence compared with, 231; Black African perspectives on, 305; Black/Afro–South Asian connections complicated by, xx; Black-identifying Ugandans empowered by, 86; British government and, 80–81; business and commercial class destroyed by, 104; citizenship status unbundled by, 114; class formation and, 50; crisis of liberalism and democracy demonstrated by, 109; endogamy disrupted by, 254; expulsion exceptionalism oversimplifying, 21–23; as global critical event, 22, 281–83; as illiberalism, 17; media coverage of, 312n10; memorializaiton and commemoration of, 304–5; Museveni apologizing for, 294–95; no government or state-led commemoration events surrounding, 168; number of expelled during, 321n96; painful memories of, 95; persistent afterlives of, 5; the present constituted by, 43–44; racial entanglement after, 62–63; racially nativist nationalism normalized by, 265; racial partitions characterizing, 13–14; representations of, 12; sense of finality about, 41; Ugandan Asian exiles impacted by, 303–4; Ugandan Asians helped by, 81–82; Ugandan Asian women displaced during, 252–53; in US academy, xviii-xix; verified citizenship status circumventing, 112–13; Western governments condemning, 82–83. *See also* expulsion exceptionalism

Asian Federation, 213

Asian merchant figure, 302

Asian minority question, 231

Asian nations, African nations cooperating with, 330n2

Asianness, 126; African identity contrasted with, 114–15; Amin, I., expunging, 106; Ugandan women activists constructing, 276. *See also* South Asianness

Asian presence: in East Africa, 36; stereotypical representation of, 62; Ugandan African conspiratorial readings of, 98. *See also* South Asian presence

"Asian" properties, in Jinja, *44*

Asians: British passports held by, *74, 77,* 80–82; colonial administration defining, 49; legal-juridical citizenship of, 232; political surveillance of, 320. *See also* Kenyan Asians; Ugandan Asians

"Asians and Africans in Ugandan Urban Life" (Taylor), 21

Asians in East Africa (Bharati), 57

Asian street vendors, stereotypical caricatures of, 204

Asian Studies Centre, at Oxford University, 304

"Asian Tigers," 331n10

Asian women, 242–43; harassment and violence toward, 248; higher education of, 255; Ugandan women activists worked with by, 269. *See also* South Asian women; Ugandan Asian women

diaspora, state-based ambitions centering, 33
disjunctive temporalities, 42
displaced population, Ugandan Asians as, 10–11
Domestic Relations Bill (DRB), 267, 274–75
domestic violence, 338n16; Asian community and, 270; femicide resulting from, 258–59; in Uganda, 264
Do the Right Thing (film), 302
double consciousness, xiv
DP (Democratic Party), 66–67
DRB (Domestic Relations Bill), 267, 274–75
Dream Half-Expressed (Mehta), 60
Dreams in a Time of War (Thiong'o), 279
D'Silva, Rhea, 290
dual citizenship, 157, 160–61
Du Bois, W. E. B., xiv, xx
Dusenbery, Verne, 319n45

EAC (East African Community), 157, 175
East Africa: Asian exodus from, 314n36; Asian presence in, 36; Bollywood films in, 338n9; British, 302, 318n12; Indian diaspora in, 211; Indian merchants expanding into, 48–49; Ugandan Asians adapting to, 57
East African Asians, in Europe and North America, 285
East African Community (EAC), 157, 175
economic growth, in African countries, 179
economics, South Asianness reconstituted by, 144
Economic War, 75, 78, 83, 235
e-governance, 147
empire, negotiating, 176–80
employment, of South Asian women, 255–56
endogamy, Asian expulsion disrupting, 254
endogamy, racial, 247, 257
entanglement, conventional approaches not attending to, 34–35
Entebbe Airport, *19*, 192
entrepreneurial culture, under Amin, I., 105–6

entrepreneurship, by community-builders, 228–29
EPZs (export processing zones), 197
ethnic citizenship, 26, 59
ethnic succession, 164
ethnographic methodologies, 37
"ethnography of events," 314n37
Europe, East African Asians in, 285
European imperialism, 16
Everyone Was Kung-Fu Fighting (Prashad), xv–xvi
exceptional noncitizen incorporation, performative rituals of, 111–18
exile, 42, 101, 114–15, 303; African Asian identity in, 12; Amin, I., in, 72, 127, 234; Patel, Praful, in, 167. *See also* Ugandan Asian exiles
expatriates, 155, 157–58, 203
expatriate staff, foreign investors hiring, 201
expropriated properties, repossession of, 137
Expropriated Properties Act, NRM reintroducing, 137
expulsion. *See specific topics*
expulsion exceptionalism, 14, 17–20, *18*, *19*, 43–45, 86–87, 305; Afro–South Asian entanglements surrounded by, 94; Amin, I. and, 109–10; Asian expulsion oversimplified by, 21–23; global visual archive of, *17*; liberal Western imaginaries centered by, 15–16; among South Asians, 281–82
Expulsion of a Minority (Twaddle), 86

Facebook groups, of Ugandan Asians, 330n69
family firms, 153, 322n97, 328n45
FDC (Forum for Democratic Change), 131, 225n2, 229–30
FDI (foreign direct investment), 176, 332n38
#Fees Must Fall movement (FMF), 288
femicide, 258–59, 264–65
Femina (magazine), 225
feminist anthropological approaches, to transcontinental Uganda, 29–31
feminist organizing, cross-racial, 266–72

feminist solidarities, Afro–South Asian, 277–78

Ferguson, James, 184–85, 195

FIDA (Uganda Association of Women Lawyers), 273

financial crisis, global (2007–8), 149, 179

Finnstrom, Sverker, 322n7

Floyd, George, 297, 301

FMF (#Fees Must Fall movement), 288

foreign businessmen, crony capitalism between NRM and, 334n58

foreign direct investment (FDI), 176, 332n38

foreign-exchange business, 119–20

foreign investment, 195–96; South-South cooperation and, 187–88; state policies around, 205–6; tax incentives for, 200–201

foreign investors: expatriate staff hired by, 201; investments pulled out of by, 182; rights and entitlements redistributed to, 198–99; South Asian presence associated with, 201–2; state officials evaluating, 200

foreign (*mzungu*), 41

Forum for Democratic Change (FDC), 131, 225n2, 229–30

Foucault, Michel, 194, 315n51, 324n26

From Citizen to Refugee (Mamdani), 312n12

FRONASA (guerrilla group), Amin, I., ousted by, 324n39

Furnivall, J. S., 51, 318n26

Ganda, the (kingdom), 116

Gandhi, Indira, 80, 323n18

Gandhi, Mohandas K., 141, 291–92, 296; Black political thought and, 297; the historical Gandhi contrasted with images of, 293; Indian proletariat influenced by, 61; in South Africa, 61–62

Gandhi Heritage and Convention Center, 294

Garvey, Marcus, 85

Gayaza School for Girls, 181

gender-based organizations, Western-based legal-juridical and carceral solutions mobilized by, 277

gender-based violence, 267, 276, 338n16

gendered insecurities, 243

gendered norms, in Indian diaspora, 253

gendered racial formations, 209, 242, 245, 277

#Ghandimustfall (GMF), 291–92, 341n23; Afro–South Asian tensions revealed by, 287; Dalits supporting, 296; India-based racist attacks on, 294

global critical event, 6, 21–25, 281–83

global financial crisis (2007–8), 149, 179

global governance, negotiating, 176–80

Global North, 13, 32, 312n7

Global South, 28, 77, 312n7

Global South neoliberalisms, 176–80

global war on terror, xxi, 28, 147

GMF. *See* #Ghandimustfall

gomesi (traditional dress), 69

governance, 25–28; Afro-Asian, 180, 187–92; colonial, 324n26; community-based, 210–14, 223; e-, 147; heteropatriarchal racially nativist communal, 252; illiberal, 27–28, 72, 75; liberal, 117–18; local, 146; logics of, 27; neoliberal, 177–78; as nonliberal, 9, 25, 27, 132; postcolonial state, 208–9

governmentality, 194, 315n51

government contacts, 121

graduated citizenship, 197

graduated sovereignty, 197

Gregory, Robert, 211

Group, Ruparelia, 304

Grovogui, Siba, 62

Gujarat (India), Ugandan Asians resettling in, 322n97

Gutkind, Peter, 57, 319n49

Haley, Nikki, 301

"half-caste," 92–93, 156, 246, 256–57, 322n1

Hand, Felicity, 245–46

Hansen, Thomas Blom, 62, 110

Hanson, Holly, 324n32

Harris, Kamala, 301

Harrison, Faye V., 298

heteropatriarchal racially nativist communal governance, 252 higher education, of Asian women, 255

Hinduism-Brahminism, 53

Hindu Marriage and Divorce Act, 275

Hindu supremacist nationalism, BJP normalizing, 215, 289

Hussein, Mohammed, 324n36

IAU. *See* Indian Association Uganda

IBF (Indian Business Forum), 227

Ibiringa, Grace, 72

identity card, Ugandan, *113*

Idi Amin: Hero or Villain? (Amin, J.), 236

Idi Amin: Lion of Africa (Moghal), 236

IFIs (international finance institutions), 137

illiberal exceptionalism, 19

illiberal governance, 27–28, 72, 75

illiberalism, 27–28; of Amin, I., 196; Asian expulsion as, 17; liberalism contrasted with, 19–20, 25

illiberal state technology, 86

illicit economies (*magendo*), 104

imaginaries, of Africa, xvii–xviii

Immigration Act (1969), 74

Immigration Department, Ministry of Internal Affairs of, 112

Immigration Office, Ugandan Asians queuing at, *84*

immigration restrictions, xiii, 21, 60, 71

Imperial Connections (Metcalf), 59

INC (Indian National Congress), 67–68

India, 296; anti-Black racism in, 290; British, 210–11, 314n36; FDI in Uganda by, 332n38; imperial conquest of, 46; Indian diaspora in relation to, 141; as market democracy, 140; Pakistan split from, 210; racism in, 289–90; Ugandan Asians forced to return to, *18*, 81. *See also* Bharatiya Janata Party; Modi, Narendra

"India-Africa Forum Summit," 333n40

India-based racist attacks, on GMF, 294

Indian-African encounters, 52–53

Indian Association of Kampala, 210

Indian Association of Uganda (IAU), 101, 173, 191, 208, 254, 327n34; anti-Asian violence responded to by, 230; BJP shaping, 222; Central Council of, 210;

gendered segregation of, 221; Indian diaspora advocated for by, 213–14; philanthropic activities of, 226; property repossession facilitated by, 220–21; reestablishment of, 219

Indian Business Forum (IBF), 227

Indian community officials, DRB resisted by, 274–75

Indian Constitution, Article 370 of, 296

Indian diaspora, 231; in African nations, 141; anticolonial consciousness in, 67–68; in East Africa, 211; expansion of, 214–15; "floating," 216–18; gendered norms in, 253; India in relation to, 141; Indian Association of Uganda advocating for, 213–14; postcolonial, 175–76; South Asian community dominated by, 284; in Uganda, 31–32

Indian diasporic entrepreneurs, schools, hospitals, and specialty medical clinics established by, 224

Indian diasporic nationalism, 174–75

Indian government, 305–6, 322n97

Indian High Commission, 335n11

Indian immigrants, to British East Africa, 318n12

Indian indentured laborers, Uganda Railway constructed by, 318n11

Indian men: African women married to, 319n49; interracial intimacies between African women, 57, 124; media coverage reducing, 270

Indian merchants, East Africa expanded into by, 48–49

Indian migrant housewives, Ugandan women activists and, 268

Indian migrant women, patriarchal violence impacting, 258

Indian (*muhindi*), 41, 93, 96–97, 157

Indian National Congress (INC), 67–68

Indian nationals, Uganda invested in by, 189

Indianness, 126, 217

Indian Ocean studies, 286

Indian Ocean trade, Indian settlement resulting from, 47–48

Indian proletariat, Gandhi influencing, 61

demographics in, 41; re-Indianization of, 214–19, 253; Ugandan Asian community in, 95

Kara, Taushif, 78

Karamoja (Uganda), 324n29

Karanja, SS, *18*

Karmali, Amirali, 324n36

Karume, Abeid, 79

Kashmir, political violence and oppression in, 289

Kasozi, A. B. K., 77, 314n31, 321n96

Kaur, Navpreet, 277

Kaur, Ravinder, 332n37

Kaur, Tanmeet, 273–74

KCCA (Kampala City Council Authority), 329n55

Kenya: Africanization in, 312n19; "nation-branding" in, 194; Uganda compared with, 159

Kenyan Asians: AAA paralleling, 238; Kenyan constitution recognizing, 233; UK resettled in by, 312n19

Kenyan constitution, Kenyan Asians recognized by, 233

Kenyan Jaluo workers, Obote expelling, 321n77

Kenyatta governments, 233

Keshodkar, Akbar, 248

Keynatta, Jomo, 82, 312n19

Kigozi, Margaret, 180–81, 185, 192–93, 332n26

King Jr., Martin Luther, 297

King, Rodney, 302

kinship, xxii, 31, 101, 141, 149, 265; biological, 227; caste-based, 55; endogamous, 31, 59; fictive, 116–17; intergenerational, 99; multigeneration, 153; patriarchal, 53–54, 56, 58, 79, 242, 244, 255–56, 265; patrilocal, 92, 253, 265; sexual, 264; transnational, 92, 94

kiwaani ("fake"), 198–202

Kiwanuka, Benedicto, 66–67

"Kony 2012" (campaign), 196

Kooky, Sharma, 258–68, 338n21, 338n23

Kwesiga, Joy, 339

KY (Kabaka Only) (Kabaka Yekka), 66, 68

Kyomuhendo, Goretti, 312n12

labor migrants, 48–49, 216, 228, 335n11

labor migration, 60

land concession, 229–32

land policy, *Constitution of the Republic of Uganda* liberalizing, 197

The Last King of Scotland (film), 11, *12*

latitudinal citizenship, 218

Lee, Christopher, 34

Lee, Spike, 302

legal documentation, 113

legal-juridical citizenship: of Asians, 232; disenchantment with, 8–9; performative rituals of, 111–18; rights and entitlements of, 20

legal-juridical citizenship status, 20, 145

Leonard, Karen, 57

Leopold, Mark, 15, 313n24, 314n31

"Let's Go Home! The Golden Jubilee Uganda Reunion" (event), *166*

liberal governance, 117–18

liberalism, 19–20, 25, 109

liberalization, 149–55

liberal nation-statehood, failure of, 23–24

liberal Western imaginaries, expulsion exceptionalism centering, 15–16

Liberation War, 127, 133, 146, 181, 327n16

local governance, NRM democratizing, 146

Lost Counties controversy, 72

Lule, Yusuf, 132, 324n39, 325n3

lumpen militariat, 106

Mabira Forest controversy, anti-Asian violence and, 229–32, 237

Madhvani, Jayant, 98

Madhvani, Meena, 98

Madhvani, Muljibhai Prabhudas, 60

Madhvani, Nimisha, 190

Madhvani Groups, 149

magendo. See illicit economies

Maini, Amar, 74

"majority minority," University of California characterized as, 299

Makerere Hospital, 261, 264

Makerere Institute of Social Research (MISR), 207, 286, 287

Makerere University, 255; colonial government founding, 280; Mamdani lecturing at, 304; racially nativist nationalism reflected by, 286–87; School of Women and Gender Studies at, 262

Makerere University professors, Joshi reacted to by, 339n31

Making a World after Empire (Lee), 34

Mamdani, Mahmood, 16, 51–53, 207, 233, 237, 286; *Citizen and Subject* by, 50, 324n26; citizenship documented by, 320n75; *From Citizen to Refugee* by, 312n12; colonial state analyzed by, 26; Makerere University lectured at by, 304; *Politics and Class Formation in Uganda* by, 49; public forums organized by, 239–40

market fundamentalism, 191

Marriage and Divorce of Mohammedans Act, 275

marriage networks, transnational, 243

marriage norms, 254

Marx, Karl, 16

material and social relations of production, social analysis and, 58–59

Mazrui, Ali, 3, 34, 83

Mbeki, Thabo, 179, 331n22

Mbembe, Achille, 110, 324n26

Mcintosh, Janet, 163

media coverage: of Amin, I., 312n10; of Asian expulsion, 312n10; Indian men and women reduced by, 270; of Joshi, 260–64

Mehta, Mahendra, 229–30

Mehta, Nanji Kalidas, 60

Mehta Groups, 149, 229–31

Melancholia for Freedom (Hansen), 62

Metcalf, Thomas, 59

methodological nationalism, 27–28

methodology, 29, 34–40, 290

middle figures, 49

migrants, 203, 312n16; Banyaruanda, 146; Black African, 54; "free" or "passenger," 48; Indian, 92, 239, 268; labor, 48–49, 216, 228, 335n11; post-1990s, 253; South Asian, 7, 33, 37, 173; twice, 12

Minister of Information, 119

Minister of Internal Affairs, 119

Minister of State for Africanization, Obote establishing, 71

Ministry for National Development (Uganda), 331n15

Ministry of Finance (Uganda), 240

Ministry of Financial Planning and Economic Development (MoFPED) (Uganda), 331n15

Ministry of Internal Affairs, Immigration Department of, 112

Ministry of Internal Affairs (Uganda), 186, 335n6

Ministry of Lands (Uganda), 186

Ministry of Trade (Uganda), 329n55

MISR (Makerere Institute of Social Research), 207, 286, 287

Miss India Uganda (competition), 225–26

Mississippi Masala (film), 11, 12, 313n23

mixed racial heritage, 91–93

Modi, Narendra, 173–74, 191, 289, 290; Kampala visited by, 215–16; nationalist and state project crafted by, 293; Ugandan Parliament visited by, 294

MoFPED (Ministry of Financial Planning and Economic Development), 331n15

Moghal, Manzhoor, 236

Morris, H. S., 54–55, 64, 210, 211

Morrison, Toni, xvi

"Move to the Left" agenda, Obote announcing, 72

muhindi (Indian), 41, 93, 96–97, 157

Mukwano Group, 151, 153, 324n36

multiracial Afro-Asian individuals, racial endogamy maintained by, 257

multiracial Afro-Asian women, with prominent roles in the national reconstruction process, 252

multiracialism, failure of, 23–24

multiracial sphere, of formal politics, 212

Munyonyo Commonwealth Resort, 173

Museveni, Yoweri Kaguta, 24, 38, 133–34, 146, 234, 324n39; Asian expulsion apologized for by, 294–95; "India-Africa Forum Summit" attended by, 333n40; Kigozi appointed by, 181; Mehta Group supported by, 229;

neoliberal culture taken up by, 150–51; presidential campaign billboards for, *195*; property repossession remarked on by, 141; returnees and, 129, 131–32, 151; revolutionary national bourgeoisie written on by, 326n15; Ugandan women promoted by, 251

Mutebi, Ronald, II, 230

Muteesa, Edward, II, 235

Mutesa, Kabaka, II (king), 65, 66, *73*

Nagar, Richa, 55–56, 152, 244–45

Nair, Mira, 11, 313n23

Nairobi National Museum, 337n28

Nakasero (Uganda), 183

Namaganda, Assumpta, 155

Namaganda, Harriet, 104

Namanve Forest, 197

NAM (Non-Aligned Movement), 61, 179, 295

Narayan, Uma, 264

national belonging, xvi–xvii

National Consultative Council (NCC), 324n39

National Identification and Registration Authority (NIRA), 227

national identity: deracialization and, 106; NRM restricting, 147; racial criteria defining, 145

nationalism, racially nativist. *See* racially nativist nationalism

national planning, by NRM, 331n15

National Resistance Army (NRA), 124, 127–28

National Resistance Movement (NRM), 24, 38, 133, 144, 169; Africanization policies maintained by, 201–2; anti-imperialist rhetoric of, 326n6; Asian business community connected with, 338n21; crony capitalism between foreign business men and, 334n58; Expropriated Properties Act reintroduced by, 137; as "hybrid regime," 315n46; Indian government tied to, 305–6; local governance democratized by, 146; national identity restricted by, 147; national planning by, 331n15; neoliberal culture taken up by, 150–51; neoliberal practice elaborated on by, 131–32; noncitizen incorporations participated in by, 283; production of security by, 325n1; racial exclusion maintained by, 136; racial formations of, 135–36; Western aid received by, 135; younger generations contending with, 322n4. *See also* Museveni, Yoweri Kaguta

nation-building, 194–95

nation-state building, through Ugandan Asians, 144

nativism, 30, 93, 205, 283, 287. *See also* racially nativist nationalism

NCC (National Consultative Council), 325

necropolitics, 324n26

Nehru, Jaharwal, 61

NEIO (New Economic International Order), 179

neocolonialism, 28

Neogy, Rajat, 68, *69*

neoliberal Afro-Asianism, 180, 187–92

Neoliberal capitalist exploitation, South-South cooperation reasserting, 179–80

neoliberal culture, 150–51

neoliberal globalization, anthropology of, 178

neoliberal governance, colonial state institutions and, 177–78

neoliberalism: citizenship impacted by, 145; racial, 154; Western imperialism and, 178

Neoliberalism as Exception (Ong), 24

neoliberalisms, Global South, 176–80

neoliberal practice, NRM elaborating on, 131–32

neoliberal racial meritocracy, 149

neoliberal universalisms, 327n16, 327n20

newcomers, 37, 95, 206–8, 216

New Economic International Order (NEIO), 179

A New System of Slavery (Tinker), 47

NGOs. *See* nongovernmental organizations

NIRA (National Identification and Registration Authority), 227

SAPs (structural adjustment programs), 134

Sarvarkar, Vinayak, 293

Schedule Three, of Constitution of the Republic of Uganda, 145–48, 232–33

School of Women and Gender Studies, at Makerere University, 262

SCOUL (Sugar Corporation of Uganda Ltd.), 229

"second slavery," 47

securitization, racialized political cultures of, 118–20

security, governmenality and, 194

security forces, state impunity escalated by, 230–31

Sembuya, Christopher, 235

sexual intimacies, interracial, 79, 123–24

sexual purity, patriarchal safeguarding of, 244–45

Al-Shabaab terrorist bombings, 325n1

Shankar, Shobana, 293

Siddi community, 290

Sikhism, xiii–xiv

Singh, Joginder "Flying Sikh," xvii

Singh, Katongole, 212

Singh, Lal, 103, 122–23, 160–61

Singh, Manmohan, 215

Singh, Mika, 224

Singh, Ram, 323n16

Singh Sabha Sikh Gurudwara, 125, 158–59

Slater, Richard, 85

small towns, Ugandan Asians in, 116–17

social analysis, material and social relations of production and, 58–59

social and communal reproduction, 120–27

sojourners, 154, 161, 203–4, 218, 228

The Souls of Black Folk (Du Bois), xiv

South Africa, Gandhi in, 61–62

Southall, Aidan, 57, 319n49

South Asia, labor migrants from, 335n11

South Asian American diaspora, 10–14, 296, 301

South Asian community, 56, 284

South Asian diaspora, 32–34

South Asian diasporic understandings, Ugandan Asian excluded from, xiii

South Asian heritage, Rwandese heritage and, 93

South Asian immigration, Amin, I., allowing, 105

South Asian/Indian presence, registers of, 42–43

South Asianness: Black African experience of, 15; economics reconstituting, 144; racial, 7–8, 15, 20, 31, 41, 124, 144, 151, 155, 192; regional racial formations of, 30–31

South Asian people, tribal recognition for, 233

South Asian presence: Black African Ugandans discussing, 20; foreign investors associated with, 201–2; visual and sensorial registers of, 43

South Asians, expulsion exceptionalism among, 281–82

South Asian studies, xix, 285

South Asian women: African indigenous women contrasted with, 271–72; employment of, 255–56; NGOs supporting, 270

South-South cooperation, 173–76, 178; BRICS and, 179, 293; foreign investment and, 187–88; neoliberal capitalist exploitation reasserted by, 179–80

sovereign authorization, 137–45

sovereign bodies, 27

sovereignty, 25–28; European/Western intellectual genealogies of, 315n52; exceptional sites of, 184–85; graduated, 197

Speke, John Hanning, 46

Srinivas, M. N., 55

Ssentamu, Robert Kyagulani, People Power, 305

Stanley, Henry Morton, 46

Stansted Airport, 17

state-based ambitions, diaspora centered in, 33

state-based cultural productions, 194–95

state-community relations, 210–14

state governance, postcolonial, 208–9

state impunity, security forces escalating, 230–31

state officials: DRB resisted by, 274–75; foreign investors evaluated by, 200; Indian, 323n18; investment promoted by, 196; passports and, 326n5; patronage to, 201, 232; Ugandan postcolonial, 28

state policies, around foreign investment, 205–6

state violence, nostalgia contrasted with, 122–23

statist political science, Uganda studies scholarship dominated by, 315n46

statues and monuments, role in memorializaiton of, 291

stayees (*rehen walley*), 32, 113, 129, 165; communal property overseen by, 219–20; returnees differentiated from, 102; urban social worlds of, 122

Stepputat, Finn, 110

Stoler, Ann, 337n4

structural adjustment programs (SAPs), 134

structural occlusion, 163

"structure of feeling," in urban Uganda, 97–98

student movements, 287, 291

study of Asians, in colonial and postcolonial Uganda, 45–52, 58–63

sub-imperial formations, 206

sub-imperialism, Indians and, 59–60, 202

Subject Races, 51, 136, 164–65

Sugar Corporation of Uganda Ltd. (SCOUL), 229

Sunak, Rishi, 302–3

Tailor, Rajni, 100–101, 210, 211, 219

Tanmeet Kaur Case, 272–77

Tanna, Sanjay, 212

Tanzania, 324n39

tax incentives, for foreign investment, 200–201

Taylor, Edgar, 14, 21, 87

technocratic norms, the political replaced by, 184–85

"Ten-Point Programme" (NRM), 133

Thind, Bhagat Singh, xvi

Thiong'o, Ngugi wa, 279

Thomas, Deborah, 8

Thompson, Gardner, 68

Tide of Fortune (Madhvani), 60

Tinker, Hugh, 47

Townsmen in the Making (Southall and Gutkind), 319n49

trade and investment conferences, 190–91

Trade Licensing Act (1969), 74

trade sector, Africanization and, 153–54, 329n52

trading licenses, 335n64

traditional African political authority, 324n32

transcontinental Afro-South Asian entanglements, 40, 297–99

transcontinental commemoration, possibilities and limitations of, 166–69

transcontinental Uganda, xiii, xxi–xxii, *xxvi*, 29–31, 282

Transition (magazine), 68, 69

transnational South Asian proletariat, 228

tribal recognition, for South Asian people, 233

Tripp, Aili Mari, 70

Trudeau, Pierre, 81

Trump, Donald, 288

Twaddle, Michael, 86

Twice Migrants (Bhachu), 312n16

UAG (Uganda Action Group), 68

Uganda: as "attractive investment destination," 190, 192–93; autochthony in, 146; Bank of, 334n57; branding of, 192–98; BRICS nations influencing, 28; beyond Buganda, 317n9; domestic violence in, 264; FDI by India in, 332n38; Indian diaspora in, 31–32; Indian nationals investing in, 189; Indians expelled from, 3; intelligentsia leaving, 323n17; intercontinental, 282; Kenya compared with, 159; labor migration in, 60; major cities and towns in, *xxvii*; Ministry of Finance of, 240; Nakasero in, 183; norms of modernity and development foiled by, 25; postcolonial, *xxvi*, 45–52, 58–63, 281; racial, 29; racial, cultural, and ethnic difference characterizing, 241; regions and traditional kingdoms of, *xxvii*; "structure of feeling" in urban,

97; transcontinental, xiii, xxi–xxii, *xxvi*, 29–31, 282; Ugandan Asians departing, *19*; underdevelopment in, 49–50; war in Northern, 322n7. *See also* Asian expulsion; colonial administration; *Constitution of the Republic of Uganda*; decolonization; foreign investment; Indian Association of Uganda; Kampala; national identity; state officials; *specific ministries*; *specific places*

Uganda Action Group (UAG), 68

Uganda Argus (newspaper), 5

Uganda Association of Women Lawyers (FIDA), 273, 276

Uganda Council of Women Congress, *248*

Uganda-India ties, in virtual/online venues, 191

Uganda Investment Authority (UIA), 176–77, 192–94, 330n8, 331n9, 332n38; investment license issued by, 334n58; Kigozi leading, 181, 185; in Nakasero, 183; public relations officers for, 196; visiting, 180–87

Ugandan African conspiratorial readings, of Asian presence, 98

Ugandan African-Indian business competition, 205

Ugandan Asian capitalist class, UPC aligning with, 72, 325n4

Ugandan Asian community, 238, 304; DAPCB tensions with, 143; dissolution of pre-expulsion, 108–9; in Kampala, 95

Ugandan Asian displacement (1972), *xxvi*

Ugandan Asian exiles, 12, 45, 142–43, 166, 231; Asian expulsion impacting, 303–4; British and Canadian nationalists celebrating, 20; Global North migrated to be, 13

Ugandan Asian family firms, 153, 322n97

Ugandan Asian Ismaili Muslim community, 140

Ugandan Asian men, Amin, I., government and, 126

Ugandan Asian refugees, 12, *17*, 101, 138

Ugandan Asian repatriation, 137–45

Ugandan Asians, *85*; African population in tension with, 208; Asian expulsion helping, 81–82; Black Africans contrasted with, 63; British High Commission discriminating against, 80; citizenship of, 74–75, 77–78; as displaced population, 10–11; East Africa adapted to by, 57; Facebook groups of, 330n69; Gujarat resettled in by, 322n97; Immigration Office queued at by, *84*; India and forced return of, *18*, 81; land concession impacting, 232; nation-state building through, 144; passports of, *113*; political participation of, 68; property assets of, 98–99; racial community securitization depended on by, 231–32; racial denizenship narrated by, 118; racial exclusion remembered by, 45; racial violence experienced by, 19–20; racial visibility sensed by, 165; relationships with the army cultivated by, 121; residences and livelihoods retained by, 119; return of, 120; rights and entitlements of, 145–46; schools, hospitals, and specialty medical clinics established by, 224; in small towns, 116–17; South Asian diasporic understandings excluding, xiii; Uganda departed by, *19*; UK Parliament expelling, 312n17. *See also* returnees; stayees

Ugandan Asians community, racial denizenship relying on, 120–21

Ugandan Asian "tycoons," 143, 150

Ugandan Asian women: archiving projects by, 306; during Asian expulsion displacing, 252–53; customary laws reaffirmed by, 272–73; return migration of, 251; in voluntary organizations, 70; workforce joined by, 249

Uganda National Congress (UNC), 66

Uganda National Liberation Front (UNLF), 324n39; Amin, I., ousted by, 127; systems violence and atrocities perpetrated by, 326n6; violence against civilians and civil war under, 132. *See also* Obote, Apollo Milton

www.ingramcontent.com/pod-product-compliance
Lightning Source LLC
Chambersburg PA
CBHW032337280326
41935CB00008B/363

9 781478 031918